First World War
and Army of Occupation
War Diary
France, Belgium and Germany

66 DIVISION
South African Brigade
Headquarters
1 September 1918 - 28 February 1919

WO95/3146

The Naval & Military Press Ltd
www.nmarchive.com
Published in association with The National Archives

Published by

The Naval & Military Press Ltd

Unit 10 Ridgewood Industrial Park,
Uckfield, East Sussex,
TN22 5QE England
Tel: +44 (0) 1825 749494

www.naval-military-press.com
www.nmarchive.com

This diary has been reprinted in facsimile from the original. Any imperfections are inevitably reproduced and the quality may fall short of modern type and cartographic standards.

Contents

Document type	Place/Title	Date From	Date To
War Diary	Lumbres Area	01/09/1918	29/09/1918
War Diary	Chuignolles	30/09/1918	30/09/1918
Operation(al) Order(s)	South Africanigrigad Operation Order No. 287	01/09/1918	01/09/1918
Miscellaneous	App 3 S.African Inf Brigade 9th Battn. M.G.C. Comdt. II Army Training Area Lumbres.		
Operation(al) Order(s)	9th Division Order No. 296 App 4	10/09/1918	10/09/1918
Miscellaneous	March Table Issued With 9th Division Order No. 296		
Miscellaneous	A Form. Messages And Signals.		
Operation(al) Order(s)	Operation Order No. 228 App 6	11/09/1918	11/09/1918
Operation(al) Order(s)	South African Brigade Operation Order No. 229 App 7	11/09/1918	11/09/1918
Operation(al) Order(s)	9th Division Order No. 297 App 8	11/09/1918	11/09/1918
Miscellaneous	March Table		
Operation(al) Order(s)	9th Division Order No. 298 App 9	12/09/1918	12/09/1918
Miscellaneous	28th Infantry Brigade South African Infantry Brigade. G.S. 28/55. 13th September 1918. App 10	13/09/1918	13/09/1918
Operation(al) Order(s)	South African Brigade Operation Order No. 230 App 11	19/09/1918	19/09/1918
Miscellaneous	66th Division. Warning Order App 12	24/09/1918	24/09/1918
Miscellaneous	C Form Messages And Signals App 13		
Operation(al) Order(s)	66th Division Order No. 87 App 14	26/09/1918	26/09/1918
Miscellaneous	March Table For Units As In Entrainment Programme "A"		
Miscellaneous	March Table For Units As In Entrainment Programme "B"		
Miscellaneous	66th Divn. G. 1052.	27/09/1918	27/09/1918
Miscellaneous	Transport Groups.		
Miscellaneous	March Table For Horse Transport Of 66th Division On Sept 27th		
Operation(al) Order(s)	South African Infantry Brigade Operation Order No. 231 App 15	28/09/1918	28/09/1918
Operation(al) Order(s)	66th Division Order No. 88 App 16	28/09/1918	28/09/1918
Miscellaneous	App 17	28/09/1918	28/09/1918
Miscellaneous	App 18	02/04/1918	02/04/1918
Miscellaneous	March Table To Accompany 66th Division Order No. 88		
Miscellaneous	A Form Messages And Signals.		
Miscellaneous	C Form Messages And Signals.		
Miscellaneous	C Form Messages And Signals. App 19		
Operation(al) Order(s)	South African Infantry Brigade Operation Order No. 233 App 20		
Miscellaneous	A Form Messages And Signals		
Miscellaneous	C Form Messages And Signals		
Miscellaneous	March Table To Accompany O.O. 233		
Miscellaneous	South African Infantry Brigade		
Miscellaneous			
Miscellaneous	Appendix "A" To narrative for October 1918		
War Diary	Chuignolles Montauban	01/10/1919	04/10/1919
War Diary	Nurlu	05/10/1919	05/10/1919
War Diary	Ronssoy	06/10/1919	07/10/1919
War Diary	Mushroom Quarry	08/10/1919	08/10/1919

War Diary	NE. of La Sablonniere	09/10/1919	10/10/1919
War Diary	500 X. NW. Of Reumont	11/10/1919	17/10/1919
War Diary	Ravine 500 X E. of Four Valley X-roads	18/10/1919	19/10/1919
War Diary	The Chateau Le Cateau	20/10/1919	31/10/1919
Operation(al) Order(s)	66th Division Order No. 92 App 1		
Miscellaneous	March Table To Accompany 68th Division Order No. 92		
Operation(al) Order(s)	South African Infantry Brigade Operation Order No. 234 App 2	03/10/1918	03/10/1918
Miscellaneous	C Form Messages And Signals		
Miscellaneous	C Form Messages And Signals App 3		
Miscellaneous	A Form Messages And Signals		
Miscellaneous	A Form Messages And Signals App 4		
Miscellaneous	A Form Messages And Signals App 5		
Miscellaneous	A Form Messages And Signals App 6		
Miscellaneous	A Form Messages And Signals		
Miscellaneous	C Form Messages And Signals		
Miscellaneous	A Form Messages And Signals App 8		
Miscellaneous	A Form Messages And Signals		
Miscellaneous	Summary Of Casualties For Period 7th To 20th Oct 1918		
Map			
Operation(al) Order(s)	South African Infantry Brigade Operation Order No. 237 App 9	06/10/1918	06/10/1918
Miscellaneous	A Form Messages And Signals App 10		
Miscellaneous	A Form Messages And Signals App 11		
Operation(al) Order(s)	South African Infantry Brigade App 12	06/10/1918	06/10/1918
Miscellaneous	App 13 South African Bde 9th Glouc. R. (Pioneers).	07/10/1918	07/10/1918
Miscellaneous	A Form Messages And Signals. App 14		
Operation(al) Order(s)	66th Division Order No. 99 App 14	07/10/1918	07/10/1918
Miscellaneous	66th Division Preliminary Order No. 1 App 16	06/10/1918	06/10/1918
Miscellaneous	66th Division Instruction No 1	05/10/1918	05/10/1918
Operation(al) Order(s)	66th Division Order No. 97 App 17	06/10/1918	06/10/1918
Miscellaneous	Issued Down To Platon Commanders.	06/10/1918	06/10/1918
Miscellaneous	South African Brigade Order 246 App 71	19/10/1918	19/10/1918
Miscellaneous	South African Brigade Order 247 App 72	19/10/1918	19/10/1918
Miscellaneous	66th Division Instruction No. 6	06/10/1918	06/10/1918
Miscellaneous	A Form. Messages And Signals.		
Miscellaneous	App 18		
Miscellaneous	A Form Messages And Signals. App 19		
Miscellaneous	Instruction No. 4 Issued Under Divl Order No. 97	06/10/1918	06/10/1918
Miscellaneous	South African Infantry Brigade Prellimanry Order No. 1 App 20	06/10/1918	06/10/1918
Miscellaneous	South African Infantry Brigade	06/01/1918	06/01/1918
Miscellaneous	South African Infantry Brigade App 21	06/10/1918	06/10/1918
Miscellaneous	App 22		
Miscellaneous	A Form Messages And Signals		
Miscellaneous	A Form Messages And Signals. App 23		
Miscellaneous	A Form Messages And Signals		
Miscellaneous	66 Divisional Order No. 100 App 24		
Miscellaneous	1st S.A.I.	09/10/1918	09/10/1918
Miscellaneous	1st SAI App 25	09/10/1918	09/10/1918
Miscellaneous	1st SAI	09/10/1918	09/10/1918
Operation(al) Order(s)	66th Division Order No. 101 App 27	09/10/1918	09/10/1918
Miscellaneous	A Form Messages And Signals. App 28		
Miscellaneous	Public Record Office		

Miscellaneous	App 29		
Miscellaneous			
Miscellaneous	A Form Messages And Signals App 29 A		
Miscellaneous	A Form Messages And Signals		
Miscellaneous	A Form Messages And Signals App 30		
Miscellaneous	A Form Messages And Signals App 31		
Miscellaneous	A & Q. App 32	11/10/1918	11/10/1918
Operation(al) Order(s)	66th Division Order No. 103	11/10/1918	11/10/1918
Miscellaneous	A Form. Messages And Signals. App 33		
Miscellaneous	A Form. Messages And Signals. App 34		
Miscellaneous	A Form. Messages And Signals. App 35		
Miscellaneous	A Form. Messages And Signals. App 36		
Miscellaneous	App 42	14/10/1918	14/10/1918
Miscellaneous	A Form Messages And Signals. App 43		
Miscellaneous	A Form Messages And Signals. App 44		
Miscellaneous	A Form Messages And Signals. App 45		
Miscellaneous	A Form Messages And Signals. App 46		
Miscellaneous			
Miscellaneous	South African Infantry Brigade App 37	11/10/1918	11/10/1918
Miscellaneous	App 38 The S A Bde		
Miscellaneous	App 39 The S A I Bde	12/10/1918	12/10/1918
Miscellaneous	S.A. Brigade. 9th Bn. Glouc. R. (Pioneers). C.R.E. Signals for information.	13/10/1918	13/10/1918
Miscellaneous	9th Bn. Glouc R. (Pioneers) App 41	14/10/1918	14/10/1918
Miscellaneous	Messages And Signals App 40		
Miscellaneous	A Form Messages And Signals.		
Miscellaneous	66th Divn.	14/10/1918	14/10/1918
Operation(al) Order(s)	66th Division Order No. 100	13/10/1918	13/10/1918
Miscellaneous	A. & Q.	16/10/1918	16/10/1918
Miscellaneous	Messages And Signals	14/10/1918	14/10/1918
Miscellaneous	189		
Miscellaneous	66th Division Instructions No 1 App 47	15/10/1918	15/10/1918
Miscellaneous	South African Bde	16/10/1918	16/10/1918
Miscellaneous	A Form. Messages And Signals.		
Miscellaneous	66th Division Instructions No 2	15/10/1918	15/10/1918
Miscellaneous	66th Division Instructions No 3	15/10/1918	15/10/1918
Operation(al) Order(s)	66th Division Instructions No 4	15/10/1918	15/10/1918
Miscellaneous	196		
Miscellaneous	Instructions No. 5	15/10/1918	15/10/1918
Miscellaneous	66th Division Instructions No. 6	16/10/1918	16/10/1918
Miscellaneous	66th Divn. G. App 47		
Miscellaneous	199		
Miscellaneous	66th Division Instructions No. 7	16/10/1918	16/10/1918
Miscellaneous	66th Division Instructions No. 8	16/12/1918	16/12/1918
Miscellaneous	R.E. Operation Order No 52 App 48	16/10/1918	16/10/1918
Miscellaneous			
Miscellaneous	Appendix "A"		
Miscellaneous	Appendix "B"-Strong Points		
Map			
Miscellaneous	Appendix "C" Communications-Bridges and Roads		
Miscellaneous	66th Division Order No. 105 App 49	16/10/1918	16/10/1918
Miscellaneous	App 50	16/10/1918	16/10/1918
Miscellaneous	App 51	16/10/1918	16/10/1918
Miscellaneous	1st S A I	16/10/1918	16/10/1918
Miscellaneous	A Form Messages And Signals. App 52		
Miscellaneous	South African Infy Bde Order No. 245 App 52		

Miscellaneous	A Form Messages And Signals. App 53		
Miscellaneous	A Form Messages And Signals.		
Miscellaneous	Messages And Signals. App 54		
Miscellaneous	A Form Messages And Signals. App 55		
Miscellaneous	A Form Messages And Signals. App 56		
Miscellaneous	A Form Messages And Signals.		
Miscellaneous	C Form Messages And Signals App 57		
Miscellaneous	A Form Messages And Signals.		
Miscellaneous	66th Division Order No. 106 App 58	17/10/1918	17/10/1918
Operation(al) Order(s)	66th Division Order No. 106	17/10/1918	17/10/1918
Operation(al) Order(s)	66th Division Order No. 108	17/10/1918	17/10/1918
Miscellaneous	Addenda To 66th Division Order 108	17/10/1918	17/10/1918
Operation(al) Order(s)	66th Division Order No. 109 App 63	18/10/1918	18/10/1918
Miscellaneous	C Form Messages And Signals.		
Miscellaneous	A Form Messages And Signals. App 59		
Miscellaneous	C Form Messages And Signals.		
Miscellaneous	C Form Messages And Signals. App 60		
Miscellaneous	A Form Messages And Signals. App 60		
Miscellaneous	A Form Messages And Signals.		
Miscellaneous	A Form Messages And Signals. App 61		
Miscellaneous	B Form Messages And Signals. App 65		
Miscellaneous	B Form Messages And Signals. App 62		
Miscellaneous	C Form Messages And Signals. App 64		
Miscellaneous	C Form. Messages And Signals.		
Miscellaneous	C Form Messages And Signals. App 66		
Miscellaneous	C Form Messages And Signals App 67	18/10/1918	18/10/1918
Operation(al) Order(s)	66th Division Order No. 110 App 68		
Miscellaneous	Tables To Accompany 66th Division Order No. 110		
Miscellaneous	C Form Messages And Signals App 69		
Miscellaneous	247		
Miscellaneous	C Form Messages And Signals.		
Miscellaneous	248		
Miscellaneous	C Form Messages And Signals		
Miscellaneous	C Form Messages And Signals App 70	19/10/1918	19/10/1918
Miscellaneous	251		
War Diary	Serain	01/11/1918	01/11/1918
War Diary	Reumont	02/11/1918	04/11/1918
War Diary	Le Cateau	05/11/1918	05/11/1918
War Diary	Pommereuil	06/11/1918	06/11/1918
War Diary	Landrecies	07/11/1918	08/11/1918
War Diary	Dompierre	08/11/1918	09/11/1918
War Diary	Solre Le Chateau	10/11/1918	10/11/1918
War Diary	Hestrud	10/11/1918	11/11/1918
War Diary	Outskirts NW of Hestrud	11/11/1918	12/11/1918
War Diary	N.W. Outskirts of Hestrud	12/11/1918	16/11/1918
War Diary	Sivry	17/11/1918	19/11/1918
War Diary	Senzeille	20/11/1918	22/11/1918
War Diary	Philippeville	23/10/1918	23/10/1918
War Diary	Bac Du Prince	24/10/1918	30/10/1918
Operation(al) Order(s)	66th Division Preliminary Order No. 111 App 1	31/10/1918	31/10/1918
Miscellaneous	South African Infantry Brigade Preliminary Operation Order No. 249 App 2	01/11/1918	01/11/1918
Miscellaneous	C Form Messages And Signals App 3		
Operation(al) Order(s)	South African Infantry Brigade Order No. 850 App 4	01/11/1918	01/11/1918
Miscellaneous	C Form Messages And Signals App 5		
Miscellaneous	C Form Messages And Signals App 6		

Miscellaneous	A Form Messages And Signals App 7		
Miscellaneous	A Form Messages And Signals App 7A		
Miscellaneous	O Form Messages And Signals App 8		
Miscellaneous	66th Division Order No. 114 App 9	04/11/1918	04/11/1918
Miscellaneous	Appendix "A" To Division Order No. 114	04/11/1918	04/11/1918
Miscellaneous	Amendment No. 1 to 66th Division Order No. 114 App 9	05/11/1918	05/11/1918
Miscellaneous			
Miscellaneous	South African Infantry Brigade Order No. 255	05/11/1918	05/11/1918
Miscellaneous	App. 12 Copy of Telegram		
Operation(al) Order(s)	66th Division Order No. 115 App 5	05/11/1918	05/11/1918
Miscellaneous	A Form Messages And Signals. App 14		
Miscellaneous	South African Brigade Order No. 256 App 15	03/11/1918	03/11/1918
Operation(al) Order(s)	66th Division Order No. 117 App 16	06/11/1918	06/11/1918
Operation(al) Order(s)	66th Division Order No. 116 App 21		
Miscellaneous	Messages And Signals App 21		
Miscellaneous	A Form Messages And Signals App 10		
Miscellaneous	C Form Messages And Signals App 11		
Miscellaneous	A Form Messages And Signals App 14		
Miscellaneous	A Form Messages And Signals App 18		
Miscellaneous	A Form Messages And Signals		
Miscellaneous	A Form Messages And Signals App 19		
Miscellaneous	C Form Messages And Signals		
Miscellaneous	A Form Messages And Signals App 20		
Miscellaneous	Extracts From 66th Div Order No. 118 App 22		
Miscellaneous	Messages And Signals		
Miscellaneous	App 24 Copy of Telegram		
Miscellaneous	Copy Of Telegram App 24		
Miscellaneous	26th Inf. Bde.		
Miscellaneous	A Form Messages And Signals App 25		
Miscellaneous	A Form Messages And Signals		
Miscellaneous	A Form Messages And Signals App 26		
Miscellaneous	A Form Messages And Signals App 27		
Operation(al) Order(s)	66th Division Order No. 120 App 28	09/11/1918	09/11/1918
Operation(al) Order(s)	66th Division Order No 121 App 29	09/11/1918	09/11/1918
Miscellaneous	Distribution		
Miscellaneous	Copy Of Telegram App 22		
Miscellaneous			
Miscellaneous	Mobile Column Order No. 1 App 29	10/11/1918	10/11/1918
Miscellaneous	A Form Messages And Signals App 30		
Miscellaneous	A Form Messages And Signals App 31		
Miscellaneous	A Form Messages And Signals		
Miscellaneous	Messages And Signals		
Miscellaneous	Messages And Signals App 32		
Miscellaneous	C Form Messages And Signals		
Miscellaneous	C Form Messages And Signals App 33		
Miscellaneous	Mobile Column Order No. 2 App 34	21/10/1918	21/10/1918
Operation(al) Order(s)	66th Division Order No. 122 App 35		
Miscellaneous	A Form Messages And Signals App 36		
Miscellaneous	A Form Messages And Signals App 37		
Miscellaneous	A Form Messages And Signals App 38		
Miscellaneous	Mobile Column Special Order App 39	11/11/1918	11/11/1918
Miscellaneous	By Aeroplane Post G.B. 14	11/11/1918	11/11/1918
Miscellaneous	G.B. 15	11/11/1918	11/11/1918
Miscellaneous	South African Infantry Brigade App 41	11/11/1918	11/11/1918
Miscellaneous	A Form Messages And Signals App 42		

Miscellaneous	C Form Messages And Signals App 43		
Miscellaneous	C Form Messages And Signals App 44		
Miscellaneous	C Form Messages And Signals		
Miscellaneous	A Form Messages And Signals. App 44	11/11/1918	11/11/1918
Miscellaneous	South African Infantry Brigade Mobile Colume Order No. 4 App 45	12/11/1918	12/11/1918
Miscellaneous	South African Infantry Brigade App 47		
Miscellaneous			
Miscellaneous	C Form Messages And Signals App 48		
Miscellaneous	C Form Messages And Signals App 49		
Miscellaneous	South African Infantry Brigade	14/11/1918	14/11/1918
Miscellaneous	South African Infantry Brigade	16/11/1918	16/11/1918
Miscellaneous	Fourth Army 293/3 (G)	13/11/1918	13/11/1918
Miscellaneous	Administrative Instructions No. 1	15/11/1918	15/11/1918
Miscellaneous	A Form Messages And Signals		
Miscellaneous	A Form Messages And Signals App 46		
Miscellaneous	South African Infantry Brigade Order No 210 App 5	15/11/1918	15/11/1918
Miscellaneous	66th Divn 7948/8/Q	16/11/1918	16/11/1918
Miscellaneous			
Miscellaneous	Appendix "A" Composition of Brigade Groups & Dispositions of Division by 18.00 November 17th	16/11/1918	16/11/1918
Miscellaneous	Appendix "X" Composition of Brigade Groups & Dispositions of Division by 18.00 November 16th	15/11/1918	15/11/1918
Miscellaneous	66th Div 7948 App 50	17/11/1918	17/11/1918
Miscellaneous	66th Division Preliminary Order No. 123 App 51	15/11/1918	15/11/1918
Miscellaneous	Reference 66th Division Order No. 123	15/11/1918	15/11/1918
Miscellaneous	South African Infantry Brigade Order No. 261 App 52	15/11/1918	15/11/1918
Miscellaneous			
Miscellaneous	March Table To Accompany Bde Order 261		
Miscellaneous	South African Infantry Brigade	17/11/1918	17/11/1918
Operation(al) Order(s)	66th Division Order No. 124 App 53	17/11/1918	17/11/1918
Miscellaneous	March Table	17/11/1918	17/11/1918
Miscellaneous	South African Infantry Brigade Order No. 312 App 54	17/11/1918	17/11/1918
Miscellaneous	March Table Issued With South African Bde Order No. 262		
Miscellaneous	March Table		
Miscellaneous	66th Division Order No. 125 App 55	12/11/1918	12/11/1918
Operation(al) Order(s)	South African Infantry Brigade Order No. 283 App 56	18/11/1918	18/11/1918
Miscellaneous	March Table Issued With South Afr Bde Order No. 263		
Miscellaneous	March Table To Accompany D.O. 126		
Operation(al) Order(s)	66th Division Order No. 126 App 57	21/11/1918	21/11/1918
Miscellaneous	C Form Messages And Signals		
Miscellaneous	South African Infantry Brigade Order 204 App 58	22/11/1918	22/11/1918
Miscellaneous	March Table Issued With South Afr Bde Order No. 264		
Miscellaneous	A Form Messages And Signals App 36		
Operation(al) Order(s)	66th Division Order No. 127 App 59	23/11/1918	23/11/1918
Miscellaneous	March Table To Accompany D.O. 127		
Miscellaneous	C Form. Messages And Signals		
Miscellaneous	South African Infantry Brigade Order No. 265 App 60	26/11/1918	26/11/1918
Miscellaneous	March Table		
Miscellaneous	66th Division G.S. 3/9 App 61	27/11/1918	27/11/1918
War Diary	Rochefort Area	15/11/1918	15/11/1918
War Diary	Marche Area	16/11/1918	16/11/1918
War Diary	Bac Du Prince	01/12/1918	14/12/1918
War Diary	Houyet Area	14/12/1918	16/12/1918
War Diary	Marche Area	17/12/1918	27/12/1918

Operation(al) Order(s)	66th Division Order No. 128 App 1	04/12/1918	04/12/1918
Miscellaneous	March Table To Accompany 66th Division Order No. 128	04/12/1918	04/12/1918
Map			
Miscellaneous	C Form. Messages And Signals. App 2		
Operation(al) Order(s)	66th Division Order No. 129 App 3	10/12/1918	10/12/1918
Miscellaneous	March Table To Accompany 66th Division Order No. 129	10/12/1918	10/12/1918
Miscellaneous	South African Infantry Brigade Order No. 266 App 4	12/12/1918	12/12/1918
Miscellaneous	March Table		
Miscellaneous	March Table	15/12/1918	15/12/1918
Miscellaneous	March Table Issued With South Afr Bde Order No. 68	16/12/1918	16/12/1918
Miscellaneous	South African Infantry Brigade App 5	16/12/1918	16/12/1918
Miscellaneous	66th Division 82/1/A. App 6	16/12/1918	16/12/1918
Miscellaneous	South African Infantry Brigade App 7	19/12/1918	19/12/1918
Miscellaneous	South African Infantry Brigade Order No 267 App 8	25/12/1918	25/12/1918
Heading	Brigade Headquarters Jan-Feb 1919		
War Diary	Marche Area	01/12/1918	29/12/1918
Miscellaneous	A Form Messages And Signals App 1		
Miscellaneous	C Form Messages And Signals App 2		
Miscellaneous	66th Division App 3	18/01/1919	18/01/1919
Miscellaneous	South African Infantry Brigade App 4		
Miscellaneous	A Form Messages And Signals App 4A		
Miscellaneous	App 5 Headquarters S. African Infantry Bde.	20/01/1919	20/01/1919
Miscellaneous	South African Infantry Brigade Order No. 268 App 6		
Miscellaneous	C Form Messages And Signals App 7		
Miscellaneous			
Miscellaneous	Messages And Signals App 8		
Operation(al) Order(s)	66th Division Order No. 130 App 8A	22/01/1919	22/01/1919
Miscellaneous	March Table To Accompany 66th Division Order No. 130		
Miscellaneous	S.A. Infantry Bde.	25/01/1919	25/01/1919
Miscellaneous	South African Infantry Brigade Order No. 269 App 9	27/01/1919	27/01/1919
Miscellaneous			
Miscellaneous	March Table		
Miscellaneous	C Form. Messages And Signals. App 10		
Miscellaneous	C Form. Messages And Signals. App 11		
Operation(al) Order(s)	66th Division Order No. 131 App 12	27/01/1919	27/01/1919
Miscellaneous	March Table To Accompany Div Order No. 131		
War Diary	Marche Area	01/02/1919	16/02/1919
War Diary	Huy Area	17/02/1919	28/02/1919
Miscellaneous	66th Division Order No. 133 App 8	08/02/1919	08/02/1919
Miscellaneous	Table Showing Locations Of Marching Units At 15.00 On Undermentional Dates.		
Miscellaneous	66th Division No. G.S. 59	10/02/1919	10/02/1919
Miscellaneous	Guards Over Abandoned German Material & C.	10/02/1919	10/02/1919
Operation(al) Order(s)	66th Division Order No. 134	13/02/1919	13/02/1919
Miscellaneous	South African Infantry Brigade Order No. 270	14/02/1919	14/02/1919
Miscellaneous	Administrative Instructions Issued In Connection With 66th Division Order No. 134 Of 13.2.19	14/02/1919	14/02/1919
Miscellaneous	Q.M.C. 691 (Q.A.) AX/54/2	27/02/1919	27/02/1919

From 9 DIV TO 66 DIV

Instructions regarding War Diaries and Intelligence Summaries are contained in F. S. Regs., Part II. and the Staff Manual respectively. Title pages will be prepared in manuscript.

WAR DIARY
or
INTELLIGENCE SUMMARY.
(Erase heading not required.)

Army Form C. 2118.

Place	Date	Hour	Summary of Events and Information	Remarks and references to Appendices
	Sept. 1918		SOUTH AFRICAN INF. BDE..	
[illegible]BRES [illegible]A~	1		Order No. 227 and Amendment issued. (app. –) (app. –)	[app. 1]
			Move of South African (C.) Bn. & S.A.L.T.M. Bty to ALQUINES Area on Sept. 2, 1918.	[app. 2]
			Division of S.A. (C) Bn. for administrative purposes amongst 1st, 2nd, and 4th. Regiments.	
	2		9th. Divn. G.S. I/243 of 1.9.18 received.	[app. 3]
			One company 9th. Bn. M.G.C. placed at disposal of S.A. Bde. for training purposes.	
	3/10		Spent in training.	
	10		9th. Divn. Order 296 received. Move of 9th. Division to II Corps Area on 11 Sept., 18. S.A. (C.) Bn. & SALTM Bty. to remain in present area.	[app. 4]
			9th. Divn. G.157 received. S.A. Bde. now includes S.A. (C.) Bn.	[app. 5]
	17		S.A. Bde. Order 228 issued. S.A. Inf. Bde. withdrawn from 9th. Divn. from 11-9-18 inclusive. Composition of Bde S.A. Bde. HQ., S.A. Bde. HQ. Signal Section 1st. SAI – SALTM Bty. 2nd. SAI 4th. SAI S.A. Field Amb. remains att. to S.A. Bde.	[app. 6]

D. D. & L., London, E.C. (A10066) Wt W5300/P713 750,000 8/18 Sch. 52 Forms/C2118/16

Army Form C. 2118.

Instructions regarding War Diaries and Intelligence Summaries are contained in F. S. Regs., Part II. and the Staff Manual respectively. Title pages will be prepared in manuscript.

WAR DIARY
or
INTELLIGENCE SUMMARY.
(Erase heading not required.)

Place	Date	Hour	Summary of Events and Information	Remarks and references to Appendices
LUMBRES Area	Sept. 18 11		S. A. Bde. Order 229 issued. 2nd. SAI and 4th. SAI to move to LUMBRES Area on 12-9-18, and SALTM Bty. to move to LUMBRES Area on 13-9-18. 9th. Divn. Order 297 received.	[App. 7] [App. 8]
	12		9th. Divn. Order 298 received.	[App. 9]
			2nd. SAI moved from the BOUVELINGHEM Area to the SENNINGHEM Area, and 4th. SAI from ALQUINES Area to COULOMBY Area. The weather was very bad and the billets not good.	
			Colonel HELBERT, Staff Officer, S.A.O.E.F., who arrived on 11th. inst., visited Brigade Units.	
	13		S.A.L.T.M. Bty. moves to LUMBRES Area.	
			S. A. Inf. Bde. was finally withdrawn from the 9th. Divn. and placed directly under VII Corps for administration.	
			2nd. Roy. Sc. Fus. and 9th. Sco. Rif. finally left the SA. Bde. and came under 28th. Inf. Bde. 9 Divn. No. G.S. 28/55 of 13-9-18 received. SA Bde. transferred to SECOND Army Reserve [VII Corps] from 13-9-18 inclusive.	[App. 10]
	14		The Brigadier-General Commanding was to have inspected 1st. SAI, but the weather was too bad to admit of any training whatever.	

39

WAR DIARY
or
INTELLIGENCE SUMMARY.
(Erase heading not required.)

Army Form C. 2118.

Instructions regarding War Diaries and Intelligence Summaries are contained in F. S. Regs., Part II. and the Staff Manual respectively. Title pages will be prepared in manuscript.

Place	Date	Hour	Summary of Events and Information	Remarks and references to Appendices
LUMBRES Area. —	Sept. 16 15		Usual Church-Parade Services were held.	
	16		The Brigadier-General Commanding inspected 2nd. SAI at 10 am., & the 4th. SAI at 11.30 am.. Both units were excellently turned out, and the men were of fine physique and well trained.	
			The Brigadier-General Commanding lectured the Officers of the 1st. and 4th. SAI. at 2 pm. and 5 pm. respectively on the "PRINCIPLES OF TRAINING."	
	17		The Brigadier-General Commanding inspected 1st. SAI at 10 am.. Men were also well turned-out, and of very good physique.	
			The 4th. SAI sent 3 coys. to do Gas Training under Second Army. Gas School at HARTLETTES.	
			2nd. SAI carried out Musketry and Range Practices.	
	18		The Brigadier-General Commanding inspected SALTM Bty. 4th. SAI carried out Range Practices, and 2nd. SAI attended Gas School at HARTLETTES.	
			1st. SAI carried out Platoon and Coy. Training.	

D. D. & L., London, E.C.
(A10266) Wt W3300/P715 750,000 2/16 Sch. 52 Forms/C2118/16

40

Army Form C. 2118.

Instructions regarding War Diaries and Intelligence Summaries are contained in F. S. Regs., Part II and the Staff Manual respectively. Title pages will be prepared in manuscript.

WAR DIARY
or
INTELLIGENCE SUMMARY.
(Erase heading not required.)

Place	Date	Hour	Summary of Events and Information	Remarks and references to Appendices
LUMBRES Area —	Sept. 18 19		VII Corps Letter G.S. 2717/5 of 18-9-18 received. S.A. Bde. transferred to 66th Division [FIRST ARMY]. [G.H.Q. O.B/2231 of 17-9-18]	
			S.A. Bde. Order 230 issued. Move of S.A. Bde. to LE CAUROY Area to join 66th Divn. [FIRST ARMY] on 22 Sept.	[App. II]
	20		SALTM Bty. practised on Range with live bombs; not a very successful shoot on account of wind. G.O.C., 66th. Divn., came over to see B.-G.C. and also Bn. commanders.	
	21		Day spent in ~~prepar~~ preparing to move to LE CAUROY Area.	
	22		Bde. entrained at WIZERNES for the new area. On arrival, Bde. HQ. billeted at - MAIZIÈRES 1st. SAI do. - GOUY-EN-TERNOIS 2nd. SAI do. - MAGNICOURT 4th. SAI } SAF Amb. } do. - AMBRINES SALTM Bty. do. - VILLERS-SUR-SIMON	

41

D. D. & L., London, E.C. (A11026) Wt W3300/P713 750,000 5/17 Sch. 52 Forms/C2118/16

-5-

Army Form C. 2118.

WAR DIARY
or
INTELLIGENCE SUMMARY.

(Erase heading not required.)

Instructions regarding War Diaries and Intelligence Summaries are contained in F. S. Regs., Part II. and the Staff Manual respectively. Title pages will be prepared in manuscript.

Place	Date	Hour	Summary of Events and Information	Remarks and references to Appendices
LE CAUROY AREA –	Sept. 18 23		The Brig.-General Comdg. went round BNS. to see that all were comfortably settled.	
	24		Training Programme issued and Training area allotted.	
	25		Route-March postponed on account of wet weather. 66th. Divn. Warning Order received and S.A. Bde. Warning Order issued. Division to be prepared to move about 27-9-18. 66 Divn. telegram G.1052 received. Divn. to move by tactical train to CORBIE Area on 28-9-18; transport by road.	[app. 12.] [app. 13.]
	26		Route March by BNS.. 66 Divn. Order 87 received. Transfer of Divn. from FIRST Army to FOURTH Army on 27-9-18. S.A. Bde Order 231 issued: S.A. Bde, [with 66 Divn.] move to CORBIE AREA on 27-9-18 – personnel by train, transport by road.	[app. 14.] [app. 15]
	27		Route March by Bde.. Afternoon spent preparing for move.	
	28		Bde. moved by tactical train: 1st. & 2nd. SAI from PETIT HOUVIN, remainder from TINQUES. On arrival whole Bde billeted at VILLERS BRETTONEUX. 66 Divn. Order 88 received. S.A. Bde. Order 232 issued. Move of Bde. Group to CHUIGNOLLES Area on 29-9-18. Amendment No. 1 to S.A. Bde. Order 232 issued.	[app. 16] [app. 17] [app. 18]

42

D. D. & L., London, E.C. (A6326) Wt. W593/776 750,000 1/16 Sch. 52 Forms/C2118/12

– 6 –

Army Form C. 2118.

Instructions regarding War Diaries and Intelligence Summaries are contained in F. S. Regs., Part II. and the Staff Manual respectively. Title pages will be prepared in manuscript.

WAR DIARY
or
INTELLIGENCE SUMMARY.
(Erase heading not required.)

Place	Date	Hour	Summary of Events and Information	Remarks and references to Appendices
CORBIE AREA –	Sept. 29		S.A. Bde. moved at 2 pm to new area:	
			Bde. HQ., 1st SAI, SALTM Bty. } at CHUIGNOLLES.	
			2nd. SAI do. FRAMERVILLE	
			4th. SAI do. RAINECOURT	
			SAF Amb. do. VAUVILLERS	
CHUIGNOLLES	30		Bde. rested during the day. 66 Divn. Order 89 received. S.A. Bde. Order 233 and Amendment issued. Move of Bde. to MONTAUBAN Area on 1st. October.	[App. 19 of App. 20]

3rd. Oct., 1918.

[signature]
Brigadier-General,
Commanding :–
South African Inf. Bde.

D. D. & L., London, E.C.
(A10266) Wt W3300/P713 750,000 2/18 Sch. 52 Forms/C2118/16

43

SOUTH AFRICAN BRIGADE. Secret

OPERATION ORDER No. 287 Copy No. 14

Ref. Army Area Map No. 6

1. The South Afr. (Comp.) BN., and S.A.L.T.M. Battery, will move by March route to the ALQUINES AREA tomorrow, 2n. inst., under further instructions to be issued by the Staff Captain.

2. Upon leaving the present area the S. Afr. (Comp.) BN. will be divided for administrative purposes amongst the 1st., 2nd., and 4th. S.A.I. now being reformed.

3. In the event of the S. Afr. Bde. being ordered/to move with the 9th. Division, the S. Afr. (Comp.) BN. will be reformed forthwith under the command of Lieut.-Col. H.H. BAMFORD, O.B.E., M.C.,

4. Brigade HQ. remains at the Chateau, LUMBRES.

Captain,
Brigade Major,
South African Brigade.

1-9-18.

Issued at
to -

1.- SA (Comp.) BN.,
2.- 2n. Roy. Sc. Fus.,
3.- 9th. Sco. Rifles,
4.- SALTM Bty.,
5.- Bde. Signal Officer,
6.- 9th. Div., "G",
7.- 107 Co., ASC.,
8.- S. Afr. Field Amb.,
9.- VII Corps, "Q",
10.- Area Comdt., LUMBRES,
11.- Area Comdt., ALQUINES,
12.- Brigade Major,
13.- Staff Captain,
14/17.- War Diary.

44

App. 2 and 3 (c)

45

S.African Inf. Brigade,
9th Battn. M.G.C.
Comdt. II Army Training Area, LUMBRES.

G.S. 1/243. 1st September, 1918.

---

1. 1 Company, 9th Battn, M.G.C., will move from present billets to BAYENGHEM LEZ SENINGHEM (3 miles W. of LUMBRES) on 3rd instant. No restriction as to time or route.

2. On arrival this Company will be attached for command and administration to S.African Inf. Brigade, and will take part in all Brigade and Battalion Tactical Exercises carried out by S.African Brigade.

3. Range accommodation will be allotted by G.O.C., S.African Brigade.

4. Billets will be allotted by Second Army Training Area Commandant, LUMBRES.

5. Demands for lorries should be made by 9th Battn., M.G.C., to 9th Division "Q" as early as possible.

T.C. Mudie,
Lieutenant Colonel,
General Staff,
9th (Scottish) Division.

Copy to "Q"

App. 4 [0]

46

SECRET.

Copy No.- 6

9th DIVISION ORDER No. 296.
****

Ref. Sheet 5a 1/100,000. 10.9.18.

1. 9th Division will be transferred from XV Corps to II Corps on 11th September, 1918 and will move into II Corps Area according to March Table overleaf.

2. Headquarters, 9th Division will close at WARDRECQUES at 11 a.m. 12th September and will open at WORMHOUDT at the same hour.

3. S.A. (Comp.) Battn. and S.A. Trench Mortar Battery will not move with 28th Inf. Brigade and will remain in their present Area.

4. ACKNOWLEDGE.

done

J.U. Hill Whitson
Lt. Colonel
aaa General Staff
9th (Scottish) Division.

Issued through Signals
at 11.30 p.m.

Copies to.-

No. 1 - 9th D.A.
2 - C.R.E.
3 - 26th Inf. Bde.
4 - 27th Inf. Bde.
5 - 28th Inf. Bde.
6 - S.A. Inf. Bde.
7 - 9th Seaforth Highrs.
8 - 9th Bn. M.G.C.
9 - 9th Train.
10 - "Q".
11 - 9th Signals.
12 - A.D.M.S.
13 - D.A.D.V.S.
14 - D.A.D.O.S.
15 - A.P.M.
16 - II Corps.
17)- XV Corps.
18)
19)- War Diary.
20)
21 - File.

MARCH TABLE ISSUED WITH 9TH DIVISION ORDER NO. 296.

Reference Sheet 5A 1/100,000.

Serial No.	Date.	Unit.	From.	To.	Route.	Remarks.
1.	11th Sept.	26th Inf. Bde. Group. (less 64th Fd. Coy.)	RACQUINGHEM Area.	LEDERZEELE Area. (Sub-area 'C')	EBBLINGHEM-LE NIEPPE-X.Roads ¼ mile N.W. of H in L'HEY.	
2.	12th Sept.	27th Inf.Bde. group.	HEURINGHEM Area.	LEDERZEELE Area. (sub-area 'C')	BLENDECQUES - ST.OMER - ST. MOMELIN.	
3	12th Sept.	9th Div. H.Q.	WARDRECQUES.	WORMHOUDT.		
4	12th Sept.	9th Seaforth Highrs.	METEREN Area.	WORMHOUDT.	CAESTRE - STEENVOORDE.	
5	12th Sept.	64th Fd. Coy.	BAILLEUL.	WORMHOUDT.	-do-	To march under orders of 9th Seaforth Hrs.
6.	12th/13th Sept.	9th D.A. (less No.3 Sect.D.A.C.)	FLETRE Area.	2nd Corps Area.		To march under orders of 2nd Corps.
7.	13th Sept.	28th Inf. Bde. (H.Q. 28th Bde, 2nd R.S.F. & 9th Sco.Rifles)	LUMBRES.	LEDERZEELE Area. (sub-area 'C')	ST OMER - ST MOMELIN.	
8.	13th Sept.	No.4 Section 9 Sig. Coy.	WARDRECQUES	LEDERZEELE Area (Sub-area 'C')		To join H.Q. 28th Bde. on arrival.

47

Serial No.	Date.	Unit.	From.	To.	Route.	Remarks.
9.	13th Septr.	78th Field Amb.	BLARINGHEM	LEDERZEELE Area (Sub-area 'C')	EBBLINGHEM - LE NIEPPE - Cross Roads ½m. N.W. of H in L'HEY.	Not to pass LYNDE Church before 10am. To join 28th I.Bde. Group on arrival.
10.	13th Septr.	63rd Field Coy.RE	LYNDE.	LEDERZEELE Area (Sub-area 'C'.	EBBLINGHEM - LE NIEPPE - Cross Roads ½m. N.W. of H in L'HEY.	To pass EBBLINGHEM Church 9.15 a.m. To join 28th I.Bde. Group on arrival.
11.	13th Septr.	9th Battn.M.G.C. (less 1 Coy.)	LA CROSSE	WORMHOUDT.		
12.	13th Septr.	1 Coy. 9th Bn. M.G.C.	LUMBRES.	LEDERZEELE Area (Sub-area 'C')	ST OMER - ST MOMELIN.	To move under orders of 28th Inf.Bde.
13.	13th Septr.	No.3 Sec. D.A.C.	WARDRECQUES.	WORMHOUDT.	EBBLINGHEM - LE NIEPPE.	To pass EBBLINGHEM Church at 9 a.m.

NOTES: 1. No restrictions as to time for above moves except where stated.

2. Distances will be maintained as in para 19 of S.S.724 (March Discipline and Traffic Control).

48

49

"A" Form.
MESSAGES AND SIGNALS.

Army Form C. 2121.
(In pads of 100.)
No. of Message..........

Prefix......... Code.......... m.	Words.	Charge.	This message is on a/c of:	Recd. at........ m.
Office of Origin and Service Instructions.	Sent		..................Service.	Date..........
By DR.	At..........m.		Offg. 5[0]	From
	To..........			
	By..........		(Signature of "Franking Officer.")	By..........

TO { 28 Inf Bde
SA Inf Bde

Sender's Number.	Day of Month.	In reply to Number.	AAA
* G.151	10		

Following wire received :-

" G.547 10th
South African Bde. not
include the South African
Composite Battn. aaa addsd
9 Div repto Q
15 Corps
10.45 p.

aaa addsd 28th Bde SA Bde, repeats
Q

From 9th Div
Place
Time

The above may be forwarded as now corrected.
Censor.

(Z) R H Hollond Major
Signature of Addressor or person authorised to telegraph in his name.

*This line, except AAA, should be erased if not required.

Wt. W 3253/P511, 500,000 Pads. 1/18. B. & S. Ltd. (E2380.)

App. 6

SOUTH AFRICAN BRIGADE

Secret

OPERATION ORDER No. 238

Copy No. 16 50

1. The South African Infantry Brigade has been withdrawn from the 9th. Division, with effect from today inclusive.

2. The 2n. Roy. Sc. Fus. and 9th. Sco. Rifles have passed to the Command of G.O.C., 28th. Infantry Brigade.

3. The S. Afr. Bde. will be composed as under, under the Comma of Brigadier-General W. .C. TANNER, C.M.G., D.S.O.,:-

S. Afr. Bde. HQ.,
S. Afr. Bde. HQ. Signal Section,
1st. S.A.I.,
2nd. S.A.I.,
4th. S.A.I.,
S. Afr. L.T.M. Battery.

4. The South African Field Ambulance will remain attached to the S. Afr. Brigade.

5. S. Afr. Bde. HQ. remains at the CHATEAU, LUMBRES, for the time being.

Captain,
Brigade Major,
South African Brigade.

Issued at 3 pm.,
11-9-18 - to

1. 1st. SAI.,
2n.2nd. SAI.,
3. 4th. SAI.,
4. SALTM Bty.,
5. Bde. Sig. Officer,
6. S.Afr. Fld. Amb.,
7. 107 Co., [illegible].,
8. Comdt., Army Areas, LUMBRES,
9. Area Comdt., LUMBRES.
10. 9th. Div. "G"
11. VII Corps "G"
12. VII Corps "A"
13. 28th. Inf. Bde.,
14. Brigade Major,
15. Staff Captain,
16/19. War Diary

app. 7

52

SOUTH AFRICAN BRIGADE. — SECRET

OPERATION ORDER No.[illegible] — Copy No. ____

Ref. Map - SELLES
1/40,000

---

1. (a) The 2nd. and 4th. BNs., S.A.I., will move by march route tomorrow, 12th. September, from the ALQUINES AREA to the LUMBRES AREA, and will be billeted as follows:

2nd. S.A.I. - SENNINGHEM
4th. S.A.I. - (COULOMBY
(SENNINGHEM

(b) The S.A.L.T.M. Battery will move by march route on the 13th. September from present billets to BAYENGHEM.

2. Time of marching is left to Commanding Officers concerned.

3. Billeting parties from the 2nd. and 4th. S.A.I. will meet the Staff Captain at the Church at SENNINGHEM at 8 am. on the 12th. inst.. Guides will meet Units at Church at COULOMBY.

4. First-line transport will move with Units.

5. No lorries are available for the move on the 12th. Sept., but Units can leave any heavy baggage they wish in present area, and lorries will if possible be obtained on the 13th. to move it.

Units must notify Bde. HQ. of their requirements by 12 noon tomorrow, 12th. inst..

A lorry will be provided for move of SALTM Bty. on the 13th. inst..

6. Bde. HQ. will remain at LUMBRES CHATEAU.

Captain,
Brigade Major,
South African Brigade.

11-9-18: Issued thro' Signals at 10 pm., to:

1. 1st. SAI.,
2. 2nd. SAI.,
3. 4th. SAI.,
4. SALTM Bty.,
5. Bde. Sig. Officer,
6. S.Afr. Fld. Amb.,
7. 107 Co., ASC.,
8. Comdt., Army Area, LUMBRES,
9. Area Comdt., LUMBRES,
10. Area Comdt., ALQUINES,
11. VII Corps "A"
12. VII Corps "G"
13. Brigade Major,
14/17. War Diary.

App. 8 [c] 51

file

SECRET.

Copy No.- 6

9th DIVISION ORDER No. 297.
****

11.9.18.

1. In continuation of 9th Division Order No. 296 of 10.9.18. Inf. Brigade Groups will move from LEDERZEELE Area to WORMHOUDT Area according to March Table overleaf.

2. (a) 9th Division Artillery will march from FLETRE Area to HAARDEKOT Area on night 12/13th September under orders issued by II Corps.

(b) Headquarters 9th Div. Artillery will be at HOUTKERQUE.

3. Royal Newfoundland Battn. on transfer shortly to Second Army will be posted to 9th Division to temporarily complete establishment of 28th Inf. Brigade and will probably detrain at ESQUELBECQ on 13th Septr.

4. (a) Para. 2 of 9th Div. Order No. 296 is cancelled.

(b) Headquarters, 9th Division will close at WARDRECQUES at 11 a.m. 12th Septr. and will open at ESQUELBECQ at the same hour.

5. ACKNOWLEDGE

done

J Elstree Whitson
Lt.Colonel
all a General Staff
9th (Scottish) Division.

Issued through Signals
at 10.45 a.m.

Copies to :-

No. 1 - 9th D.A.
2 - C.R.E.
3 - 26th Inf. Bde.
4 - 27th Inf. Bde.
5 - 28th Inf. Bde.
6 - S.A. Inf. Bde.
7 - 9th Seaforth Highrs.
8 - 9th Bn. M.G.C.
9 - 9th Train.
10 - "Q".
11 - 9th Signals.
12 - A.D.M.S.
13 - D.A.D.V.S.
14 - D.A.D.O.S.
15 - A.P.M.
16 - II Corps.
17-18- XV Corps.
19 9th Div. Reception Camp
20 - Area Comdt. LEDERZEELE.
21 - " " WORMHOUDT.
22-23- War Diary.
24 - File.

MARCH TABLE (issued with 9th Div. Order No. 297 of 11.9.18.

Item.	Date.	Unit.	From	To.	Route.	Remarks.
1.	12th Sept.	26th Inf. Bde. Group (less 64th Field Coy. R.E.)	LEDERZEELE Area (Sub-Area "C")	WORMHOUDT Area.	L'ERKELSBRUGGE - ZEGGERS CAPPEL - ESQUELBECQ.	
2.	13th Sept.	27th Inf. Bde. Group.	-do-	-do-	-do-	
3.	14th Sept.	28th Inf. Bde. Group.	-do-	-do-	-do-	
4.	14th Sept.	F Coy. 9th Bn. M.G.C.	-do-	-do-	-do-	

Note.- No restrictions as to times.

53

App 9.[•] 54

SECRET.

Copy No 6

9th DIVISION ORDER No. 298. 12.9.18.

1. Serial Nos. 7 and 12 of March Table issued with 9th Div. Order 296 and Serial Nos. 3 and 4 of March Table issued with 9th Division Order 297 are cancelled.

2. (a) Personnel of 28th Inf. Bde. (Headquarters 28th Inf. Bde., 2nd Bn. R.Scots Fuslrs., ~~and~~ 9th Bn. Sco. Rifles and 28th T.M. Battery) and personnel of 1 Coy. 9th Bn. M.G.C. (to move under orders of 28th Inf. Bde.) will move from LUMBRES to WORMHOUDT Area by train on 13th September.

(b) Entraining Station will be LUMBRES.

(c) Detailed orders for move by train will be issued by "Q".

3. Transport of 28th Inf. Brigade, and of 1 Coy. 9th Bn.M.G.C. will move by road on 13th Septr. from LUMBRES to ESQUELBECQ.
Route:- ST OMER - ST MOMELIN - L'ERKELSBRUGGE - ZEGGERS CAPPEL.
Not to pass L'ERKELSBRUGGE before 2 p.m.

4. 63rd Field Coy. R.E., No. 4 Section 9th Div. Signal Coy., and 76th Field Ambulance will march from LEDERZEELE Area (sub-area "C") to WORMHOUDT Area on 14th September under orders of O.C. 63rd Field Coy. R.E. and will join 28th Inf. Bde. Group on arrival.
Route:- L'ERKELSBRUGGE - ZEGGERS CAPPEL.
No restrictions as to time.

5. Reference Item 2 of March Table issued with Order 297, Route of 27th Inf. Bde. Group will be Road junction ¼ mile S.W. of B in BROXEELE - L'ERKELSBRUGGE and 27th Inf. Bde. Group will be clear of L'ERKELSBRUGGE by 12 noon.

6. 28th I.Bde. 9th Bn.MGC. C.R.E. ADMS. Signals will acknowledge.

T. E. L. Hill Whitson
Lieutenant Colonel,
att. G.S. General Staff,
9th (Scottish) Division.

Issued through Signals at 1.45 p.m.

Copies to:-

No. 1 to 9th D.A.	12 to A.D.M.S.
2 to C.R.E.	13 to D.A.D.V.S.
3 to 26th Inf. Bde.	14 to D.A.D.O.S.
4 to 27th Inf. Bde.	15 to A.P.M.
5 to 28th Inf. Bde.	16 to II Corps.
6 to S.A. Inf. Bde.	17-18 XV Corps.
7 to 9th Seaforth Highrs.	19 to 9th Div.Recep.Camp.
8 to 9th Bn. M.G.C.	20 to A.Commdt.LEDERZEELE.
9 to 9th Div. Train.	21 to " " WORMHOUDT.
10 to "Q".	22-23 War Diary.
11 to 9th Signals.	24 to File.

App. 10 [o]
55

S E C R E T.

28th Infantry Brigade.
South African Infantry Brigade.

G.S. 28/55. 13th September 1918.

1. Paragraph 3 of 9th Division, G.S. 28/53 of 10th September (as amended by G.S. 28/53 of 11/9/18) is cancelled.

2. South African Brigade will cease to be under command of 9th Division from 13th September inclusive and will pass into Second Army Reserve, administered by VII Corps.

13/9/18.

[signature] Lieut.Colonel.
General Staff.
9th (Scottish) Division.

Copies to:-
II Corps.
XV Corps.
"Q".
9th Signals.
9th D.A.
C.R.E.
26th Inf. Bde.
27th Inf. Bde.
9th Seaforth Highrs.
9th Battn. M.G.C.
9th Div. Train.
A.D.M.S.
D.A.D.V.S.

SOUTH AFRICAN BRIGADE
OPERATION ORDER NO.23

Secret.
Copy No...14.

19/9/18. app. 11

1- The 66th. Division (less Artillery) is being concentrated in the LE CAUROY Area (First Army).

2. The South African Infantry Brigade Group will be transferred by rail to First Army on 22nd. Sept., to join the 66 th. Division.

3. The South African Infantry Brigade Group will entrain at WIZERNES and detrain at TINQUES.

4. Administrative Instructions will be issued by the Staff Captain.

5 acknowledge

Issued thro' Signals
at 7pm. to:-

Major,
Brigade Major,
South African Brigade.

Nos.1/3 to 1st.2nd.4th.Regts.
4. S.A.L.T.M.Bty.
5. S.A.F.Amb.
6. VII Corps 'G'
7. 66th. Division.
8. Bde. Sig. Officer.
9. Bde. Major.
10. Staff Captain

No.11 to VII Corps 'A'
12 Area Comdt.LUMBRES.
13 Comdt. Army Areas LUMBRES.
14/17 War Diary.
18 Office Copy.

56

App. 12 [c]

58

<u>SECRET.</u> <u>66th DIVISION.</u>

W A R N I N G   O R D E R .

The Division will be prepared to move from present area on or about September 27th.

Lieut-Colonel.
General Staff.
66th Division.

D.H.Q.,
24-9-18.

<u>Distribution.</u>

"Q".
Signals.
C.R.E.,
198th Inf. Bde.
199th Inf, Bde.
S. A. Brigade.
Divl. Train.
A.D.M.S.
D.A.D.V.S.
Camp Commandant.
D.A.D.O.S.
A.P.M.
D.G.O.
66th M.T. Coy.

App. 13 [c]

"C" Form.

Army Form C. 2121.
(In books of 100.)

MESSAGES AND SIGNALS.

No. of Message ________

Prefix SM Code ___ Words 30	Received	Sent, or sent out.	Office Stamp.
£ s. d.	From GZX	At ____ m.	25/9/18
Charges to Collect	By GD	To ____	
Service Instructions		By ____	

Handed in at GZX Office 11.10p m. Received 11.41p m.

TO	South African Bde

* Sender's Number	Day of Month.	In reply to Number	AAA
G 1052	25		

The	Division	will	move
by	tactical	train	to
CORBIE	Area	on	Sept
28th	aaa	Transport	will
move	by	Road	staging
night	27th	/28th aaa	Details
follow			

FROM	66 Div
PLACE & TIME	

* This line should be erased if not required.

(7432)—W 302—100,000—10/9/17—E. P. Co.—(E1503).

app. 14 [o]

S E C R E T .

Copy No. 10

59

66th DIVISION ORDER No. 87.

26th September 1918.

1. The 66th Division (less Artillery) accompanied by Divisional M.T. Coy. (less 2 Sections) will be transferred from First Army to Fourth Army commencing 27th September.

On arrival in Fourth Army area the Division will be accommodated in the CORBIE area and will be administered by XIII Corps.

2. Dismounted personnel will move by tactical train entraining at TINQUES and PETIT HOUVIN on 28th September under instructions to be issued by 66th Division "Q".

Detraining Station - CORBIE.

Orders for the march of Units to entrainment stations will be issued later.

3. Horse transport, under orders of Major G.M.KIDD M.C. 5th R. Innis. Fus., will move by road on September 27th in accordance with attached march table.

4. M.T. Coy. (less 2 sections) and all other motor vehicles will move by road on 28th September, an Officer reporting in advance to S.M.T.O. XIII Corps, VILLERS BOCAGE.

5. Divisional Headquarters will close at LE CAUROY and open at CORBIE at 2 p.m. on 28th September.

6. ACKNOWLEDGE.

F.P. Nosworthy
Lieut-Colonel.
General Staff.
66th Division.

DISTRIBUTION.

Copy No. 1 War Diary.
2 " "
3 File.
4 'A' and 'Q'.
5. Signals.
6 C.R.A.
7 C.R.E.
8 198th Inf. Bde.
9 199th Inf. Bde.
10 S.A.Brigade.
11 Divl. Train A.S.C.
12 A.D.M.S.
13 D.A.D.V.S.
14 Camp Commandant.
15 66th M.T.Coy.
16 D.A.D.O.S.
17 D.A.P.M.
18 D.G.O.
19 First Army.
20 Fourth Army.
21 VIII Corps.
22 " "
23 XIII Corps.
24 " "
25. A.D.C.

MARCH TABLE FOR UNITS AS IN ENTRAINMENT PROGRAMME "A".

Serial No.	Unit.	From.	To.	Route.	Starting time.	Remarks.
1.	9th Glouc. R.	PENIN.	TINQUES.	-	8.0 a.m.	
2.	199th Inf.Bde.HQ.	IZEL-LEZ-HAMEAU.	TINQUES.	Road going north from IZEL as far as ST.POL-ARRAS road.	7.10 a.m.	
3.	5th Conn.Rang.	-do-	TINQUES.	-do- -do-	7.15 a.m.	
4.	18th (LHY) K. L'pool R.	GIVENCHY-LE-NOBLE.	TINQUES.	PENIN.	8.30 a.m.	
5.	9th Manch. R.	MANIN.	TINQUES.	PENIN.	8.15 a.m.	
6.	149 L.T.M.Batt.	VILLERS SIR SIMON.	TINQUES.	PENIN.	8.40 a.m.	
7.	2/3rd E.L.Fd.Amb.	IZEL-LEZ-HAMEAU.	TINQUES.	Road going N. from IZEL as far as ST.POL - ARRAS Road.	9.0 a.m.	
8.	S.A. Bde. H.Q.	MAIZIERES.	TINQUES.	AVERDOINGT.	10.30 a.m.	
9.	4th Bn.S.A.Regt.	AMBRINES.	TINQUES.	MAZIERES - AVERDOINGT.	10.20 a.m.	
10.	6th Bn. Lan.Fus.	LIGNEREUIL.	TINQUES.	AMBRINES - PENIN.	10.15 a.m.	
11.	S.A. L.T.M.Batt.	VILLERS SIR SIMON.	TINQUES.	PENIN.	11.15 a.m.	

MARCH TABLE FOR UNITS AS IN ENTRAINMENT PROGRAMME "B".

Ser.No.	Unit.	From.	To.	Route.	Startg.time.	Remarks.
12.	1st Bn S.A.Regt.	GOUY EN TERNOISE.	PETIT HOUVIN.	MONTS EN TERNOIS.	7.15 a.m.	
13.	2nd Bn.S.A.Regt.	MAGNICOURT.	-do-	MONTS EN TERNOIS.	7.15 a.m.	
14.	S.A. Fld. Amb.	AMBRINES.	-do-	MAGNICOURT - MONTS EN TERNOIS.	7.0 a.m.	
15.	430th F.Co.R.E.	SARS LES BOIS.	-do-	-do- -do-	8.30 a.m.	
16.	431st F.Co.R.E.	BERLENCOURT.	-do-	SARS LES BOIS - MAGNICOURT.- MONTS EN TERNOIS.	8.15 a.m.	
17.	432nd F.Co.R.E.	DENIER.	-do-	-do- -do- -do-	8.15 a.m.	
18.	H.Q., R.E.	LE CAUROY.	-do-	ETREE WAMIN-HOUVIN-HOUVIGNEUL - MONCHEAUX.	8.00 a.m.	
19.	D.H.Q. incldg. Div. Emp. Coy.	LE CAUROY.	-do-	-do- -do-	8.05 a.m.	
20.	Div. Sig. Co.	LE CAUROY.	-do-	-do- -do-	8.10 a.m.	
21.	6th R.Dub. Fus.	LIENCOURT.	-do-	SARS LES BOIS-MONTS EN TERNOIS.	7.00 a.m.	
22.	198th Inf.Bde.HQ.	GRAND RULLECOURT.	-do-	LIENCOURT-SARS LES BOIS - MONTS EN TERNOIS.	9.00 a.m.	
23.	5th R.Innis.Fus.	-do-	-do-	-do- -do-	9.05 a.m.	
24.	198 L.T.M.Batt.	VILLERS SIR SIMON.	-do-	AMBRINES - MAIZIERES - MONTS EN TERNOIS.	9.40 a.m.	To be clear of AMBRINES by 10.15
25. 2/2	Field Amb.	BLAVINCOURT.	-do-	DENIER-SARS LES BOIS - MONTS EN TERNOIS.	10.00 a.m.	
26.	Mob.Vet.Sect.	LE CAUROY.	-do-	ETREE WAMIN -HOUVIN-HOUVIGNEUL-MONCHEAUX.	8.15 a.m.	

62

63

SECRET.

66th Divn.
G. 1052.

"A" and "Q".
Signals.
C.R.E.
198th Inf. Bde.
199th Inf. Bde.

South African Bde.
Div. Train A.S.C.
A.D.M.S.
Camp Commandant.
A.D.C.

Reference Divisional Order No. 87, para. 2, and entrainment programme forwarded under 66th Division No. 7252/Q. of 26.9.18, dismounted personnel will march to stations as in attached tables.

P.A.

Lieut-Colonel,
General Staff,
66th Division.

D.H.Q.,
27.9.18.

TRANSPORT GROUPS.

Div. H.Q. Group.	198th Bde.	199th Bde.	S.A. Bde.
Divisional Headquarters.	Bde.H.Q. & Sig. Sect.	Bde. H.Q. & Sig.Sect.	Bde.H.Q. & Sig.Sect.
H.Q. & No.1 Sect.Div.Sig.Co.	6th Lan. Fus.	18th (LHY) K.L'pool R.	1st Bn. S.A.Regt.
H.Q. & 3 F. Cos. R.E.	5th R.Innis.Fus.	9th Manch. R.	2nd Bn. S.A. Regt.
S.A.A. Section of D.A.C.	6th R.Dub.Fus.	5th Conn.Rang.	4th Bn. S.A. Regt.
H.Q. Divl. Train.	2/2nd E.L.Fld.Amb.	9th Bn.Glouc. R. (Pioneers).	S.A. Fld. Amb.
Mob. Vet. Sect.	543 Coy.A.S.C.	2/3rd E.L. Fld.Amb.	542 Coy. A.S.C.
		544 Coy. A.S.C.	S.A. L.T.M.B.

****

65

MARCH TABLE FOR HORSE TRANSPORT of 66th DIVISION on SEPT. 27th.

(To accompany 66th Division Order 87. of 26.9.18.)

Serial No.	Group.	From.	To.	Route.	Remarks.
1.	Div.H.Q. Group.	Billets.	RAINCHEVAL.	Cross roads 1200 yds S.of BEAUDRICOURT CHURCH - LE SOUICH - LUCHEUX-HALLOY - ORVILLE - MARIEUX.	Under Maj. P.H.SHARPE, R.E. To be clear of BEAUDRICOURT CHURCH by 9.0 a.m.
2.	198th Bde. Group.	Billets.	RAINCHEVAL.	GRAND RULLECOURT-HUMBERCOURT-MONDICOURT-PAS- THIEVRES - MARIEUX.	Under 198th Bde.Transport Officer. To be clear of GRAND RULLECOURT by 9.0 am
3.	199th Bde. Group.	Billets.	MARIEUX.	Same as for Serial No. 2.	Under 199th Bde.Transport Officer. NOT to enter GRAND RULLECOURT before 9.30 a.m.
4.	S.A. Bde. Group.	Billets.	MARIEUX.	ETRÉE-WAMIN and then as for Serial No. 1.	Under S.A. Bde.Transport Officer. NOT to enter BEAUDRICOURT before 9.30 a.m.

NOTE ~~1.~~ ~~Groups as per reverse.~~

1 2. Distances will be maintained in accordance with S.S. 724. Gaps of 50 yds will be left between each section of 12 vehicles.

2 3. March will be continued on Sept. 28th to CORBIE Area via TOUTENCOURT, under orders to be issued by Major G.M. KIDD, M.C., 5th R. Innis. Fus.

3 4. Billets will be obtained from Town Major of MARIEUX ~~and RAINCHEVAL~~.

4 5. An Officer from each Group will report to Major D.V.M.BALDERS, M.C., D.A.A.G., 66th Divn. at CORBIE Station at 12 noon on 28th Sept.

5 6. Personnel will be rationed by their units for consumption 28th Sept. Forage for consumption 28th Sept. will be issued by Divl. Train on termination of march on 27th Sept. Rations and forage for consumption 29th Sept. will be issued on arrival at final destination.

****

App. 15. 66

Secret

SOUTH AFRICAN INFANTRY BRIGADE

Copy No. 14

Ref. Maps -
Lens 11
Amiens 17

OPERATION ORDER No. 231

28 Sept., '18

1. The 66th. Division (less Artillery), accompanied by Divl. MT. Coy. (less 2 sections) will be transferred from First Army to Fourth Army, commencing Sept. 27th.

2. S. African Inf. Bde. Group will move, personnel by train, transport by road, to the CORBIE AREA.

3. Personnel will entrain at TINQUES and PETIT HOUVIN on Sept. 28th., and detrain at CORBIE.

4. All orders for march of Transport and administrative arrangements will be made by Staff Captain.

5. Orders for the march of Units to entraining stations will be issued later.

6. ACKNOWLEDGE.

Major,
Brigade Major,
South African Inf. Bde.

Issued at 11.30 pm.,
to -

1. 1st. SAI
2. 2nd. SAI
3. 4th. SAI
4. SALTM Bty
5. S.A.Fld. Amb.
5. Bde. Signal Off.,
6. 542 Co., ASC.
7. 430 Fld. Co., RE,
8. 66th. Division
9. Area Cdt., Maizieres,
10. 198 Inf. Bde.
11. 199 Inf. Bde.
12. Staff Captain
13. Brigade Major
14/17. War Diary.

al

Unit	S.P.	Time	To	Route	REMARKS
2n. SAI	Church, MAGNICOURT sur CAUCHE	8.15 am.	MARIEUX	ESTREE WAMIN - X-rds. 1200 yds. S. of BEAUDRICOURT Church LE SOUICH - LUCHEUX - HALLOY - ORVILLE - MARIEUX.	1. Transport will stage night 27th/ Sept. at MARIEUX.
1st.SAI	do.	8.20 am.	do.		
4th.SAI	do.	8.25 am.	do.		
S.A.F.Amb.	do.	8.30 am.	do.		
Bde.HQ. SALTMB 548 Co.ASC	do.	8.35 am.	do.		2. Not to enter BEAUDRICOURT before .[illegible]

1. Distances will be maintained in accordance with SS.724. Gaps of 50 yds. [illegible] be left between each section of 12 vehicles.
2. March will be continued on Sept. 28 to CORBIE Area via TOUTENCOURT, under orders to be issued by Maj. G.M. KIDD, MC., 5th. R. Innis. Fus..
3. Billets will be obtained from Town Major of MARIEUX.
4. An Officer from each group will report to Maj. D.V.M. BALDERS, MC., DAAG., 66th. Divn., at CORBIE Statn. at 12 noon on 28th. Sept.,
5. Personnel will be rationed by their Units for consumption 28th. Sept.. Forage for consumption 28th. Sept. will be issued by Divl. Train on termination of March on 27th. Sept.. Rations and forage for consumption 29th. Sept. will be issued on arrival at final destination.

67

66-16 [o]

S E C R E T.

Copy No....10

68

66th DIVISION ORDER No. 88.

28th September 1918.

1. The 66th Division (less Artillery) will march 29th Septemb to MERICOURT and HARBONNIERES Areas as in attached March Table.

2. Distances will be observed on march as laid down in S.S.72

3. Billetting arrangements will be issued by "Q".

4. M.T. Company will move under orders of Div. "Q".

5. Divisional Headquarters will close at CORBIE at 2.0 p.m. and open at MORCOURT at same hour.

6. ACKNOWLEDGE.

W H Guinness.
Lieut-Colonel,
General Staff,
66th Division.

DISTRIBUTION.

copy No. 1 War Diary.
2 " "
3 File.
4 "A" and "Q".
5 Signals.
6 C.R.A.
7 C.R.E.
8 198th Inf. Bde.
9 199th Inf. Bde.
10 S.A. Bde.
11 Divl. Train A.S.C.
12 A.D.M.S.
13 D.A.D.V.S.
14 Camp Commandant.
15 66th M.T. Coy.
16 D.A.D.O.S.
17 D.A.P.M.
18 D.G.O.
19 Fourth Army.
20 XIII Corps.
21 "
22 A.D.C.

Ser.No.	Unit.	From.	To.	Route.	Remarks.
4.	<u>R.E. Group.</u> 9th Glouc.R.(Pioneers). 430th F. Co. R.E. 431st F. Co. R.E. 432nd F. Co, R.E.	HAMELET and VAIRE Sous areas. CORBIE.	CAPPY Sub-area.	HAMEL - SAILLY-LAURETTE - BRAY sur-SOMME.	To be clear of VAIRE Sous CORBIE by 11.0 a.m.
5.	<u>Divl. H.Q. Group.</u> Divl. Headquarters. H.Q. & No.1 Sec.Div.Sig. Coy. S.A.A.Sect. of D.A.C. H.Q. Div.Train. Mobile Vet. Sect.	CORBIE Area.	MORCOURT Sub-area.	HAMEL - CERISY.	To march under orders of Camp Commandant.

<u>NOTE</u>.- It is left to the discretion of O.C. Groups to send parties on direct to destination without moving to billets allotted for night 28th/29th, in case any trains are so late as to make this desirable. Any such parties must either join their groups on the march, or alternatively clear CORBIE by 9.30 a.m.

69

SECRET.

app. 17

SOUTH AFRICAN BRIGADE ORDER NO. [illegible]

Copy No. ....

Map Ref.
AMIENS 17 1/100,000

28th. Sept.1918. 61

1. The South African Brigade Group will move tomorrow (29th. instant) to the CHUIGNOLLES Area.
2. The move will take place in accordance with attached March Table.
3. 1st. Line Transport will march with Units.
4. Billetting parties to report to Staff Captain at Church at CHUIGNOLLES at 11am. tomorrow.
5. Same lorries as were used today will be available tomorrow.
6. Reports to Brigade H.Q. at CHATEAU VILLERS en BRETONNEUX till 10-15am., afterwards to Head of column.
7. Acknowledge.

Issued thro' Signals
at 11.0 .pm.

[signature] Major,
Bde. Major,
South African Bde.

Copies to:-

1/3	to 1st., 2nd. and 4th. Rgts.	No. 9	Bde.Signal Off.
4.	S.A.L.T.M.Bty.	10/11	66th. Division.
5.	S.A.F.A.	12/13	War Diary.
6.	542 Coy. A.S.C.	14	Staff Captain
7.	198 Inf. Bde.	15/16	Office Copies.
8.	199 Inf. Bde.		

MARCH TABLE.

Serial No.	Unit.	Starting Point.	Time.	Route.	Remarks.
1.	Bde. H.Qrs) Sig. Section)	X Roads N.of L. in VILLERS BRETONNEUX	10-5am.	LA MOTTE Santerre	100 yards interval to be maintained between Companies and between Units and their Transport. 500 yards between battalions and 20 yards between every 12 vehicles. Usual Clock Hour Halts.
2.	S.A.L.T.M.Bty.		10-7am.		
3.	1st. S.A.I.		10-10am.		
4.	2nd. S.A.I.		10-25am.		
5.	4th. S.A.I.		10-40am.		
6.	S.A.Fd.Ambl.		11-5am.		
7.	542 Coy. A.S.C.		11-15am.		

App. 18 70

SOUTH AFRICAN BRIGADE.

Corrigenda No. 1 to South African Brigade Order No. 282.

Transport will be Brigaded and March to new Billeting Area under the orders of Lt. Johnson, 4th. S.A.Infantry.

Starting point

X Roads North of L. in VILLERS BRETONNEUX.

Time. 1.0pm.

On arrival in New area all A.A.L.Gs., will be mounted and positions reported to B.H.Qrs.

8/[illegible]/18.

Major,
Brigade Major,
South African Brigade.

MARCH TABLE TO ACCOMPANY 66th DIVISION ORDER No. 88.

Ser.No.	Unit.	From.	To.	Route.	Remarks.
1.	South African Bde. Group. Bde.H.Q. & Sig.Sect. 1st Bn S.A.Regt. 2nd Bn. S.A.Regt. 4th Bn. S.A. Regt. S.A. Fld. Ambulance. 542 Coy. A.S.C. S.A. L.T.M.Batt.	VILLERS BRETONNEUX Sub-area.	CHUIGNOLLES Sub-area.	LA MOTTE-EN-SANTERRE - PROYART.	To be clear of western end of LA MOTTE by 12.30 p.m.
2.	199th Brigade Group. Bde. H.Q. and Sig. Sect. 18th (IHY) K.L'pool R. 9th Manch. R. 5th Conn. Rang. 2/3rd E.L. Fld. Amb. 541 Coy. A.S.C. 199 L.T.M.Batt.	CORBIE Area.	PROYART Sub-area.	FOUILLOY - LA MOTTE-EN-SANTERRE.	Not to enter LA MOTTE before 12.30 p.m. and to be clear of western end by 1.45 p.m.
3.	198th Brigade Group. Bde. H.Q. and Sig.Sect. 6th Lan. Fus. 5th R. Innis. Fus. 6th R. Dub. Fus. 2/2nd E.L. Fld. Amb. 543 Coy. A.S.C.	CORBIE Area.	HARBONNIERES Area.	LA MOTTE-EN-SANTERRE - BAYONVILLERS.	Not to enter LA MOTTE before 1.45 p.m.

72

Army Form C. 2121
(in pads of 100).

"A" Form
MESSAGES AND SIGNALS.

No. of Message..................

Prefix........Code........m.	Words / Charge	This message is on a/c of:	Recd. at........m.
Office of Origin and Service Instructions.	Sent	..........Service.	Date..........
Copy	At........m.		From..........
	To..........		
	By..........	(Signature of "Franking Officer.")	By..........

TO 1st SAI / SAFA
2nd " / SALTMB
4th " / 542 Coy ASC

Sender's Number.	Day of Month.	In reply to Number.	AAA
*	29		

Reference SA Bde Orders No 232 of 28th aaa On account of lateness of arrival of Battalions Brigade will march tomorrow at 2.5 pm instead of 10.5 am aaa Therefore all Units will march exactly four hours later than laid down on march table aaa Billeting parties will meet Staff Captain at noon instead of 10 am

From S. A. Bde.
Place *
Time 2.30 am.

The above may be forwarded as now corrected. (Z) (Sgd) E Barlow Major Bde Major

Censor. Signature of Addressor or person authorised to telegraph in his name.

* This line should be erased if not required.

(12968.) Wt. W12952/M1294. 187,500 Pads. 1/17 McC. & Co., Ltd. (E. 818.)

Army Form C. 2123.
(In books of 100.)

"C" FORM.
MESSAGES AND SIGNALS.

No. of Message..........

Prefix.........Code......Words..........	Received.	Sent, or sent out.	Office Stamp.
£ s. d. Charges to Collect	From.......... By..........	At..........m.	73
Service Instructions		To.......... By..........	

Handed in at..........Office..........m. Received..........m.

TO (2)

* Sender's Number.	Day of Month.	In reply to Number.	AAA
4th Bde	[illegible]	Group	to
CAPPY	to	the	[illegible]
of	HARBONNIERES	by	12
noon	not	to	[illegible]
PROYART	before	12	noon
aaa	Route	along	S
bank	of	Canal	[illegible]
FROISSY	&	CAPPY	[illegible]
road	not	marked	on
map	aaa	19th	Bde
[illegible]	[illegible]	2nd	[illegible]
[illegible]	marching	to	CHUIGNOLLES
[illegible]	to	be	complete
by	2	pm	aaa
[illegible]	group	will	march
to	[illegible]	area	on
[illegible]	[illegible]	[illegible]	[illegible]

FROM
PLACE & TIME

* This line should be erased if not required.

(16629) Wt535/M1970. 300,000 Pads. 4/17. McC. & Co., Ltd. (E1218).

App. 19 C of J 73A

"C" FORM.
MESSAGES AND SIGNALS.

Army Form C. 2123.
(In books of 100.)

No. of Message....................

Prefix..........Code........Words....112	Received.	Sent, or sent out.	Office Stamp.
£ s. d.	From..[illegible]	At..................m.	B.A.
Charges to Collect	By..[illegible]	To..................	30.9.18
Service Instructions		By..................	

Handed in at..........[illegible]..........Office..10.18..m. Received..10.40..m.

TO	5 A Bde

* Sender's Number.	Day of Month.	In reply to Number.	AAA
C F 79	30		

Following	moves	will	take
place	Oct	1st	AAA
5	A	Bde	Group
to	MONTAUBAN	Suzanne	[illegible]
BRAY	and	MARICOURT	to
be	N	of	Canal
de	la	SOMME	by
10.45	am	AAA	[illegible]
Bde	Group	to	MARICOURT
[illegible]	the	Bde	head
of	Column	to	cross
Canal	at	11	and
AAA	Div	to	Group
to	MONTAUBAN	[illegible]	[illegible]
&	MARICOURT	head	of
Column	to	cross	Canal
at	12.30	pm	AAA

FROM	
PLACE & TIME	

* This line should be erased if not required.

(19629) Wt125/M1970. 300,000 Pads. 4/17. McC. & Co., Ltd. (E1213).

app 20

76

Secret

SOUTH AFRICAN INFANTRY BRIGADE

OPERATION ORDER

- No. 233 -

Copy No.

Sept., 1918

Ref. Maps -
AMIENS 17 - 1/100,000
LENS 11 - 1/100,000

---

1. The S. African Bde. Group will move by March Route tomorrow to billets in the M?NTAUBAN Area.

2. The move will be carried out in accordance with the attached March Table.

3. Transport will move with Units.

4. Advance parties will meet Staff Captain at 10.30 am. tomorrow, 1st. Oct., at X-rds. W. of 'M' in MARICOURT.

5. Guides will meet Units at X-rds. W. of 'M' in MARICOURT.

6. Reports to Bde. HQ., CHUIGNOLLES, until 9 am. - afterwards to head of column.

7. ACKNOWLEDGE.

Major,
Brigade Major,
South African Inf. Bde..

Issued at 11pm. thro' Signals
to 1. 1st. SAI
2. 2nd. SAI
3. 4th. SAI
4. SALTM Bty
5. SA Fld. Amb.
6. Bde. Sig. Off.
7. 532 Co. ASC
8. 66th. Division
9. Area Cdt., CHUIGNOLLES
10. 198 Inf. Bde.
11. 199 Inf. Bde.
12. Staff Captain
13. Bde. Major
14/17 - War Diary.

"A" Form

MESSAGES AND SIGNALS.

No. of Message.........

Prefix............ Code......... ......m. Office of Origin and Service Instructions.	Words / Charge Sent At..............m. To.............. By..............	*This message is on a/c of:* ....Service. (Signature of "Franking Officer.")	Recd. at......... Date......... From ......74 By.........

TO { Recipients of S A Bde O. 233

Sender's Number.	Day of Month.	In reply to Number.	AAA
* O.233/1.	1		

Amendment	to	S A Bde	O 233
In	column	Starting	Point
for	Serial	Nos	1
to	3	read	X-rds
300	yds	W	of
CHUIGNOLLES		Church	and
for	Serial	Nos	4
to	6	read	X rds
E	of	E	in
FRAMERVILLE.			

From S A Bde.

Place

Time

The above may be forwarded as now corrected. (Z) (Sgd) E. [illegible]

Censor. Signature of Addressor or person authorised to telegraph in his name.

* This line should be erased if not required.

(18965.) Wt. W12952/M1294. 187,500 Pads. 1/17 McC. & Co., Ltd. (E. 818.)

Army Form C. 2121.
(In books of 100.)

"C" FORM.
MESSAGES AND SIGNALS.

No. of Message................

Prefix........Code......Words........... £ s. d. Charges to Collect	Received. From............... By................	Sent, or sent out. At..............m. To.............. By..............	Office Stamp. 75
Service Instructions			

Handed in at..Office..............m. Received..............m.

TO (3)

* Sender's Number.	Day of Month.	In reply to Number.	AAA
1st	Lines	advanced	parties
of	1	S M	[illegible]
[illegible]	Ades.	[illegible]	DRAG
at	Cross	Roads	[illegible]
N	of	MARICOURT	at
10 30	am	[illegible]	Bde
will	obtain	billets	from
Area	Cdt	(CAPPY)	advanced
parties	[illegible]	at	10
am	[illegible]	Div	HQ close
Maricourt	&	open	at
HARBONNIERES	at	12	noon
[illegible]	[illegible]		

(DRAG)

FROM
PLACE & TIME 66 Div

* This line should be erased if not required.

(18639) Wt528/M1970. 300,000 Pads. 4/17. McC. & Co., Ltd. (E1213).

Ref. Maps -
A[illegible]ENS 17 - 1/100,000
L[illegible] QQ - 1/100,000

MARCH TABLE to accompany O.O. 2[illegible]3

Serial No.	Unit	Starting Place	Starting Point Time	ROUTE	Remarks
1.	Bde. HQ. & Sig. Co.	X-rds. 500 yds. E of CHUIG-NOLLES Church	0910	BRAY-sur-SOMME - then direct road to MARICOURT.	Distances of 100 yds. between Coys. & Transport of Units. -
2.	1st. SAI		0913		
3.	SALTM Bty.		0919		
4.	2nd. SAI	X-rds. W of 'E' in FRAMER-VILLE	0815		- 500 yds. between Bns. -
5.	4th. SAI		0831		25 [illegible] yds. between every 6 vehicles.
6.	SAFA		0840		
[illegible]	[illegible]48 Co. ASC	As for B.H.Q.	*		

* To march under orders of O.C. Coy., but to be clear of Starting point by 0900.

77

78

SOUTH AFRICAN

INFANTRY BRIGADE

NARRATIVE of the Operations carried out by the Brigade subsequent to the reconstitution of the Brigade on the 11th. September, 1918....

79

During the opening days of Oct. the Bde. moved from CHUIGNOLLES to MONTAUBAN, NURLU, and RONSSOY, arriving in the RONSSOY area on the morning of 5th. Oct.. The Bde. Group consisted of:-

1st. SAI
2nd. SAI
4th. SAI
SALTM Bty.
S. Afr. Fld. Amb.,
430 Field Co., RE..

Oct. 6th. On the 6th. Oct., warning was received that the Bde. would take part in a major operation of the Fourth Army, to be commenced on a date to be notified later, and to be carried out in conjunction with an American Corps on the Right and the Third Army on the Left. The share of the operation allotted to the 66th. Div. was to attack on a line running from SE. to NW. through the Eastern outskirts of BEAUREVOIR, the S. Afr. Bde. (on the Right) and the 198 Inf. Bde. (on the Left) forming the Divl. assaulting troops. Each of these Bdes. was to attack on a two-BN. front; S. Afr. Bde. being made responsible for the section from the Cemetery SE. of BEAUREVOIR (in B.17.a.) to a point in the Northern outskirts of BEAUREVOIR (abdut B.4.c.2.6). In the S. Afr. Bde. disposition, the 2nd. SAI and 4th. SAI (on the Right and Left respectively) were the assaulting troops, with 1st. SAI in support. The accompanying map shows the Bde. and Inter-BN. boundaries with the First objective (RED line) and second objective (GREEN line) of the opening operations.

Zero hour and day were ultimately notified for 05.10 on 8th. Oct., and during the morning of Oct. 7th. the three BNs. of SAI., together with Bde. HQ., moved from the RONSSOY area to a section of the HINDENBURG line near BONY, as a preliminary step towards occupying their battle positions.

Oct. 7th. At 21.00 on Oct. 7th. the Bde. moved off to their assembly positions which had previously been taped out.

Oct. 8th. By 03.30 on Oct. 8th., the assembly, (which was covered by the 25th. Div.) had been completed, Bde. HQ. being then in MUSHROOM QUARRY. Unfortunately, the assembly was not completed without loss, as at about 01.00 a heavy enemy barrage came down to the West of the assembly line, causing numerous casualties amongst all three BN., Lt.-Col. BAMFORD, OBE., MC., Commanding the 2nd. SAI., being among the wounded.

At the appointed time, the assaulting BN.s of the Bde. moved forward to the attack under cover of an effective creeping barrage, and despite a stubborn resistance on the part of the enemy - mainly by MG. fire - rapid progress was made.

The first objective, the RED line - was reached and consolidated by the S. Afr. Bde. at about 07.00..

Bde. HQ. moved forward LA SABBLONIERE.

As indicating the strength of the enemy opposition up to the capture of the first objective, it may be mentioned that the enemy made full use of the strong defensive positions afforded by sunken roads and trenches, particularly in the area of attack of the Right BN. (2nd. SAI.)

80

The USIGNY RAVINE also constituted a formidable obstacle but thanks to the assistance of a Tank the capture of this position did not involve any material delay in the general advance. In many cases the enemy machine-gunners resisted until they were either killed or captured, the enemy losses in this stage of the fighting being substantial, both in men and material - the latter including five field-pieces, of which four were captured as the result of some clever individual work by an Officer and a few men. These guns were subsequently turned on the enemy, and utilised in harassing his retirement.

The first objective - the RED line - having been captured, the 199 Inf. Bde. took up the attack as previously arranged, leapfrogging through the S. Afr. Inf. Bde. and 198 Inf. Bde., which at 13.00 received orders to reorganise in readiness for a continuation of the operations on the succeeding day; the 199 Bde. meantime proceeding with the capture of the second objective - the GREEN line - which included the town of SERAIN. By this time S. Afr. Bde. HQ. had been moved forward to a point N. of the X-r_s. NE. of LA SABLONNIERE.

About 23.00 on 8th. Oct., orders were received regarding the operations to be carried out on the following day. These operations contemplated that the Divl. troops would press forward to the capture of MARETZ, the assaulting forces being provided by 198 and 199 Inf. Bdes., with the S. Afr. Inf. Bde. in Div. Reserve. After MARETZ had been secured the S. Afr. Bde. was to take up the attack, and press on to the capture of MAUROIS, consolidating on the E. outskirts of that town.

The S. Afr. Bde. dispositions for the operations of Oct. 9th. were the same as for the 8th., viz., the attack to be carried out on a two-BN. front, 2nd. SAI on the Right and 4th. SAI on the Left, with the 1st. SAI in support.

During the night of the 8/9th. Oct., enemy bombing 'planes were very active over the area captured, but they did no material damage.

Oct. 9th. The Div. advance on Oct. 9 opened as arranged, and the 198 and 199 Inf. Bdes. reached the day's first objective, which was a line running from SE. to NW. through the E. outskirts of MARETZ, without much difficulty.

About 10.30 the S. Afr. Bde. took up their appointed share in these operations, as already indicated, and leapfrogged through the 198 and 199 Inf. Bdes., continuing the attack on the Divl. front through MAUROIS and HONNECHY.

The S. Afr. Bde. and Inter-BN. boundaries in this further advance, and the Bde. objective (BLUE line) were as shown on the appended map. In the meantime Bde. HQ. had been moving forward successively to PETITE FOLIE FME., AVELU, L'EPINETTE, and to field at P.20.d.2.3., just W. of Rly. near MAUROIS.

By 14.30 the S. Afr. Bde. had reached its objective E. of MAUROIS. The main feature of the advance to this objective, as was the case in the previous day's operations, was the determined resistance offered by enemy MGs., well placed tactically at points from which effective oblique fire could be directed. This opposition, as was anticipated, was strongest in the neighbourhood of the BOIS de GATTIGNY, and on the Rly. embankment immediately to the W. of the wood. But the attacking BNs. quickly adopted tactics for outflanking the enemy positions, and with the assistance of a couple of armoured cars succeeded in overcoming these obstacles, their losses being wholly disproportionate to the strength of the positions captured.

Contrary to expectations, the villages of MAUROIS and HONNECHY constituted only slight obstacles in the final stages of the day's advance.

One feature of the day's operations was not contemplated by the Opération Order, but was justified by the circumstances. At about 12.00 the Left attacking BN. of the Bde. (4th. SAI) was approaching the W. outskirts of BERTRY. The town was not within the S. Afr. Bde.'s objective, but as the advance of the co-operating forces on the Bde.'s Left flank seemed to have been checked, and as the BERTRY area dominated a section of the Bde.'s objective, the 4th. SAI. cleared up this area before occupying its section of the day's objective.

Whilst clearing the village of BERTRY an enemy motor-car containing an Officer was captured, in running order. The Officer, who was wounded, stated his mission was that of firing mines and charges which had been placed at various points to retard our advance. The following morning a party was sent to recover the car, but found that it had been removed.

The BN. in Bde. Reserve (1st. SAI) was not subjected to demands during the earlier stages of the day's operations, but as the situation cleared and it became apparent that the enemy resistance was weakening, orders were received for the S. Afr. Bde. to push on and capture REUMONT and to establish and an outpost line around the NE. extremities of that village, including BOICRIES FME.. For the purposes of this supplementary operation, 1st. SAI., which had, during the earlier stages of the day's advance, remained in Bde. Reserve at AVELU, was ordered (at 14.30) to move up at once in support of the other two BNs., which, as already narrated, had established themselves on the objective E. of MAUROIS and HONNECHY. In pursuance of this order 1st. SAI. moved up to positions along the Rly. line SW. of MAUROIS, and at 19.30 2 coys. of this BN. went forward to the MAUROIS area in support of 2nd. SAI.. Two hours later 1st. SAI. went forward and without opposition completed the supplementary operation by occupying REUMONT and establishing the required outpost line covering the village, thus relieving the 3rd. Cav. Div., which had during the afternoon of the 9th. worked up to these positions.

The day's work was most creditable to the Bde., the enemy suffering heavily both in men and material.

__Oct. 10th.__

Nothing of importance happened on the 10th. Oct.. The 3 BNs. of the Bde. moved into billets in REUMONT and MAUROIS, the Div. advance being continued by 198 and 199 Inf. Bdes., which passed through the S. Afr. Inf. Bde. at 05.00.. During the day the enemy bombarded the REUMONT area with gas and HE. shells, which caused some casualties to 1st. SAI..In the evening, Bde. HQ. was carried to a point in the NW. outskirts of REUMONT, and at the same time 2nd. and 4th. SAI. moved out a short distance to the NE. of REUMONT, where they occupied positions S. and N. respectively of the main road to LE CATEAU, 1st. SAI remaining in REUMONT.

__Oct 11th.__

On the 11th Oct. orders were received that the Bde. would move up that night to relieve the other two Bdes. of the 66th Divn. (198 and 199 Bdes.) which, after passing through the S. Afr. Bde. on the previous morning, had occupied a line immediately to the W. of LE CATEAU. For the S.African Bde. this proved to be the opening move of a period of continuous fighting of the most arduous and exhausting character. Indeed it is no exaggeration to assert that what the Officers and men of the Bde. had to endure, and what they accomplished during the period 11th. to 12th. Oct., will compare favourably with the most memorable exploits recorded in the annals of the Bde...

The German retirement on the Western front had reached a stage where it became essential for the enemy to hold up the Allied advance E. of LE CATEAU and the river SELLE. Otherwise the enemy's difficulties in extricating his forces and withdrawing them to his new lines of resistance would be greatly increased. By this time, as already narrated, the 66th. Div. had fought its way up to the Western extremities of LE CATEAU, so that the Divn. now began to feel the stiffening of the enemy resistance, due to the causes just mentioned. As it turned out, the S. Afr. Inf. Bde. had to shoulder a share in the task of overcoming the stiffening resistance on the part of the enemy.

In accordance with orders, the Bde. on the night of the 11th. Oct., moved up from REUMONT area and relieved the 198 and 199 Inf. Bdes. in the line W. of LE CATEAU. The disposition of the Bde. was as follows:

1st. SAI. relieved the line BNs. of both the 198 and 199 Bdes., the 2nd. and 4th. SAI. being in support on the Right and Left respectively.

The co-operating Units on the Right and Left of the Bde. were provided by troops of the 33rd. and 25th. Divisions.

Bde. HQ. moved forward the same evening to a position in Q.7.b..

Oct. 12 - 14 From the 12th. to the 15th., the 1st. SAI. had some difficulty in pushing forward the line N. of LE CATEAU to the bank of the SELLE river, as the valley of this river was dominated by the enemy positions on the Eastern bank, and by the houses in the Northern outskirts of LE CATEAU. Strong enemy patrols were very active along the Western bank of the SELLE stream between LE CATEAU and MONTAY, and in pushing forward the line in this vicinity the 1st. SAI. lost some 20 Officers, NCOs., and men killed and wounded, and a post of 1 NCO. and 7 men was reported missing. The enemy continued to be troublesome ~~xxxxxxx~~ amongst the numerous houses along the Western banks of the stream.

Oct.15 On Oct. 15th., orders were received for the Bde. to attack E. of the river SELLE in conjunction with the 50th. Divn. on the Right, with assembly positions on the E. bank, and objectives as shown by RED and GREEN lines on Map "B".

The BN. boundary is shown by a BLACK line, and it will be noticed that each BN. had to open out considerably as it proceeded from its assembly to its objective.

As the area W. of the river had not been cleared, the 1st. SAI. were ordered to attack at 5.45 pm. on the 16th., make good all posts on the E. bank to enable 8 bridges to be thrown across the river, by which the assaulting BNs. were to reach the assembly positions.

83

This attack was successfully accomplished, and the necessary posts established. On crossing the river it was found that a strong wire entanglement had been erected along the E. bank of the river, through which the parties sent to cover the erection of the bridges were required to cut their way and prepare openings for the assembly of the assaulting BNs..

At 8 pm. the assaulting BNs., 4th. SAI. on Right, 2nd. SAI. on Left, moved forward to selected positions near the river, and Bde. HQ. moved up to the Ravine about 500 yards North of the Four-Valleys cross-roads..

One coy. of the 1st. SAI. had been detailed to follow the 2nd. SAI. in the attack, and form a defensive flank to the N. between the Railway embankment and the river.

Zero hour had been fixed for the 50th. Div. at 5.20 am., and for the Bde. at 8.5 am.. This difference of time was due to the fact that the 50th. Divn. had a great deal of ground to cover before it was able to get into line with the 66th. Divn..

Assembly:

The assembly of the assaulting troops was carried out as soon as the necessary bridging of the stream had been completed; this, however, was necessarily slow across the light foot-bridge and through the gaps in the wire on the far bank of the river.

The enemy positions along the railway bank and northern outskirts of LE CATEAU were within close range of the positions of assembly, but in addition to this he had pushed out a line of outposts armed with MGs. along the road immediately East of the river, and was at several points within 50 yards of our assembly positions.

The enemy outposts were very active, and did much to retard the progress of the assembly. However, this was complete at 4.30 am., when the troops did all in their power to consolidate their positions before daybreak. Time, however, did not permit of more than a scanty preparation in the way of trenches to protect that assaulting troops between dawn and 8.5 am., at which latter hour they were to attack.

Fortunately, just before dawn, nature provided excellent cover from view, in the shape of a heavy mist which entirely prevented the enemy from obtaining observation of our concentration, and resulted in his barrage falling just over our line.

84

At 5 am all was in readiness, and at 8-5 am, under cover of artillery and MG. barrage, and hidden by a thick mist, the Battns. advanced to the attack. From the outset, thick belts of single and double-apron wire were encountered, and in face of heavy MG. fire from front, right rear, and left flank (the enemy appeared to still hold posts in LE CATEAU) the attack was carried forward, all the wire having been cut by hand, as the barrage had not touched it on account of its proximity to the assembly positions.

After proceeding about 100 yards, a sunken road, protected by a palisade, was encountered, and the right Battn. was held up for some time here, suffering many casualties before being able to go on.

The Left Battn., who had discovered a CT which ran underneath the wire almost up to the Rly Embankment, had been able to get forward more quickly, and announced at 9-15 that they had reached their objective. By 9-30 both Battns. had secured the first objective and had pushed out patrols in front, only to be compelled to recall them on account of the heavy MG fire to which they were subjected.

1st S.A.I. was now called upon to reinforce each Battn. with a Coy. on account of the severe losses sustained, and one Btn. of 198 Bde. was sent forward to mop up LE CATEAU itself.

Later in the day the last Coy. of 1st S.A.I. was sent up to the left flank, which appeared to be in danger of being enveloped.

The 50th Divn., who were to capture the Railway triangle and make contact with the Right BN. was met by strong opposition. 198 Bde. were therefore ordered to take over part of the line from the right Battn., and if the 50th Divn. were successful in establishing themselves in the Railway Triangle during the night, the attack to the final objective was to be carried out in the morning.

The 50th Divn., not being successful, this operation was cancelled, and the Bde. proceeded with the work of consolidating the Railway Embankment during the 18th.

About 5 pm orders were issued for the S.A.Bde. to be relieved by the 199 Bde. This relief was to be made upon the condition that a further line be established and secured. Owing to the lateness of the hour, it was recommended that the relief should be cancelled, and this was approved. The further line was then established and secured during the night. Unfortunately a portion of the 1st S.A.I. was relieved before this could be prevented, and these troops had to be recalled to relieve the relief.

Next day (Oct.19th) Bde. H.Qrs. moved up to the Chateau just N. of LE CATEAU, which had been H.Qrs. for all three BNs. during the operations and during night 19/20th the Bde. was relieved and the next morning proceeded to rest billets in SERAIN.

The South African Light Trench Mortar Battery had been left behind at BONY during the first phase of the operations from BEAUREVOIR to REUMONT, and their services were first required on the 14th Oct., when they moved up and took up positions on the left flank, where they did excellent work in destroying enemy MGs.

On the morning of the 18th, 2 guns were sent up to the Right flank, and here again good work was done, although good posit- for the guns were not easy to obtain, as on the Left it was found necessary to move their positions on several occasio-

During the period of these operations - viz., from 8th. October to 11th. November - no reinforcements from the Depot in England reached the Brigade, and consequently, from the 9th. Oct. onwards the tasks allotted to the Brigade had to be undertaken with Battalions very depleted in numbers.

The first draft arrived at HESTRUD on the evening of 11th. November, eight hours after hostilities had ceased. This draft, however, only consisted of some 500, all ranks, being approximately one-third of the Brigade's requirements, whilst at this time some 4,000 men of all categories were then at the WOKING Depot.

Reference must be made to the very keen desire and splendid efforts of the Officers and men of this final draft to reach the Brigade in time to be of assistance. After leaving railhead they pushed on with all possible speed, and on one particular day accomplished a march of some 23 miles.

APPENDIX "A"

To narrative for October, 1 9 1 8

CASUALTIES

	Off.	OR.
Killed	6	155
Wounded	40	982
Died of Wounds	1	29
Missing	1	46
Gassed	-	17
TOTAL	47	1227

CAPTURES

Prisoners	Off. 4; ORs., 1238
MGs.	567
LTMs.	19
Field Guns	22
Anti-tank Guns	4
Bicycles	15
Lorries	1
Motor-cars	3

ATTACHED TROOPS:

Operations of Oct. 8th.
83rd. Bde. R.F.A.
1 18prd. Bty. of 112th. Bde. RFA.
x"B" Coy., 1st. Tank BN. (less 1 Section)
430 Field Co., RE.
"B" Co., 25th. BN., MGC..

Operations of Oct. 9th.
23rd. Bde., RFA.
"B" Co., 25th. BN., MGC.
430 Field Co., RE.
1 troops, Northumberland Hussars.
1 Section, XIII Corps Cyclists.

Operations of Oct. 17th.
82nd. Bde., RFA.
1 Coy., 25th. BN., MGC.
"C" Section (4 guns) No. 1 Spec. Co., RE.

*****

Army Form C. 21..

WAR DIARY
or
INTELLIGENCE SUMMARY.
(Erase heading not required.)

Instructions regarding War Diaries and Intelligence Summaries are contained in F. S. Regs., Part II. and the Staff Manual respectively. Title pages will be prepared in manuscript.

Place	Date	Hour	Summary of Events and Information	Remarks and references to Appendices
CHUIGNOLLES	Oct 1.		S.Afr. Bde. moved to MONTAUBAN.	
MONTAUBAN	2.		Training in attack practice.	
	3.		do do do Division Warning Order received - Move by road on 4/10/18.	~~App. 1 (o)~~
			Division Order No 92 received - Move to COMBLES on 4/10/18.	App. 1 (o)
			Issued - Warning Order to move on 4/10/18; S.Afr. Bde. Order No 234 - Bde to move to COMBLES on 4/10/18.	App. 2
	4.		Bde. moved to COMBLES in morning. Received Div. Order No. 93 - Move to NURLU.	App. 3 (o)
			Bde. Order No. 235 issued. Bde to move to NURLU 4/10/18.	App. 4
			Bde. moved during evening to NURLU.	
NURLU.	5.		Div. Order No. 94 received and Bde. Order 236 issued. Bde to move to RONSSOY area 5/10/18.	App. 5 (o) App. 6.
			Bde. moved to RONSSOY.	
RONSSOY.	6.		Div. Order 95 and Add. received. Move to LE CATELET-MAUROIS line. Bde. Warning order issued - Bde. to move ay 12.00, 6/10/18.	App. 7 (o)
			Div. Order 96 received. Amending destination in Order 95. S.A.Bde to HINDENBURG line, Squares A.9. & 15.a.and b.	App. 8 (o)
			Bde. Order 237 issued. Bde to move to LE CATELET-MAUROIS line.	App. 9.
			Div. G.X.9 received. Moves in D.O. 95 and 96 postponed 24 hours.	App.10.(o)
Additional to 6th See page 2.			Bde. B.S. 55 issued postponing moves in Order 237 24 hours.	App.11.
			Amendment to Bde. Order 237 issued. Bde to move to HINDENBURG line, Squares A.9.& 15.a.and b.	App.12.
			Brig-General Commanding went forward to reconnoitre the front with Commanding Officers.	
do	7.		Bde. Major and Officers from each Battn. went up to BEAUREVOIR to reconnoitre positions for putting down assembly tapes for starting point of attack. Each Regt. sent up parties to find out best routes to forward positions. At 9 p.m. Regts moved forward to their assembly positions.	
			Bde. H.Q. moved from RONSSOY to HINDENBURG line near BONY at 10 a.m.	
			Div. G.X. 9 received. Hour and day for forthcoming operations - 05.10, Oct. 8.	App.13(o)
			Div. Order 99 received - Hour at which troops of 66th Div. are to be formed up: re-withdrawal of 25th Div.	App.14 (o)
			Bde. Prelim. Order No. 2 issued confirming Prelim. Order No. 1, with exception of amendments. Bde. B.S.62 issued ordering Bns. to move to assembly positions. ~~BMX~~ 2 issued, instruction re Contact planes. "If anly slight resistance is met on GREEN line being taken, 198 and S.A.Bdes. may be required to go through again on a two Battn. front".	App.15.

270

Instructions regarding War Diaries and Intelligence Summaries are contained in F. S. Regs., Part II. and the Staff Manual respectively. Title pages will be prepared in manuscript.

WAR DIARY
or
INTELLIGENCE SUMMARY.
(Erase heading not required.)

Army Form C. 2118.

Place	Date	Hour	Summary of Events and Information	Remarks and references to Appendices
Ada.	Oct. 6th.		Div. Prelim. Order 1 received. Scheme of action of Div. in major operations to be undertaken shortly. (Instructions 1, 2, 4 and 6 also received)	App.16.(o)
			Div. Order 97 received. Orders for attack by Div. on 8/10/18.	App.17.(o)
			Div. Order 98 received. Moves to take place on 7/10/18. S.A.Bde. as in Order 98.	App.18.(o)
			Bde. B.S.37 issued. Moves ordered in Bde. Order 237 to take place on 7/10/18.	App.19.
			Bde. Prelim. Order No. 1 issued. Action of S.A.Bde. in major operations to take place shortly.	App.20.
			Bde. BM. 926 issued. Officers to be detailed by Bns. to reconnoitre assembly positions at 6 a.m. 7/10/18.	App.21.
MUSHROOM QUARRY.	8		Bde. H.Q. moved to MUSHROOM QUARRY. Col. BAMFORD, O.C. 2nd S.A.I., reported badly wounded at 2 a.m. Both assaulting Battns. in position at 4.15 a.m. Attacked at 5.10 a.m. Both Battns had to face strong M.G. fire at commencement; reported ~~both~~ objectives gained - 4th S.A.I. at 7.30 a.m. 2nd S.A.I. at 6.50 a.m. Bde H.Q. moved at 7.30 a.m. to LA SABIONNIERRE.	
			199th Inf. Bde. passed through at proper time.	
			Bde .H.Q. moved to N. of X-roads N.E. of LA SABIONIERRE. Heavily bombed from 6.30 pm. until midnight by aeroplanes.	
			Div. Order 99 received. Line captured by Div on 8/10/18. Ordering further advance on 9/10/18. Second objective - Line through P.18.central, P.23.central, to be taken by S.A.Bde.	App.22 (o)
			Div. GB.15 received. Zero hour for operations of 9/10/18.	App.23 (o)
			Div. Order 100 received, giving Divl. front. S.A.Bde to be in Divl. Reserve.	App.24 (o)
NE. of LA SABIONNIERE	9		Bde. BMX.14 issued, ordering continuance of advance 9-10-18; objective of Bde., second objective as given. Attack by 2nd. SAI. on right and 4th. SAI. on left.. 1st. SAI in support. Bde. to move forward keeping in touch with 198 and 199 Bdes..	App.25
			Bde. passed through 198 and 199 Bdes. at about 10.30 am.. 2nd. SAI on right were hung up at railway embankment by MG. fire, but gradually forced the position and reached objective at about 2.20 pm.. 4th. SAI on left were subjected to MG. fire on their left; they reached their objective at about same time as 2nd. SAI.. Bde. HQ. moved to PETITE FOLIE FME.; at 10 am. to farmhouse near AVELU; at noon to L'EPINETTE, and at 4 pm. to field near railway embankment.	
			Bde. BMX. 25 issued; infantry to push forward NE. of REUMONT, morning of 10-10-18; 2 coys. of 1st. SAI. to reinforce front line SE. of the MAUROIS - REUMONT road. At 5.30 am. 10-10-18 1st. SAI. to attack and capture REUMONT and BOIORIES FME., and thence along tracks running through P.18.b.4.3. - P.18.d.9.4. - P.18. .20.00 - P.23.d.1.8.	App.26

D. D. & L., London, E.C. (19340) Wt W3300/P713 750,000 5/18 E 2686 Forms/C2118/16.

Instructions regarding War Diaries and Intelligence Summaries are contained in F. S. Regs., Part II. and the Staff Manual respectively. Title pages will be prepared in manuscript.

WAR DIARY
or
INTELLIGENCE SUMMARY.
(Erase heading not required.)

Army Form C. 2118.

Place	Date	Hour	Summary of Events and Information	Remarks and references to Appendices
	9		Div. Order 101 received. Bde. to take over REUMONT and ground in P.12.c. & d., Q.7.c. & d., and Q.13.a. & c., from 3rd. Cav. Div.. Bde. to be in Div. Reserve, 10-10-18, and to be prepared to follow up after 198 and 199 Bdes. had passed through.	App.27(o)
			Bde. BMX.26 issued, cancelling BMX. 25. 'Cavalry have captured REUMONT and TROISVILLES;1st. SAI. to take over REUMONT from cavalry and establish posts in Q.13.c., Q.7.c. & d., and P.12.c.' This was done, and 1st. SAI. reported arrival at REUMONT at 2 am. without incident.	App.28
			4th. SAI reported at about 10 pm. that they had taken the village of BERTRY, owing to progress through P.21. and P.15. being impossible on account of heavy MG. fire from the village. Detachment of FG. horse and an armoured car rendered assistance in capturing BERTRY.	
	10.		Div. Order 102 received; action to be taken by 198 and 199 Bdes. consequent on result of operations of 17th. and 33rd. Divs..	App.29(o)
			Bde. BMX. 30 issued.. Div. to continue advance, 10-10-18.. Bde. to be in Div. Reserve, and to be prepared to move from present positions on receipt of order. 199 Bde. to pass through S. Afr. Bde. outposts at 5.0 am. and continue the advance: 1st. SAI. billeted in REUMONT 2nd. SAI do. } MAUROIS 4th. SAI }	App 29 A.
			About midday, verbal order received from Div. to move ~~from~~ two BNs. E. of REUMONT, Right BN. to watch carefully Rt. Div. flank, where 25 Div. reported hung up at BENIN. Bde. BMX. 31 issued; '2nd. SAI to move forthwith to a position in Q.7.a. & d. and get into touch with 25 Div.; 4th. SAI. to move to position in P.6.a. and P.12.b.; 1st. SAI. to remain at REUMONT.'	App.30
			Bde. Warning Order issued; Units to hold themselves in readiness to move up at about 5.30 pm.	App.31
			Bde. HQ. moved at 6.30 pm. to about 600x. NW. of REUMONT.. 2nd. SAI. reported at about 10.45pm. that patrols had returned at 8.30 pm. that they could not get into touch with 25 Div..	
600x. NW. of REUMONT	11		Div. order 104 received.. Bde. to take over Div. front on night 11-10-18. Line - K.16.d.4.2., along S. bank of SELLE to K.23.c.9.0., along W. bank of river through LE CATEAU, to K.34.d.0.0. to Q.3.a.5.5.. Bde. to prepare to attack K.11.c.5.5., K.17.b.5.5., K.18.central, on 12-10-18, to establish posts at once on N. bank of river, K.27.b.& d., K.16.c. & d..	App.32(o)
			Div. GB.50 received. Administrative boundaries and moves of various Units.. Div.G.114 received;'Corps on Left will attack 12-10-18.. 66 Div. to throw forward Left flank to K.17.a.'	App.33(o) App.34(o)
			Div. G.116 received. Field artillery to be used to assist in obtaining objectives given in Order 103.	App.35(o)
			Bde. BMX.33 issued. Orders for relief of 198 and 199 Bdes. on night 11-10-18.	App.36
			1~~st.~~ [struck through]	

Army Form C. 2118.

Instructions regarding War Diaries and Intelligence Summaries are contained in F. S. Regs., Part II. and the Staff Manual respectively. Title pages will be prepared in manuscript.

WAR DIARY
or
INTELLIGENCE SUMMARY.

(Erase heading not required.)

Place	Date	Hour	Summary of Events and Information	Remarks and references to Appendices
	11		1st. SAI. ordered to establish line of posts on N. bank of LA SELLE river, approx K.22.b. & d., K.16.c. & d., and attack by BNs. to take place probably 12-10-18: Objectives - K.11.c.5.5., K.17.b.5.5., K.18.central, but further orders would be issued. If possible, advantage to be taken of attack by 33rd. Div. by securing high ground in K.11.c. and K.17.b..	App.37
500x. NW. of REUMONT	12		Relief by 1st. SAI completed 11.30 pm. 11-10-18, and by 4th. SAI. at about 4.30 am.12-10-18.	
			1st. SAI. reported that an attempt to cross the stream by A and B. coys. during the night failed owing to heavy MG. fire from railway bank K.16.d. and K.22.b.. Recommended that railway bank be subjected to artillery fire. Cancellation of artillery arrangements for 5.30 am. asked for.. Report by 1st. SAI. timed 3.45 am.. at 5.45 am. 1st. SAI. reported that bridge was not completed until after 3.15 am.. Bde. BMX.40 issued. "Bridges are being thrown over LA SELLE river, and these are to be held. They will be commanded by LGs. and MGs. by day, and by posts on further bank by night. High ground in K.27.b. & d. to be strengthened by Pioneer BN.."	App.38 App.39 App.40
			1st. SAI ordered to make another attempt to cross river at 10.30 am.. General Officer Commanding Bde., however, went up to see the position, and finding the river too deep to ford, decided it was useless to make the attempt. As 33 Div. had been thrown back after crossing river, 66 Div. postponed action until Rt. flank came up.	
			Weather very wet, and during the night locality of Bde. HQ. was shelled heavily with gas-shells.	
do.	13		A wet day; situation quiet. During the afternoon a post of the 1st. SAI. at K.34.b.40.85. was captured by the enemy. A patrol searched in the vicinity, but found only rifles and packs.	
do.	14		Div. G.1112 received. 9 Gloucesters (Pnrs.) attached to S. Afr. Bde.	App.41(o)
			Bde. Order 243 issued: 2nd. SAI. to relieve 2n. North. Fus. (150 Bde.): 9 Gloucesters to relieve 2 coys. 1st. SAI. in line on left: 2 coys. 1st. SAI. thus relieved to move into support, leaving 2 coys. in line.. 4th. SAI. to take up positions vacated by 2nd. SAI. in Q.7.b.. Bde. BMX. 48 issued; re Order 243, Left Div. boundary from 14-10-18 to be P.6.central to K.21.c.0.0. - rd. junction K.22.a.2.1. (excl. to 66 Div.) - K.17.d.9.6. - K.12.central.. 9 Gloucesters not to take over N. of this, as was originally intended, and 1st. SAI. to withdraw any of their troops N. of the boundary. Bde. BMX. 49 issued; re BMX.48; 9th. Gloucesters to establish an interlocked post with 115 Bde. on their Left.	App.42 App.43 App.44
			Situation during day was quiet. Above reliefs reported complete by 10.30 pm..	

4 5 8

WAR DIARY
or
INTELLIGENCE SUMMARY.
(Erase heading not required.)

Army Form C. 2118.

Instructions regarding War Diaries and Intelligence Summaries are contained in F. S. Regs., Part II. and the Staff Manual respectively. Title pages will be prepared in manuscript.

Place	Date	Hour	Summary of Events and Information	Remarks and references to Appendices
500x. NW.of REUMONT	15		Brigadier General Commanding ordered the erection of bridges over river SELLE during night 14/15, but RE. failed to accomplish this on account of patrol encounters near river. Enemy posts definitely proved to be on our side of the river.	
			1st. SAI. were ordered to clear their side of the river of enemy posts or patrols during the evening.	
			Bde. BS.99 issued; 'to prevent enemy from crossing to W. bank of SELLE river, front line will be reinforced at night.'	App.45
			Bde. BMX.54 issued.-'9th. Gloucesters to take over from 1st. SAI. on night of 15-10-18 the portion of line to the S. of their present boundary as far as line running through K.28.c.5.7. to rd. junction in K.28.b.3.5. - K.23.c.2.1.. 1st. SAI. to withdraw troops thus relieved to support line.'	App.46
			During day, situation quiet. Intermittent shelling and slight gas-shelling.	
	16		Received - Divn. Order 104 G.118 G.1120 G.1120/1 Instructions 1 - 8 and Amendments. } Orders for attack on 17-10-18.	App.47(o)
			CRE. Order 52 received.	App.48(o)
			Divn. Order 105 received - further orders for attack on 17-10-18.	App.49(o)
			430 Field Co., RE., Instructions received, ordering construction of strong points at K.29.c.8.9. and K.23.c.1.2..	App.50(o)
			Bde. Order 244 issued, and Amendment; orders for attack on 17-10-18. 1st. Objective - K.29.a.1.8. - K.29.central - K.36.d.0.5. (RED Line).. 2nd. Objective (BLUE Line).. 4th. SAI. to attack on the Right and 2nd. SAI. on the Left. One coy. 1st. SAI. to follow 2nd. SAI. and on capture of RED Line to clear Railway Line in NE. direction as far as RICHEMONT STREAM, and throw back a defence flank to SELLE river. Remaining coys. of 1st. SAI. to K.28.b. & d., and come back into Bde. Reserve. 1st. SAI. to place posts on E. side of river to protect N. and S. flanks of troops during assembly.	App.51
			At 5.45 pm., 16-10-18, 1st. SAI. to attack and clear the line of the SELLE river to cover construction of bridges which the RE. had been ordered to throw across during the night to enable the infantry to form up on the E. bank.	
			Bde. ~~BMX. 105~~ BS105. issued, informing 1st. SAI. of artillery arrangements. 1st. SAI. to arrange for consolidation as soon as possible and push covering parties over to protect construction of bridges.	App.52

D. D. & L., London, E.C. (20540) Wt W5300/P713 750,000 3/15 E 2688 Forms/C2118/16.

274

Army Form C. 2118.

Instructions regarding War Diaries and Intelligence Summaries are contained in F. S. Regs., Part II. and the Staff Manual respectively. Title pages will be prepared in manuscript.

WAR DIARY
or
INTELLIGENCE SUMMARY.
(Erase heading not required.)

6

Place	Date	Hour	Summary of Events and Information	Remarks and references to Appendices
	16		Bde. order 245 issued; relief of 2nd. SAI. and 9th. Gloucesters by 198 Bde. in portion of line: 2nd. SAI. to move to K.26.a. & b., K.25.d., and K.26.a.. 9th. Gloucesters to move to MAUROIS. 4th. SAI. to move to positions K.27.c., K.33.a. & c., K.32.b. and K.33.a.. Minor operation of clearing the W. bank of the SELLE river was carried out at 5.45 pm. without loss, and 2nd. and 4th. SAI. moved up at about 7.30 pm. to the river to be ready to cross when bridges were constructed.	App. 52A
			Bde. HQ. moved to position in ravine about 500x. E. of Four-Valley X-rds..	
	17		At 2 am. the bridges were put across the river, and 2nd. and 4th. SAI. crossed to their assembly positions. All was in readiness by 5 am.. A heavy mist covered the attack. 4th. SAI. reported a strongly-wired road from K.29.a.3.2. to K.29.c.0.3., which was held by enemy MGs., and which had not been touched by our barrage. At 10 am. 2nd. SAI. reported that information had been given by casualties to effect that the railway line had been secured.	
			At 10.20 am. 2nd. SAI. reported Second objective had been reached, but troops had had to retire to railway line; it was also reported that enemy MGs. were firing from houses in village in rear, and also from house in left rear (from MONTAY).	
			At 11 am. 1st. SAI. reported that A coy. had been placed at disposal of 4th. SAI. owing to severe casualties having been sustained by latter regt.. At 1.18 pm. 4th. SAI. reported that touch had not been obtained with 50 Div.. At 1.26 pm. 1st. SAI. reported that a further coy. had been sent forward to reinforce left of 2nd. SAI..	
			Bde. BMX. 89 to Divn. "Villages making position extremely difficult on our Right. Rly. from K.35.c.2.4. to K.35.b.1.5. is not in our possession. We hold railway from K.29.a.7.0. to K.36.b.1. . approx.. Have 1 coy. still in reserve on road in K.29.d."	App. 53
			Later message (BMX.91) informed Div. that situation remained as reported in BMX.89, except that reserve coy. had been moved to position K.28.b.80.95 to K.29.a.20.35. in order to protect left flank, which had been threatened. At 2.50 4th. SAI. reported that last reserve coy. of 1st. SAI. had been sent up to Left flank, which was being enveloped.	App 54.
			Div. GB.95 received: "Artillery fire being brought to bear on rly. between K.35.central and K.35.c.9.3. from 5 pm. to 5.45 pm.. When artillery fire lifts at 5.45 pm., rly. from K.35. central to Div. boundary at K.35.c.9.3. is to be made good."	App. 55(c)
			Bde. BMX.96 issued. Line to be secured as Bde. portion of Div. Line of resistance - rly. crossing K.23.c.1.3. - K.35.central, with defensive flank along river in K.23.c. and K.22.d., and also through BAILLON FME. to river.. 1st. SAI. to undertake occupation of the rly. to North as far as K.23.c.1.3. and provision of defensive flank along line of RICHEMONT STREAM to its junction with the SELLE river.	App. 56

275

D. D. & L., London, E.C. (A9540) Wt W3300/P713 750,000 3/18 Forms/C2118/16.

Instructions regarding War Diaries and Intelligence Summaries are contained in F. S. Regs., Part II. and the Staff Manual respectively. Title pages will be prepared in manuscript.

INTELLIGENCE SUMMARY.

(Erase heading not required.)

Place	Date	Hour	Summary of Events and Information	Remarks and references to Appendices
Ravine 500x. E. of Four-Valley X-roads.			2nd. SAI. ~~would~~ will provide defensive flank from BAILLON FME. to SELLE river.	App.[illegible]
			Div. Order 106 received. Line to be consolidated by Bde.	App.58 (o)
			Div. Order 107 received. Operations to be carried out on 18-10-18.	App.59 (o)
			Div. G.126, ~~[illegible]~~ GB.97, and Order 108 received; cancels Order 107 - Operations for 18-10-18, contingent on 59 Div. capturing railway triangle.	App 57(o)
			Div. G.128, 130, and 131 received; action to be taken by Bde. vide BMX.96 above. 9th. Gloucesters to relieve 5th. Innis. Fus. and come undersorders of SA Bde.	App.60 (o)
			Bde. BMX. 98 issued; action of Bde. on 18-10-19 is dependant on whether rly. triangle is captured. If not captured, code-word "REFUSAL" would be sent.	App 60 (A)
do.	18		Code-word "REFUSAL" received from Div. (G.129) and sent out (BMX.90).	App.61(o)
			Div. Order ~~[illegible]~~ 109 received; adjustment of N. boundary of Div. and relief of 9th. Gloucesters on night 19/19th..	App.62 App.63(o)
			Div.G.131 received. 9th. Gloucesters come under command of 199 Bde. forthwith.	App.64(o)
			Received - Divn. ~~[illegible]~~ G.134, 137, 138, 140, 144; Orders for relief of Bde. by ~~[illegible]~~ by 199 Bde., provided SA. Bde. had secured line K.36.a.1.9. to K.23.c.1.3..	App.65(o)
			Div. G.146 received; 'reports indicate enemy is retiring. Leading Bdes. will push out strong patrols and maintain touch with enemy. Troops not to advance E. of RICHEMONT stream.'	App.66(o)
			Div. G.147 received; relief of SA. Bde. by 199 Bde. cancelled, reason for cancellation being that the objectives marked on the map with the original Order had been shown as RED and GREEN on the map, and had become confused in the Order, as the Div. referred to these lines in reverse order.	App.67(o)
			Bdes. were now ordered verbally to carry on the take final objective, wjich could easily have been done before, but for confused order. Final objective was taken during the night.	
do.	19		Bde. HQ. moved to Chateau, LE CATEAU. Situation quiet.	
			Div. Order 110 received; relief of Div. by 18th. Div., night 20/21st. Oct.	App.68(o)
			Div. G (unnumbered) received. '25th. Div. taking over night 19-10-18 front to K.36.d.6.0.. 199 Bde. will take over remainder of Div. front.	App.69(o)
			Div. G.152 received. 'After dusk 199 Bde. to relieve SA Bde. in front line.'	App.70(o)
			Bde. Order 246 issued; relief of Bde. by 199 Bde. night 19/20th.. 1st. SAI. to move to NE. edge of LE CATEAU; 2nd. and 4th. SAI. and SALTM Bty. to REUMONT.' Relief completed at about 1 am.	App.71
			Bde. Order 247 issued.. Bde. to move to SERAIN on 20-10-18.	App.72

276

Army Form C. 2118.

Instructions regarding War Diaries and Intelligence Summaries are contained in F. S. Regs., Part II. and the Staff Manual respectively. Title pages will be prepared in manuscript.

WAR DIARY
or
INTELLIGENCE SUMMARY.
(Erase heading not required.)

Place	Date	Hour	Summary of Events and Information	Remarks and references to Appendices
The Chateau, LE CATEAU.	20		Bde. moved to SERAIN.	
	21 - 31		Bde. at SERAIN; route marches carried out on 25th. and 28th., and Bde. took part in Divl. Scheme on Oct. 31st.. Remainder of time spent in re-organising and re-equipping, and t raining under BN. arrangements. A copy of the narrative for the month is attached	

[signature]
Brigadier-General,
Commanding -
South Afr. Inf. Bde..

277

App. 1 (O)

87

SECRET.

Copy No. 10

66th DIVISION ORDER No. 92.

3rd October 1918.

1. The 66th Division will move by road tomorrow, 4th October, in accordance with attached March Table

Move to be complete by 13.00.

2. Billets from Area Commandants concerned.

3. Orders for move of 9th Glouc. R. (Pioneers) will be issued separately.

4. Divisional Headquarters will close MONTAUBAN and open COMBLES at 11.00 October 4th.

5. ACKNOWLEDGE.

Done

F.P. [signature]

Lieut-Colonel,
General Staff,
66th Division.

Issued at 12:40.

DISTRIBUTION.

Copy No. 1.	War Diary.	13	A.D.M.S.
2	" "	14	D.A.D.V.S.
3	File.	15	Camp Commdt.
4	'A' and 'Q'.	16	66th M.T.Coy.
5	Signals.	17	D.A.D.O.S.
6	C.R.A.	18	D.A.P.M.
7	C.R.E.	19	D.G.O.
8	198th Inf. Bde.	20	S.A.A.Sec. D.A.C.
9	199th Inf. Bde.	21	Fourth Army.
10	South African Bde.	22	XIII Corps.
11	9th Bn. Glouc.R.(Pioneers).	23	" "
12	Divl. Train A.S.C.	24	A.D.C.

*****

MARCH TABLE TO ACCOMPANY 66th DIVISION ORDER No. 92.

Serial No.	UNIT.	FROM.	TO.	ROUTE.	REMARKS.
1.	Divl. H.Q. Group.	MONTAUBAN.	COMBLES.	GUILLEMONT	Under orders of Camp Commandant. Head of Column to pass cross roads S.28.c.1.6 at 10.30.
2.	198th Bde. Group.	GUILLEMONT.	MOISLAINS.	COMBLES - BOUCHAVESNES.	To be clear of GUILLEMONT by 10.00.
3.	199th Bde. Group.	MARICOURT.	MAUREPAS.	HARDECOURT AUX-BOIS.	To be clear of present billets by 10.00.
4.	S.A. Bde. Group.	MONTAUBAN.	COMBLES.	GUILLEMONT.	Head of column to pass cross roads S.28.c.1.6 at 09.00.

87A

Groups as per D.O. 88.

app 2.

SOUTH AFRICAN INFANTRY BRIGADE — Secret 14 88

Ref. Maps - FRANCE, 57c :1/40000

OPERATION ORDER 234

Copy No. 13
3-10-18

1. The South African Inf. Bde. Group will move by March Route tomorrow, 4th. Oct., to the COMBLES Area, in accordance with the attached March Table.

2. First-line Transport will march with Units.

3. The Staff Captain will make all administrative and billeting arrangements.

4. Locations of Units in new Area will be notified to this Office immediately on arrival.

5. Reports to Bde. HQ., MONTAUBAN, until 9 am.; afterwards on line of march, until arrival at COMBLES.

6. ACKNOWLEDGE.

Issued thro' Signals at 15.30

[signature] Major,
Brigade Major,
South African Inf. Bde..

to 1. 1st. SAI
2. 2nd. SAI
3. 4th. SAI
4. SALTM Bty
5. SAFld.Amb.
6. 542 Co.ASC
7. 66th. Divn.
8. Area Cdt., ~~MONTAUBAN~~ GERMAN REGIMENT
9. [illegible]
10. 198 Inf.Bde.
11. 199 Inf. Bde.
11. Bde. Sig. Off.
12. Staff Captain,
13. Brigade Major,
14/18. War Diary.

MARCH TABLE

Serial No.	Unit	Starting Point Place	Starting Point Time	ROUTE	REMARKS
1.	Bde.HQ.& Sigs.	X-rds.	09.00	SW Corner of BERNAFAY WOOD - GUILLEMONT	Distances: 100x between Coys.& transport of Units. - 500x between BNs; 25x between every 6 vehicles.
2.	4th. SAI		09.05		
3.	1st. SAI	S.28.	09.19		
4.	2nd. SAI	c.1.6	09.35		
5.	SALTM Bty.		10.01		
6.	SAF Amb.		10.04		
7.	542 Co.ASC		10.10		

Clock-hour halts.

Army Form C. 2123.
(In books of 100.)

"C" FORM.
MESSAGES AND SIGNALS.

No. of Message..............

Prefix.........Code......Words...........	Received.	Sent, or sent out.	Office Stamp.
£ s. d.	From...............	At...............m.	
Charges to Collect	By...............	To...............	
Service Instructions		By...............	

Handed in at..Office..............m. Received..............m.

TO 2)

* Sender's Number.	Day of Month.	In reply to Number.	AAA
93.			

As	early	as	possible
aaa	Divn	will	move
again	5th	Oct	after
09.00			

FROM AHSE

PLACE & TIME 1700

* This line should be erased if not required.

(19629) W1528/M1970. 300,000 Pads. 4/17. McC. & Co., Ltd. (E1213).

90

App 3 (1)

"C" Form. Army Form C. 2123.
(In books of 100.)

MESSAGES AND SIGNALS. No. of Message............

Prefix...... Code...... Words 57 £ s. d. Charges to Collect	Received. From MFF By	Sent, or sent out. At..............m. To........... By...........	Office Stamp. S2A. 4/10/18 1736

Service Instructions

Handed in at MFSE Office 1720 m. Received 1736 m.

TO: Jefe

* Sender's Number.	Day of Month.	In reply to Number.	AAA
93	4		

Following moves will take place today aaa SA Bde Group to NURLU Head not to pass cross roads in COMBLES T.28 central before 20.00 aaa route via MOISLAINS aaa 198th Bde Group to MOISLAINS via COMBLES Head to pass cross roads in T.20.c at 18.30 aaa 9th Glos R. to MOISLAINS to be clear of Combles by 18.45 aaa Billets of ... to [illegible] area MOISLAINS [illegible] NURLU [illegible]

FROM

PLACE & TIME

* This line should be erased if not required.

(10629) Wt328/M1970. 300,000 Pads. 4/17. McC. & Co., Ltd. (E1213).

91

"A" Form
MESSAGES AND SIGNALS.

Army Form C. 21
(In pads of 100)

No. of Message............

Prefix.............Code..............m.	Words	Charge.	This message is on a/c of:	Recd. at......m.
Office of Origin and Service Instructions	Sent		..........................Service.	Date.............
	At ....m.			From ....
	To			
	By		(Signature of "Franking Officer")	By...............

TO 2.

Sender's Number.	Day of Month.	In reply to Number.	AAA

Route MOISLAINS.

3 First line transport will march with Elints.

4. Bde H.Q. will close at 19.45 at BOILEAUX WOOD and open at NURLU on arrival.

5 Acknowledge.

From S A Bde
Place
Time

The above may be forwarded as now corrected. (Z) (Sgd) E Barlow Major, Bde Major

Censor. Signature of Addressor or person authorised to telegraph in his name

* This line should be erased if not required.

Wt. W3253/ P.511 27/2 H. & K. Ltd. (E. 2634)

92

App 4

"A" Form
MESSAGES AND SIGNALS

Army Form C. 2121
(In pads of 100.)

No. of Message..........

Prefix..........Code..........m. | Words | Charge.
Office of Origin and Service Instructions

Sent
At ....m.
To ....
By ....

This message is on a/c of: ....Service.
(Signature of "Franking Officer")

Recd. at......m.
Date..........
From ....
By..........

TO			
	1st SAI	SAFA	B50.
	2nd SAI	SALTMB	
	4th SAI	542 Coy ASC	

Sender's Number.	Day of Month.	In reply to Number.	AAA
Order 235	4		

Ref Map LENS 11.
AMIENS 17.

1. S.A. Bde Group will march this evening to NURLU as follows. Starting point main Rd SE Corner of BOILEAUX WOOD
Time 19.45

2 Order of March

Bde H.Q. Signal Sect	19.45
SALTMB	19.48
2nd SAI	20.01
1st SAI	20.17
4th SAI	20.23
542 Coy ASC	20.45

SAFA will join Column on march immediately in front of 542nd Coy ASC.

From
Place
Time
The above may be forwarded as now corrected. (Z)
Censor. Signature of Addressor or person authorised to telegraph in his name
* This line should be erased if not required.

Order No. 1625. Wt. W3253/ P 511. 27/2 H. & K. Ltd. (E. 2634)

94

"A" Form

Army Form C. 2121
(In pads of 100.)

MESSAGES AND SIGNALS.

No. of Message: Opps (0)

Prefix............Code............m. | Words | Charge.

Office of Origin and Service Instructions

Sent
At ....m.
To ....
By ....

This message is on a/c of:
............Service.
(Signature of "Franking Officer")

Recd. at......m.
Date..........
From ....
By..........

TO

Sender's Number. | Day of Month. | In reply to Number. | AAA

66th Division
Order 94
mislaid

From
Place
Time

The above may be forwarded as now corrected. (Z)

Censor. Signature of Addressor or person authorised to telegraph in his name

* This line should be erased if not required.

Order No. 1625. Wt. W3253/ P 511. 27/2 H. & K.

"A" Form

Army Form C. 2121
(In pads of 100.)

MESSAGES AND SIGNALS.

No. of Message..........

Prefix......Code......m.	Words	Charge.	This message is on a/c of:	Recd. at......m.
Office of Origin and Service Instructions	Sent		App 6 ......Service.	Date
	At ......m.			From
	To			
	By		(Signature of "Franking Officer")	By......

TO
1st SAI	B.S.O.	542nd Coy ASC.
2nd "	SALTMB.	
4th "	SAFA.	

Sender's Number.	Day of Month.	In reply to Number.	AAA
Order 236.	5		

Ref 62C 1/40000

The SA Bde Group will move by March Route today to RONSSOY area

2. The Brigade will march as under –

BHQ + Signal Section	09.15
SALTMB	09.18
1st SAI	09.21
4th SAI	~~10.04~~ 09.37
2nd SAI	10.04
SAFA	10.20
542 Coy ASC	10.25

[illegible]

Route LIERAMONT – VILLERS FAUCON.

3. First line transport will march with Units.

4. Lorries will be retained for todays move. One extra lorry will report to each Unit at ~~[illegible]~~ 07.30

5. Billeting parties will report to Staff

From Captain at Area Commandants

Place Office at RONSSOY at 09.00.

6. Time Blankets + Great-Coats will be

The above may be forwarded as now corrected. (Z)

Censor.

Signature of Addressor or person authorised to telegraph in his name

* This line should be erased if not required.

Order No. 1625. Wt. W3253/ P 511. 27/2. H. & K., Ltd. (E. 2634)

"A" Form
Army Form C. 2121
(In pads of 100.)

MESSAGES AND SIGNALS.

No. of Message...........

Prefix............Code...............m.	Words	Charge.	This message is on a/c of:	Recd. at......m.
Office of Origin and Service Instructions	Sent		..........................Service.	Date............
	At ....m.			From ....
	To			
	By		(Signature of "Franking Officer")	By..............

TO 2.

Sender's Number.	Day of Month.	In reply to Number.	AAA

Carried on lorries.

7. B teams & spares will return to MOISLAINS under orders of Major CLERK, 4th SAI & report to Billet Warden for accommodation. Major CLERK will remain in command of these teams.

8. Battalions will furnish a return to this Office by 17.00 5th October showing distribution of personnel on going into action. This return will be made out as per pro forma attached.

9. Bde HQ will close at NURLU at 09.15 & open at RONSSOY on arrival.

10. Acknowledge.

From S. A. Bde
Place
Time

The above may be forwarded as now corrected. (Z)

Censor.

F. Heal[illegible] Major
Bde Major

Signature of Addressor or person authorised to telegraph in his name

* This line should be erased if not required.

Order No. 1625. Wt. W3253/ P 511. 27/2. H. & K., Ltd. (E. 2634)

95

"A" Form. Army Form C. 2121 (In pads of 100.)

MESSAGES AND SIGNALS.

No. of Message............

Prefix..........Code..........m.	Words	Charge.	This message is on a/c of:	Recd. at......m.
Office of Origin and Service Instructions	Sent		..........Service.	Date......
	At ....m.			From 97
	To			
	By		(Signature of "Franking Officer")	By..........

TO

Sender's Number.	Day of Month.	In reply to Number.	AAA
Add to O. 236.			

Bde will march in BATTLE ORDER today & surplus kit will be dumped at Bde H.Q. at NURLU under guards to be detailed from Battalion B teams.

Personnel ~~[illegible]~~ of B teams must be rationed for consumption 5th.

From 5. 14. Bde.

Place

Time

The above may be forwarded as now corrected. (Z)

Censor.

L [illegible] Major. Bde Major

Signature of Addressor or person authorised to telegraph in his name

* This line should be erased if not required.

Order No. 1625. Wt. W3253/ P 511. 27/2. H. & K., Ltd. (E. 2634)

Army Form C. 2123.
(In books of 100.)

"C" FORM.

MESSAGES AND SIGNALS.

No. of Message ....

App 7(b)

Prefix ..... Code ..... Words	Received.	Sent, or sent out.	Office Stamp.
£ s. d.	From	At .....m.	SIGNALS
Charges to Collect	By	To	
Service Instructions		By	

Handed in at .... Office 10.35 m. Received .... m.

TO	SA Bde	93

*Sender's Number.	Day of Month.	In reply to Number.	AAA
GX 10	1		

Ref	DO 95	5th	aaa
DHQ	will	remain	at
RONSSOY	until	further	notice
aaa	addsd	all	concerned

FROM
PLACE & TIME

66 Divn
10.05

* This line should be erased if not required.

(9899) Wt. .../M1970. 100,000 Pads. 4/17. McC. & Co., Ltd. (E1218).

"A" Form
MESSAGES AND SIGNALS.

Army Form C. 2121 (In pads of 100)

S.A. Bde

Priority

App 8 (b)

98

TO 198th Bde. 199th Bde. S.A.Bde. Train. ASC Sigs. CRE. A.D.M.S. DAPM. C.C. D.A.D.O.S. S.A.Scot.DAG. 13th Corps. 4th Army.

Sender's Number.	Day of Month.	In reply to Number.	AAA
G.G. 0.0.96.	6.		

Destinations mentioned in aaa 00.95 of yesterday are amended as follows aaa S.A. Bde to HINDENBURG LINE Square A.9 and 15 A.& B aaa 199 Bde HINDENBURG LINE Southwards from A.15 C & D aaa Tow Path & Chambers in Canal Tunnel running South from A 3.d.5.1 been examined for mines and is now available aaa Good entrance also at about A.15.d.90. aaa Norther half alloted to xx S.A.Bde. and southern half to 199th Bde aaa 198th Bde to LE CATELET NAUROY line about LE CATELET aaa Acknowledge.

A 14 d 95.15

From 66th Div.
Place
Time 09.40

(Sd) Walter Guinness
Lt Col.

The above may be forwarded as now corrected.

Censor. Signature of Addressor or person authorised to telegraph in his name.

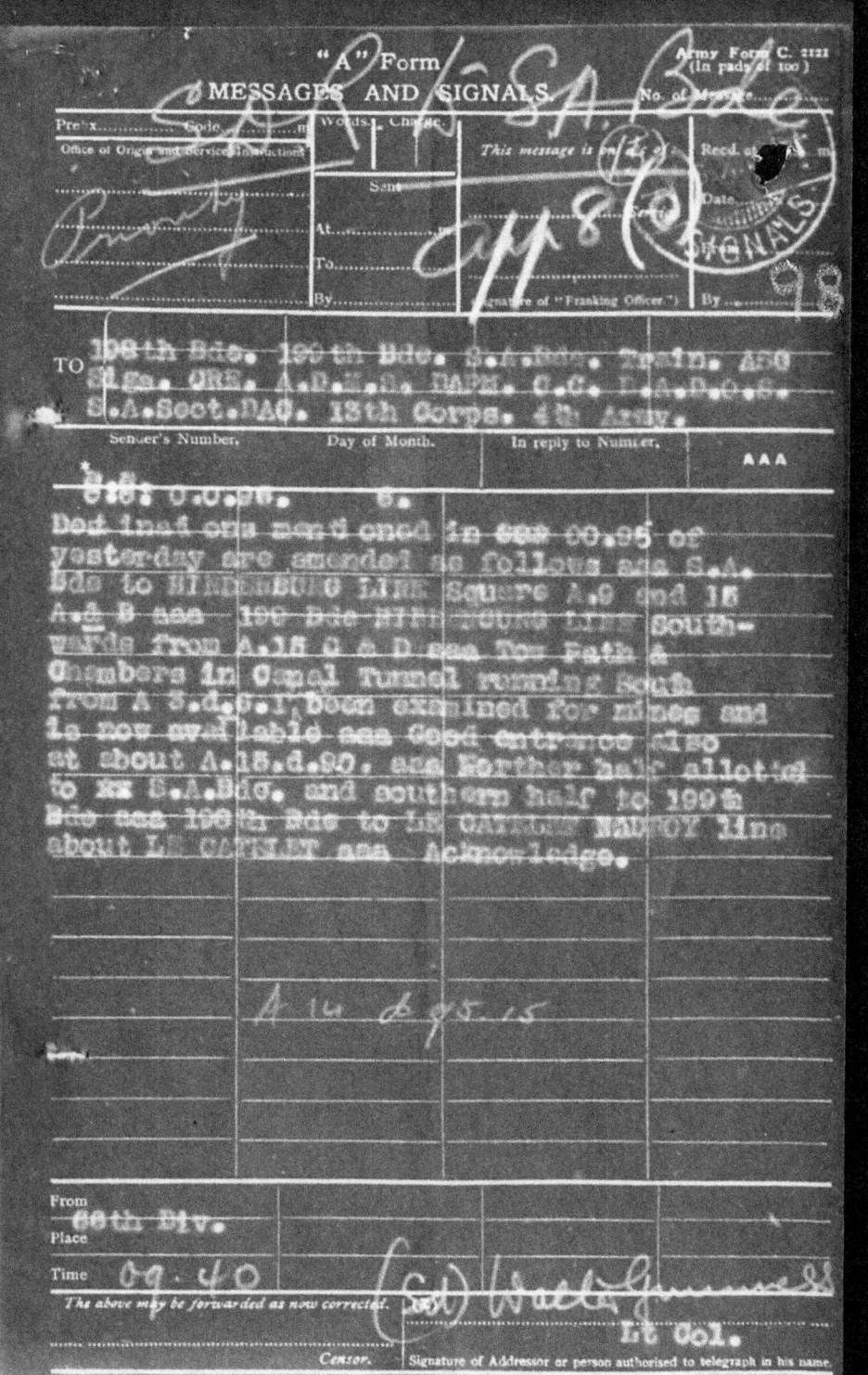

"A" Form

Army Form C. 2121
(In pads of 100.)

MESSAGES AND SIGNALS.

No. of Message..........

Prefix.............Code.............m.	Words / Charge.	This message is on a/c of:	Recd. at ....
Office of Origin and Service Instructions	Sent	..........Service.	Date..........
	At ....m.		From 99
	To		
	By	(Signature of "Franking Officer")*	By..........

TO: 198 Bde 199 Bde. S.A. Bde. Q Train Sigs
CRE ADMS DAPM Camp Comndt. ~~DADOS~~
AAA SRC, DAC, 13th Corps [illegible]

Sender's Number.	Day of Month.	In reply to Number.	AAA
G.O.85	5		

The following moves will take place 6th Oct AAA
199 Bde Group to HINDENBURG LINE S. OF BONY
via LONGAVESNES & RONSSOY Head to pass X roads
D.29.d. at 12.30 AAA 9th Glous. to GUILLEMONT
FARM A.13.b. same route to be clear of billets
by 11.00 AAA 198 Bde Group to GOUY via RONSSOY
to enter RONSSOY at 13.15 AAA S.A. Bde Group
to LE CATELET-NAUROY Line Squares 22 23 & 17
to be clear of RONSSOY at 15.00 AAA Field
Coys RE. less bridging equipment will join
Bde. Groups not later than 17.00 to be clear
of VILLERS FAUCON by 10.00 AAA 25th M.G. Bn.
about GILLEMONT FARM A.13.b. not to enter
RONSSOY before 16.00 AAA Transport and Train
Coys will move through RONSSOY sending an Offr.
to D/H/Q RONSSOY to ascertain their destin
ation AAA Advanced DHQ will open at BONY at
A.16.d.8.6. at 14.00

From
Place 66th Div.
Time

The above may be forwarded as now corrected. (Z)

Censor.

Signature of Addressor or person authorised to telegraph in his name

Lt. Col.

* This line should be erased if not required.

[illegible]

Summary of Casualties for period 7th to 20th Oct., 1918

1	2		3		4		5		6		7		8		9
Date	Killed in Action		Wounded		Wounded and remaining at duty		Missing		Died from wounds and included in Column 3		Total (not including Column 6)				Remarks
	OFF	O/R	OFF.	O/Rs	OFF	O/Rs	OFF	O/R.	OFF.	O/Rs	OFF	O/Rs			
7th Oct., 18	–	–	–	3	–	–	–	–	–	–	–	3			
8th " "	–	28	4	151	2	2	–	–	–	5	6	181			
9th " "	1	23	1	70	3	1	–	–	–	4	5	94			
10th " "	–	–	–	10	2	1	–	–	–	1	2	11			
11th " "	–	–	–	1	–	–	–	–	–	–	–	1			
12th " "	–	–	–	25	–	–	–	–	–	–	–	25			
13th " "	–	–	1	6	–	–	–	–	–	–	1	6			
14th " "	–	–	–	1	–	3	–	–	–	–	–	4			
15th " "	–	–	–	4	–	–	–	–	–	–	–	4			
16th " "	–	–	1	6	–	–	–	–	–	–	1	6			
17th " "	–	23	4	91	–	12	–	–	–	1	4	126			
18th " "	–	5	–	17	–	6	–	–	–	–	–	28			
19th " "	–	1	–	3	–	–	–	–	–	–	–	4			
20th " "	–	–	–	–	–	–	–	–	–	–	–	–			
Totals	1	80	11	388	7	25	–	–	–	11	19	493			

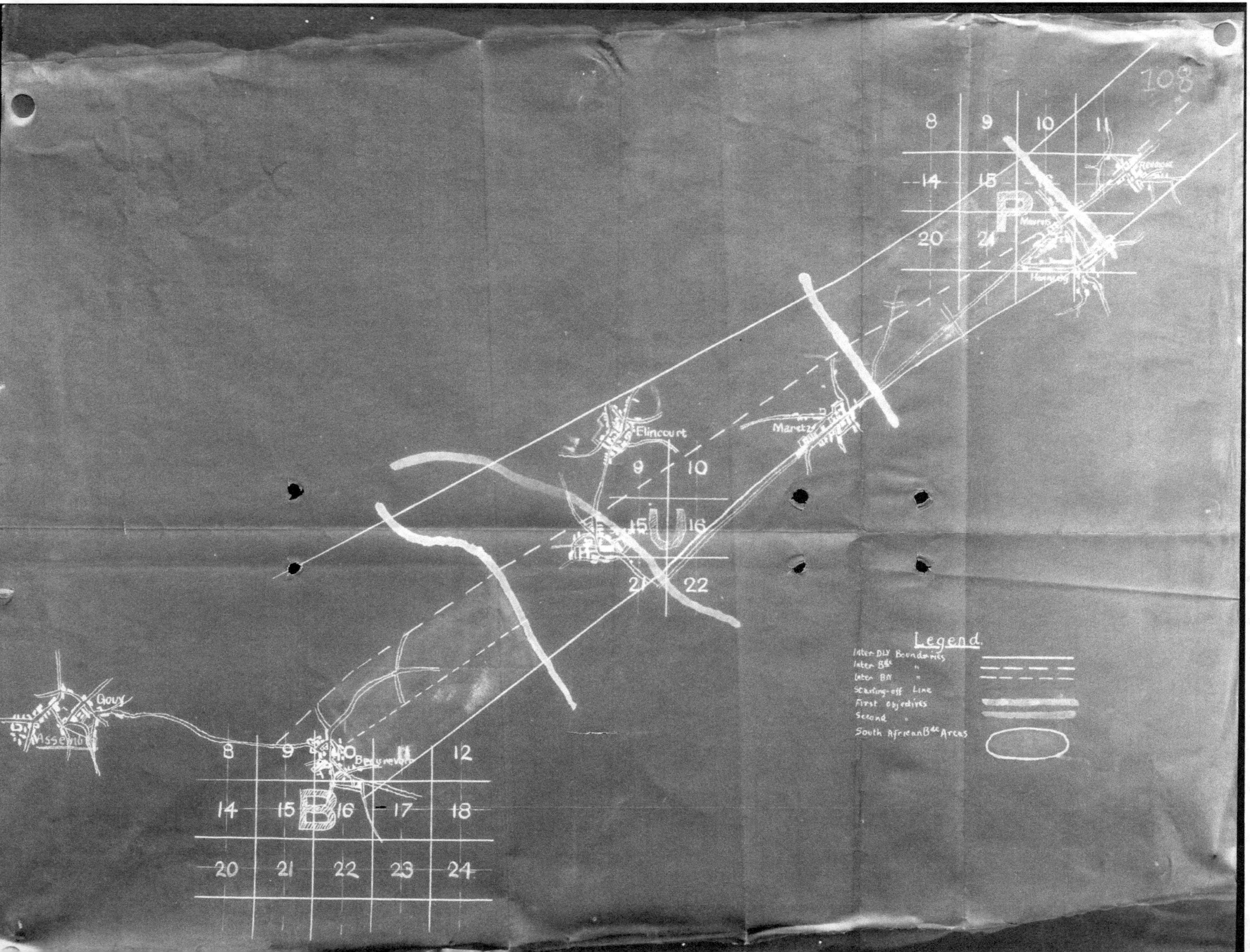
108
Elincourt
Maretz
Gouy
B
U
P
Legend
Inter-Div Boundaries
Inter Bde "
Inter Bn "
Starting-off Line
First objectives
Second "
South African Bde Areas

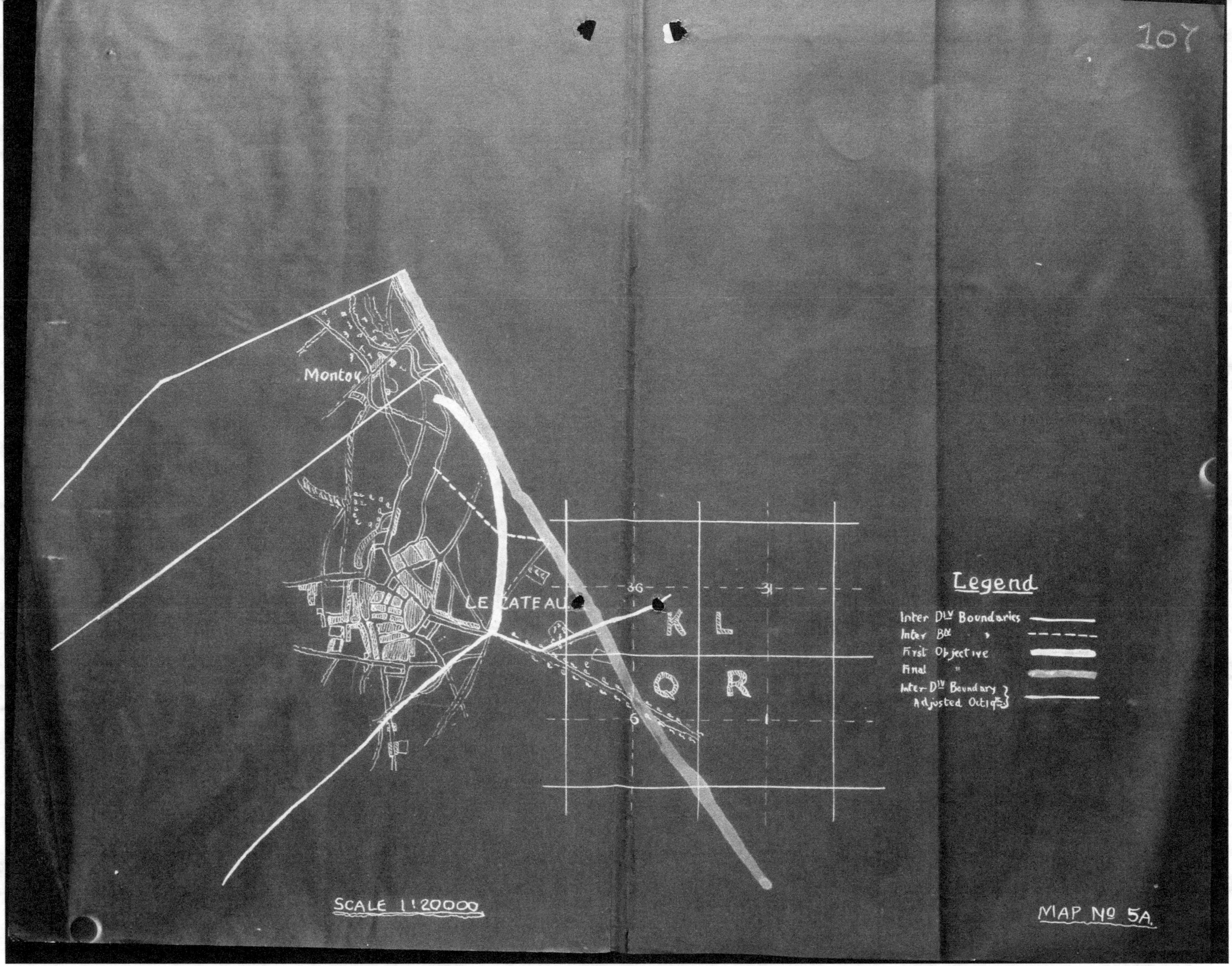
Montoy
LE CATEAU
36
31
6
1
K
L
Q
R
Legend
Inter D^{iv} Boundaries
Inter B^{de} "
First Objective
Final "
Inter-D^{iv} Boundary Adjusted Oct 19th
SCALE 1:20000
MAP No 5A.

100

app 9.

SECRET

S OUTH AFRICAN INFANTRY BRIGADE

Copy No. 13

Reference Map - MONT BREHAIN, 1/2 ,

OPERATION ORDER No. 237

6.10.18

1. The South African Inf. Bde. Group will move by March Route today, Oct .6th., to the LE CATELET - NAUROY line, squares 22, 23, and 17 .

2. The move will take place as under -

Bde. HQ. & Sig. Section	.....	12
SALTM Bty	.....	1203
2nd. SAI	.....	1206
1st. SAI	.....	1221
4th. SAI	.....	1236

S A F Amb. .. Under orders to be issued later
542 Co., ASC., will move under its own arrangements.

Location on reaching new quarters to be notified at once to Brigade HQ..

Starting Point- X-rds. F.21.c.20.95,

Route - GILLEMONT - BONY..

~~3. Each Unit of Bde. Group will send an Officer to Divl. HQ., RONSSOY, as soon as possible, to ascertain destination of Transport and Train Company.~~

3~~4~~. Staff Captain will meet Parties from Units at 1300 at A.15.d.9.6..

4~~5~~. Brigade H Q. will close at RONSSOY at 12 and open at A.17.c.5.7. on arrival.

5~~6~~. Great-coats will be carried.

6~~7~~. ACKNOWLEDGE .

Major,
Brigade Major.
South African Inf. Bde..

Issued thro' Signals at 1 45, to -
1. 1st. SAI ✓
2. 2nd. SAI ✓
3. 4th. SAI
4. SALTM Bty. ✓
5. SAFLd. Amb. ✓
6. 542 Co. ASC ✓
7. 66th. Divn. ✓
8. 198 Inf. Bde. ✓
9. 199 Inf. Bde.. ✓
10. Bde. Sig. Off..
11. Staff Captain,
12. Bde. Major, ✓
13/16. War Diary
17. File.

"A" Form. 102 19

Army Form C.2121 (in pads of 100).

No. of Message

MESSAGES AND SIGNALS.

Prefix .... Code .... m. | Words | Charge

Office of Origin and Service Instructions.

Sent

At .... m.

To ....

By ....

This message is on a/c of .... Service.

(Signature of "Franking Officer.") GM 10 (8)

Recd. at .... m.

Date

From

By

Stamp: 6.X.18 FF SIGNALS

TO S A Bde.

Sender's Number.	Day of Month.	In reply to Number.	AAA
* G X 9	6		

Move of troops as ordered in D.O 95 and D.O 96 postponed 24 hours aaa Advanced parties will proceed as ordered aaa addsd all concerned

From 66 Divn

Place

Time 0955

The above may be forwarded as now corrected. (Z)

Censor. Signature of Addressor or person authorised to telegraph in his name.

* This line should be erased if not required.

750,000. W 2183 M309. H. W & V., Ld. 6/16.

103

"A" Form
MESSAGES AND SIGNALS.

Army Form C. 2121
(In pads of 100.)

No. of Message ....

Prefix .... Code .... m. | Words | Charge.

Office of Origin and Service Instructions: Copy

Sent
At .... m.
To ....
By ....

This message is on a/c of: App
.... Service.
(Signature of "Franking Officer")

Recd. at ......m.
Date ....
From ....
By ....

TO		
1st SAI	SALTMB.	BSO.
2nd SAI	SAFA	
4th SAI	542 Coy ASC	

Sender's Number.	Day of Month.	In reply to Number.	AAA
B.S. 55	6		

Move	of	troops	as
ordered	in	Bde	Order
234	postponed	24	hours
AAA.	Advanced	parties	will
meet	Staff	Captain	at
Cross	Roads	A.14.d.95.15.	
at	12.30	today.	

From S A Bde.
Place
Time

The above may be forwarded as now corrected. (Z) (Sgd) E Barlow Major Bde Major.

Censor. Signature of Addressor or person authorised to telegraph in his name

* This line should be erased if not required.

Order No. 1625. Wt. W3253/ P 511. 27/2 H. & K. Ltd. (E. 2634)

SOUTH AFRICAN INFANTRY BRIGADE app 12

SECRET
Copy No.
6.10.18

AMENDMENT No. 1 to Bde. O. ORDER No.237.

---

1. For para. 1 read - 'South African Inf. Bde. will move by March Route today, Oct. 6th., to the HINDENBURG Line, Squares A.9., 15.A. and B..

2. ~~For~~ Para. 2 ~~read~~ - Order of March is amended as under -

'Bde. HQ. and Sig. Sectn.	....	1200
SALTM Bty.	....	1203
4th. SAI	.....	1205
1st. SAI	....	1217
2nd. SAI	....	1230

SAFAmb. will move under its own arrangements.'

3. For para. 4 read - 'Staff Captain will meet parties from Units at 1230 at X-rds. at A.14.d.95.15.

[signature]
Major, Brigade Major,
South African Inf. Bde..

Issued to all Recipients of Bde. O. 237 - at 1100.

104

S E C R E T.

66th Divn.
G.X. 9.

105

app 13(0)

Signals.
C.R.E.
C.R.A. 18th Divn.
198th Inf. Bde.
199th Inf. Bde.
South African Bde.
9th Glouc. R. (Pioneers).
25th Bn. M.G.C.
76th Bde. R.G.A.
89th Bde. R.G.A.
A.D.M.S.

The hour and day of Zero for forthcoming operations by Fourth Army will be 05.10 October 8th.

2. ACKNOWLEDGE.

done

[signature]

Lieut-Colonel,
General Staff,
66th Division.

D.H.Q.,
7.10.18.

"A" Form.
Army Form C. 2121.
(In pads of 100.)

MESSAGES AND SIGNALS.

No. of Message..............

Code.......m	Words.	Charge.	This message is on a/c of:	Recd. at ......m.
Office of Origin and Service Instructions.	Sent		............Service.	Date
	At........m.			From
	To........			By........
	By........		(Signature of "Franking Officer.")	

TO { 198th Bde. 25th Divn.
199th Inf. Bde.
S.A. Bde.

* Sender's Number.	Day of Month.	In reply to Number.	AAA
45.	7		

Reference 66th D.O. 90 AAA For para 8
substitute following All troops of 25th Divn
will be withdrawn at Zero minus 2 hours
independently of relief AAA B.Gs.C. will arrang
to let all units of 25th Divn on their front
know if they themselves are in position before
this hour in order that the latter may at once
be withdrawn

From 66th Divn.
Place
Time

The above may be forwarded as now corrected. (Z)

Censor. Lt-Col. GS.
Signature of Addressor or person authorised to telegraph in his name.

* This line should be erased if not required.

(3790.) Wt. W 492/M 1647. 650,000 Pads. 5/17. H.W.&V., Ld. (E. 1187.)

App' 14(8)
106

Copy No. 9

SECRET.

66th DIVISION ORDER No. 99.

1. 66th Division will be formed up on the line T.27.d.0.3 (GOUZEAUCOURT Farm and enclosure exclusive to 66th Division) to B.17.a.10.40, by Zero minus 2 hours, at which hour all posts of 25th Division in front of this Line will be withdrawn.

2. 198th and South African Bdes will be responsible for their own protection from Zero minus 2 hours onwards.

3. Troops of 25th Division actually relieved by troops of 66th Division will be withdrawn on relief.
B.Gs.C. will arrange the above directly with Brigade Commanders of the 25th Division concerned.

4. 74th Inf. Bde. H.Qrs are in BEAUREVOIR Line about B.13.b.3.7 or B.14.c..
75th Inf. Bde. and 7th Inf. Bde. H.Qrs are at B.26.a.8.5.
74th Inf. Bde. are holding Left of front.
75th Inf. Bde. are holding Right of front.

5. Command of front to be held by Division will pass from G.O.C. 25th Division to G.O.C. 66th Division at Zero minus 2 hours.

6. Division will be informed when all troops of 198th and S.A. Bdes are formed up, by code word "MOSQUITO".

7. Contact aeroplanes will call for flares at zero plus 2.35, zero plus 4 hors and zero plus 5 hours.

8. If only slight resistance is met with, on GREEN Line being taken, 198th and S.A. Bdes may be required to go through again on a two battalion front, each Brigade about 2000 yds frontage
Dividing line U.14.central - U.9.d.central.

9. If enemy is found to have retreated during today, 198th and South African Bdes may be called upon to take over line and follow him up, each on a two battalion front.

10. ACKNOWLEDGE.

Issued at 15:00

[signature]
Lieut-Colonel,
General Staff,
66th Division.

D.H.Q.,
7.10.18.

DISTRIBUTION.

Copy No. 1	War Diary.	10	9th Glouc. R.(Pioneers).
2	" "	11	25th Division.
3	File.	12	25th Bn. M.G.C.
4	Signals.	13	XIII Corps.
5	C.R.E.	14	76th Bde. R.G.A.
6	C.R.A. 18th Divn.	15	89th Bde. R.G.A.
7	198th Inf. Bde.	16	1st Tank Bn.
8	199th Inf. Bde.	17	3rd (Light) Tank Bn.
9	South African Bde.	18	35th Squadron R.A.F.
		19	A.D.C.
		20.	50th Divn.

109

(Contd.)

(8) ZERO. Zero hour will be notified in writing from Bde H.Q.RS. at 19. 30 .am. on the 7th. OCTOBER

(9) SYNCHRONISATION OF WATCHES.

Watches will be Synchroni at Bde H.Q.rs. MUSHROOM QUARRY at 19.00 and 21.00 on the 7th. Oct. All units will send representatives at these hours.

HEAD QUARTERS. After the capture of the Red Line, Bde H.Qrs. will move to the vicinity of the Xroads in 4.5.a.

[signature]

for Major,
Brigade Major,
South African Brigade.

7th. October. 1916.

To all receipents off Preliminary Oder No. 1.

Issued at 1230.

App 16(0)

S E C R E T.

Copy No. 10.

66th DIVISION PRELIMINARY ORDER No. 1.

1.
GENERAL PLAN.

With a view to increasing the breach in the enemy's defences, major operations are about to be taken in a general north-easterly direction by the Third and Fourth Armies; the objectives and tactical boundaries of XIII Corps are as shown on the attached map.

38th Division (V Corps) will be operating on the northern flank, and 30th American Division (American 2nd Corps) on the southern flank of the XIII Corps.

The attack will probably take place on the morning of.........October.

2.
CORPS PLAN.

It is presumed that by the above day our front line will run approximately east of VILLERS FARM (T.20.b.), - east of GOUZEAUCOURT FARM (T.26.d.) - east of BEAUREVOIR.

(a) The attack to the RED Line will be made by the 66th Division on a two Brigade front in conjunction with one Brigade from 25th Division on the Right, and one Brigade from the 50th Division on the Left.

The task of the latter Brigade will be to protect the Left flank of the Corps, and to co-operate with the 38th Division in the capture of VILLERS OUTREAUX.

(b) After the capture of the RED Line the intention is to exploit the situation northwards from LES MARLICHES (T.17.c.) along spur T.11.central, also to capture SERAIN, in conjunction with 2nd American Corps, who will take PREMONT. If, therefore, the operation is successful, the position at the end of the day should be as shown by the GREEN Line.

3.
DIVISIONAL PLAN OF ATTACK.

The 66th Division will attack with South African Brigade on the Right, and the 198th Inf. Bde. on the Left, each Brigade being on a two battalion front. The 199th Inf. Bde. will follow up the attack, and after the capture of the RED Line will pass through the 198th and South African Bdes. in order to seize SERAIN and secure the high ground in U.7., U.14., U.15., and U.21. *

4.
DIVIDING LINES.

(a) Between Bde. of 25th Division and South African Bde. B.16.b.9.7 (Cemetery) to U.25.d.8.4.
(b) Between S.A. Bde. and 198th Bde. B.9.a.6.2 (BELLEVUE FARM), T.28.d.4.1.(cross roads) - T.21.b.65.15.
(c) Between 198th Bde. and 50th Division, T.27.c.5.5 - T.22.d.1.9.- T.17.a.1.3.

5.
ASSEMBLY.

(a) By 14.00 on "Y" day Brigades will be disposed as follows :-

198th Bde.	LE CATELET - NAUROY Line.
S.A. Bde.	HINDENBURG LINE North of BONY.
199th Bde.	HINDENBURG LINE South of BONY.

On Y/Z night 198th and South African Bdes will move forward in time to complete their forming up by Zero minus 2 hours. Further information will be issued concerning

/forward...

* After capture of RED LINE, 198 Bde. will push forward on the left and secure the high ground about T.11.

forward routes and forming up lines which, however, should be reconnoitred at once by Bdes concerned.

(b) 199th Bde. with 432nd F. Co. R.E. will move forward at Zero minus 1½ hours from the HINDENBURG Line, along a track which is being prepared from HINDENBURG Line in A.21.d. to road at A.23.b.9.0, - A.18.d.0.0. - north of TORRENS CANAL (B.19.a.and b.) - MUSHROOM QUARRY (B.20.a.5.8.) - BELLEVUE FARM. Bde and Field Co. will then deploy along and in rear of BEAUREVOIR - GUISANCOURT road, whence they will move forward and exploit the situation so soon as G.O.C. 199th Bde. has assured himself that the general advance to the RED Line has been successful.

6. CONSOLIDATION. (a) Each objective or line gained will be consolidated by assaulting troops at once.

(b) Strong points will be constructed by Bdes about the following positions :-

198th Bde.

(1) LES MARLICHES FARM (T.17.c.3.7.).
(2) T.11.b.2.1.
(3) T.11.c.7.3.
(4) T.12.b.2.2.

199th Bde.

(1) U.7.central.
(2) U.8.c.4.3.
(3) About Mill U.14.b.9.8.
(4) U.15.d.0.8.
(5) U.21.b.0.6.

South African Bde.

(1) U.19.c.2.3.
(2) U.19.b.8.1
(3) U.20.d.1.3.
(4) U.21.a.3.2.
(5) U.30.b.0.3.
(6) U.26.c.0.5.
(7) C.1.a.3.7.

7. RESERVES. (a) Until the 199th Bde moves forward from the BEAUREVOIR - GUISANCOURT road to exploit the situation, the Division Reserve will consist of :-

199th Inf. Bde.
432 F. Co. R.E.
9th Glouc. R.(Pioneers) (at MONT ST. MARTIN).

B.G.C. 199th Bde. will therefore arrange to keep in constant communication with D.H.Q. whom he will inform of his intention to advance.

(b) Directly on capture of RED Line, if they have already used all their three battalions, B.Gs.C. 198th and S.A. Bdes will withdraw one battalion into Bde. Reserve, reporting its position to D.H.Q.

(c) 9th Glouc.R. (Pioneers) will be in Divisional Reserve until GREEN Line has been secured.

/ (d)......

(d) 20 machine guns from 25th Bn. M.G.C. will be in Divisional Reserve in Valley B.5.central, after capture of RED Line.

(e) 6 mark V Tanks will concentrate in valley B.5.cent. after capture of RED Line

8. ARTILLERY. 1. The attack to the first objective will be preceded by a strong barrage. This barrage will come down and rest for 3 minutes 100 yards in front of enemy outpost line. It will then move forward by lifts of 100 yards in 3 minutes for 1200 yards. It will then slow down to 100 yards in 4 minutes until it reaches a line 500 yards in front of first objective.(RED Line). The barrage will then dwell for 30 minutes, when it will lift and the second phase of the attack will commence.

The attack from the RED Line will be supported by Mobile Field Artillery, which will move forward with a view to supporting the infantry over open sights. Details of Field Artillery barrage and employment of Corps H.A. will be forwarded later.

The 112th Bde. R.F.A. has been detailed for the close support of the 66th Division through-out the action. Of this One 18-pr Battery R.F.A. will be attached to each of South African and 198th Bdes. The remainder of the Bde. R.F.A. will, after capture of the RED Line, support the advance of the 199th Infantry Bde. to the GREEN Line. The O.C. 112th Bde. R.F.A. will arrange to have his H.Q. close alongside the H.Q. of 199th Inf. Bde. from Zero minus 1 hour onwards.

9. TANKS. 16 mark V and 11 whippet Tanks have been detailed to support the attack of the Division.

Details will be issued separately.

10. R.E. and PIONEERS. 430, 431, and 432 F. Cos. R.E. will be attached to S.A., 198th and 199th Inf. Bdes., respectively, from 17.00 Oct. 7th. They will assist in the construction of the strong points detailed in para. 6, under arrangements to be made direct between O.C. F. Cos. and Bdes. concerned.

After capture of GREEN Line, and on receipt of orders from D.H.Q., the 9th Bn. Glouc. R.(Pioneers) will repair th GRANDCOURT - LORMISSET - BEAUREVOIR - LA SABLONNIERE - LA FOLIE FARM road. Secondly, the GOUY-BEAUREVOIR road.

11. SIGNAL COMMUNICATIONS. (a) The Divisional Axial Line of Communication will be BONY - A.17.c.5.8 - B.19.a.8.0 - B.14.a.5.8 - BELLEVUE FARM - T.28.b.5.3 - LA FOLIE FARM - SERAIN.

O.C. Signals will arrange for transmission of all reports forwarded to any of the above positions. Brigades and other formations should select H.Q. as near as possibl to this line during the advance.

(b) Visual. / Pigeon. / Wireless. } Details will be communicated later.

12. HEADQUARTERS. Advanced Divisional Headquarters will be established on "Y" day at BONY, A.15.d.2.8 at noon

On Y/Z night and on Z day Divisional Advanced Report Centres will be established as follows :-

Till Zero. -	At A.17.c.5.7.
At Zero plus 30 mins -	About B.13.central.
On the RED Line being captured.	LA SABLONNIERE.
On capture of SERAIN.-	LA FOLIE FARM.

/S.A. Bde....

12.
HEADQUARTERS. (cont).

S.A. Bde. - ON Y day. A.17.c.5.7.
At Zero. MUSHROOM QUARRY. B.20.a.5.8.
199th Bde. - Until Zero minus 1 hour. A.21.b.2.6.
At Zero. MUSHROOM QUARRY. B.20.a.5.8.

13. Further instructions will be issued on this order later, including :-

(a) Definite details about forming up lines.
(b) Information concerning enemy.
(c) Artillery arrangements.
(d) Smoke.
(e) Machine guns.
(f) Aircraft.
(g) Tanks.

13. ACKNOWLEDGE.

F.P. Nosworthy

Lieut-Colonel,
General Staff,
66th Division.

D.H.Q.,
6.10.18.

Issued through Signals at 23.59.

DISTRIBUTION.

copy No.	1	War Diary.	11	25th Division.
	2	" "	12	50th Division.
	3	File.	13	18th Division.
	4	"Q".	14	XIII Corps.
	5	"		
	6	Signals.	16	25th M.G. Bn.
	7	C.R.E.	17	35th Squad. R.A.F.
	8	198th Inf. Bde.	18	1st Tank Battn.
	9	199th Inf. Bde.	19	3rd Light Tank Battn.
	10	S.A. Bde.	20	76th Bde. R.G.A.
			21	89th Bde. R.G.A.

22. A.D.C.

66th DIVISION INSTRUCTION No. 1.

Distribution :- down to Company Commanders.

INTELLIGENCE ARRANGEMENTS DURING BATTLE.

The following procedure will be adopted.

1. **Summaries.** No Summary will be called for, but a short general outline of the day's operations will be either wired or telephoned to D.H.Q. by 6 p.m. each evening. This outline will include the action taken by enemy artillery and aircraft; movement on rail and road; any work on defences observed.

2. **Identifications.** Early information as to identity of prisoners is essential. As batches of prisoners arrive at Bde. H.Q., men from different units will be given slips (as attached) to fill in. Number of prisoners, approx., identification, time and place of capture will then be wired to Division and Corps "I" by priority wire.

An identification wire should read as follows :-

"20 prisoners 5th Coy. 1st I.R. 185 Divn captured in "G.16.a. about 10 am.".

3. **Disposal of Prisoners.** Prisoners will be sent down to Divl. P.O.W. Cage as soon as possible after capture for examination by the D.I.O.
In the case of a number of prisoners being employed in carrying down our stretcher cases from the front line, samples of each unit will be detached and sent down to the Cage at once - the stretcher bearing party arriving later.

4. **Escorts.** Regimental escorts are responsible for conducting prisoners as far back as Bde. H.Q. where they will be given signed receipts for the numbers taken over from them: The disposal of prisoners in rear of Bde. H.Q. will be carried out under Divisional arrangements.

5. **Documents.**

(a) Officers and N.C.Os will be searched immediately after capture. All documents found on them will be sent down by the escort who will hand them over to the Bde. Intelligence Officer at Bde. H.Q.

(b) Documents will not be taken from other ranks until arrival at Corps Cage.

(c) Paybooks, identity discs and personal belongings will NOT be taken from prisoners.

(d) THE RETENTION OF ANY CAPTURED DOCUMENTS IS STRICTLY FORBIDDEN. Documents of interest will be returned to units if desired, after they have been examined. Individuals desiring the return of any document should write their name and unit on the back or envelope of the document.

(e) Escorts and guards should be warned to take special precautions to prevent prisoners from destroying papers.

/6. Separa

114

6.
Separation of Officers, N.C. Os and men.

Care will be taken that officers, N.C.Os and privates are separated at once, and no communication allowed to pass between the groups.

7.
Searchers.

Each Brigade will detail two searchers who will systematically search the battlefield, enemy positions, H.Q., dead, etc., for papers, documents, maps, etc., have them packed in sandbags, and forwarded as quickly as possible to the Divisional Cage.

This personnel should be armed with handy weapons and carry torches.

8.
General.

It is most important that the transmission of prisoners and documents back to Corps Cages should proceed as rapidly as possible. Detailed examination of prisoners and documents is undertaken at Corps H.Q. Examination by lower formations is to be confined strictly to items of immediate tactical importance, i.e., Enemy Intentions, dispositions, and the location of supports and reserves.

No attempt should be made to examine any other documents but MAPS.

F.P. [signature]
Lieut-Colonel,
General Staff,
66th Division.

D.H.Q.,
WD 5.10.18.

app 14 (O) 116

S E C R E T.

Copy No....9.

66th DIVISION ORDER No. 97.

Reference attached 1/20,000 combined sheet.

1. In accordance with instructions already issued, the 66th Division will attack and capture the line shown in Green on attached map.

The 7th Bde. (25th Division) will attack on the Right of the 66th Division, and the 149th Bde. (50th Division) on the Left. The task of the latter Brigade is to co-operate with the V Corps for the capture of VILLERS OUTREAUX, and at the same time to protect the northern flank of the 66th Division.

2. The operation will be carried out on the morning of 8th October, at an hour which will be notified later.

3. The final objective will be reached in two bounds.

(a) First objective - RED Line.
Practice trench U.25.central - U.19.c.6.5 - U.19.a.1.6 - T.18.d.1.1 - T.17.d.4.4 - LES MARLICHES FARM inclusive.

(b) Final objective - GREEN Line.
U.22.c.1.6 - SERAIN - U.7.central - U.11.central.

4. (a) 66th Division will attack and capture the RED Line, with South African Bde. on the Right and 198th Bde. on the Left.- the dividing line between Bdes is shown on attached map.

The attack will be preceded by a strong artillery barrage and supported by tanks.

As soon as the barrage ceases, 198th Bde. will push forward to capture the remainder of the WALINCOURT - AUDIGNY Line as far north as T.11.central, and will secure the high ground about T.11.central.

(b) The attack on the GREEN Line will be carried out by 199th Bde. who will advance through the RED Line half an hour after the latter has been secured.

5. Details for the assembly of troops have already been issued.

The infantry jumping off line will run from B.17.a.8.0 in a straight line to T.27.c. 7.8, and the barrage will come down at Zero 200 yards in front of that line.

Assaulting troops will be formed up on the jumping off line; infantry posts established in front of this line will be withdrawn during night 7th/8th October under arrangements to be made by 25th and 50th Divisions.

6. Artillery.

The attack of the Division will be covered by the 18th Divisional Artillery Group, consisting of 82nd and 83rd Bdes R.F.A., of 18th Div. ~~Artillery~~ R.F.A., 290th and 291st Bdes. R.F.A. of 58th Div. R.F.A., 65th, 84th and 150th Army Bdes R.F.A., also by the 76th Bde. R.G.A. and 89th Bde. R.G.A.

Battle Headquarters of the above will be notified later.

The 82nd, 84th, 290th and 294th Bdes will cover the Left of the Division. The 83rd, 65th and 150th Bdes will cover the Right of the Division.

Arrangements have been made for one gun, firing on dividing line between attacking Bdes., to fire one smoke shell every other lift.

7. **Tanks.**
The attack will be supported by Whippet and Mk. 5 Tanks.

8. **Headquarters.**

Advanced Divisional Headquarters will open at BONY, A.15.d.2.8, at 14.00 on October 7th, and at A.17.c.5.8 at Zero hour.

9. ACKNOWLEDGE.

Walter Guinness.
Lieut-Colonel,
General Staff,
66th Division.

D.H.Q.,
6.10.18.

Issued through Signals at..........

DISTRIBUTION.

Copy No. 1.	War Diary.	11	25th Bn. M.G.C.
2	" "	12	25th Division.
3	File.	13	50th Division.
4	"Q".	14	C.R.A. 18th Divn.
5	Signals.	15	35th Squad. R.A.F.
6	C.R.E.	16	1st Tank Battalion.
7	198th Inf. Bde.	17	3rd (Light) Tank Battn.
8	199th Inf. Bde.	18	76th Bde. R.G.A.
9	South African Bde.	19	89th Bde. R.G.A.
10	9th Glouc.R.(Pioneers).	20	XIII Corps
21	A.D.C.	22	A.D.M.S.

SECRET. Issued down to Platoon Commanders.

INSTRUCTION No. 2. Issued under Divl.Order No. 97.

AIRCRAFT.

1. Contact aeroplanes of 35th Squadron R.A.F. will fly along the line at each objective and will call for flares by sounding a succession of "A's" on the Klaxon Horn, and by firing a White Very light.
If the aeroplane fails to mark the line accurately, it will repeat its call ten minutes later.

2. Troops in the advanced line will answer these calls as follows :-

(a) By lighting Red ground flares, 3 of which in tin are to be carried by every N.C.O. and section commander.
(b) By firing Very lights, if possible, 3 in succession.
(c) By flashing pocket torches in a westerly direction.
(d) By using as reflectors pieces of tin sewn inside flap of box respirator, or carried separately.
(e) By waving ground sheets or helmets.

3. The urgent importance of replying to calls of contact aeroplanes must be impressed on all troops. By this means only can formations be furnished with information enabling them to deal with hostile resistance and to exploit success.
Failure to respond to calls also forces aeroplanes to fly so low as to suffer heavy casualties in pilots and machines. It may also lead to artillery fire being turned on to localities which though occupied by our troops are supposed to be hostile owing to lack of information. At the same time it must be understood that THOSE IN REAR POSITIONS ARE NEVER TO ANSWER CALLS FOR SIGNALS.

4. Red flares show best against dark backgrounds such as the shadow at the bottom of a shell hole or trench.

5. COUNTER ATTACK PLANES.

(a) From Zero hour, counter-attack planes will be constantly in the air with the object of observing hostile concentrations or abnormal movement.

/(b) In the event

(b) In the event of an enemy concentration indicating a counter-attack. the counter-attack aeroplane will signal this information to the artillery by wireless. In the case of counter-attack actually developing a white PARACHUTE flare will be fired by the aeroplane in the direction of the troops moving for the impending counter-attack, for the information of the infantry.

Red lights fired from counter-attack machines indicates targets for artillery and other aircraft and must not be confused with the above.

6. MARKINGS ON PLANES.

The following will be the markings of machines allotted to special duties :-

(a) Contact patrol machine - Rectangular panels 2 feet by 1 foot on both lower planes about 3 feet from the fuselage and a streamer on the tail.

(b) Machines working with the Tanks - Black band under the tail.

7. Smoke bombs may be dropped from aircraft to screen the advance of our infantry and tanks.

Walter Guinness
Lieut-Colonel,
General Staff,
66th Division.

D.H.Q.,
6.10.18.

SECRET   App. 71   122

SOUTH AFRICAN BRIGADE ORDER 246

1. (a) The 66th. Div. will be relieved by the 18th. Div. commencing night 20/21 Oct..
   (b) The S. Afr. Bde. will be relieved in the line tonight 19/20th. by the 199 Bde..

2. The relief will be carried out as follows:
   4th. Rgt. and 1 coy. of 1st. Rgt. by 9th. Manchesters.
   2nd. Rgt. and 3 coys. of 1st. Rgt. by 18th. K. L'pool Rgt.

3. On relief, 1st. SAI. will move to billets in cellars to be reconnoitred by them in NE. edge of LE CATEAU, and 2nd. SAI, 4th. SAI, and SALTM Bty., to billets in REUMONT.

4. All details, such as guides, etc., to be arranged between Commanding Officers.

5. Staff Captain will make all necessary billeting and administrative arrangements.

6. Locations of Units and their HQ. will be reported to Bde. HQ. as soon as possible on arrival at their new areas.

7. Bde. HQ. will remain at the Chateau, LE CATEAU.

8. Completion of relief will be notified to Bde. HQ. by code - "RATIONS UP".

9. Command will pass, on completion of relief.

10. ACKNOWLEDGE.

(sd) E. BARLOW, Major,
Bde. Major, S. Afr. Inf. Bde..

19-10-18

Secret   App. 72   121

SOUTH AFRICAN BRIGADE ORDER 247

Ref. 57B.1/40,000

1. 66 Div. (less arty., 9th. Glosters, 3 coys. RE.) will be relieved from the line by 18th. Div. night 20/21st. October.
2. S. Afr. Bde. will move tomorrow to billets in SERAIN area in accordance with attached March Table.
3. Billets and administrative arrangements will be made by Staff Captain, who will also provide for move of transport.
4. Units will notify Bde. HQ. location of their HQ. on arrival in new areas.
5. Bde. HQ. closes at the Chateau, LE CATEAU, at 10.30 am., and opens at SERAIN on arrival.

(sd) E. BARLOW, Major,
Bde. Major, S. Afr. Inf. Bde..

19-10-18

MARCH TABLE

Serial No.	Unit	Starting Time	Point Place.	Route	Remarks
1.	SALTM Bty.	10.30	Road junction P.17.a.8.6.	REUMONT - MAUROIS - MARETZ	Distances 100x between Coys., 500x between BNs.
2.	2nd. SAI	10.35			
3.	4th. SAI	11.00			
4.	1st. SAI	11.15			
5.	Bde. HQ.) Signals)	11.30			

S E C R E T. Not to be taken into action. C

Distbn: down to Bn Commdrs.

60th DIVISION INSTRUCTION No. 6. Issued under D.O. No.97.

120

1. GENERAL.

1. The main chain of communication will run along the line BONY - Dugout A.17.c.5.6 in trench - dugout B.19.a.?.0 - trench B.1?.a.5.5 (near LONGUSSET FARM) - approximately B.9.a.cent (or in BELLEVUE FARM) - T.2?.b.5.3 - PTE FOLIE FARM - SERAIN.

2. Signal offices will be established at each of those points, forming Divisional Reports centres. Liaison between infantry and artillery will also be carried out through this channel.

3. In order to prevent the enemy gaining any warning of the intended operations, all communications forward of the NAUROY - LE CATELET Ridge will be carried out by despatch carrier only until Zero hour.

4. After Zero all messages will be sent in "clear" (except those relating to casualties, location of reserves, and directions of counter-attacks, in the case of our own troops), and the Code Calls given in the Training Manual Signalling will be used.

5. At Zero Advanced Divisional H.Q. will be established in trench at A.17.c.5.6.

II WIRES.

(1) Before Zero two lines will be run from Adv. D.H.Q., to BELLEVUE Signal Office.
These will be continued on as soon after Zero as practicable as far as LA FOLIE FARM Signal Office.
(2) The only other cables, except artillery lines, will be those laid by infantry Brigades after their objectives have been reached.

III WIRELESS.

(1) Spark wireless sets will be established at Adv. D.H.Q. and BELLEVUE Signal Office before Zero, these will remain in position throughout operations.
(2) Loop wireless sets will be established as follows :-

(a) Before Zero at BELLEVUE.
(b) After Zero at T.2?.b. and LA FOLIE Signal Office
(c) Each Bn of 19?th Inf.Bde. will carry a loop set which will move with Bn.H.Q. and keep in touch with Bde. H.Q.

(3) C.W. Wireless sets for Artillery use are not available.
(4) Power buzzer and amplifier communications will not be established.

IV. VISUAL.

1. Visual Stations will be established at each of the Division Report Centres, the calls will be as follows :-

A.17.c.	Y F P R
B.19.a.	C T P R
B.1?.a.	L H T
BELLEVUE	B V F
T.2?.b.	T T B
LA FOLIE FARM.	L F L

2. Machine gun O.P's will be established as follows :-

B.11.c.1.6.	For fire on area round USIGNY RAVINE and sunken road in B.5.d.
B.?.a.7.9.	For fire on area round LA SABLONNIERE.
T.27.b.5.3.	For fire on area round LE VERGER.

For fire forward of this, the Independent (A) Machine Gun Company will be in touch with one of the Divisional Report Centres.
Infantry wanting support from M.G.C. will call up any of these O.P's, whose call will be "M.G", or send a message to the nearest report centre.

(3) Infantry Companies and Battalions will keep touch throughout by visual with Bn. and Bde. H.Qrs.

123

(4) By night infantry working to infantry or machine guns, will use red screens on lamps, and artillery to artillery will use yellow screens, but when calling up opposite arms the colour of the arm to be called up will be used.

V. MESSAGE CARRIERS

(1) Motor cyclists.
One will remain with each Infantry Bde. H.Q., the remainder will be distributed in pairs along the chain of communications as far as the roads are passable.
(2) Push cyclists.
Two will be distributed at each post along the axial chain beyond the limit reached by the motor cyclists.
Each Brigade will keep six at H.Q. ready for use.
(3) Mounted orderlies.
Six will be available for use along the main chain for portions where roads are in bad condition.
Each Infantry Bde will have five available at H.Q.
(4) Runners will be held at Infantry and Artillery Bde., Battery, and Battn H.Q. as required, artillery providing their own runners where necessary.
All units keeping in touch with the axial line of communication will send two runners to remain at that Signal office on the axial line, with which they are keeping touch at the time.

VI PIGEONS.

(1) There are at present none available, if any become available in time to be of use priority of issue will be given as follows :-

Whippets.
199th Inf. Bde. H.Qrs.
Other Inf. Bde. H.Qrs.
Bn. H.Qrsof 199th Inf. Bde.
Other Bn. H.Qrs.
Artillery F.O.O's.

VII. AEROPLANES.

(1) There will be an aeroplane flying all day prepared to take signals by POPHAM PANEL, from units on the ground.
(2) This plane will be marked by two streamers on each wing.
(3) Units will put out their aeroplane discs, T.Panel, and T.M.S. Code Call on arrival in any position; when communicating with the aeroplane they will show the call up signal which will be acknowledged by the aeroplane on the Klaxon Horn repeating the Code Call three times. Each group being acknowledged by the general answer.
(4) These messages will be dropped at the Adv. D.H.Q. Dropping Station at A.17.c.6.8.

VIII. LIGHT SIGNALS.

(1) Ground flares will be lighted as in 66th Divn Instructions.
(2) Rockets.
S.O.S. Signal will be GREEN
GREEN
RED.

IX. CODES &c.

(1) No special cypher codes will be arranged as messages may be sent in clear.
(2) The T.M.S. Code calls of units are as follows :-

/66th D.H.Q.

66th Div. H.Q.	Y F F
Adv. 66th D.H.Q.	Y F F R
198th Inf. Bde.	Z S H
6th Lan. Fus.	L F F
5th R.Innis.Fus.	I F E
6th R.Dub.Fus.	D F F
199th Inf. Bde.	Z S I
18th K.L.R.	K L R
9th Manch.R.	M A N 1
5th Conn.Rang.	C R E
South African Bde.	S Z A
1st S.A. Regt.	A S A
2nd do.	B S A
4th do.	D S A
9th Glouc.R.(Pioneers)	G L I

X. ACKNOWLEDGE.

Lieut-Colonel,
General Staff,
66th Division.

D.H.Q.,
6.10.18.

DISTRIBUTION.

War Diary.	50th Division.
War Diary.	18th Division.
File.	XIII Corps.
"Q".	25th M.G. Bn.
Signals.	35th Squad. R.A.F.
C.R.E.	1st Tank Bn.
198th Inf. Bde.	3rd (Light) Tank Bn.
199th Inf. Bde.	76th Bde. R.G.A.
S.A. Bde.	89th Bde. R.G.A.
25th Division.	A.D.C.

==============

124

"A" Form.

MESSAGES AND SIGNALS.

Army Form C. 2121.
(In pads of 100.)

No. of Message ....

Prefix ...... Code ...... m.	Words. 21	Charge.	This message is on a/c of:	Recd. at ...... m.
Office of Origin and Service Instructions.	Sent		...... Service.	Date
4FF SA Bde	...... m.			From
	To			By
	By		(Signature of "Franking Officer.")	

TO

Sender's Number.	Day of Month.	In reply to Number.	AAA
*			

From	
Place	
Time	

The above may be forwarded as now corrected.	(Z)
Censor.	Signature of Addressor or person authorised to telegraph in his name.

* This line should be erased if not required.

(3795.) Wt. W492/M1647. 650,000 Pads. 5/17. H.W. & V., Ld. (E. 1187.)

Prefix .... Code .... m

Office of Origin and Service Instructions.

Sent

At .... m.

To ....

By ....

This message is on a/c of:

125 .... Service.

OHP

(Signature of "Franking Officer.")

Recd. at .... m.

Date 18 (0)

From ....

By ....

TO "Q" Signals. C.R.E. 198th Bde. 199th Bde. S.A. Bde. Train ASC 9th Glouc. R. ADMS DADVS DAPM Camp Commdt. 66th M.T. Coy. SAA Sex. DAC DGO 4th Army 13th Cps

Sender's Number.	Day of Month.	In reply to Number.	
* D.O.98.	6		AAA

F Following moves will take place 7th Oct. AAA S.A. Bde. Group to HINDENBURG Line as in O.O.96 of 6th Oct. to be clear of RONSSOY at 10.30 AAA 198th Bde. Group to HINDENBURG Line as in O.O. 96 Head to enter RONSSOY at 11.00 AAA 199th Bde Group to LE CATELET ~~HEAD TO~~ head to pass LONGAVESNES CHURCH at 10.30 AAA 25th M.G. Bn. about GILLEMONT FARM to enter RONSSOY at [illegible].00 AAA Instructions about the destination of transport and train Coys are being issued by Divn "Q" AAA F.Cos. R.E. will come under orders of Bde. Groups at 17.00 until when demands for work must be submitted through C.R.E. AAA Advanced D.H.Q. will open at BONY about A.15.d.2.6 at 14.00 AAA Moves of Field Ambulances will be ordered by A.D.M.S. AAA ACKNOWLEDGE

From 66th Divn.

Place

Time

The above may be forwarded as now corrected.

(Z)

Censor.

Lt-Col. GS.

Signature of Addressor or person authorised to telegraph in his name.

* This line should be erased if not required.

(3796.) Wt. W 492/M1647. 650,000 Pads. 5/17. H.W. & V., Ld. (E. 1187.)

126

"A" Form
MESSAGES AND SIGNALS.

Army Form C. 2121
(In pads of 100.)

No. of Message..........

Prefix..............Code..............m. | Words | Charge
Office of Origin and Service Instructions: Copy

Sent
At ....m.
To
By

This message is on a/c of: App 19 Service.
(Signature of "Franking Officer")

Recd. at......m.
Date
From
By

TO 1st SAI	SALTMB	BSO.
2nd SAI	SAFA	
4th SAI	542 Coy ASC	

Sender's Number.	Day of Month.	In reply to Number.	AAA
BS 54	6		

Moves	will	take	place
tomorrow	Oct	7	as
ordered	in	Bde	Or[illegible]
237	the	only	alteration
being	that	time	of
passing	starting	point	for
each	Unit	will	be
two	and	half	hours
earlier	the	clock	hour
halt	at	09.30	being
taken	in	consideration.	

From SA Bde
Place
Time

The above may be forwarded as now corrected. (Z) (Sgd) E Barton
Major

Censor. Signature of Addressor or person authorised to telegraph in his name

* This line should be erased if not required.

128

SECRET.

INSTRUCTION No. 4. Issued under Divl. Order No. 97.

TANKS.

1. Allotment.

Nature.	Unit.	No. of Tanks.	Commander.	Attached to.
Heavies. (Mk. 5.)	'C' Coy., 1st Tank Bn.	12 (less 4 to 25th Divn.)	Major HISKIN.	S.A. Bde. Brig-General W.E.C.TANNER, C.M.G., D.S.O.
do.	'A' Coy. 1st Tank Bn.	8	Major BOXER.	198th Bde. Brig-General A.J.HUNTER, D.S.O., M.C.
Whippets (medium Mk A).	'E' Coy. 3rd Light Tank Bn.	11	Major C.H. MAY, M.C.	199th Bde. Brig+General G.C.WILLIAMS, D.S.O.

2. Tanks accompanying 198th and S.A. Bdes will follow the infantry attack and will co-operate against any point that infantry fail to get under the barrage. They may not be required up to the RED Line, and are on no account to be pushed ahead of, or level with the infantry, the object being to minimise any possible loss of tanks by uselessly exposing them to enemy fire where the infantry do not need their assistance.

On the capture of the RED Line 3 tanks from each company will be immediately withdrawn into Divisional Reserve in valley about B.5.central. Remaining tanks of company attached to 198th Bde. will be available for exploitation of area allotted to that Brigade. The remaining tanks (5) of company allotted to South African Bde. will operate against LES FOLIES and SERAIN as necessary. While the barrage is dwelling beyond the RED Line all tanks attached to either Bde will be withdrawn out of view on to reverse slopes or into depressions.

On capture of SERAIN all tanks will concentrate in valley about B.5.central. The 6 tanks in Divisional Reserve, together with troops in Divisional Reserve (1 Bn. Pioneers), and 20 machine guns, will be prepared at any time after capture of RED Line to deal with any attempted counter-attack from the North.

3. Whippets accompanying 199th Bde will time their arrival so as to cross the RED Line when the barrage lifts. They will then move forward at top speed to work round and attack SERAIN.

As soon as final objective has been made good they will concentrate in valley about U.19. and 20. and wait there until consolidation is complete, when they will be ordered to withdraw

/4. Tank.....

129

4. Tank Commanders will get into touch with B.Gs.C. to whom they are attached, after 14.00 7th Oct. as follows :-

S.A. Bde. HINDENBURG Line about A.15.b.central.
199th Bde. HINDENBURG Line about A.16.c.0.1.
198th Bde. In LE CATELET - NAUROY Line about LE CATELET.

They will arrange routes and times with them.

5. Following signals will be used :-

From Infantry to Tanks.

Helmet on top of rifle = Tank wanted here.(rifle to be pointed in direction where Tank is required.).

From Tanks to Infantry. =

Red and Yellow Flag	= "Am broken down - don't wait".
Green and White Flag.	= "Come on to mop up".
Tricolour.	= "Am withdrawing from action for supplies".

F.P. Thornbury

Lieut-Colonel,
General Staff,
66th Division.

D.H.Q.,
6.10.18.

DISTRIBUTION.

War Diary (2 copies).	50th Division.
File	18th Division.
"Q".	XIII Corps.
Signals.	25th M.G. Battalion.
C.R.E.	35th Squadron R.A.F.
198th Inf. Bde.	1st Tank Battn. (3 copies).
199th Inf. Bde.	3rd Light Tank Battn.(2 copies).
South African Bde.	76th Bde. R.G.A.
25th Division.	89th Bde. R.G.A.

A.D.C.

****

app 20 130

Reference - MONT BREHAIN 1/20,000

SOUTH AFRICAN INFANTRY BRIGADE

PRELIMINARY ORDER No. 1

SECRET

Copy No. 15

6.10.18

I.

(a) - With a view to increasing the breach in the enemy's defences, Major Operations are about to be taken in a general North-easterly direction by the Third and Fourth Armies.

(b) - The 66 th. Divn. will attack the RED LINE with the South African Inf. Bde. on the Right, and the 198th. Inf. Bde. on the Left - each on a two/BN. frontage. The 199th. Inf. Bde. will follow this attack, and after the capture of the RED LINE will pass through the S. Afr. and 198th. Bdes. in order to seize the GREEN LINE (SERAIN and the high ground in U.13, U.14, and U.26.)

(c) - The attack to the RED LINE will be made by the 66th.Divn in conjunction with one Bde. from the 25th. Divn. on the Right of the S. Afr. Bde., and one Bde. from the 50th. Divn. on the Left of the 198th. Bde..

(d) - The task of the Bde. of the 50th. Divn. will be to protect the Left Flank of the Corps, and to co-operate with the 38th.Divn. in the capture of VILLERS OUTREAUX.

(e) - The capture of SERAIN will be carried out in conjunction with the 2nd. American Corps, who will take PREMONT.

II. INTENTION

The S. Afr. Inf. Bde. will attack in normal formation with the 2nd. Regt. on the Right, the 4th. Regt. on the Left, and the 1st. Regt. in Support.

III. BOUNDARIES

The Brigade Boundaries are shown in RED on the reference. The dividing lines between the attacking BNs. is shown in BROWN.

IV. ASSEMBLY

(a) - The position of assembly for the two assaulting BNs. is that approximately shown on the reference in BLACK. The support BN. will assemble immediately in rear of the assaulting BNs., along the NE edge of BEAUREVOIR VILLAGE.

The BLACK Line referred to above is immediately in rear (b) of our present front line, held by troops of the 25th.Divn..

(b) BN. Commanders will arrange for the position of assembly to be reconnoitred, as well as the necessary lines of approach, tomorrow the 7th inst..

(c) - Each BN. will detail a responsible Officer to accompany the Bde. Major tomorrow morning, starting at 6 am. from Bde. HQ., for the purpose of reconnoitring the positions of assembly. These Officers will be prepared to tape the positions on the evening of 'Y-Z' Night.

(d) - The two assaulting BNs. will each detail six reliable NCOs. to reconnoitre routes-between MUSHROOM QUARRY and their positions of assembly who will be prepared to guide the Tanks-allotted to the Bde. from their positions of readiness to the assembly positions on 'Y-Z' night.

These N COs. will be required to travel in the Tanks during the attack for the purpose of keeping touch between the Tanks and the Infantry.

131

(c) - On 'Y-Z' night, Bns. will be required to complete the assembly by ZERO minus 2 hours.

V. ATTACK.
(a) - The Bns will attack in normal formation, preceded by the Tanks and closely follow the creeping barrage to the RED objective.

(b) In order to assist the rapid exploitation of the situation and the capture of the GREEN LINE, the O.C., 2nd. Regt. will, assisted by the Tanks, arrange to capture and hold LES FOLIES as soon as the protective barrage ceases.

(c) When the 199th. Bde. has passed through the RED LINE, the O.C., 2nd. Regt., will arrange for two Platoons to occupy and hold the high ground in U.26. a. and b..

(d) The Supporting Bn. will follow in support of the attacking Bns., paying particular attention to the protection of their flanks, and on the arrival of the assaulting Bns. at their objective will occupy a supporting position approximately along the line of the track running through C.1.a., U.25.c., T.30.d., T.30.a., and thence to the Left Bde. boundary about T.23.d.7.5..

VI. ARTILLERY.
(a) The attack on the RED LINE will be made under cover of a strong barrage. This barrage will come down and rest for 3 mins. 200 yards in front of the Infantry forming-up tapes. It will then move forward by lifts of 100 yards in 3 mins. for 1200 yards, and then slow down to 100 yards in 4 mins. until it reaches a line 300 yards in front of the RED LINE.
A protective barrage will dwell 300 yards in advance of the RED LINE for 30 mins., when it will lift and the second phase of the attack will commence.

(b) The attack on the RED LINE will be further supported by a mobile Field Battery which will move forward with the Bns., one section in support of each Bn., to give supporting fire over open sights.
Details of Field Artillery barrage and employment of Corps Heavy Artillery will be supplied later.
The Section Commander of these supporting F.A. Sections will be in close touch with the Bn. commander concerned.

VII. TANKS.
VIII (a) 12 Mark V. Tanks will accompany the S.Afr. Bde. in the attack on the RED LINE, and will be disposed under the order of Tank Squadron Commander on the Bde. Front, six with each attacking Bn..
(b) The Tanks will pay particular attention to probable opposition at LA SABBLONNIERE, PETIT FOLIE FM., and MAREST FM..
(c) After the protective barrage has ceased, two Tanks will be prepared to assist the 2nd. Regt. in capture of LES FOLIES.

VIII. MACHINE GUNS.
25th. MG. BN. (attached to 66th. Divn.) will be disposed as follows -

(a) 4 guns	will deal with	USIGNY RAVINE (B.12.a.)	
4	do.	SABBLONNIERE (B.4.b)	
4	do.	Copse & dug-outs N. of SABBLONNIERE.	
4	do.	T.28.d. and T.29.c.	
4	do.	PETIT VERGER FM. (T.22.d.)	

These 20 guns will co-ordinate their barrage with Artillery programme, allowing necessary clearances.
They will be in position by midnight 'Y-Z' night.

VIII (Contd)

After ceasing fire on above targets they will concentrate in the valley B.5. central, and be in Divl. Reserve. They will then be prepared to deal with any counter-attack from a northerly direction.

(b) 16 guns will concentrate at B.13.b.3.0. by 1900 on Y-Z night, sending liaison officer to MUSHROOM QUARRY to keep in touch with assembly of infantry.

After ZERO they will advance with the infantry of S.A. and 198th. Bdes., and will take up positions from which they will be able to deal with the following points by direct fire -

4 guns	on	HAMAGE FM. (T.24.c.)
4	do.	PETIT FOLIE FM. (U.19.c.0.3.)
4	do.	LES FOLIES (U.19.d.)
4	do.	REDOUBT about U.25.central.

On capture of RED LINE these guns will remain laid on above targets until further orders.

(c) 6 guns each are allotted to 198th. and S. Afr. Bdes. These guns will be given definite tasks beforehand by B.G.C's. concerned, which they will carry out under their own Officers.

On capture of RED LINE they will take up suitable defensive positions to secure this line in case of counter-attack.

IX. CONSOLIDATION.

(a) Each objective or line gained will be consolidated by the assaulting troops at once. The importance of continuing this work, even after other troops have passed through any particular line cannot be too strongly impressed on all concerned.

(b) Strong points will be constructed near the following positions -

1. Cross roads - U.25.c.
2. PETIT FOLIE FM. - U.19.c.
3. U.26.c.) - Protecting Right flank.
4. U.26.a.)
5. LES FOLIES.

(c) To assist in the construction of the above strong points, two sections of 430th. Field Co., R.E., will be attached to the Right assaulting Bn., one section to the Left assaulting Bn., and one in Reserve in rear of the Supporting Bn..

X. COMMUNICATIONS.

(a) The Divl. ~~xxxxxx~~ axial line of communication will be the road - BONY - A.17.c.5.5. - LORNISSET - BELLEVUE FM - LA SABBLONIERE - LA FOLIE FM..

(b) Runner-posts will be established at suitable intervals along this line.

(c) Details of Visual Signalling will be communicated later.

XI. LIAISON ~~xxx~~ Bn. Commanders will exercise the usual care in keeping up liaison with troops on their flanks by means of interlocked posts.

133

<u>SOUTH AFRICAN INFANTRY BRIGADE</u> <u>SECRET</u>

Ref. Map - <u>ADMINISTRATIVE INSTRUCTIONS in connection with Preliminary Order No. 1...</u> <u>6.10.18</u>

MONT BREHAIN,
1/20,000

<u>Ammunition Supply.</u>

Small dumps of SAA and No.36 grenades will be established at each BN.HQ. on the night of the 7/8 Oct..

Indents for further supplies should be submitted to Staff Captain, who will arrange to forward material to BN. HQ..

<u>Rations</u>

Each man will carry 2 days' rations, i.e., Rations for Z day and iron rations.

<u>Water</u>

40 petrol tins of water will be dumped at each BN. HQ. on the night of the 7/8 Oct..

<u>Prisoners of War</u>

Units will provide escorts for prisoners as far as Bde. HQ., where they will be taken over by Divl. escorts.

<u>Stragglers' Posts</u>

Stragglers' Posts, consisting of 1 NCO and 3 men, will be established at - B.14.b.8.5.

These men will be provided from surplus men of 4th. SAI., and will report to Staff Captain at MUSHROOM QUARRY at 8 pm. on night 7/8 Oct..

[signature]

Captain,
Staff Captain,
<u>South African Inf. Bde..</u>

To all Recipients of
<u>Preliminary Order No. 1</u>

134

XII. HEADQUARTERS.

Bde. HQ. will be established on Y day at A.17.c.5. 7. , and at ZERO, at MUSHROOM QUARRY.

Major,
Brigade Major,
South African Inf. Bde.

Issued through Signals at
23.45 to -
1. 1st SAI
2. 2nd SAI
3. 4th. SAI
4. S.A.L.T.M. Bty.
5. 66th. Divn.
6. 198 Inf. Bde.
7. 199 Inf. Bde.
8. Bde. Signal Offc.
9. 25th. MG. BN.
10. 432 Field Co. RE
11. Tank Squadron
12. Staff Captain,
13. Bde. Major,
14/17. War Diary.

App. 21

SOUTH AFRICAN INFANTRY BRIGADE

1355

1st. SAI
2nd. SAI
4th. SAI

Each BN. will detail a responsible Officer to meet the Brigade Major at 6 am. tomorrow morning at Bde. HQ. for the purpose of reconnoitring positions of assembly.

These Officers will be prepared to tape positions on Y-Z night.

(sd) E. BARLOW, Major,
Bde. Major, S. Afr. Inf. Bde..

6-10-18

	Sent	This message is on a/c of:	Recd. at
	At.............m.	Service	Date
	To..............	App. 22 (O)	From
	By..............	(Signature of "Franking Officer.")	By 136

TO: 198th Bde — 18th Div Arty — 35th Sqn R.A.F. — File
199th Bde — Signals — 1st Tank Bn — Q
S.A. Bde — 25th M.G. Bn — 25th Division — 13th Corps

* Sender's Number.	Day of Month.	In reply to Number.	AAA
DO99	8th		

The Division today captured all its objectives penetrating the enemy positions to a maximum depth of 6200 yds on a 3000 yards front aaa Prisoners estimated about 700 Casualties except for barrage on jumping off position were very small aaa 5 different enemy divisions were identified aaa

Line now runs La LAMPE FARM U 7 central, U 8 b 0 5, Windmill U 8 d 9 3 U 15 Central to Roman Road ~~U 21 b 9 2~~ U 22 a 4 7 aaa

The advance will be continued tomorrow 9th October aaa 13th Corps with 66th Division on left and 25th Division on right aaa

~~[illegible]~~

From
Place
Time

The above may be forwarded as now corrected. (Z)

Censor. Signature of Addressor or person authorised to telegraph in his name.

* This line should be erased if not required.

(379L.) Wt. W492/M1647. 650,000 Pads. 3/17. H.W. & V., Ld. (E. 1187.)

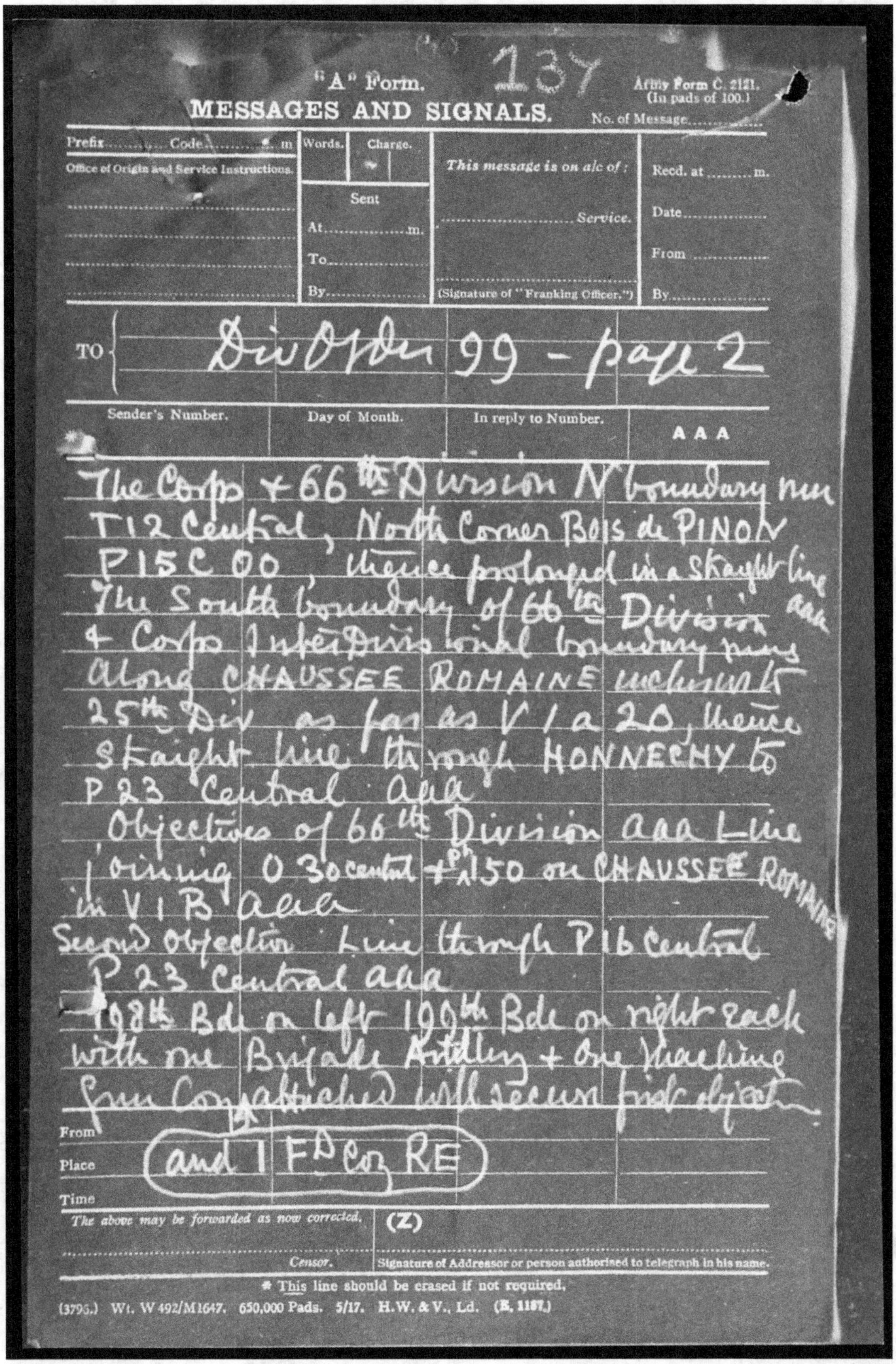

137

"A" Form.
MESSAGES AND SIGNALS.

Army Form C. 2121.
(In pads of 100.)
No. of Message..............

Prefix........ Code........ m	Words.	Charge.	This message is on a/c of:	Recd. at ....m.
Office of Origin and Service Instructions.	Sent		.... Service.	Date..............
	At..........m.			From ....
	To..........			
	By..........		(Signature of "Franking Officer.")	By..............

TO { Div Order 99 - page 2

Sender's Number.	Day of Month.	In reply to Number.	AAA

The Corps + 66th Division N boundary now T12 Central, North Corner BOIS de PINON P15C 00, thence prolonged in a straight line The South boundary of 66th Division aaa & Corps Inter Divisional boundary runs along CHAUSSEE ROMAINE inclusive to 25th Div as far as V1a 20, thence straight line through HONNECHY to P23 Central aaa

Objectives of 66th Division aaa Line joining O30 central + Pt 150 on CHAUSSEE ROMAINE in V1B aaa

Second Objective Line through P16 central P23 Central aaa

198th Bde on left 199th Bde on right each with one Brigade Artillery + one Machine Gun Coy attached and 1 Fd Coy RE will secure first objective

From
Place
Time

The above may be forwarded as now corrected. (Z)

Censor. Signature of Addressor or person authorised to telegraph in his name.

* This line should be erased if not required.

(3795.) Wt. W 492/M1647. 650,000 Pads. 5/17. H.W. & V., Ld. (E. 1187.)

"A" Form.

MESSAGES AND SIGNALS.

Army Form C. 2121 (In pads of 100.)

No. of Message..........

Prefix..........Code..........m | Words. | Charge.

Office of Origin and Service Instructions.

SBG

Sent At.......... To.......... By..........

This message is on a/c of: ....Service.

app 23 (0)

(Signature of "Franking Officer.")

Recd. at ....m. Date.......... From.......... By..........

TO			
198 Bde	18 Div Arty	35 Sqn RAF	File
199 Bde	Signals	1st Tank Bn	Q
54 Bde	25 MG Bn	25 Div	13 Corps

Sender's Number: G.1515 | Day of Month: 8 | In reply to Number. | AAA

Reference Div order 99 of today have since been informed by Corps that Zero hour will be 0520. AAA Presume Corps CRA arranging a shoot therefore be prepared to attack at this hour which will be Zero hour unless you are notified to the contrary

Axial line of communication for tomorrow will be PETIT FOLIE FARM – North of SERAIN to FARM U10a52 – l'EPINETTE O36b67 – COPSE P20a

In accordance with wishes of 25th Div Heavy Arty will start to lift off S.W. exits of MARETZ 06.15 & will go back through village at rate 100 yards every 4 minutes

From

Place

Time

The above may be forwarded as now corrected. (Z)

Censor. | Signature of Addressor or person authorised to telegraph in his name.

* This line should be erased if not required.

H. W. & V. Ld. (E. 1187.)

"A" Form.

MESSAGES AND SIGNALS.

Army Form C. 2121.
(In pads of 100.)

No. of Message..............

Prefix.......... Code.......... m. Office of Origin and Service Instructions.	Words. Charge. Sent At..........m. To.......... By..........	This message is on a/c of: .... Service. (Signature of "Franking Officer.")	Recd. at ....m. Date.......... From.......... By..........

139

TO { 66th Div Order No 99 page 3

Sender's Number.	Day of Month.	In reply to Number.	AAA

*

Inter Brigade boundary line through MILL in U 14 b & point where stream cuts first objective in P 31 a inclusive to 199th Bde.

S.A. Brigade will take 2nd objective with one Brigade Artillery & one M.G. Coy & 1 RE Coy attached leap frogging 198 & 199 Bdes on first objective AAA

Until first objective S.A. Bde will be in Divisional Reserve AAA

On passing 2nd objective 199 Bde will move as support to S.A. Bde, 198 Bde will be in Divisional Reserve AAA

Artillery Bdes M.G. & Field Coys affiliated to Infy Bdes will be the same as today.

From

Place

Time

The above may be forwarded as now corrected. (Z)

Censor. Signature of Addressor or person authorised to telegraph in his name.

* This line should be erased if not required.

(3796.) Wt. W 492/M1647. 650,000 Pads. 5/17. H.W. & V., Ld. (E. 1187.)

Army Form C. 2121.
(In pads of 100.)

MESSAGES AND SIGNALS.

No. of Message ....

Prefix .... Code .... m	Words.	Charge.	This message is on a/c of:	Recd. at .... m.
Office of Origin and Service Instructions.	Sent		.... Service.	Date
	At .... m.			From 140
	To			
	By		(Signature of "Franking Officer.")	By ....

TO { 66th Div Order No 99 page 4

Sender's Number.	Day of Month.	In reply to Number.	AAA

BGCs 198 & 199 will make U3 central U10 central their first bound and will arrange to attack ~~[illegible]~~ at 5 A.M. tomorrow 9th aaa

CRA is arranging to engage ELINCOURT and 160 contours ground in U10 & U16 from 4.30 to 5 A.M.

BGC 198 Bde will consider turning ELINCOURT from the South by passing through 199th Bde after the latter has completed his first bound aaa

All units will at once fill up their ammunition & water aaa

No Tanks are available as yet to assist but it is hoped to obtain 2 heavies for each Bde aaa

Divl. H.Q. are at BELLEVUE FARM until first objective has been reached aaa

From

Place

Time

The above may be forwarded as now corrected. (Z)

.... Censor. Signature of Addressor or person authorised to telegraph in his name.

* This line should be erased if not required.

(3796.) Wt. W492/M1647. 650,000 Pads. 5/17. H.W. & V., Ld. (E. 1187.)

...SSAGES AND SIGNALS. (In pads of 100.) No. of Message........

Prefix........ Code........ m | Words. | Charge. | This message is on a/c of: ....Service. (Signature of "Franking Officer.") | Recd. at ....m. Date........ From .... By........

Office of Origin and Service Instructions.

Sent At........m. To........ By........

TO { 66th Div! Arty No. 99 pm 15

Sender's Number. | Day of Month. | In reply to Number. | AAA

198 Bde H.Q. Les MARLICHES FARM (T17c)
199 Bde H.Q. T 29 c 97
S. A Bde H.Q. T 29 c 96
SAA Section is at BONY (near DHQ)
18th DA BEAUREVOIR (B9d47)
~~Divisional Advanced Report Centre~~
Pt. FOLIE FARM U 19 c 0 2

ACKNOWLEDGE

F.P. Lowthy [?] Capt

From
Place
Time 8.10 PM

The above may be forwarded as now corrected. (Z)

Censor. Signature of Addressor or person authorised to telegraph in his name.

* This line should be erased if not required.

(3795.) Wt. W 492/M1647. 650,000 Pads. 5/17. H.W.&V., Ld. (E. 1187.)

"A" Form.

Army Form C. 2121
(In pads of 100.)

MESSAGES AND SIGNALS.

No. of Message...........

Prefix........ Code........ m | Words. | Charge.

Office of Origin and Service Instructions.

Sent
At..........m.
To..........
By..........

This message is on a/c of:
.... Service.
(Signature of "Franking Officer.")

Recd. ......m.
Date......
From......
By......

TO

242

Sender's Number.	Day of Month.	In reply to Number.	AAA

Prisoners of War Cage 9th October will be at BELLEVUE FARM aaa ~~[illegible]~~ It is important owing to difficulties of communication that succeeding H.Q. should be located ~~[illegible]~~ on or near to Axial line of Communications

From 66th Div
Place
Time

The above may be forwarded as now corrected. (Z)

Censor. Signature of Addressor or person authorised to telegraph in his name.

* This line should be erased if not required.

(3796.) Wt. W 492/M1647. 650,000 Pads. 5/17. H.W.&V., Ld. (E. 1187.)

App 24(0) 143

Copy No.

SECRET.

66th Divisional Order No 100.

1
SITUATION. From all reports received the attack by the Third & Fourth Armies appears to have been a complete success. Practically all objectives have been taken; Cavalry have gone through, and the enemy is reported to be retreating in disorder.

2 After clearing up the situation about SERAINS 199th Inf. Bde will push forward and consolidate on the General line - U.16.a.1.0 - where touch will be maintained with 25th Divn - U.15.c. - U.9.c.0.6 - U.8.central - U.7.central. GREEN LINE. 198th Inf. Bde, after capture of LES MARLICHES Fm., will gain touch with 38th Divn in the WARLINCOURT - AUDIGNY Line. Arrangements have been made by 50th Divn for the withdrawal of their troops from the line so soon as this contact is obtained.

3 On completion of above the divisional front will be divided into the following sectors under arrangements to be made direct between B.Gs.C concerned:-

199th Bde. PONCHAUX - MARTZ road exclusive (about U.16.c.2.0) to SERAINS - ELINCOURT road exclusive. (about U.8.d.8.6).

198th Bde. SERAINS - ELINCOURT road inclusive (about U.8.d.8.6) to Northern Corps Boundary thence back to WARLINCOURT - AUDIGNY Line where contact is obtained with 38th Divn.

S.A. Bde. Will concentrate in Divl. Reserve in the valley about B.29. central.

198th and 199th Bdes. will hold their fronts with one or two Battalions, 3rd battalion of each Bde. will be disposed in support in the WARLINCOURT - AUDIGNY line

4
MACHINE GUNS. 'D' Coy. 25th Bn M.G.C. will remain affiliated to the 199th Bde and will be disposed defensively in depth between the GREEN and the RED Line.

'A' Coy. 25th Bn. M.G.C. will be attached to 198th

Bde and will be similarly disposed for defence of Left Sector

25' Bn. M.G.C., less 'A' and 'D' Coys. will concentrate in Divl. Reserve about SABLONNIERE

5 ARTILLERY. Artillery Bdes will remain affiliated as at present with the exception of the Bde. RFA. at present attached to S.A. Bde. which will be withdrawn under arrangements to be made by C.R.A. 18' Divl. Artillery

6 CONSOLIDATION. So soon as the line detailed in para 2. is gained, this will be consolidated with a series of wired posts including strong points near the following localities

U. 16 c. 2. o. 1
U. 15. cent.
U. 9 c. o 6.
SERAINS.
U. 8. a. 3. o.
U. 7 central
T. 12. central
T. 11. central
LES MARLICHES. FARM.
LES FOLIE
U 26. central

The posts will be manned by definite garrisons.

7 TRANSPORT. Transport is being sent up and Bdes will send guides to meet it at

~~BELLE VUE. FARM at.~~

LORMISSET CROSS ROADS at ...

8. Ack. by bearer

F. ... [signature]

Lieut. Colonel
General Staff
66' Division

Issued at. 3.15 P.M.
D.S.B.
8. 10. 18.

By cyclist orderly
~~199 Inf Bde~~
199 do
S.A. ..

145

Copy.

1st S.A.I.
2nd S.A.I.
4th S.A.I.

In accordance with order B.M.X. 14 the South African Bde will be prepared to move forward and keep touch with 198th and 199th Inf. Bde. in their advance in order to follow through these Brigades without delay in securing the 2nd objective.
Axial line of communication for today will be PETIT FOLIE FARM - N. of SERAIN to Farm U.a.5.2. - L'Epinette - O.36.b.6.7. - Copse P.20.d.
Boundary between 2nd and 4th Bns. P.31.a.00.02. straight line thro P.26.central., P.21.d.4.4. to MAUROIS REUMONT Road, road inclusive to 4th S.A.I.

02.00

9/10/18.

1st. SAI
2nd. SAI
4th. SAI BMX.14 9-10-18

App. 25 146

1.(a) Divn. today captured all its objectives, penetrating the enemy positions to maximum depth of 6200x. on a 3000x front. Prisoners about 700.

(b) Line now runs to LAMPE FME., U.7.central, U.8.b.0.5.,Windmill U.8.d.9.3., U.15.central., to Roman rd., U.22.a.4.7..

(c)Advance will be continued today by XIII Corps, 66 Div. on Left, 25 Div. on right.

(d) Corps and 66 Div. boundary runs: T.12.central, N. corner, BOIS DE PINON, P.15.c.0.0., thence in straight line. S. boundary 66 Div. runs along CHAUSSEE ROMAINE inc. to 25 Div. as far as V.1.a.2.0., thence straight line through HONNECHY to P.23.cent..

2. First objective 66 Div. is line joining U.30.cent. and point 150 on CHAUSSEE ROMAINE in V.1.b.. Second objective is line running through P.16.cent. and P.23.cent..

2.(a) S. Afr. Bde. will take second objective, leapfrogging thro' 198 and 199 Bde. after these Bdes. have taken 1st. objective.

(b) Until 1st objective is taken, SA Bde. will be in Divl. Reserve. On taking 2nd. objective, 199 Bde. will move as support to SA Bde. and 198 Bde. will be in Divl. Reserve.

3. Attack of 2nd. objective will be made with 2n. BN. on right, 4th. BN. on left, and 1st. BN. in support. Each BN. will have attached to it the same Field guns, MGs., and section of Fld. Co., RE., as yesterday morning. No tanks are available as yet to assist but it is hoped to obtain two heavies for each BN..

4. BN.s will at once replenish their water and ammunition.

5. Bde. HQ. will remain for the present at T.29.c.90.95..

6. ACKNOWLEDGE.

7. Zero hour, 05.20..

(sd) E. BARLOW, Major,
Bde. Major, S. Afr. Inf. Bde..

01.30

App. 26

1st. SAI
18 Div. Arty..

247

BMX.25 9-10-18

1. Information: According to information from 3rd. Cav. Div., cavalry are well in advance of REUMONT but the high ground in Q.27.b. & d. is still held by the enemy on the right of our position NE. of MAUROIS.
2. Intention: It was intended to push our infantry line forward this evening NE. of REUMONT, but as this could not be undertaken before nightfall it will be done tomorrow morning.
3. OC., 1st. SAI will detail 2 coys. to reinforce our front line SE. of the MAUROIS - REUMONT road.
4. At 05.30 tomorrow morning 1st. SAI. will attack and capture the village of REUMONT, including BOICRIES FME., and thence along tracks running through P.18.b.4.3. 4 P.18.d.9.4 - P.18.d.20.00 - P.23.d.1.8..
5. It is probable 199 Inf. Bde. will pass through REUMONT at an early hour in the morning, and the intention is to assist by seizing this jumping off point.
6. Artillery fire from one FA. Bde. will be put down on BOICRIES FME., Q.13.c., P.24.b. & d., from 95.30 to 06.30..
7. OC., 2nd. SAI., has been instructed to supply the necessary guides to conduct the two coys. to reinforce the front line tonight, and arrangements will be made for the remainder of the BN. to be in position for the attack on REUMONT tomorrow morning.
8. ACKNOWLEDGE.

8.15 pm..

(sd) E. BARLOW, Major,
Bde. Major, S. Afr. Inf. Bde..

App 29 (8)

SECRET.

Copy No 148

66th DIVISION ORDER No. 101.

1. The Division have again had a most successful day and have advanced their line to a maximum depth of 12,000 yds on an average breadth of 2,500 yds.
The Physical fitness of all ranks, and the way in which units made efficient arrangements and carried out orders at comparitively short notice was satisfactory.

2. Cavalry have passed through TROIS VILLES and REUMONT today in a north-easterly direction.
The Corps will continue the advance tomorrow.

3. In confirmation and continuation of verbal instructions from G.O.C. to B.Gs.C. Brigades, South African Bde. will take over REUMONT and ground in P.12.c. and d., Q.7.c.and d., Q.13.a.and c., from Third Cavalry Division immediately.
South African Bde to be in Divisional Reserve on 10th October.
199th Bde. will move at 03.00 to pass through S.A. Bde outposts at 05.00, and continue the advance on the general objective Q.6.cent. K.36.central, K.23.central, K.16.central.

4. Divisional and Brigade boundaries will be as follows :-

(a) With 25th Division on the Right, a line between P.23.central and K.29.central.

(b) With 33rd Division on the Left, a line between P.11.central and K.16.central.

Touch will be gained with 25th Division on the Right and 33rd Division on the Left in this objective.

5. 198th Bde. will move at 03.00 and advance in support of 199th Bde.
When both Brigades have passed through South African Bde., the latter will be prepared to move forward on receipt of orders from Division.

6. Two heavy tanks are allotted to 199th Bde. O.C. 1st Tank Bn. and B.G.C. 199th Bde. have made all arrangements.

7. Machine Guns will be allotted to Brigades as for today.

8. One troop of Northumberland Hussars will be attached to each Inf. Bde. These will be used either as a troop or split up and attached to Infantry units for local protection and reconnaissance.
One section of Corps cyclists will be attached to each Bde. H.Q. These will be used for reconnaissance and for mounted orderly work.
Yeomany and cyclists will report as under :-

For 198th and 199th Bdes. At 199th Bde. H.Q. L'EPPINETTE O.36.b.5.7. at 02.30. 10th Oct
198th Bde. will send guides there to meet troops allotted to them.

For S.A. Bde. they will report at P.21d.1.4 at 03.00.

149

9. R.E. Coys will be withdrawn from 198th and S.A. Bdes and pass to command of C.R.E. at 03.30., 10th October.

10. Axial line of communications for tomorrow will be from LE PINETTE - REUMONT CHURCH - Q.1.central - Point 150 in K.27.d. - K.23.a. central.

11. Dropping station for aeroplanes will be about U.10b.8.2.

12. Prisoners of War Cage will be established at north-eastern end of MARETZ and will proceed by lorry leaving D.H.Q. at 06.00. 10th October.

13. Advanced D.H.Q. will open at U.10.b.8.2. at 12.00.

14. ACKNOWLEDGE.

Walter Guinness
Lieut-Colonel,
General Staff,
66th Division.

Issued at 20.15.

D.H.Q.,
9.10.18.

DISTRIBUTION.

Copy No.	1	War Diary.
	2	" "
	3	File.
	4	"Q".
	5	Signals.
	6	C.R.A. 18th Divn.
	7	C.R.E.
	8	198th Inf. Bde.
	9	199th Inf. Bde.
	10	South African Bde.
	11	A.D.M.S.
	12	D.A.P.M.
	13	XIII Corps.
	14	25th Division.
	15	33rd Division.
	16	3rd Cav. Divn.
	17	1st Tank Bn.
	18	25th Bn M.G.C.
	19	35th Squad. R.A.F.
	20	Detachment, North'd Hus.
	21	Detachment Corps Cyclists
	22	A.D.C.

****

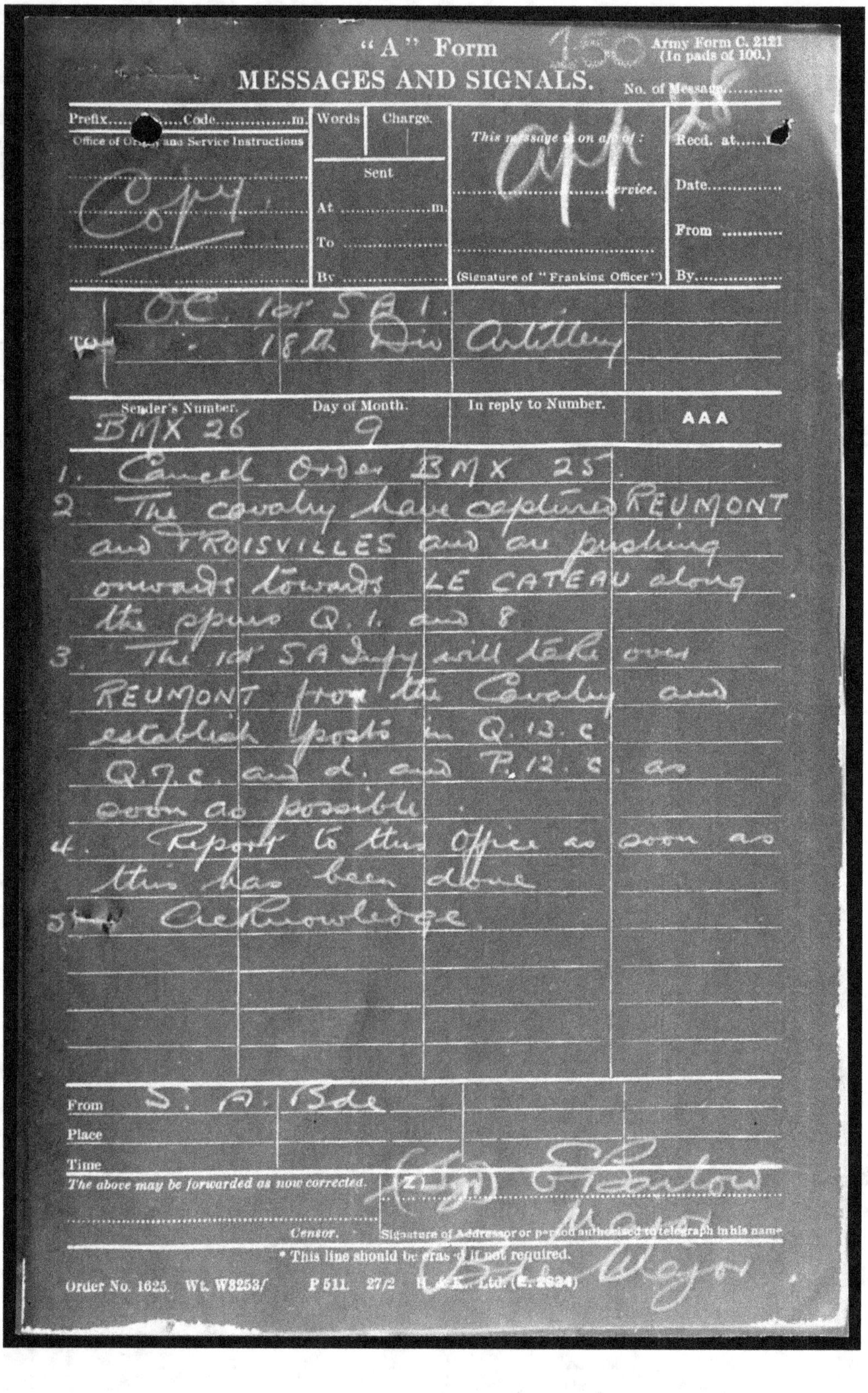

"A" Form 150 Army Form C. 2121 (In pads of 100.)

MESSAGES AND SIGNALS. No. of Message 28

Prefix...... Code...... m. Office of Origin and Service Instructions	Words	Charge	This message is on a/c of:	Recd. at...... m.
Copy.	Sent At ...... m. To ...... By		App ...... Service. (Signature of "Franking Officer")	Date...... From ...... By......

TO O.C. 1st S.A.I.
" 18th Div Artillery

Sender's Number.	Day of Month.	In reply to Number.	AAA
BMX 26	9		

1. Cancel Order BMX 25
2. The cavalry have captured REUMONT and TROISVILLES and are pushing onwards towards LE CATEAU along the spurs Q.1. and 8
3. The 1st SA Infy will take over REUMONT from the Cavalry and establish posts in Q.13.c Q.7.c. and d. and P.12.c. as soon as possible.
4. Report to this Office as soon as this has been done
5. Acknowledge.

From S. A. Bde
Place
Time

The above may be forwarded as now corrected. (Z) (Sgd) E Barlow Major

Censor. Signature of Addressor or person authorised to telegraph in his name

* This line should be erased if not required.

Order No. 1625. Wt. W8253/ P 511. 27/2 H. & K. Ltd. (E. 2634) Bde Major.

PUBLIC RECORD OFFICE

Reference WO 95/3146

DUE TO A FAULTY DEXTER MACHINE.

FOLIOS 151-159 DO NOT EXIST

Prefix .... Code .... m | Words. | Charge. | This message is on a/c of: | Recd. .... m.

Office of Origin and Service Instructions.

Sent

At .... m.

To ....

By ....

.... Service.

app 29 (0)

(Signature of "Franking Officer.")

Date ....

From ....

By 167

TO 198th Bde — 19th DA — 25 Divn
199th Bde — Signals — 33 Divn
SA Bde ✓ — 13 Corps

Sender's Number.	Day of Month.	In reply to Number.	AAA
* DO 102	10th		

No definite information as regards result of attack by 17th & 33rd Divisions at 1700 today on high ground in K3 - K10 - K17 could be obtained from 33rd Div at 2230 AAA

If the above attack has succeeded in establishing itself on ridge with its right about K17 central 198 Bde will secure the general line about K17 central - K23c 1060 along SELLE River on West bank to K29a 00 AAA 199 Bde from this point K23d 70 K35c 74 Q5a 79 along Rly to Q4b 16 Q4a 68, Q3b 77 along track to point 143 (cross roads) AAA

From

Place

Time

The above may be forwarded as now corrected. (Z)

Censor. Signature of Addressor or person authorised to telegraph in his name.

* This line should be erased if not required.

(3796.) Wt. W 492/M1647. 650,000 Pads. 3/17. H. W. & V., Ld. (E. 1187.)

Prefix ...... Code ...... m. Words ...... Charge

Office of Origin and Service Instructions.

Sent
At ...... m.
To ......
By ......

This message is on a/c of:
...... Service.
(Signature of "Franking Officer.")

Recd. at ...... m.
Date ......
From ......
By ......

TO 162

Sender's Number.	Day of Month.	In reply to Number.	AAA
*			

Both brigades will attack simultaneously under a combined Arty & M.G. creeping barrage AAA All details and Zero hour will be arranged between Brigadiers AAA H.A. liaison officer will be ordered to report forthwith to 199th Bde H.Q. [illegible] Q7a7h AAA

If the aforesaid operation has not been successful 198 Bde will consolidate and improve its position wherever possible. 199th Bde will exploit situation in LE CATEAU as BGC sees fit.

All units will be warned to reduce movement by day to the minimum AAA Above in confirmation of verbal orders to BGC 199 Bde

~~Advd Div HQ will open at Mon de PIERRE~~

~~P4d at 0800 AAA~~

From

Place 66th Div

Time 1230

The above may be forwarded as now corrected. (Z)

Censor. ...... Signature of Addressor or person authorised to telegraph in his name. [signature] Lt Col

* This line should be erased if not required.

(3796.) Wt. W 492/M1647. 650,000 Pads. 5/17. H. W. & V., Ld. (E. 1187.)

"A" Form
Army Form C. 2121
(In pads of 100.)

MESSAGES AND SIGNALS.

No. of Message...........

Prefix............ Code............m. | Words | Charge.
Office of Origin and Service Instructions

Sent
At ....m.
To ....
By ....

This message is on a/c of: App 29A
...............Service.
(Signature of "Franking Officer")

Recd. at ....m.
Date ....
From ....
By 163

TO
1st S A I — C Coy 25th M G Co
2nd S A I — 83rd Bde R F A
4th S A I — OC Detach with the

Sender's Number.	Day of Month.	In reply to Number.	AAA
BMX 30	10		

1 (a) The Division have again had a most successful day & have advanced their line to a maximum depth of 12000 yds on an average breadth of 2,500 yds.
The splendid behaviour of all ranks & the way in which units made efficient arrangements & carried out orders at very short notice was satisfactory.
(b) Cavalry passed through TROIS VILLES and REUMONT today in an N.E direction.
(c) The 66th Div will continue the advance today.
(d) The Divl and Bde boundaries will be as follows —

From
Place
Time

The above may be forwarded as now corrected. (Z)
Censor. Signature of Addressor or person authorised to telegraph in his name

* This line should be erased if not required.

Order No. 1625. Wt. W3253/ P 511. 27/2. H. & K., Ltd. (E. 2634).

MESSAGES AND SIGNALS. No. of Message............

Prefix............Code..............m.	Words / Charge.	This message is on a/c of:	Recd. at......m.
Office of Origin and Service Instructions	Sent	...........................Service.	Date............
	At ....m.		From ....
	To		
	By	(Signature of "Franking Officer")	By..............

TO

Sender's Number.	Day of Month.	In reply to Number.	AAA
	2		166

(1) with 25th Div on the right a line between P 23 central and K 29 central
(2) with 33rd Div on the left a line between P 11 central and K 16 central
(3) Touch will be gained with 25th Div on the right & 33rd Div on left on this objective
(4) S A Bde will be in Div Reserve today.
199 Bde are moving at 03.00 to pass through S A Bde outposts at 05.00 continuing the advance on the general objective Q 6 central K 36 central K 23 central K 16 central
198 Bde move at 03.00 to

From
Place
Time

The above may be forwarded as now corrected. (Z)

Censor. Signature of Addressor or person authorised to telegraph in his name

* This line should be erased if not required.

Order No. 1625. Wt. W3253/ P 511. 27/2. H. & K., Ltd. (E. 2634).

"A" Form — Army Form C. 2121 (In pads of 100.)

MESSAGES AND SIGNALS.

No. of Message..........

164

Prefix..........Code..........m.	Words	Charge.	This message is on a/c of:	Recd. at......m.
Office of Origin and Service Instructions*	Sent		..........Service.	Date..........
	At ....m.			From ....
	To			
	By		(Signature of "Franking Officer")	By..........

TO 3

Sender's Number.	Day of Month.	In reply to Number.	AAA

to advance in support 199 Bde

2. The S A Bde Group will be prepared to move from present positions immediately on receipt of further orders

3. Bns must call in any posts and get together so as to be able to move if necessary as a body by march route

4. Detailed instructions as regards move will be issued later.

ACKNOWLEDGE

From S A Bde

Place

Time 09 00

The above may be forwarded as now corrected. (Z)

..........Censor.

[illegible] Major, Bde Major

Signature of Addressor or person authorised to telegraph in his name

* This line should be erased if not required.

Order No. 1625. Wt. W3253/ P 511. 27/2. H. & K., Ltd. (E. 2634).

165

"A" Form
Army Form C. 2121
(In pads of 100.)

MESSAGES AND SIGNALS.

No. of Message............

Prefix............Code..............m.	Words	Charge.	This message is on a/c of: OHS Service.	Recd. at......m.
Office of Origin and Service Instructions	Sent		(Signature of "Franking Officer")	Date..............
	At ....m.			From ....
	To			By....................
	By			

TO
1st S.A.I.
2nd S.A.I.
4th S.A.I.

Sender's Number.	Day of Month.	In reply to Number.	AAA
BM.x 31	10		

With reference to S.A. Bde BM.x30 the 2nd S.A.I. will move up forthwith to a position in Q.7.a + d and endeavour to get into touch with 25th Div who are believed held up on right aaa 4th S.A.I. will move up to a position in P.6.d and P.12.b aaa 1st S.A.I. will remain at REUMONT aaa 2nd + 4th will report H.Q. when Bns in position. 2nd also to report when in touch with 25th Div aaa Bde H.Q will remain at present location aaa Add to B.M.x30. Axis line of communication to-day is L'EPINETTE – REUMONT CHURCH – Q.1 central – Point 150 in K.27.d – K.23.a central aaa Acknowledge. Copies to C Coy 35 M.G.C 83 Bde RFA 66 Div. + O.C. Det. North. Hsrs

From
Place
Time 13.00

The above may be forwarded as now corrected. (Z)

Censor. Signature of Addresser or person authorised to telegraph in his name

* This line should be erased if not required.

Order No. 1825. Wt. W2252/ P511. 27/2. H. & K., Ltd. (E. 2834).

"A" Form (In pads of 100.)

MESSAGES AND SIGNALS.

No. of Message............

Prefix..............Code..............m. | Words | Charge.

Office of Origin and Service Instructions

Sent
At ....m.
To ....
By ....

This message is on a/c of: App 31 ....Service.

(Signature of "Franking Officer")

Recd. at......m.
Date..........
From 160
By............

TO
1st S.A.I. | C Coy ... |
2nd | 83rd Bde R.F.A. |
4th | Detachment North. Hrs. |

Sender's Number.	Day of Month.	In reply to Number.	AAA
[illegible]	15.		

Units should hold themselves in readiness to move up at ~~any time~~ about 17.30.

From S.A. Bde
Place
Time

[illegible signature]

The above may be forwarded as now corrected. (Z)

Censor. Signature of Addressor or person authorised to telegraph in his name

* This line should be erased if not required.

Amendment to Divl Order No. 108. **66th Divn.**

3x22(0)

app 32(0)

167

A & Q.	35th Squad. R.A.F.
Signals.	1st Tank Bn.
C.R.A. 18th D.A.	76th Bde. R.G.A.
C.R.E.	80th Bde. R.G.A.
198th Inf Bde.	O.C. Detachment Corps Cyclists.
199th Inf. Bde.	O.C. Squadron Corps Cavalry
South African Bde.	33rd Division.
Train A.S.C.	50th Division.
A.D.M.S.	9th Gloucester Regt.

XIII Corps.

The following amendments will be made to Divisional Order 108:-

Para.2. 6th Line.
For K.21.a.0.0. substitute K.20.a.0.0.
Para 3. 6th line.
For "On relief 198th Bde." substitute "on relief 199th Bde".
Para 3. 7th line.
For "199th Bde.H.Q." substitute "198th Bde H.Q."

(Sd) Walter Grunnell [?]

Lieut Colonel
General Staff 66th Division.

D.G.S.
11/10/18.

168

S E C R E T.

Copy No....9..........

66th DIVISION ORDER No. 103.

11/10/18

1.
INFORMATION. (a). Present line held by the Division runs K.16.d.4.2. along southern bank of SELLE to K.23.c.0.0., thence along western bank of Reiver through le CATEAU to K.34.D.0.0., thence to Q.3.a.5.5., Q.2.d.0.0.

100th Brigade reached railway line in places East of le CATEAU yesterday evening but after heavy fighting was unable to establish itself there, attack on South having been postponed.

(b). The enemy is holding the high ground N.E. of the SELLE River, and the line of the railway East of the SELLE River to Q.10.c.

Two Regiments of the 17th Reserve Division have been identified about le CATEAU. This Division was brought down from Flanders and thrown into the battle after 7 weeks rest yesterday aftxerday afternoon.

2.
BOUNDARIES. The 50th Division is taking over from the 25th Division. The Corps Northern and Southern boundaries remain as before.

The inetr-Divisional boundary will now run P.23.c., K.34.a.5.2., thence due East along road to point when it crosses SELLE River, thence North along Western bank of SELLE River to K.21.a.0.0., thence to road junction K.23.b.7.0., along riad to K.18.central. (road inclusive to 66th Division).

3.
RELIEF. South African Brigade with two affiliated M.G. Coys., 1 Troop Northumberland Hussars, 1 Section Cyclists, 2 Brigades of Field Artillery (those now attached to 198th and 199th Brigades) will take over the Divisional front to-night, relief to be completed as soon as possible after dark. All details will be arranged direct between Brigadiers. On relief 199th Brigade will be withdrawn into REUMONT; 199th Brigade H.Q., and two Battalions REUMONT; 1 Battalion in positions accupied by S.A.Brigade in Q.7.

198th Brigade will be at 2 hours notice. Remaining 2 M.G. Companies will be withdrawn into Divisional Reserve in MAUROIS.

Squadron of Northumberland Hussars will come under orders of S.A. Brigade at 05.00 morning 12th instant.

4.
INTENTIONS. South African Brigade will at once make preparations to attack the objective K.11.c.5.5., K.17.b.5.5., K.18. central on 12th. B.G.C., S.A. Brigade will beforehand by vigorous patrolling establish himself on the Northern banks of the River K.22.b. & d., K.16.c. & d.

The 50th Division has as its objective the high ground N.E. and E. of le CATEAU, Squares K.29, K.35, K.36. Corps on the North and South will also continue their advance.

5.
HEADQUARTERS. Divisional Headquarters will be at l'EPINETTE (0.36.b.8.8 and MARETZ. N. of Roman road. Battle H.Q., MOOLIN de PIERRE P.4.d.9.5.

ACKNOWLEDGE.

[signature]

Lieut-Colonel.
General Staff.
66th Division.

App 87 & 84
Attack on N tomorrow morning

"A" Form. Army Form C. 2121.
(In pads of 100.)

MESSAGES AND SIGNALS.

No. of Message..............

Prefix.......... Code.............. m | Words. | Charge. | This message is on a/c of: | Recd. at .... m.

Office of Origin and Service Instructions.

Sent

At..............m.

To..............

By..............

app Service. 33 (0)

(Signature of "Franking Officer.")

Date

From 172

By..............

TO G. Signals, CR.A. 18th Div. Arty. CRE. 198th Bde. 199th Bde S.A.A.Sec. Train, A.D.M.S., 50th Divns, 9th Glouc. R. XIII Corps.

Sender's Number.	Day of Month.	In reply to Number.	AAA
* 25th Bn. M.G.C. G.B.59.	11		

Following are the administrative boundaries for the Divisional Area aaa Corps northern boundary on left aaa On right K.34.a.0.0. K.18. c.0.0. cross roads V.1.a.2.0. portion of MARETZ north of main road aaa Reserve Division area south west MARETZ to the line GUISANCOURT Farm BEAUREVOIR inclusive aaa Moves will take place tomorrow as follows aaa 198 Bde to MAUROIS 199 Bde all in REUMONT aaa D.H.Q. and Divl Troops MARETZ north of Roman Road aaa M.G. Bn. less two companies MAUROIS 9 Glouc R. REUMONT all moves to be completed by 15.00 aaa B.G.C. 198 Bde to arrange with B.G.C. 149 Bde direct aaa Order for 198 Bde to be at two hours notice is cancelled aaa After move 199 Bde will be at two hours notice.

From

Place 66th Div.

Time 09.30

The above may be forwarded as now corrected. (Z)

Censor. Signature of Addressor or person authorised to telegraph in his name.

Lt-Col. G.S.

* This line should be erased if not required.

(3198.) Wt. W 12952/M1294. 375,000 Pads. 1/17. H. W. & V., Ld. (E. 818.)

"A" Form.
Army Form C. 2121.
(In pads of 100.)

MESSAGES AND SIGNALS.

No. of Message

Prefix ... Code ... m	Words. 23	Charge.	This message is on a/c of: app 34 (Service)	Recd. at ... m.
Office of Origin and Service Instructions. DR	Sent At 01.25 m. To ... By ...		(Signature of "Franking Officer.")	From ... By ...

TO S.A ... 18 D.A. 178

Sender's Number.	Day of Month.	In reply to Number.	AAA
G 114	4		

Corps	wires	are	Corps
...	left	attack	tomorrow
objectives	K 17	K 10	153
AAA	66	Div	will
conform	by	...	forward
left	flank	to	join
up	...	K 17a	

From 66 Div

Place

Time 01.10

The above may be forwarded as now corrected. (Z)

Censor. Signature of Addressor or person authorised to telegraph in his name.

* This line should be erased if not required.

(3796.) Wt. W 492/M1647. 650,000 Pads. 5/17. H.W. & V., Ld. (E. 1187.)

Form C. 2121.
(In pads of 100.)

"A" Form.

MESSAGES AND SIGNALS.

No. of Message............ 177

Prefix........ Code........ m.	Words.	Charge.	This message is on a/c of:	Recd. at .... m.
Office of Origin and Service Instructions.	Sent		.... Service.	Date
	At........ m.			From
	To........			
	By........		(Signature of "Franking Officer.")	By

App 35 (O)

TO { S.A. Bde

Sender's Number.	Day of Month.	In reply to Number.	AAA
* G 115	4		

Heavy Arty. will deal with squares L 19 a & c K 24 d K 29 (particular attention being paid to Rly. embankment) K 35 a & b to cover and assist operation of 33rd Div. Arty. will open fire at 5 a.m. & cease firing at 5.45 a.m. You will utilize your two F. Arty. Bdes. to assist you in attaining if possible your objective as given in para. 4 of D.O. 153 of date. The operation of the whole Corps on your left should offer you a favourable opportunity of doing so.

From 66 Div

Place

Time

The above may be forwarded as now corrected. (Z)

J. P. [illegible] Lt Col

Censor. Signature of Addressor or person authorised to telegraph in his name.

* This line should be erased if not required.

(3796.) Wt. W 492/M1647. 650,000 Pads. 5/17. H.W.&V., Ld. (E. 1187.)

174

"A" Form
MESSAGES AND SIGNALS.

Army Form C. 2121
(In pads of 100.)

No. of Message 36

Prefix ... Code ... m.	Words	Charge	This message is on a/c of:	Recd. at ... m.
Office of Origin and Service Instructions	Sent		App ... Service.	Date ...
Copy	At ... m.			From ...
	To ...			
	By ...		(Signature of "Franking Officer")	By ...

TO 1st SA I
2nd SA I
4th SA I

Sender's Number.	Day of Month.	In reply to Number.	AAA
BM/X 36	11.		

1. The South African Bde will relieve the 198th & 199th Bde in the line tonight, 11th inst.
2. The relief will be carried out as follows

2 Coys 1st SA I	Liverpool Regt in front line		199 Bde
2 Coys 1st SA I	Lancs Fusrs " "		198 Bde
2nd Regt SA I	Manchesters in support		199th Bde
4th Regt SA I	Inniskilling Fusrs in support		198th Bde

3 Guides from above Bns of 198th & 199th Bdes will be on main road NE of REUMONT about P.18.a.35,95. at 8 pm.
4. Completion of relief will be notified to Bde H.Q. by code word O.K.
5 Command will pass at 9 pm.
6. B.H.Q. will open at Q.7.b.3.2. at the above hour.
7 Acknowledge.

From S A Bde.
Place
Time

*The above may be forwarded as now corrected. (Z) (Sgd) E Barlow Major
Censor.* Signature of Addressor or person authorised to telegraph in his name
Bde Major.

* This line should be erased if not required.

Order No. 1625 Wt. W3253/ P 511. 27/2 H. & K. Ltd. (E. 2634)

Appx 42.

[5. African Brigade Order 243.

SECRET.

Ref. 57B. 1/40,000 Copy No. 9.

14 - 10 - 18.

1. The following reliefs and alterations of dispositions will take place tonight:-

2nd SAI will relieve 2nd Northumberland Fusiliers (150th Bde).

9th Gloucester R. (Pioneers) will relieve the 2 Coys of 1st S.A.I. in line on left.

2 Coys. 1st S.A.I. relieved by 9th Gloucester R. (Pioneers) will take up positions in support of 2 Coys. 1st SAI remaining in line.

4th SAI will withdraw from present positions to those now occupied by 2nd SAI in Q.7.b.

2 All detail arrangements such as provision of guides, etc. will be made between C.O.C concerned.

3 Completion of relief will be signalled to Bde HQ. by Code word · Rations up.

4. 9th Gloucester Rgt. (less B Team) will be temporarily attached to the S.A. Bde while in the line.

"A" Form
Army Form C. 2121
(In pads of 100.)

MESSAGES AND SIGNALS.

No. of Message..........

Prefix..........Code..........m. Words Charge.
Office of Origin and Service Instructions
Sent
At ....m.
To ....
By ....
This message is on a/c of:
App. 43.
(Signature of "Franking Officer")
Recd. at ......m.
Date..........
From ....
By..........

TO { 1st S A I
9th Gloucesters

Sender's Number.	Day of Month	In reply to Number.	AAA
Bde 48	14		

Reference Bde Order 243 of today the left Divisional Boundary is from today P 6 Central to K. 21. c. 0. 0. thence to Road junction K. 22. a. 2. 1 (exclusive to 66th Div) – K. 17. d. 0. 6 – K. 12. Central aaa 9th Gloucesters are not to take over N of this as originally instructed and 1st S A I should withdraw any troops they have N of this boundary

From S A Bde
Place
Time 1610

The above may be forwarded as now corrected (Z) (Sd) E Barlow Major

Censor. Signature of Addressor or person authorised to telegraph in his name
Bde Maj.

* This line should be erased if not required.

Order No. 1625 Wt. W3253/ P 511 27/2 H. & K., Ltd. (E. 2634)

"A" Form
MESSAGES AND SIGNALS.

Army Form
(In pads of 1

No. of Message........

Prefix..........Code..........m. | Words | Charge.

Office of Origin and Service Instructions

Sent
At ....m.
To ....
By ....

This message is on a/c of:
..........Service.
App 44
(Signature of "Franking Officer")

Recd. at......m.
Date.
From
By... 173

TO { 9th. Gloucesters.
115th. Bde

Sender's Number.	Day of Month.	In reply to Number.	AAA
BMX 49	14.		

Ref my BMX 48 of to-day and
you will establish an interlock
post with the 115th. Bde on
your left.
Addsd 9th. Gloucesters. rptd
115th. Inf. Bde. for
information

From
Place L.H. Bde.
Time

The above may be forwarded as now corrected. (Z)

Censor. Signature of Addressor or person authorised to telegraph in his name

* This line should be erased if not required.

Order No. 1625. Wt. W3253/ P 511. 27/2. H. & K., Ltd. (E. 2634).

"A" Form

Army Form C. 2121 (In pads of 100.)

MESSAGES AND SIGNALS.

No. of Message 45

Prefix .... Code .... m.	Words	Charge.	This message is on a/c of:	Recd. at ......m.
Office of Origin and Service Instructions	Sent		App 45	Date ....
	At .... m.		.... Service.	From ....
	To			
	By		(Signature of "Franking Officer")	By ....

TO: 1st S.H.
2nd S.H. 9th Gloucesters.

Sender's Number.	Day of Month.	In reply to Number.	AAA
BS 99	15.		

In order to prevent enemy from crossing to the west bank of the LASELLE stream please arrange to so thicken up your front line at night as to cover the line of the stream and prevent his patrols from crossing to our side

From [illegible] Bde
Place
Time

The above may be forwarded as now corrected. (Z)

.... Censor. Signature of Addressor or person authorised to telegraph in his name

* This line should be erased if not required.

Order No. 1625. Wt. W3253/ P 511. 27/2. H. & K., Ltd. (E. 2634).

(In pads of 100.)

MESSAGES AND SIGNALS.

No. of Message..........

Prefix..........Code..........m.	Words	Charge	This message is on a/c of:	Recd. at..........m.
Office of Origin and Service Instructions	Sent		..........Service.	Date..........
	At..........m.		App 46	From..........
	To..........			
	By..........		(Signature of "Franking Officer.")	By..........

TO { 1st SAI.
9th Gloucester Regt

Sender's Number.	Day of Month.	In reply to Number	AAA
BMx54	15th		

1. The 9th Gloucesters will ~~arrange~~ to take over tonight from the First S.A.I. the portion of line to the South of their present Boundary as far as ~~Road junction~~ ~~K28~~ line running through K28c5.7 – road junction in K28b3.5 – K23c21

2. Details to be arranged between C.O.s

3. 1st SAI will withdraw troops thus relieved to Support line.

4. 9th Gloucester will render to this office fresh disposition of troops by 10 a.m. 16th inst.

From 5 Completion of relief will be notified

Place by Code Word "Going Strong"

Time 6 Acknowledge

The above may be forwarded as now corrected. (Z)

.... Censor.

Signature of Addressor or person authorised to telegraph in his name

* This line should be erased if not required.

2

5. Liaison will be maintained with 150th Bde by 2nd S.A.I. by means of an interlocking post.

6. Exact disposition of troops must be forwarded to this Office by 10 am tomorrow (12th inst)

7. Acknowledge

(Sgd) E. Barlow
Major
Bde Major
S. African Bde

Distribution.

1. 1st SAI
2. 2nd SAI
3. 4th SAI
4. 9th Gloucester R.
5. Bde Signal Officer
6. 66 Division
7. 150th Inf Bde
8. 115th "

Secret

App. 37

180

SOUTH AFRICAN INFANTRY BRIGADE

1st. SAI.

Ref. Sheet 57B:1/40,000

1. 33rd. Divn. is making an attack on the left of the line you are taking over tonight to obtain the high ground NE. of the LA SELLE river.
2. You will as soon as possible establish a line of posts on the Northern bank of the SELLE, approx K.22.b. & d., K.16.c. & d..
3. An attack by your BN. will be made probably tomorrow, 12 inst., for which further orders will be issued, and the selected objective is that shown on the reference in BLUE, viz., K.11.c.5.5., K.17.b. 5.5., K.18.central.
4. The attack referred to in para. 3 will be carried out in conjunction with the 50 Div. on your right. The objective in the case of this Division is the high ground NE. and N. E. of LE CATEAU, squares K.29., K.35., K.36.. Corps on the North and South will also continue their advance.
5. If an opportunity presents it sekf to cooperate with the attack of 33rd. Div. tomorrow morning, 12 inst., it might be possible to gain the high ground in K.11.c. and K.17.b., and thus materially assist in gaining the attack with the 50th. Div..
6. Boundaries and objectives are marked in BLUE on the reference.
7. Particular care will be taken to protect the right flank, which will be somewhat exposed until 50th. Div. advance their line.
8. Arrangements will be made with the FA. Bdes. in support to put down a barrage across the front and the right flank of your objective tomorrow morning at 05.30.. This barrage will open some 300x. NE. of the rly. line and will creep forward at the rate of 100x. in 3 minutes. A protective barrage will stand some 100x. beyond the front and right flank for half-an-hour.

(sd) W. TANNER,
Brigadier-General,
Cmdg., S. Afr. Inf. Bde..

06-10,
11-10-18

The S A Bde

App 38.

181

The O.C. A & B. Coys report that they are unable to get across stream owing to heavy M.G. fire from railway bank in K 16 d & K 22 b. Recommend that railway bank be subjected to artillery fire this morning to enable us to pass it later. Please cancel artillery arrangements for 0530.

0.345.

[illegible] Lt Col.
1st S A I

The S A I Bde. App 39 182

Did you not receive my message asking you to cancel barrage. Have instructed M.G. to remain here as they will be wanted this afternoon. Bridge was not completed until after 0315 & M.G. fire was very heavy from Railway embankment. Very heavy barrage put down by enemy at 0445 & continued when our barrage opened. Is dying down now.

0545

12/10/18

[illegible] Lt Col.
1st S A I

Will give you news of how things are going on left as soon as I can ascertain

183

S.A.Brigade.
9th Bn. Glouc. R. (Pioneers).
C.R.E.)
Signals) for information.

66th Div.
G1112

Reference 66th Division Order No. 104 of 13th October:-

1. From 14th October inclusive, the 9th Glouc. R. (Pioneers) (less "B" Team) ~~will~~ under Capt. A.N.SUGGIT, will be temporarily attached to the South African Infantry Brigade and will take over the sector of the line from Road Junction K.28.d.6.8. to Northern Divisional Boundary under orders of B.G.C. S.A.Brigade.

2. Capt. A.N.SUGGIT with necessary advanced parties will report to H.Q. S.A.Inf. Bde. (Q.7.a.7.4.) at 09-30 October 14th.

3. Lieut-Colonel E.P.NARES M.C., and "B" Teams will proceed to MARETZ on October 14th reporting on arrival to 66th Div. "Q" for billets and further instructions.

4. ACKNOWLEDGE.

Done

Lieut-Colonel.
General Staff.
66th Division.

D.H.Q.,
13-10-18.

app 41(0)

184

66th Divn.
~~G.1112x~~
G.1112.

9th Bn. Glouc. R. (Pioneers).
S.A. Brigade.
Q.
C.R.E.
Signals.

The following amendments will be made to 66th Division G.1112 of 13th October:-

(a) For Captain A.N. SUGGIT read Major E.F.B.WITTS, D.S.O.

(b) Para. 3 is cancelled.

Lieut Colonel E.P. NARES, M.C. and 'B' Team plus surplus personnel not required by S.A. Brigade will remain at REUMONT and carry on their normal work under instructions of C.R.E.

F.P. Lawnthey

Lieut Colonel.
General Staff, 66th Division.

D.H.Q.
14th Oct. 1918.

185

(In pads of 100.)

MESSAGES AND SIGNALS.

No. of Message..........

Prefix.......... Code.......... m.	Words	Charge.	This message is on a/c of:	Recd. at......m.
Office of Origin and Service Instructions	Sent		App 40. Service	Date..........
....	At ....m.		....	From ....
....	To		....	
....	By		(Signature of "Franking Officer")	By..........

TO			
1st SAI	66 Div		
2nd SAI	25 Bn MGC		
4th SAI			

Sender's Number.	Day of Month.	In reply to Number.	AAA
BMX 40	12		

Bridges are being thrown over the R. SELLE stream at points to be selected and these bridges will be held so as to ensure a crossing at any time which may be required.

By day they will be commanded by the [illegible] in those lines and at night by posts on the further bank. They will also be made use of for passing patrols over for the purpose of keeping touch with the enemy and obtaining identifications.

The high ground in K 29 b and d and 33 central is known to be strengthened by the defences

From			
Place			
Time			

The above may be forwarded as now corrected. (Z)

Censor. Signature of Addressor or person authorised to telegraph in his name

* This line should be erased if not required.

Order No. 1625. Wt. W3253/ P 511 27/2 H. & K., Ltd. (E. 2634).

Army Form C. 2121
(In pads of 100.)

MESSAGES AND SIGNALS.

No. of Message............

Prefix.............Code...............m. Office of Origin and Service Instructions	Words / Charge. Sent At ....m. To .... By	This message is on a/c of: ....Service. (Signature of "Franking Officer")	Recd. at......m. Date........ From 176 By........

TO Z

Sender's Number.	Day of Month.	In reply to Number.	AAA

working to be undertaken by the Pioneer Battn.
The line will be strongly held by the liberal use of M.Gs and Lewis Guns and the men ~~[illegible]~~ in the front line reduced as far as possible.

From S.A. Bde
Place
Time

The above may be forwarded as now corrected. (Z) [illegible] Major Bde Major

Censor. Signature of Addressor or person authorised to telegraph in his name

* This line should be erased if not required.

Order No. 1625. Wt. W3253/ P 511. 27/2. H. & K., Ltd. (E. 2634).

S E C R E T.

66th Divn.
S1120

In continuation of 66th Division Order No. 104 dated 13th October 1918.

1. Reference para. 2 - Third Army will not co-operate on the North.

2. Para. 5 is cancelled.

3. Reference para. 6:-

The objective will be secured as follows:-

(a) By mid-day on 15th Oct., South African Brigade will arrange to have completed a thorough reconnaissance of all possible crossings of the river in K.34 and select a site for bridging in K.28.d. They will also secure by posts on the east bank any bridges which still remain intact. Result to be reported to D.H.Q. by 17.00 15th October.

(b) On night 15th/16th they will further consolidate all crossings secured on night 14th/15th and will arrange for the bridging of any other crossings necessary for the operation.
In addition they will occupy a definite portion of the town by infiltration of patrols and establishment of a picquet line.

(c) At Zero the assaulting Battalions will be formed up East of the river covered by the previously established line of picquets and at Zero plus 2 to 3 hours (according to the time taken by the 50th Division to gain their intermediate objective) will advance and capture the RED line.
After a pause of half an hour on the RED line, they will seize the BLUE line, final objective.

ACKNOWLEDGE.

Walter Guinness
Lieut Colonel.
General Staff, 66th Division.

D.H.Q.
14th Oct. 1918.

Issued to:-

A & Q.
Signals.
18th Div. Arty.
C.R.E.
South African Bde.
25th Bn. M.G.C.
9th Bn. Glouc. R.
50th Division.
A.P.C.

SECRET. Copy No. 10

66th DIVISION ORDER No. 10[illegible] 13th October 1918.

Reference 1/20,000 sheets 57b (N.E. and S.E.) (Edition 2A)
(Note. Grid lines on above 1/20,000 sheets differ slightly from Grids on 1/40,000 sheets).

1. To maintain the pressure on the enemy, and to increase the difficulties of his withdrawal the Fourth Army will carry out a further operation at an early date.

2. The attack of the XIII Corps will be carried out by the 50th Division on the Right and 66th Division on Left. It is not yet known whether the Third Army will co-operate on the North.

3. (a) The dividing line between 66th and 50th Divisions will be the road P.18.b.5.5. - Q.9.c.8.4. - Q.4.b.4.0 (road exclusive to 66th Division). - Thence a straight line to road junction K.35.d.0.3 (inclusive to 66th Division) - thence along road through K.35.d.6.0. to cross roads K.36.d.7.9.

(b) The dividing line between 66th Division and Third Army will be a line P.6.central - K.21.c.C.0. - road junction K.22.a.2.1. (exclusive to 66th Division) - K.17.d.0.6. - K.12.a.central.

4. The above alterations to the Divisional Sector will be made during the night 14/15th October under arrangements to be made direct between B.G.C. S.A. Inf. Bde. (H.Q. Q.7.a.7.4.) with B.Gs.C. ~~199th~~ 150th Inf. Bde. (H.Q. HONNECHY) and 115th Inf. Bde. (H.Q. TROISVILLES P.4.b.8.8.).
Necessary readjustments to be completed by 22 o'clock.

5. ~~The 100th Bn M.G. Corps will relieve the 25th Bn M.G. Corps in the 66th Divisional Sector by 06.00 on October 15th. Details to be arranged between Os.C. direct in consultation with S.A. Bde.~~
~~From 06.00 on October 15th, 25th Bn M.G. Corps will be attached to 50th Division.~~

6. The S.A. Bde will prepare at once for the capture of the objective

K.29.a.1.8. - K.29.central - K.36.d.0.5.

7. In the event of the enemy withdrawing before the above operation takes place, troops will advance at once and secure the line of the Railway in K.29. and K.35.

8. ACKNOWLEDGE.

F.P. Nosworthy
Lieut-Colonel,
General Staff,
66th Division.

DISTRIBUTION.

Copy No.	1	War Diary.
"	2	" "
	3	File.
	4	'A' and 'Q'.
	5	Signals.
	6	18th Divl. Arty.
	7	C.R.E.
	8	198th Inf. Bde.
	9	199th Inf. Bde.
	10	South African Bde.
	11	25th Bn M.G.C.
	12	100th Bn M.G.C.
	13	9th Bn Glouc R.
	14	A.D.M.S.
	15	D.A.P.M.
	16	XIII Corps.
	17	38th Division.
	18	50th Division.
	19	A.D.C.

188

S E C R E T.

66th Divn.
G.1120/1

A. & Q.	South African Bde.
Signals.	25th Bn. M.G. Corps.
18th Divl Arty.	9th Bn. Glouc. R.
C.R.E.	A.D.M.S.
198th Inf. Bde.	D.A.P.M.
199th Inf. Bde.	C Section No.1 Special Coy.R.E.

Reference 66th Division Order No. 104 dated 13th October 1918 and Instructions 1 - 8 issued under same.

ZERO day will be October 17th 1918.

ZERO HOUR will be 05.20 am

Acknowledge on attached slip and return receipt by bearer.

J. Marriott
Captain.
General Staff, 66th Division.

D.H.Q.
16th October 1918.

MESSAGES AND SIGNALS. No. of Message

Prefix .... Code .... Words .... / £ s. d. / Charges to Collect	Received. From .... By	Sent, or sent out. At .... m. To .... By	Office Stamp. SZA 14.10.18

Service Instructions.

Handed in at .... Office 1330 m. Received 1440 m.

TO [illegible]

*Sender's Number.	Day of Month.	In reply to Number.	AAA
118	14		

[illegible]	[illegible]	[illegible]	[illegible]
[illegible]	[illegible]	[illegible]	[illegible]
[illegible]	[illegible]	[illegible]	10.40

FROM [illegible]

189

S E C R E T.

app 47(0)
190

66th DIVISION INSTRUCTIONS NO.1.

Issued under 66th Division Order No. 104 dated 13/10/18.

1. 66th Division G.1128 of 14th Oct. is cancelled.
The advance of the 66th Division to its final objective (RED Line) K.29.a.1.8. - K.29.central - K.36.d.0.5., will be effected by an enveloping movement of LE CATEAU from the North in conjunction with the advance of the 50th Division in the South.

2. The point of junction of the attacking troops of the 66th and 50th Divisions will be K.35.c.9.3.
The attack of the 66th Division will be so timed that the front line troops of both Divisions arrive at the above point at the same time.

3. The forming up line of the 66th Division will be just east of the River SELLE from approximately K.28.d.9.1. to K.29.a.2.3.
The advance will then be made under a creeping barrage in a S.E. direction with the right flank advancing along the road K.34.b.95.73. - K.35.c.80.50., and thence, after junction with the 50th Division, along the Divisional boundary as laid down in D.O.104.
The left of the attack will advance through BAILLON FARM K.29.a inclusive to the level crossing K.29.c.85.90 where a strong point will be formed to protect the left of the Division.
After the line of the Railway has been captured and contact obtained with the left of the 50th Division, the advance will be continued in an easterly direction pivoting on the level crossing K.29.c.85.90 until the final objective is gained.
The railway line as far as K.23.c.1.2 will be cleared by a special party directly the final objective has been captured, a further defensive flank being thrown back along the stream from K.23.c.1.2 to K.22.d.7.2.

3. Exact time tables, barrage programmes and arrangements for masking various localities with smoke and gas, will be issued separately. Zero of 66th Division will be approximately 2 hours later than Zero of 50th Division.

4. The C.R.E. will arrange to have at least 8 bridges thrown across the River SELLE on Y/Z night between the points K.28.d.8.1 and K.29.a.3.4.
As an important factor of the operation is surprise, it is essential that no indications should be given to the enemy that the bridging of the River SELLE between these points is contemplated. On the other hand attempts will be made to bridge the River west of LE CATEAU and active patrolling in this direction carried on in order to lead the enemy to believe that a direct advance through the town is intended.

5. Div. Battle H.Q. will be established at P.4.d.4.9.
South African Bde Battle H.Q. will be established in the Ravine about K.27.c.6.2.
C.R.E. will arrange for adequate splinter proof accommodation to be constructed for the latter place by ~~midnight on Y/Z night.~~ 18.00 on 16th Oct
O.C. Signals will arrange for direct communication to be maintained between Division and Brigade Battle Headquarters. from 19.00 on 16th Oct

6. acknowledge
done.

F.P. [signature]
Lieut Colonel.
General Staff, 66th Division.

D.H.Q.
15th Oct. 1918.

DISTRIBUTION.

A & Q.
Signals.
18th Divl. Arty.
38th Division.
C.R.E.
198th Inf. Bde.
S.A. Brigade.
XIII Corps.
50th Division.
A.D.C.
25th Bn. M.G.C.
9th Bn. Glouc. R.
A.D.M.S.

191

SECRET.

South African Bde.
18th Divl. Artillery.
25th Bn M.G.C.

66th Divn.
1126

Reference Instructions Nos. 2 and 4 (Artillery and Machine Guns) of 15th October :-

Artillery and Machine Gun Fire will cease along Railway Line as far as K.23.c.1.2. at Zero plus 144 minutes to enable a party to clear this up as mentioned in Instructions No. 1 of 15th. at end of para. 3.

D.H.Q.,
16.10.18.

Lieut-Colonel,
General Staff,
66th Division.

"A" Form.

MESSAGES AND SIGNALS.

Army Form C. 2121.
(In pads of 100.)

192

Prefix	Code	m	Words.	Charge.	This message is on a/c of:	Recd. at ....m.
Office of Origin and Service Instructions.			Sent		Service.	Date
CDR			At ....m.			From
			To			
			By		(Signature of "Franking Officer.")	By

No. of Message.

TO — S A Bde

Sender's Number.	Day of Month.	In reply to Number.	AAA
* GB55	16th		

Reference Instructions No2 of yesterday (Artillery) Opening barrage will be put down 200 yards in front of Infantry forming up line and not as stated in paragraph 6

From 66th Div.

Place

Time

The above may be forwarded as now corrected. (Z)

Censor. Signature of Addressor or person authorised to telegraph in his name. [signature] Guinness Lt Col

* This line should be erased if not required.

(3796.) Wt. W 492/M1647. 650,000 Pads. 5/17. H.W. & V., Ld. (E. 1187.)

193

S E C R E T

66th DIVISION INSTRUCTIONS No 2.

Issued under 66th Division Order No. 104 dated 13.10.18.

ARTILLERY.

1. The following Field Artillery will support the attack of the 66th Division :-

(a) 18th D.A. Group. - C.R.A. Brig-Genl.T.C. SEAGRAM, D.S.O.
65th Army Brigade R.F.A.
84th Army Brigade R.F.A.
82nd Bde. R.F.A.
83rd Bde. R.F.A.

(b) Heavy artillery to be detailed by XIII Corps.

2. The preliminary bombardment will be spread over 48 hours previous to the attack, and will be accompanied by strong harassing fire. There will be no hurricane bombardment immediately preceding the assault.

3. On Y/Z night, and not later than 03.00 on Z day, the valleys of River RICHEMONT in K.23.d., K.24., and K.30.b., and also the area to the west of POMMEREUIL (L.25.central) will be bombarded with Lethal shell.

4. At Zero an intense bombardment by all natures will be opened on the areas in square K.35. and squares K.29. and 22. within the safety limits of the River SELLE.

From Zero plus 15 minutes the bombardment will drop to slow rate of fire and the area to be covered by the advance of the Division will be systematically searched backwards and forwards, special attention being paid to the cuttings and embankments of the railway, and to the ground immediately to the west of this line where wire is suspected.

A similar artillery programme supported by M.G. fire will be carried out simultaneously by the 38th Division on the area to the north of the Divisional sector in order to deceive the enemy as to the extent and location of the infantry attack.

5. From Zero plus one hour until assaulting infantry is formed up east of the SELLE, a proportion of smoke will be mixed in the bombardment of the north-east and eastern outskirts of LE CATEAU; on the area between the SELLE and the railway north of BAILLON Farm; and on the slopes of the spur N.E of MONTAY.

6. At Zero plus 129 mins a strong barrage will be put down ~~300~~ 200 yds in front of the Infantry forming up line. The barrage will remain stationary for 15 mins and will then advance by lifts of 100 yards at the rate of 100 yards in 3 mins, straight through to a distance of 300 yds in front of the final objective.

There will be no halt on the railway line.

There will be a pause of 3 hours in front of the final objective after which the barrage will again advance on the Right flank of the Division in order to allow the 50th Division to advance to their final objective.

139. 1.1 T44

Ack

F.P. Nosworthy
Lieut-Colonel,
General Staff, 66th Division.

D.H.Q.,
15.10.18.

DISTRIBUTION.

Copy	'A' & 'Q'.	198th Inf. Bde.	XIII Corps.
	Signals.	199th Inf. Bde.	38th Division.
	18th Div.Arty.	S. A. Bde.	50th Division.
	C.R.E.	25th Bn M.G.C.	A.D.C.

Duplicate 194

SECRET.

66th DIVISION INSTRUCTIONS No. 3.

ISSUED UNDER DIVISION ORDER No 104 dated 13.10.18.

PRELIMINARY MOVES AND DISPOSITIONS AT ZERO.

1. 198th Inf. Bde. will move up to REUMONT. Move to be completed by 12.00 hours 16th. 198th Bde. Transport Lines will return to area previously occupied S.W. of REUMONT.

2. The following dispositions will be taken up at dusk on 16th:-

(a) 198th Bde.H.Q. will take over present S.A.Bde. H.Q. in Q.7.b.
(b) S.A. Bde. H.Q. will move to K.27.c.
(c) 198th Bde will take over those portions of the front
  (i) From the Northern Divisional Boundary inclusive, to the Romnn Road inclusive.
  (ii) From CAMBRAI - LE CATEAU Road inclusive to Southern Divisional Boundary.
(d) The valley in 27.a. and c. and 26.b. and d. will be exclusively at the disposal of South African Bde.

Relief will be completed as soon as possible after dusk on 16th October.

3. 9th Glouc. R. on relief will concentrate in billets in [illegible] MAUROIS.
That portion of the Régiment not in the line will be clear of REUMONT by 10.00

4. From Zero onwards. 199th Bde. and 9th Glouc.R.(Pioneers) will be ready to move at one hour's notice.

5. ACKNOWLEDGE.

F.P. Nosworthy
Lieut-Colonel,
General Staff,
66th Division.

D.H.Q.,
15.10.18.

DISTRIBUTION.

Copy No 1	War Diary.
2	" "
3	File.
4	'A' and 'Q'
5	Signals.
6	18th Divl Arty.
7	C.R.E.
8	198th Inf. Bde.
9	199th Inf. Bde.
10	South African Bde.
11	25th Bn M.G.C.
12	9th Bn Glouc. R.
13	Divl Train A.S.C.
14	A.D.M.S.
15	D.A.P.M.
16	A.P.M. XIII Corps.
17	XIII Corps.
18	38th Division.
19	50th Division.
20	A.D.C.

195

SECRET.

66th DIVISION INSTRUCTIONS No. 3.

ISSUED UNDER DIVISION ORDER No 104 dated 13.10.18.

PRELIMINARY MOVES AND DISPOSITIONS AT ZERO.

1. 198th Inf. Bde. will move up to REUMONT. Move to be completed by 12.00 hours 16th. 198th Bde. Transport Lines will return to area previously occupied S.W. of REUMONT.

2. The following dispositions will be taken up at dusk on 16th:-

(a) 198th Bde.H.Q. will take over present S.A.Bde. H.Q. in Q.7.b.
(b) S.A. Bde. H.Q. will move to K.27.c.
(c) 198th Bde will take over those portions of the front
 (i) From the Northern Divisional Boundary inclusive, to the Roman Road inclusive.
 (ii) From CAMBRAI - LE CATEAU Road inclusive to Southern Divisional Boundary.
(d) The valley in 27.a. and c. and 26.b. and d. will be exclusively at the disposal of South African Bde.

Relief will be completed as soon as possible after dusk on 16th October.

3. 9th Glouc. R. on relief will concentrate in billets in MAUROIS.
That portion of the Regiment not in the line will be clear of REUMONT by 10.00

4. From Zero onwards. 199th Bde. and 9th Glouc.R.(Pioneers) will be ready to move at one hour's notice.

5. ACKNOWLEDGE.

F.P. [signature]
Lieut-Colonel,
General Staff,
66th Division.

D.H.Q.,
15.10.18.

DISTRIBUTION.

Copy No 1 War Diary.
2 " "
3 File.
4 'A' and 'Q'
5 Signals.
6 18th Divl Arty.
7 C.R.E.
8 198th Inf. Bde.
9 199th Inf. Bde.
10 South African Bde.
11 25th Bn M.G.C.
12 9th Bn Glouc. R.
13 Divl Train A.S.C.
14 A.D.M.S.
15 D.A.P.M.
16 A.P.M. XIII Corps.
17 XIII Corps.
18 38th Division.
19 50th Division.
20 A.D.C.

S E C R E T.

66th DIVISION INSTRUCTIONS No. 4.

Issued under 66th Division Order No. 104 dated 13/10/18

MACHINE GUNS.

1. The 25th Bn. M.G. Corps reinforced by 2 Coys 18th Bn. M.G.Corps will support the attack of the Division.

2. 2 Coys of the 25th Bn.M.G.Corps and 2 Coys of 18th Bn. M.G.Corps will be used for supplementing the artiller, barrage and will co-ordinate their barrage with the artillery programme allowing the necessary clearances. *
From Zero onwards these guns will maintain a slow rate of fire from selected localities, particular attention being paid to the Railway cuttings and embankment in K.35, K.29., K.23., and K.22 as far North as the Divisional boundary.
A steady rate of fire will also be maintained on the South and South-east slopes of the SPUR N.E. of MONTAY until half-an hour after the capture of the RED Line.

3. 1 Company 25th Bn. M.G.Corps will concentrate on Y/Z night in the neighbourhood of K.33. where they will advance at Z plus 2¼ hours to positions from which they can effectively strengthen the defence of the RED Line as soon as the latter is captured.
Details will be arranged by O.C. 25th Bn. M.G. Corpswith the South African Brigade direct.
This Company will maintain a liaison officer at South African Brigade H.Q. from Zero minus 1 hour until the completion of the operation.

4. 1 Company 25th Bn. M.G.Corps will be in Divisional Reserve ready to take up defensive positions west of the River SELLE from which fire can be brought to bear up the Valley of the River Richemont.

5. After the completion of the barrage programme the 2 Coys 25th Bn. M.G.Corps mentioned in para. 2 will come into Divisional reserve.
Machine Guns at present sited for the defence of the Divisional sector will not move into their barrage positions before 20.00 on Y/Z night.

ACKNOWLEDGE.

F.P. Nosworthy
Lieut Colonel.
General Staff, 66th Division.

D.H.Q.
15th Oct. 1918.

DISTRIBUTION.

A & Q.
Signals.
18th Divl. Arty.
C.R.E.
South African Bde.
A.D.C.
25th Bn. M.G.Corps.
9th Bn. Glouc. R.
XIII Corps.
38th Division.
50th Division.

196

197

SECRET.

INSTRUCTIONS No 5.

In continuation of 66th DIVISION INSTRUCTIONS Nos 1 and 3.

198th Inf.Bde. 1. B.G.C. 198th Infantry Brigade will be responsible for the mopping up of LE CATEAU inside the area :-

Railway crossing Q.4.b.4.1. - bridge Q.4.b.15.90.- R. SELLE to junction K.28.d.8.1. - road K.28.d.9.1. to K.35.c.9.3.- Southern boundary of Division from K.35.c.9.3. to Q.4.b.4.1.

He will effect this by passing two Companies Infantry across the SELLE at Zero plus 3 hours by the bridges to be constructed between K.28.d.8.1. and K.29.a.1.3. and by entering the village from the N.E. or EAST.

After clearing the above area, these two Coys will secure and hold the eastern exits of the village.

2. 198th Inf. Bde. will detail one complete battalion to be in Divisional Reserve from Zero onwards. Unit and location to be reported to D.H.Q. by 17.00 October 16th.

After Zero, this battalion will not be moved without orders from Divisional Headquarters.

R.Es and Pioneers. 3. C.R.E. will arrange for the follwoing :-

(a) Strong points to be constructed about level crossing K.29.c.8.9. and about K.23.c.1.2. immediately after the capture of these localities by the infantry.
(b) Strong Points about K.35.c.9.3. and K.35.d.0.8.
(c) Repair of bridges over R. SELLE at Q.4.b.1.8. and K.34.b.0.1. to take wheeled traffic.
(d) Repair and clearing of the CAMBRAI - LE CATEAU - BASUEL road through LE CATEAU.

4" Stokes Mortars 4 C. Section (4 guns) No. 1. Special Coy. R.E., under Lieut. C.F. HARRY will take up positions on X/Y night about K.34.a.6.9. and will smoke the area round BAILLON Farm and northwards from Zero plus one hour till Zero plus 129 minutes, care being taken not to shell within safety limits of the infantry forming up line.

At Zero plus 129 mins the fire of these mortars will be lifted so as to smoke the valley in K.23.c. and d.

Lieut. C.F. HARRY will report to H.Q. South African Bde. at 21.00 on Y day.

5. ACKNOWLEDGE.

F.P. Isworthy
Lieut-Colonel,
General Staff, 66th Division.

D.H.Q.,
15.10.18.

DISTRIBUTION.

Copy No 1	War Diary.	11	25th Bn M. G.C.
2	" "	12	9th Bn Glouc. R.
3	File.	13	Divl.Train A.S.C.
4	'A' and 'Q'.	14	A.D.M.S.
5	Signals.	15	D.A.P.M.
6	18th Divl.Arty.	16	A.P.M. XIII Corps.
7	C.R.E.	17	XIII Corps.
8	198th Inf. Bde.	18	38th Division.
9	199th Inf. Bde.	19	50th Division.
10	South African Bde.	20	A.D.C.

198

S E C R E T.

66th DIVISION INSTRUCTIONS NO.6.

Issued under 66th Division Order No. 104 dated 13/10/18.

AIRCRAFT.

1. 35th Squadron R.A.F. will co-operate as follows:-

(a) Contact patrols will be sent out at the following hours:-

(i) Zero plus 1 hour 36 minutes.
NO REPLY WILL BE GIVEN TO THIS AEROPLANE.

(ii) Zero plus 3 hours 10 minutes.
Troops on the final objective or most advanced line gained will show Red flares, tin discs, flash torches, or make other signs of recognition.

(iii) Zero plus 4 hours 10 minutes.
To verify (ii) above.

(iv) Just before dusk to obtain final dispositions at the end of the day.

(b) A Counter-attack patrol will be up continuously throughout the day. Should a counter-attack develop, this plane will drop WHITE PARACHUTE lights immediately over the counter-attacking troops.

(c) Phosphorous bombs will be dropped from Zero onwards to smoke the following localities:-

(i) High ground in Squares L.19.c. & d., L.25.a and L.26.b.

(ii) High ground in L.26.c. and L.32.a & c.

2. MARKINGS ON PLANES.

The following will be the markings of machines allotted to special duties:-

(a) Contact patrol machine - Rectangular panels 2 feet by 1 foot on both lower planes about 3 feet from the fuselage and a streamer on the tail.

(b) Machines working with the Tanks - Black band under the tail.

3. DROPPING GROUNDS.

Divisional Dropping ground (marked X) will be established at P.4.d.2.6.
South African Brigade Dropping Ground (marked 6ZSH) will be established at K.27.c.1.1.

F.P. [signature]
Lieut Colonel.
General Staff, 66th Division.

D.H.Q.
16th Oct. 1918.

DISTRIBUTION.

'A' & 'Q'. | 198th Inf. Bde. | VIII Corps.
Signals. | 199th Inf. Bde. | 38th Division.
18th Div. Artly. — S.A. Bde. | 50th Division.
C.R.E. | 25 Bn M.G.C. | 35 Squad. R.A.F.

SECRET. 66th Divn.
G.

app 47(o)

In continuation of 66th Division Order 104

dated 13th.

1. Reference para 2. (c) Third Army will not co-operate in the North.

2. Para 5 is cancelled.

3. Para 6:

The objective will be secured as follows :-

(a) By 07.00 on 15th B.G.C. South African Bde will arrange to have completed a thorough reconnaissance of all possible crossings of the river in K.34. and select a site for bridging in K.28.d. He will also secure by posts on the east bank any bridges which still remain intact.

Result to be reported to D.H.Q. by 12.00 15th October.

(b) On night 15th/16th he will further consolidate all crossings secured on night 14th/15th and will arrange for the bridging of any other crossings necessary for the operation.

In addition he will occupy a definite portion of the town by infiltration of patrols.

(c) On night 16th/17th he will similarly occupy the whole of the town up to GREEN Line (first objective vide attached map).

(d) At Zero he will seize and secure any portions of the GREEN Line (first objective) not yet captured and will advance thence tox the red line after a pause of from two to three hours.

After a pause of half an hour on the RED Line he will seize the BLUE Line, final objective.

199

200

S E C R E T.

66th DIVISION INSTRUCTIONS No.7.

Issued under 66th Division Order No. 104 dated 13/10/18.

SYNCHRONISATION OF WATCHES.

An Officer from 66th Divisional H.Q. will call at 18th Divl Artillery H.Q. at 18.35 16th October bringing correct time.

Watches will be synchronised by a representative from Division at 198th Brigade H.Q. in the Orchard at Q.7,a.7.4. (turning off Roman road by anti-aircraft guns) at 19.30 hours 16th October.

Following will send representatives, each with 2 watches:-

198th Brigade.
199th Brigade.
South African Bde.
25th Bn. M.G.C.
9th Bn. Glouc. R.
C Section No.1 Special Coy.R.E.
C.R.E.

ACKNOWLEDGE.

Lieut Colonel.
General Staff, 66th Division.

D.H.Q.
16th Oct. 1918.

DISTRIBUTION.

A & Q.
Signals.
C.R.E.
18th Divl Arty.
198th Brigade.
199th Brigade.
South African Bde.
25th Bn. M.G.C.
9th Bn. Glouc. R.
C S ction No.1 Special Coy.R.E.
A.D.C.

S E C R E T. 201

66th DIVISION INSTRUCTIONS NO. 8.

Issued under 66th Division Order No. 104 dated 13/10/18.

CO-OPERATION WITH 50TH DIVISION.

1. The attack of the 66th Division will not be launched until it can be fairly assumed that the 50th Division has gained their Intermediate objective, i.e. the line Q.4.d.4.1. - Q.24.c.0.5.

2. This Intermediate Objective is to be taken by the 151st Inf. Bde (H.Q. Q.19.central) crossing the stream in Q.28.a. & c and attacking on a 3 Battalion front.
   According to barrage time-table the line should be gained by Zero plus 95 minutes.

3. The following measures will be taken to ensure that information concerning the capture of this line will be obtained as early as possible.

   (a) The Contact Aeroplane which will call for flares on 50th Division Intermediate line at Zero plus 1 hour 36 minutes will drop duplicate copies of its report at S.A. Brigade H.Q. (K.27.c.1.1.) and at Div. H.Q. (P.4.d.2.6.).

   (b) This aeroplane will also signal by wireless which will be picked up by Divisional and 18th D.A. Masts the Code call "G.O.C., G.O.C., G.O.C. DOTTED" so soon as the above line has been captured.

   (c) G.S.O 2 66th Division and 4 mounted Orderlies (from Northumberland Hussars) to report to H.Q. 151st Inf. Bde (Q.19.central) by Zero minus 2 hours; best route between H.Qrs S.A. and 149th Inf. Bdes to be reconnoitred forthwith.
   Situation reports will be sent by these Orderlies to S.A. Brigade at Zero, Zero plus 1 hour and Zero plus 1½ hours.

   (d) O.C. 66th Div. Signals will arrange for Visual Communication to be established between the two Brigades concerned.

4. The Red Line of 50th Division will be taken by the 149th Inf. Bde.
   Headquarters of 149th Inf. Bde will be at Q.19.central from Zero until capture of Intermediate Line when it will move to Q.20.b.8.5.
   Posts will be established by this Brigade at K.35.c.8.3 and K.36.d.4.8.
   S.A. Brigade will detail one platoon to follow close in rear of the right flank of the attack with the special mission of connecting up with the left of the 149th Inf. Bde at the above posts.

5. 50th Division Report Centre will be at HONNECHY Station Q.29.d. until after capture of Red line when it will be established at Farm Q.19.central.

6. ACKNOWLEDGE.

F.P. [signature]
Lieut Colonel.
General Staff, 66th Division.

D.H.Q.
16th Oct. 1918.

Distribution.

'A' & 'Q'.	G.R.C.	35th Squadron R.A.F.	50th Divn.
Signals.	198th Bde.	25th Bn. M.G.C.	XIII Corps.
18th Div Arty	199th Bde	9th Bn Gloucester R.	38th Divn.
	S.A. Brigade		

SECRET. App 48(8) Copy No.......

202

66th DIVISIONAL ENGINEERS.

R.E.OPERATION ORDER NO. 52 (16-10-18).

1. R.E.Operation Order No. 51 dated 11-10-18 is cancelled.

2. The advance of the 66th Division to its final objective (RED LINE) K.29.a.1.8. - K.29. Central - K.36.d.0.5. will be effected by an enveloping movement of LE CATEAU from the North in conjunction with the advance of the 50th Division in the South.

3. The point of junction of the attacking troops of the 66th and 50th Divisions will be K.35.c.9.3.
The attack of the 66th Division will be so timed that the front line troops of both Divisions arrive at the above pint at the same time.

4. R.E. and PIONEERS.

The 431 and 432 Field Companies, assisted by Pioneers, will throw eight bridges across River SELLE on Y/Z night between the points K.26.d.8.1. and K.29.a.3.4. (see appendix 'A'). The important factor of the operation is surprise. It is essential that no indication should be given to the enemy that the bridging of the River SELLE between these points is contemplated. Every precaution, will, therefore, be taken to select bridging sites, which as far as possible afford cover and screen the actual bridges.
A duckboard bridge was placed last night at K.34.b.0.1. in a prominent position in order to make the enemy believe that a direct advance through the town is contemplated.

The 430 Field Co. R.E., assisted by Pioneers, will construct Platoon Strong Points at K.29.c.8.9. and K.23.c.1.2. immediately after the capture of those positions by the Infantry (see Apendix 'B').

The 431st Field Company, assisted by Pioneers, will construct a Strong Point for Platoon at K.35.c.9.3. (See appendix 'B').

The 430th & 432nd Field Co. will construct bridges over the River SELLE at Q.4.b.1.8. and K.34.b.0.1. respectively to take 1st Line Transport. (See appendix 'C').

Pionners will repair and clear the CAMBRAI-LE CATEAU - BAZUEL Road through LE CATEAU (See appendix 'C').

5. LOCATIONS: Regimental Aid posts are being established at K.27.c.4.8. - K.27.c.8.6. - P.18.a.7.4.

Relay Posts - Cross Roads K.33.a.4.6. and posts at 1000 yards interval along the REUMONT-MAUROIS Road to A.D.S.

A.D.S. - MAUROIS - P.22. b. 5.6.

6. Div. Battle H.Q. will be established at P.4.d.4.9.
S.A.Brigade Battle H.Q. are being established in the RAVINE about K.27.c.4.6. where 430 Fld. Co. have prepared splinter-proof accommodation.
198th Brigade are moving to present S.A.Brigade H.Q. in Q.7.b.
C.R.E. and Field Co. H.Q. remain as at present.
9th Bn. Gloucester Regt. (Pioneers) have moved to MAUROIS. P.22.b.9.1

7. ACKNOWLEDGE.

C.S. DAVIES.

Lieut Colonel R.E.
C.R.E. 66th Division.

Distribution.

Copy No. 1. - 66th Div. 'G'
" 2 - 430th Fld. Co. R.E.
" 3 - 431st Field Co. R.E.
" 4 - 432nd Field Co. R.E.
" 5 - 9th Bn. Gloucester Regt (Pioneers)
" 6 - C.R.A.
" 7 - C.E. XIII Corps.
" 8 - 198 Inf. Bde.
" 9 - 199 Inf. Bde.
" 10 - South African Bde.
" 11 - File.
" 12 - War Diary.
" 13 - " "

204

3a. The forming up line of the 66th. Division will be just East of the River SELLE from approximately K.28.d.[illegible].1. to K.29.a.2.3.
The advance will then be made under a creeping barrage in a S.E. direction with the right flank advancing along the road K.34.b.95.75. - K.35.c.90.50., and thence, after junction with the 50th. Division, along the Divisional boundary as laid down in R.E.R.O. No. 81 dated 11.10.18.
The left of the attack will advance through BAILLON FARM K.29.a inclusive to the level crossing K.29.c.85.90. where a strong point will be formed to protect the left of the Division.
After the line of the Railway has been captured and contact obtained with the left of the 50th. Division, the advance will be continued in an easterly direction pivoting on the level crossing K.29.c.85.90. until the final objective is gained.
The railway line as far as K.23.c.1.2. will be cleared by a special party directly the final objective has been captured, a further defensive flank being thrown back along the stream from K.23.c.1.2. to K.22.d.7.2.

APPENDIX 'A'

BRIDGES TO BE THROWN ACROSS RIVER SELLE ON NIGHT OF 16th./17th.

Unit constructing Bridges.	No. of Bridges.	Points to be bridged.	Bridging Parties.	When parties proceed.	Remarks.
431st. Fld. Co. R.E. assisted by 9th Bn. Gloucester Regt. (Pioneers)	4.	At 4 points evenly spaced sites to be selected by R.E. Officer in charge, between K.29.c.1.9. and K.29.c.3.4.	1 Officer R.E. 1 Officer, Gloucester R. and 1 party per bridge consisting - 10 R.E. 15 Gloucester R.	On receipt of orders from C.R.E.	Owing to the fact that Pioneer Battalion Reserve Coy. (which find all parties detailed on this table) has not been relieved in time to return to billets, the following arrangements will be made. O.C., 9th. Gloucester Regt. will detail 8 groups of 60 O.R. for carrying bridges - each group of 60 will detail 4 parties of 15 each. Each group will send 2 orderlies to S.A. Bde. H.Q. by 10.30 hours where they will be met by 2 orderlies from 431 & 432 Fd. Coys. respectively. The Fd. Coy. orderlies will collect their respective groups & take them to the bridges to be carried into position. Here the whole party will report to the R.E. Officer in charge.
432nd. Fld. Co. R.E. assisted by 9th. Bn. Gloucester Regt. (Pnrs.)	4.	At 4 points evenly spaced, sites to be selected by R.E. Officer in charge, between K.29.d.3.1. and K.29.c.09.75.	do.	do.	

Note 1. In event of situation being such that bridging tonight is impossible, it will be carried out at ZERO under barrage. Should this difficulty arise every endeavour must be made to inform Division.

2. Following arrangements have been made - 1st. S.A. Bn. H.Q. in house at K.33.c.4.8. are providing 2 guides on application at Bn. H.Q. - 1 for each Bridging group - to take their groups to the ~~[illegible]~~ road in K.33.b. & d. opposite river to be bridged.

205

APPENDIX 'B' - STRONG POINTS.

1. Strong points for a garrison of 1 Platoon will be constructed at about level crossing K.29.c.8.9. at about K.23.c.1.2. and at about K.35.c.9.3.

2. Each strong point will consist of a group of 5 disconnected lengths of trench, 10 yards long, 3 feet wide at top fire step at -3 deepened behind firesteps to -5. Care must be taken when siting to avoid enfilade enemy fire from high ground. The 10 yard legs should if necessary bend in the centre, thus - 

3. On completion, they will be handed over to the Infantry, after which digging party will return to their respective H.Q. Until handed over, they will be manned and fought by the digging party.

4. DIGGING PARTY. Each man will carry 120 rounds of ammunition, 70 rounds of which will be handed over by each man on relief.

S.P. at	Coy. responsible for siting.	Party to dig.	When complete hand over to	Rendezvous.	Time.	Despatched by.	Remarks.
K.29.c.8.9. K.23.c.1.2.	450 Fd.Co. 450 Fd.Co.	1 R.E. Off.) 10 R.E. 15 9th Gloster Rgt. O.R. 1 Pnr. Off.) 10 R.E. 15 9th Gloster Rgt. O.R.	Inf. of S.A. Bde.	S.A.Bde H.Q. at about K.27.c.4.6.	07.30	B.G.C. S.A.Bde when situation is sufficiently clear.	9th Gloster Pnr. Co. providing these parties is remaining for the night near S.A.Bde H.Q. and will send 2 Orderlies to S.A Bde H.Q. at 07.00 hrs on 17th. where they will report to Officer of 450 Fd. Co. on his arrival.
K.35.c.9.3.	431 Fd.Co.	1 R.E.Officer 1 9th Glosster Officer. 10 R.E. O.R. 15 9th Gloster Regt. O.R.	Inf. of 198 Bde.	REUMONT R.E. Off. will report to 198 Bde H.Q.	09.30	B.G.C. 198 Bde when situation is sufficiently clear.	Arrangements to be made direct between C.O. 9th Gloster Rgt. and O.C.431st Fld.Co. for meeting of R.E. and P.r. Personnel.

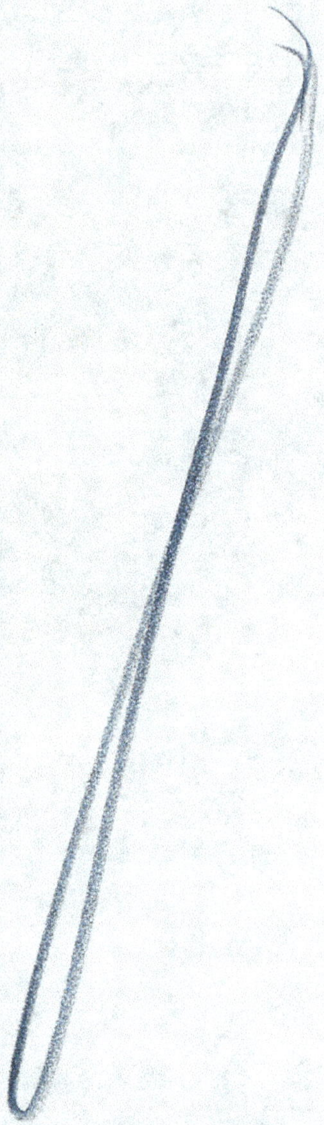

APPENDIX 'C'

COMMUNICATIONS- BRIDGES AND ROADS.

BRIDGES.

Bridges for 1st Line Transport will be constructed at Q.4.b.1.8. and K.34.b.0.1.

Site.	By whom erected.	Type.	Work to commence at	Remarks.
Q.4.b.1.8.	430 Fd.Co.	Weldon Trestles.	On receipt of orders from C.R.E.	When selecting site for bridges the following points must be considered - At both these places the Corps are going erect a Class 'A' Bridge. Therefore, the line of road must be left. Also it may be necessary to put up a Bridge for mechanicaltransport before the Corps Bridge is complete. Spaces should be left for this if possible.
K.34.b.0.1.	432nd Fd.Co	do.	do.	

Roads.

The 9th Bn. Gloucester Regt (Pioneers) will have 2 platoons standing by ready to proceed to repair and clear up CAMBRAI - LE CATEAU - BAZEUL Road through LE CATEAU, on receipt of orders from this Office.

An additional 2 Platoons will clear and repair the REUMONT - LE CATEAU Road and fill in craters at about K.27.d.9.9. and K.33.c.6.5. and as soon as the situation permits at the discretion of O.C. 9th Bn.Gloucester Regt. (Pioneers)

app 49(o)
208
10

SECRET.

Copy No.......

66th DIVISION ORDER No. 105.

16th October 1918.

ATTACK. 1. In accordance with instructions already issued, the 66th Division will attack tomorrow, 17th October, in conjunction with the 50th Division on the Right

Zero will be at 05.20

OBJECTIVE. 2. The objective of the Division will be the line K.36.d.4.6., - K.29.central - K.29.a.1.8. A defensive flank will be formed on the left through BAILLON FARM (K.29.a.), and, after the final objective has been captured, the Railway line will be cleared as far as K.23.c.1.2., so as to allow a further defensive flank being thrown back along the stream from K.23.c.1.2. to K.22.d.7.2.

TROOPS. 3. The attack will be carried out by the South African Infantry Brigade with one Company 25th Bn. M.G.Corps and will be supported by artillery and machine gun barrages in accordance with instructions already issued.

The 198th Infantry Brigade (less 1 Battalion) with one company 25th Bn. M.G. Corps will be responsible for the mopping up of LE CATEAU and for the defence of the Village after the final objective has been obtained.

The 199th Infantry Brigade and one Battalion 198th Infantry Brigade will be retained in Divisional Reserve.

HEADQUARTERS. 4. Headquarters will be established as follows:-

	Adv. D.H.Q.	P.4.d.4.9. from ZERO.
K 27.c.3.2.	S.A. Inf. Bde.	K.27.c.3.1. from 19.00 on 16th Oct.
	198th Inf. Bde.	Q.7.a.8.4. from ZERO.

5. ACKNOWLEDGE.

[signature]
Lieut Colonel.
General Staff, 66th Division.

DISTRIBUTION.

Copy No. 1	War Diary.	Copy No. 12	25th Bn. M.G.C.
" " 2	" "	13	9th Bn. Glouc. R.
3	File.	14	D.A.P.M.
4	A & Q.	15	AP.M.X111 Corps.
5.	Signals.	16	38th Division.
6	18th Divl. Arty.	17	50th Division.
7.	C.R.E.	18	35th Squad. R.A.F
8.	198th Inf. Bde.	19	X111 Corps.
9	199th Inf. Bde.	20	C Sec.No.1 Special Coy. R.E.
10	S.A. Brigade.	21	A.D.C.
11	A.D.M.S.		

209

app 50(0)

SECRET.

~~[illegible] GREEN~~

S. A. Bde (For information)

You will construct two strong points at the following places

K 29 c 8 9

K 23 c 1 2

2. You will take a party of 10 sappers with 10 shovels & 5 picks for each strong point & report to S.A. Bde HQ. in caverns at Q.27c at 07.30 on 17 inst.

Two parties each consisting of 1 Officer & 15 Pioneers with 15 shovels & 7 picks will meet you there for assisting in construction of strong points.

3. You will report immediately on arrival to the G.O.C. S.A. Bde & will obtain from him (a) instructions as to when the situation is sufficiently clear for your parties to proceed with the work. You

the instruction as to whom you are to hand over the strong points when completed.

4. Each strong pt. will consist of 5 lengths of trench each 10 yds long & of the following section.

5. ~~Each strong point will consist of~~
After handing over these strong points to the Infantry as instructed by G.O.C. 5th Bde you will return with your parties to Bn H.Q. at MARIOG.

6. Until the strong point is handed over it will be manned by the sappers & pioneers.

6. Skeleton equipment with 120 rounds of ammunition & reserve rations carried.

16:10:18

[illegible] Major R.E.
Comdg. [illegible] R.E.

SECRET. Copy No. 10.

App 51.

South African Brigade Order No 244.

16.10.18. 211

Maps Sheet 57b N.E.

1 Information

(a) To maintain pressure and increase difficulties of enemy withdrawal, Fourth Army will carry out further operations at an early date.

(b) The attack of the XIII Corps will be carried out by 50th Division on the right, 66th Division on the left. It is not yet known whether the Third Army will co-operate on the north.

(c) The 50th Division on our right will attack the line of the road running from the S.W. end of the [illegible] CATEAU – Q.4.b. thence through Q.4.d., Q.10.b. and ... Q.11.d. ... Q.33.b.d. as their first objective and then attack the [illegible] line shown on the ... as their 2nd objective. It is probable that our attack on the [illegible] line will synchronise with the advance of the 50th Division from their 1st to their 2nd objective.

2 Boundaries

(a) The dividing line between the 50th & 66th Divisions shown in red on the ... is P.15.b.5.5 – Q.9.a.8.4 – Q.4.b.4.0 (road) (inclusive to 66th Division) – thence straight line to road junction L.31.d.0.1 (inclusive to 66th Division) thence following road through K.35.d.6.0 to ... road K.30.d.7.9.

(b) The dividing line between 66th Division and Third Army also shown in red on the ... is F.6. central, K.2.c.0.0. road junction K.12.c.2.2. (inclusive to 66th Division) – K.17.d.0.5. – K.22 central.

3 The advance of the 66th Division to the first objective (road line) K.29.a.1.7. – K.29. central – K.36.a.0.3 will be effected by an enveloping movement of LE CATEAU from the North in conjunction with the advance of the 50th Division on the South.

4 The point of junction of the attacking troops of the 66th Division & the 50th Division will be K.35.c.9.3. The attack of the 66th Division will be so timed that the front line troops of both Divisions ... arrive ... points at the same time.

5 The forming up line of the 66th Division will be ... bank of the ... SELLE ... K.35.a.9.1 to K.29.... ...

made under a creeping barrage in a S.E. direction with the right flank advancing along the road K 34 b 95.75 – K 35 c 80.30 [illegible] after junction with the 50th Division along the Divisional boundary as shown on the [illegible].

The left of the attack will advance through BAILLON Farm K 29 a [illegible] to the level crossing K 29 c 85.90 where a strong point will be formed to protect the left of the Division.

After the line of the railway (Red line) has been captured and contact obtained with the 50th Division the advance will be continued in an Easterly direction pivoting on the level crossing K 29 c 85.90 until the first objective (Blue line) is gained.

The railway line as far N.W as K 23 c 1.2 will be cleared by a special party directly the first objective has been captured & a further defensive flank will be thrown out along the stream from K 23 c 1.2 to K 22 d 7.2

6 At 5.45 pm this evening 16th inst the OC 1st SAI will arrange to attack & clear the line of the SELLE river in order to cover the construction of the necessary bridges to enable the attacking troops to form up on Y/Z night.

In order to hold the line of the river & cover the exits of the bridges the OC 1st SAI will arrange to consolidate this line as soon as captured & when the bridges have been completed will hold with strong posts Eastern exits of the bridges.

7 The 4th & 2nd SAI will carry out the attack on the Division front & will assemble on the Eastern bank of the SELLE Stream on Y/Z night

8 The 4th SAI will attack on the right & the 2nd SAI on the left

9 The dividing line between the 4th & 2nd will be that shown in Black eg K 29 c 00.70 – K 29 c 75.00 – K 35 b 00.50 – K 35 b 70.60

10 The OC 1st SAI will detail one Company to follow the 2nd SAI left flank & upon the capture of the red line this Company will [illegible] in a N.E. direction

SECRET

214

1st SAI
2nd SAI
4th SAI

The following amendments are to be made to the x Instructions issued herewith

---

Barrage will open at ZERO & go through the programme as far as the Railway line & then disperse on various targets. It will return to the starting line at Zero + 150 minutes remaining 15 minutes in front of our assembly position & then move on at the rate 100 x in 3 minutes.

Should the 50th Division not reach 1st objective we will in any case seize the line of the railway; in this event the code word [illegible] 'REFUSAL' will mean that the Railway line will be the final objective and not the Blue Line. If the code word is not received then the two objectives will be carried.

The moment it is known that the 1st SAI have been successful in obtaining the line of LE SELLE River the R.E. parties will push on with the construction of the bridges & the 2nd & 4th SAI will be prepared to carry out their assembly EAST of the river & dig themselves in.

Z day 17th Oct. 1918
ZERO hour 5.20 am is the jumping off time of the 50th Division - our jumping off time is ZERO plus 165 minutes viz 8.5 am.

[signature]
Capt.
for Bde Major
1st SA Infty Bde

16/10/18

x Copies of Div Instrs.

as far as the RICHEMONT stream and thence back a defensive flank along the line of this stream to the SELLE river.

11. The remaining three companies of the 1st S.A.I. will as soon as the assembly is complete withdraw to the line of the road in K 28 b & d and K 34 b and constitute Bde Reserve.

12. Exact time, Artillery barrage programmes, & arrangements for masking various localities with smoke and gas will be issued separately.

13. Y/Z night and Zero hour will be notified later. Zero of the 66th Division will be approximately 2 hours later than Zero of 50th Division.

14. C.R.E. is arranging to throw at least 8 bridges over the SELLE river on Y/Z night between the points K 27 a 8 1 and K 29 c 3 4.

15. "B" & "C" Coys. 25th Bn M.G.C. will co-operate from selected positions on high ground West of the River.

16. As an important feature of the operation is surprise it is essential that no indications should be given to the enemy that bridging of the SELLE river at the points named is contemplated. On the other hand attempts will be made to bridge the river East of LE CATEAU and active patrolling in this direction carried on in order to lead the enemy to believe that a direct advance through the town is intended.

17. 1st S.A.I. will arrange to place posts on the East side of the river on the Northern & Southern flanks of the position of assembly to cover the flanks of the attacking troops during assembly.

18. S.A. Inf. Bde H.Q. will be established at about K 27 c 3 7

19. Acknowledge.

Distribution.

1. C.O. 1st S.A.I.
2. C.O. 2nd S.A.I.
3. " 4th S.A.I.
4. " [illegible]
5. [illegible]
6. [illegible]
7. & 66 Division
8. & 198 Inf Bde
9. " 199 Inf Bde

[signature]
Major
Bde Major
S. African Bde

"A" Form

MESSAGES AND SIGNALS.

No. of Message..........

Prefix.......Code.......m. Office of Origin and Service Instructions	Words	Charge.	This message is on a/c of:	Recd. at......m.
	Sent		App 52 Service.	Date. 217
	At ....m.			From
	To			
	By		(Signature of "Franking Officer")	By

TO O.C.
10th S.A.S.

Sender's Number.	Day of Month.	In reply to Number.	AAA
B.S. 105	16.		

With reference to your attack on the line of the River SELLE this evening at 5.45 pm arrangements have been made with the Artillery to shell the triangle during the day and this evening the guns ~~they~~ will fire on this again for 5 minutes before your Zero hour & then lift on to the line of the river for another five minutes thence to the line of the Railway until 6.45 pm.

You will arrange for your troops to consolidate as soon as possible and push covering parties over to cover construction of the bridges.

The time given to the Artillery will be sent you by wire

From

Place

Time

The above may be forwarded as now corrected. (Z)

Censor. Signature of Addressor or person authorised to telegraph in his name

* This line should be erased if not required.

Order No. 1625 Wt. W3253/ P 511 27/2 H. & K., Ltd. (E. 2634)

South African Infy Bde
Order No 245

App 52A
219

Reference
57C N.E.

1. The S.A. Bde will be relieved by the 198 Bde in the line tonight in the following portion of Army front.
(a) From the N Divisional Bdy. inclusive to the Roman Rd. inclusive.
(b) From Cambrai - Le Cateau Rd. inclusive to S. Divisional Bdy
(2) The relief will be carried out as under -
2nd. S.A.I by 2 Coys Dublins in K 33 c + d
1 Coy Inniskillings in Q 8
9th Gloucesters by Inniskillings less 2 Coys.
Relief to be completed as soon as possible after dusk.
3. On completion of relief the 2nd. S.A.I will move to reconnaitre positions in Ravine in K 26 a + b. and about main road in K 25 d. and K 26 c
The 9th. Gloucesters on relief will reconnaitre in billets in MAUROIS

218

3

4. The 4th SAI will move up after dusk to reconnoitre positions in ravine in K27c and K33 a 4c and about main road in K32b & K33 a.

5. All details such as supply of guides etc will be arranged between O.C's.

6. Reliefs will be notified to B.H.Q. by code word "Cookers ARRIVED"

7. Bde H.Q will close at Q7 b32 at 1800 & open at K27 C 3 7 at 1900 Bns. will notify Bde of new H.Q as soon as possible

8. Acknowledge

Issued through Signals at 1400 to

1. - 1 SAI
2. - 2 SAI
3. - 4 SAI
4. - 9 Gloucesters
5. - 66 Div
6. B.S.O.
7. 198 Infy Bde
8. 199
9. 25 M.G. Coy.
10. 18 Div Art.

"A" Form
Army Form C. 2121
(In pads of 100.)

MESSAGES AND SIGNALS.

No. of Message............

Prefix.......... Code.......... m. Office of Origin and Service Instructions	Words	Charge.	This message is on a/c of: .... Service. app 53 (Signature of "Franking Officer")	Recd. at......m. Date.......... From.......... By..........
	Sent At ....m. To .... By			

TO { MESE 221

Sender's Number.	Day of Month.	In reply to Number.	AAA
BMX 89	17th		

The [illegible] is making [illegible] extremely difficult on our right the railway from K35C 8.4 to K35 B1.5 is in our possession & should like Artillery fire brought to bear on it as I would arrange

From
Place
Time

The above may be forwarded as now corrected

"A" Form
Army Form C. 2121
(In pads of 100.)

Army Form C. 2121
(In pads of 100.)

"A" Form
MESSAGES AND SIGNALS.

No. of Message...........

Prefix........Code..............m.	Words	Charge.	This message is on a/c of:	Recd. at......m.
Office of Origin and Service Instructions	Sent		............................Service.	Date..............
	At ....m.			From 220
	To			
	By		(Signature of "Franking Officer")	By................

TO (2)

Sender's Number.	Day of Month.	In reply to Number.	AAA

[illegible]

From			
Place			
Time			

The above may be forwarded as now corrected. (Z)

"A" Form Army Form C. 2121 (In pads of 100.)

MESSAGES AND SIGNALS.

No. of Message..........

Prefix.......... Code.......... m. | Words | Charge.

Office of Origin and Service Instructions

Sent

At ....m.

To ....

By ....

This message is on a/c of:

..........Service.

(Signature of "Franking Officer")

Recd. at......m.

Date..........

From..........

By..........

App 854

216

TO MESE

Sender's Number.	Day of Month.	In reply to Number.	AAA
B1791	17		

Situation remains as reported in my B1789 except that Reserve Company has been moved position between K28b 80.95 to K29a 20.35 in order to protect left flank which has been threatened AAA

Intelligence Officer is out to

From

Place

Time

The above may be forwarded as now corrected. (Z)

Censor. Signature of Addressor or person authorised to telegraph in his name

* This line should be erased if not required.

Order No. 1625. Wt. W3253/ P 511. 27/2. H. & K., Ltd. (E. 2634).

"A" Form
Army Form C. 2121
(In pads of 100.)

MESSAGES AND SIGNALS.

No. of Message..........

Prefix.......Code.......m.	Words	Charge.	This message is on a/c of:	Recd. at.......m.
Office of Origin and Service Instructions	Sent		app 55 (O) ......Service.	Date..........
	At ....m.			From ....
	To			
	By		(Signature of "Franking Officer")	By..230

TO { South African Brigade

Sender's Number.	Day of Month.	In reply to Number.	AAA
GB 95	17th		

Reference BM X 89 Artillery fire is being brought to bear on Railway between K35 central & K35c93 from 1700 to 1745

At the same time 50th Division are going to make good Railway Trench.

When Artillery fire lifts at 1745 G.O.C. wishes you to make good Railway from K35 central to Div. boundary at K35c93

From 66th Div
Place
Time 16.25

The above may be forwarded as now corrected. (Z) Walter Guinness Lt Col
....
Censor. Signature of Addressor or person authorised to telegraph in his name

* This line should be erased if not required.

Order No. 1625. Wt. W3253/ P 511. 27/2. H. & K., Ltd. (E. 262

MESSAGES AND SIGNALS.

No. of Message............

Prefix..........Code..........m.	Words	Charge.	This message is on a/c of:	Recd. at......m.
Office of Origin and Service Instructions			..........Service.	Date .... 9/10?
	Sent		app 56	From ....
	At ....m.			By ....
	To		(Signature of "Franking Officer.")	
	By			

TO { FEDO ZERO ZESA

Sender's Number.	Day of Month.	In reply to Number.	AAA
BM 6?	9		

50th Division holds general line on ST SOUPLET – LE CATEAU Railway Station on 9/10 being disposed in following line right to forward? as the Division line of resistance.

(a) 150? Bde [illegible] along K 32 c 1.3 – K 35 central to the defensive flank along ridge K 32 c & K 32 d and then through BAILLON farm & [illegible]

(b) 149? Bde K 5 central (exclusive) along railway embankment to K 31 c 9.2 then along South Divisional boundary through

From			
Place			
Time			

The above may be forwarded as now corrected. (Z)

.... Censor. Signature of Addressor or person authorised to telegraph in his name

* This line should be erased if not required.

Order No. 1625. Wt. W3253/ P 511. 27/2. H. & K., Ltd. (E. 2634).

MESSAGES AND SIGNALS.

No. of Message..........

Prefix..........Code..............m.	Words	Charge.	*This message is on a/c of:*	Recd. at......m.
Office of Origin and Service Instructions	Sent		..........................*Service.*	Date..............
....	At ....m.			From ....
....	To		....	
....	By		(Signature of "Franking Officer")	By................

TO (2) 227

Sender's Number.	Day of Month.	In reply to Number.	AAA

946 [illegible] SELLE [illegible]

[illegible]

From			
Place			
Time			

* The above may be forwarded as now corrected. (Z)

....

Censor. Signature of Addressor or person authorised to telegraph in his name

* This line should be erased if not required.

Order No. 1625. Wt. W3253/ P 511. 27/2. H. & K., Ltd. (E. 2634).

app 27(b)

Army Form C. 2123.
(In books of 100.)

"C" Form.

MESSAGES AND SIGNALS.

No. of Message ______

Prefix ___ Code ___ Words ___	Received.	Sent, or sent out.	Office Stamp.
£ s. d. Charges to Collect	From [illegible] By [illegible]	At ______ m. To ______ By ______	[illegible]
Service Instructions 118 pty (?)			

Handed in at [illegible] Office [illegible] m. Received [illegible] m.

TO [illegible] 222

* Sender's Number	Day of Month.	In reply to Number	AAA
G 1216	17		

DO 107 a [illegible] and 198 Inf Bdes will be prepared to continue the attack tomorrow to finish objective in event of railway triangle Q.5.a being captured tonight aaa Details follow [illegible] aaa [illegible] No 3 of Bdes

[illegible]

FROM 66 Div

PLACE & TIME

* This line should be erased if not required.

“A” Form

Army Form C. 2121
(In pads of 100.)

MESSAGES AND SIGNALS.

No. of Message..........

Prefix..........Code..........m. Office of Origin and Service Instructions	Words / Charge. Sent At ....m. To .... By	*This message is on a/c of:* ....*Service.* .... (Signature of "Franking Officer")	Recd. at......m. Date.......... From .... By 229

TO 3

Sender's Number.	Day of Month.	In reply to Number.	AAA

Tanks	aaa	Have	one
Company	still	in	reserve
on	road	in	K.28.d

[illegible signature]

From

Place

Time

The above may be forwarded as now corrected. (Z)

....
Censor.

Signature of Addressor or person authorised to telegraph in his name.

* This line should be erased if not required.

Order No. 1625. Wt. W3253/ P 511. 27/2. H. & K., Ltd. (E. 2634).

Army Form C. 2121.
(In pads of 100.)

...AGES AND SIGNALS.

No. of Message.........

Code..........m.	Words.	Charge.	This message is on a/c of:	Recd. at.......m.
...ace of Origin and Service Instructions.	Sent		..................Service.	Date..........
	At..........m.			From..........
	To..........			
	By..........		(Signature of "Franking Officer.")	By..........

TO. 223

Sender's Number.	Day of Month.	In reply to Number.	AAA
*			

199 Brigade are taking over all the line west of the river except that held by 9th Gloucesters so whole of 198 & SA Bdes will be available for the attack aa Attack will be contingent on the capture of the railway triangle tonight by 50th Divn AAA If this attack fails code word refusal will be sent ~~AAA~~ In which case SA and 198 Bdes will conform with Divisional order 106 AAA Barrage will be put down at zero plus 33 minutes on line 200 yards east

From			
Place			
Time			

The above may be forwarded as now corrected. (Z)

Censor. Signature of Addressor or person authorised to telegraph in his name.

*This line, except AAA, should be erased if not required.

Wt. W 3253/P511. 500,000 Pads. 1/18. B. & S. Ltd. (E2389.)

A Form.
MESSAGES AND SIGNALS.
(In p...)
No. of Message......

Prefix...... Code...... m.	Words.	Charge.	This message is on a/c of:	Recd. at...... m.
Office of Origin and Service Instructions.	Sent		......Service.	Date......
	At......m.			From......
	To......			
	By......		(Signature of "Franking Officer.")	By

TO 224

Sender's Number.	Day of Month.	In reply to Number.	AAA

of railway embankment will dwell for six minutes and will then move back at the rate of 100 yards in three minutes to a line 300 yards east of red line AAA it will cease at Zero plus ~~[illegible]~~ 75 minutes

Please acknowledge by initialling envelope

From 66th Div
Place
Time 23.55

The above may be forwarded as now corrected. (Z)

Censor. Signature of Addressor or person authorised to telegraph in his name. [illegible signature] Lt Col

*This line, except AAA, should be erased if not required.

Wt. W 3253/P511. 500,000 Pads. 1/18. B. & S. Ltd. (E2389.)

...orm. Army Form C. 2121.
(In pads of 100.)

MESSAGES AND SIGNALS.

No. of Message........

Prefix ...... Code ...... m.	Words.	Charge.	This message is on a/c of:	Recd. at ...... m.
Office of Origin and Service Instructions.	Sent		.... Service.	Date ....
	At .... m.			From ....
	To			
	By		Signature of "Franking Officer."	By ....

TO SA Bde & 198 Bde. 225

Sender's Number.	Day of Month.	In reply to Number.	AAA
G B97	17th		

The following order has been telephoned from Divn and is repeated to you in case original sent by DR has not yet arrived AAA The attack will be continued tomorrow morning objective K 26 D 36 K 29 A 70 K 23 C 12 AAA Dividing line between SA and 198 Brigade cross roads K 36 A 55 95 AAA Zero will be at 05.30 AAA Assaulting troops will be in position on jumping off line by 04.30 AAA

From
Place
Time

The above may be forwarded as now corrected. (Z)
Censor. Signature of Addressor or person authorised to telegraph in his name.

*This line, except **AAA**, should be erased if not required.

Wt. W 3253/P511. 500,000 Pads. 1/18. B. & S. Ltd. (E2389.)

MESSAGES AND SIGNALS.

Prefix ...... Code .... m. Office of Origin and Service Instructions	Words	Charge.	This message is on a/c of: .... Service. (Signature of "Franking Officer")	Recd. at ......m. Date .... From .... By ....
	Sent At ....m. To .... By			

TO (3) 226

Sender's Number.	Day of Month.	In reply to Number.	AAA

completion of these tasks will be reported to Bde Hdqrs by Coys and [illegible]

Barnes [illegible]

From			
Place			
Time			

The above may be forwarded as now corrected. (Z) .... Censor. Signature of Addressor or person authorised to telegraph in his name

* This line should be erased if not required.

Order No. 1625. Wt. W3253/ P 511. 27/2. H. & K., Ltd. (E. 2634).

Corrected copy   App 58(O)

SECRET.   Copy No. 10

231

66th DIVISION ORDER NO. 106.

17th October 1918

1. 50th Division now hold the general line of the St.SOUPLET - LE CATEAU Railway. The situation round the Station in Q.10 being obscure.

2. 66th Division will at once consolidate and securo with Machine Guns the following line which will be the Divisional main line of resistance :-

(a). S.A.Brigade.
Railway embankment from River crossing K.23.c.1.3. - river in K.35.central inclusive; with defensive flank along K.23.c. and K.22.d. and also through BAILLON FARM to the River.

(b) 198th Brigade.
K.35. central exclusive - along Railway embankment to K.35.c.9.3. thence back along Southern Divisional Boundary through Q.4.b.3.0. to River SELLE. In addition the LE CATEAU - BASUEL ~~BAILLON~~ Road will be secured by a strong forward post as far east as the road junction Q.35.d.6.0.
198th Brigade will ensure that the mopping up of LE CATEAU is thoroughly completed before dusk, also the capture of any portion of the above objective not yet taken.

3. Patrols will be pushed well out in front of the above main line of resistance and advance posts established in any such suitable localities as buildings etc.

4. MACHINE GUNS.
The Machine Gun Companies at present affiliated to S.A. and 198th Brigades will remain at the disposal of the B.G's C. concerned.
The remaining 2 Companies 25th Bn. M.G.C. and 2 Companies 18th Bn. M.G.C. under O.C. 25th Bn. M.G.C. will take up suitable defensive positions from which they can effectually cover the Divisional front.

5. PIONEERS.
9th Bn. Gloucester Regt. less B. Teams under Major E.F.B.WITTS, D. will relieve 5th R.Innis. Fus. (less 2 Companies) in the line between the Divisional Northern Boundary and the Roman Road inclusive. The relief to be complete as soon after dusk as possible. 9th Bn. Glouc. Regt. (Pioneers) B Teams plus 1 Battalion 199th Brigade will move immediately to REUMONT where they will be in Divisional Reserve.
The 6th Bn. Lan.Fus. is released from Divisional Reserve and placed at the disposal of B.G.C. 198th Bde.

6. ARTILLERY S.O.S.
Artillery S.O.S. lines will run as follows :-
K.23.c.3.3. - K.29.b.2.0. - K.36a.a.6.0. - K.35.d.9.0. - Q.5.a.7. -Q4.d.8.8

7. Headquarters, S.A. and 198th Bdes. will remain in their present locations.
Advanced D.H.Q., will close at P.4.d.4.9. at 17.00 after which time all reports should be sent to D.H.Q. MARETZ.

232

8. S.A. and 198th Brigades will report by wire when they have taken over and secured their respective fronts by the code word 'HOME'.

9. ACKNOWLEDGE.

F.P. Wormsby

Lieut-Colonel.
General Staff.
66th Division.

DISTRIBUTION.

Copy No. 1.	War Diary.	13	25th Bn. M.G.C.
2.	- do -	14	18th Bn. M.G.C.
3.	File.	15	D.A.P.M.
4	A. & Q.	16	A.P.M. XIII Corps.
5	Signals.	17	38th Division.
6	18th Div.Arty.	18	50th Division.
7	C.R.E.	19	35th Squad. R.A.F.
8	198th Inf.Bde.	20.	XIII Corps.
9	199th - do -	21.	A.D.C.
10	S.A. Brigade.		
11	Divl.Train.		
12	A.D.M.S.		

\# NOTE.
50th Division are now arranging to capture Station in Q.10., and Railway Triangle in Q.5.a. under a barrage.

SECRET.

Copy No. 10.

233

66th DIVISION ORDER No. 106.

17th October 1918.

1. 50th Division now hold the general line of the St. SOUPLET - LE CATEAU Railway. The situation round the Station in Q.10 being obscure. *

2. 66th Division will at once consolidate and secure with Machine Guns the following line which will be the Divisional main line of resistance:-

(a). S.A. Brigade.
Railway embankment from River crossing K.23.c.1.3. - K. 35. central inclusive; with defensive flank along river K.23.c. and K.22.d. and also through BAILLON FARM to the River.

(b). 198th Brigade.
K.35.central exclusive - along Railway embankment to K.35.c.9.3. thence back along Southern Divisional Boundary through Q.4.b.3.0. to River SELLE. In addition the LECATEAU - BAILLON Road will be secured by a strong forward post as far east as the road junstion [illegible]35.d.6.0. Q.35.d.60

198th Brigade will ensure that the mopping [illegible] of LE CATEAU is thoroughly completed before dus[illegible] the capture of any portion of the above objective [illegible] yet taken

3. Patrols will be pushed well out in front of th[illegible] main line of resistance and advance posts established [illegible] such suitable localities as buildings etc.,

4. MACHINE GUNS.
The Machine Guns Companies at present affiliated to S.A. and 198th Brigades will remain at the disposal of the B.G's C. concerned.
The remaining 2 Companies 25th Bn. M.G.C. and 2 Companies 18th Bn. M.G.C. under O.C. 25th Bn. M.G.C. will take up suitable defensive positions from which they can effectually cover the Divisional front.

5. PIONEERS. 9th Bn. Glouc. R. less B Teams (under Major E.F.B. WITTS D. will relieve 5th R. Innis. Fus. (less 2 Companies) in the line be the Divisional Northern Boundary and the Roman Road inclusive. The relief to be complete as soon after dusk as possible. 9th B Glouc. R. (Pioneers) B Teams plus 1 Battalion 199th Bde. will move immediately to REUMONT where they will be in Divisional Reserve.
The 6th Bn. Lan. Fus. is released from Divisional Reserve and placed at the disposal of B.G.C. 198th Brigade.

6. ARTILLERY S.O.S.
Artillery S.O.S. lines will run as follows:-
K.23.c.3.3. - K.29.b.2.0. - K.36.a.0.0. - K.35.d.9.0. - Q.5.a.7.9. - Q.4.d.5.8.

7. Headquarters S.A. and 198th Brigades will remain in their present locations.
Advanced D.H.Q., will close at P.4.d.4.9. at 17.00 after which time all reports should be sent to D.H.Q., MARETZ.

234

SECRET

Copy No. 10 . . . . . .

17th Oct. 1918.

66th DIVISION ORDER No. 108.

1. Division Order 107 of 17th instant is cancelled.

2. The action of the 66th Division to-morrow, 18th Oct., is dependant on whether the Railway Triangle Q.5.a. is captured by the 50th Division tonight or not.

3. If the Railway Triangle is captured;

(a). The 198th and S.A. Infantry Brigades will continue the attack to-morrow Oct. 18th in conjunction with the 50th Division.
Divisional Objective "Line K.36.d.3.6. - K.29.a.7.0. K.23.c.1.2.
50th Divisional Objective "K.36.d.3.6. - Q.6.b.7.1. - BASUEL.

Dividing line between 66th and 50th Division - as at present laid down.
Dividing line between S.A. and 198th Brigades - K.35.central - cross roads K.36.a.05.95.

Zero will be 05.30.

(b). The assaulting troops of the 198th and S.A. Brigades will form up by 04.30 on the Railway Line and advance under barrage, details of which will be notified separately.

(c). 199th Infantry Brigade will be disposed by Zero as follows:-
1 Bn disposed along the North East and South East outskirts of LE CATEAU for the defence of the village against counter-attack.
1 Bn. distributed defensively West of the River SELLE from the Cemetery (K.28.b.7.4. exclusive) to the Southern Divisional boundary.
1 Bn. in Q.7. (in Divisional Reserve)

(d) The 2 attacking Brigades will therefore be relieved of all responsibility for the defence of the area West of the River SELLE and of the Village of LE CATEAU in itself.

(e) The 198th and S.A. Brigades will use all their available troops, if necessary, for the capture of the RED LINE.
199th Brigade will probably be used to exploit the situation later in the day, and in any case to take over Divisional front on night of 18/19th October.

(f). Headquarters S.A. Brigade will remain at K.27.c.5.2.
Headquarters 198th Brigade will opn at Zero plus 1½ hours about K. 33.c.3.0, where arrangements are being made for accommodation and communication.
Headquarters 199th Brigade will open at Zero at Q.7.a.8.4. (alongside present 198th Brigade Headquarters)

235

4. If the Railway Triangle in Q.5.a. is not captured tonight, the fact will be notified to all concerned by the Code Word "REFUSAL".

(a). In this case S.A. and 198th Infantry Brigades will conform with the orders laid down in Division Order No. 106.

(b) 199th Brigade will be disposed by Zero as follows:-

Brigade H.Q. plus 1 Bn. REUMONT
1 Bn. Q.7.
1 Bn West of River SELLE from Cemetery (K.28.b.7.4.) exculusive to Southern Divisional Boundary.

5. Acknowledge.

F.P. Nosworthy
Lieut. Colonel
General Staff.
66th Division.

DISTRIBUTION

Copy No.1. War Diary.
2 do
3 File
4 A & Q
5 Signals
6 18th Div. Art.
7. C.R.E.
8 198th Inf. Bde.
9 199th Inf. Bde.
10 S.A. Bde.
11 9th Glouct R.
12. A.D.M.S.
13. 25th Bn. M.G.C.
14. D.A.P.M.
15. 38 th Division.
16. 50th Division.
17 35 Squad R.A.F.
18 X111 Corps.
19 A.D.C.
20 G.S.O.2.

ADDENDUM. TO 66th DIVISION ORDER 108

Artillery

Barrage will come down Zero plus 33 minutes on a line 200 yards East of Railway embankment and will dwell there for 6 minutes when it will advance by 100 yards lifts at the rate of 100 yards in three minutes until the final protective barrage is reached.

The Barrage will gain protective line at Zero plus 75 minutes and will continue on this line at a slow rate until Zero plus $2\frac{1}{2}$ hours.

2. MACHINE GUNS.

The Companies of the 25th M.G.C. at present attached to S.A. and 198th Infantry Brigades will remain with these Brigades for consolidation in depth between the river SELLE and the final objective.

Two Companies 25th Bn. M.G.C. and two Companies of 18th Bn. M.G.C. will be employed on barrage.

On capture of final objective the two Companies 18th Bn. M.G.C. will relieve the two Companies 25th Bn. M.G.C. in K.27. taking up the defensive positions to cover left flank of the Division.

On relief these two Companies 25th Bn. M.G.C. will be withdrawn into Divisional Reserve at REUMONT.

3. ACKNOWLEDGE.

F.P. Nosworthy

Lieut Colonel
General Staff.
66th Division.

17.10.18.

Issued to all recipients of D.O.108.

ET.

app 63(0) 10

Copy No. ....
236

66th DIVISION ORDER NO. 109. 18th Oct. 1918.

1. The North Boundary of XIII Corps and 66th Division will be adjusted as follows from 06.00 on 19th instant:-

J.36.d.3.0. - Cross Roads K.32.d.2.4. - Cross Roads K.28.b.3.8. - Railway Bridge K.23.c.2.3. all inclusive to V Corps - thence K.18.central - L.7.central - L.2.central.

2. XIII Corps retain running rights over the REUMONT - MONTAY Road.

3. On night 18th/19th, 113th Inf. Bde. of 38th Division will relieve 9th Glouc.R(Pioneers) in the sector from present Divisional Northern Boundary as far South as the line K.27.d.3.0. - K.23.central.

4. On completion of relief, which will be notified to Div. H.Q. by code word "COMPLETE", the command of sector from line K.27.d.3.0. - K.23.central Northwards will pass from G.O.C. 66th Division to G.O.C. 38th Division.

5. After relief, 9th Glouc.R.(Pioneers) will be withdrawn to REUMONT and will continue their normal work under instructions from C.R.E.

6. 38th Division, 199th Inf. Bde. and S.A.Bde. to acknowledge.

F.P. Twomby [signature]

Lieut.-Colonel.
General Staff.
66th Division.

DISTRIBUTION.

Copy No. 1. War Diary.
2. do.
3 File.
4. A & Q.
5. Signals.
6. 18th Div. Arty.
7. C.R.E.
8. 198th Inf. Bde.
9. 199th do.
10. S.A.Bde.
11. 9th Glouc.R.(Pioneers) (thro' 199th Inf.Bde.)
12. A.D.M.S.
13. 25th Bn. M.G.C.
14. D.A.P.M.
15. 38th Divn.
16. 50th Divn.
17. 35th Squad R.A.F.
18. XIII Corps.
19. A.D.C.
20. G.S.O. 2.

"C" FORM.
MESSAGES AND SIGNALS.

Army Form C. 2123
(In Books of 100.)

No. of Message.........

Prefix...... Code...... Words........	Received.	Sent, or sent out.	Office Stamp.
£ s. d. Charges to Collect	From......... By.........	At.........m. To......... By.........	Y-F 17 X.18. TELEGRAPHS
Service Instructions Priority			237

Handed in at 6th Div Office 1518 m. Received 1535 m.

TO Jefe

* Sender's Number.	Day of Month.	In reply to Number.	AAA
GC 128	17		

JEFE S...	will	secure	rly
line	from	K23c	to
K35 Central	inclusive	aaa	SOHU
will	take	over	and
secure	rly	from	K35
central –	K35c93	– Q4b30	with
forward	post	towards	road
junction	K35d60	aaa	BGC's
will	arrange	details	direct
aaa	SOHU 198	Bn will	clear
LE CATEAU		before	dusk
aaa	Two	Coys	FEHA 5 Inf Bns
holding	line	N	of Jefe
will	be	relieved	by
two	Coys	FETI	under
2nd	i/c	at	dusk
aaa	MOQI	now	at

FROM
PLACE & TIME 6 Lan Fus

* This line should be erased if not required.

(19629) Wt528/M1970. 300,000 Pads. 4/17. McC. & Co., Ltd. (E1213).

Army Form C. 2123.
(In books of 100.)

"C" FORM.

MESSAGES AND SIGNALS.

No. of Message

Prefix......Code......Words......	Received.	Sent, or sent out.	Office Stamp.
£ s. d.	From......	At......m	ARMY Y-FB 17.X.18. TELEGRAPHS
Charges to Collect	By......	To......	
Service Instructions		By......	

238

Handed in at......Office......m. Received......m.

TO

*Sender's Number.	Day of Month.	In reply to Number.	AAA
disposal	SOHU 1981	aaa	Detail
follow	aaa	ack	aaa
addsd	SUHU	JEFE	FETI
repeated	18	DA	CRE
SABE	and	Corps	SESI

FROM 66 Div

PLACE & TIME 1510

*This line should be erased if not required.

(19629) Wt528/M1970. 300,000 Pads. 4/17. McC. & Co., Ltd. (E1213).

"A" Form.

MESSAGES AND SIGNALS.

Army Form C. 2121.
(In pads of 100.)

No. of Message ....

Prefix ...... Code ...... m	Words.	Charge.	This message is on a/c of:	Recd. at ...... m.
Office of Origin and Service Instructions. SD ...	Sent At ...... m. To ...... By		App 39 (0) ...... Service. (Signature of "Franking Officer.")	Date ...... From ...... By 240

TO { Signals. 18th D.A. C.R.E. 198 Bde. 199 Bde. S.A. Bde. 9 Glouc R. A.D.M.S. 25 Bn. M.G.C. 10... D.A.P.M. ... , 38 Div. 33 Squad. RAF, ... Corps. **AAA**

Sender's Number.	Day of Month.	In reply to Number.
D.O.107.	17.	

Subject to Railway line from K.29.a.7.0. to Railway Triangle in Q.5.a. inclusive being taken by ... tonight 199 Inf. Bde will continue the adva[nce] Oct. 18th in conjunction with 50th Div on right a[aa] Objective of 199 Bde line K.36.d.2.6. K.29.a.7.0 aaa Objective 50th Div. from K.36.a.2.6. north of BASUEL aaa Zero 05.30 aaa 199 Bde will move u[p] via bridges over SELLE K.28.d, 29.c. and a. and will assemble by 04.00 along Railway line with right flank on LE CATEAU - BASUEL Road inclusive aaa Advance will be made under creeping artiller[y] and machine Gun barrages aaa Details later aaa Headquarters 199th Inf. Bde at Zero Q.7.a.7.4. aaa 199 Bde Advance report centre will be established at Q.33.c.3.0. ~~and D.H.Q. will remain at MARETZ.~~ from ZERO + 2 hours AAA.

D.H.Q. will remain at MARETZ aaa ack

From

Place 66th Div.

Time

The above may be forwarded as now corrected. (Z)

Censor. Signature of Addressor or person authorised to telegraph in his name.

H. McCarthy Lt-Col G.S.

* This line should be erased if not required.

(3198.) Wt. W 12952/M1294. 375,000 Pads. 1/17. H. W. & V., Ld. (E. 818.)

"C" Form.
MESSAGES AND SIGNALS.

Army Form C. 2123.
(In books of 100.)

No. of Message ....

Prefix ...... Code ...... Words	Received.	Sent, or sent out.	Office Stamp.
£ s. d. Charges to Collect	From ...... By	At ......m. To ...... By	241
Service Instructions: Priority 3 Bde			

Handed in at 66 Divn Office 1555 m. Received 1606 m.

TO JEFE

* Sender's Number	Day of Month.	In reply to Number.	AAA
GC130	17		

Ref	GC/128	for	two
Corps	FETI	substitute	FETI
less	B	teams	aaa
Addressed	JEFE	SUHU	FETI
repeated	18	DA	CRE
SESI	SABE	and	Corps.

FROM PLACE & TIME: Phese 1550

* This line should be erased if not required.

(3557.) Wt. W528—M1970. 25m., 100 lvs. 5/17. J. H., Ltd (E.)

Army Form C. 2123.
(In books of 100.)

"C" FORM.
MESSAGES AND SIGNALS.

No. of Message..............

Prefix.........Code......Words........... £ s. d. Charges to Collect	Received. From.......... By..........	Sent, or sent out. At..........m. To.......... By..........	Office Stamp. Y-FR 17.X.18. TELEGRAPHS

Service Instructions

239

Handed in at..........Office..........m. Received..........m.

60 (6)

TO Jefe

Aff

* Sender's Number.	Day of Month.	In reply to Number.	AAA
GC131	17		

Ref	GC128	on	completion
of	relief	FETI	less
B	Teams	will	come
under	orders	of	G O C
JEFE	aaa	added	JEFE
SUHU 198	FETI	repted	CRE
SESI	SABE		

FROM PLACE & TIME Mese 16-15

* This line should be erased if not required.

(19629) Wt528/M1970. 300,000 Pads. 4/17. McC. & Co., Ltd. (E1213).

"A" Form

MESSAGES AND SIGNALS.

Army Form C. 2121 (In pads of 100.)

No. of Message App 60A

Prefix .... Code .... m.	Words	Charge.	This message is on a/c of:	Recd. at ......m.
Office of Origin and Service Instructions: Appx	Sent At ......m. To ...... By		......Service. (Signature of "Franking Officer")	Date ...... From ...... By 242

TO 1st SAI
2nd SAI
4th SAI

Sender's Number.	Day of Month.	In reply to Number.	AAA
BMX 98	18.		

1. The action of 86 Divn tomorrow is dependent on whether the Railway triangle is captured tonight by 50th Div or not

2. If triangle is captured –
198th & SA Bde will continue attack today in conjunction with 50th Div.
Divisional Objective –
from K.36.d.3.6. – K.29.a.7.0. – K.23.c.1.2.
Dividing line between S.A. & 198th Bdes –
K.35 cent – X roads – K.36.a.05.95.

3. The 2nd Bn SAI will attack on the left with 1st SAI extending their flank along the Railway embankment to the North
The 4th SAI will attack on the right

From
Place
Time

The above may be forwarded as now corrected. (Z)

Censor. Signature of Addressor or person authorised to telegraph in his name

* This line should be erased if not required.

Order No. 1625 Wt. W3253/ P 511. 27/2 H. & K. Ltd. (E. 2634)

"A" Form.

MESSAGES AND SIGNALS.

Army Form C. 2121
(In pads of 100.)

No. of Message..........

Prefix..............Code..............m. | Words | Charge.

Office of Origin and Service Instructions

Sent
At ....m.
To ....
By ....

This message is on a/c of:
..........................*Service.*
(Signature of "Franking Officer")

Recd. at......m.
Date..............
From ....
By..........244

TO 2

Sender's Number.	Day of Month.	In reply to Number.	AAA
BMX 98	18		

Boundaries between Battns will remain the same.

4. Assaulting troops will form up by 04.30 on the railway line & advance under barrage details to be notified later.

5. S A Bde will use all available men if necessary for capture of RED line

6. If Railway triangle is not captured tonight the fact will be notified by Code word "Refusal" in which case S A Bde will conform with orders laid down in BMX 96 of 17th.

7. Bde HQ will remain the same

8. Acknowledge

From JEFE (S A Bde)
Place
Time

The above may be forwarded as now corrected. (Z) (Sgd) E Barker? Major

Censor. Signature of Addressor or person authorised to telegraph in his name

* This line should be erased if not required.

Order No. 1025. Wt. W3253/ P 511. 27/2 H. & K. Ltd. (E. 2634)

MESSAGES AND SIGNALS. No. of Message..................

Prefix .... Code .... Words	Received.	Sent, or sent out.	Office Stamp.
Charges to Collect £ s. d.	From .... By	At .... m. To .... By	61
Service Instructions 10/4	Apr		243

Handed in at Priority [illegible] Office [illegible] m. Received [illegible] m.

TO Tele

* Sender's Number	Day of Month	In reply to Number	AAA
G129	18		

Ref	66	DO	108
Para	4	aaa	REFUSAL
aaa	ack	by	wire

FROM 66 Div

PLACE & TIME 0040

* This line should be erased if not required.

(3557.) Wt. W528—M1970. 25m., 100 lvs. 5/17. J. H., Ltd. (E.)

(1086) Wt.W16552/M1615 250,000 Pads. 21/3/17. J.R.&C. E 685 Forms C2122/6.

"B" Form. 252

Army Form C2122
(In pads of 150)

MESSAGES AND SIGNALS.

No. of Message ....

Prefix SM Code 1836 m.	Received	Sent	Office Stamp
Office of Origin and Service Instructions. Y F F Priority / **Words** 83	At 1608 m.	At .... m.	[illegible]
	From Y F F	To [illegible]	
	By [illegible]	By [illegible]	

App

TO Tele

Sender's Number.	Day of Month.	In reply to Number.	AAA
G134	18		
199	Bde	will	relieve
SA	Bde	in	line
after	dusk	tonight	and
take	over	[illegible]	[illegible]
from	K23C1.3	to	K36
Central	aaa	199	Bde
Hq	will	move	to
K27C6.2	aaa	Details	to
be	arranged	between	BGCS
direct	aaa	To	be
distinctly	understood	that	SA
and	198	Bde	will
hand	over	RED	LINE
intact	on	their	respective
points	aaa	On	relief
SA	Bde	will	[illegible]

From to HONNECHY aaa Added 3 Bdes
Place who will ack [illegible] S A [illegible]
Time Sigs [illegible]

* This line should be erased if not required.

No. of Message............

..........Code..........m.	Words	Charge.	This message is on a/c of :	Recd. at......m.
Office of Origin and Service Instructions	Sent		..........Service.	Date 62
	At ....m.		app	From 245
	To			By..........
	By		(Signature of "Franking Officer")	

TO

Sender's Number.	Day of Month.	In reply to Number.	AAA

REFUSAL

From

Place

Time

The above may be forwarded as now corrected.

Censor.

(Z)

Signature of Addressor or person authorised to telegraph in his name

* This line should be erased if not required.

Order No. 1625. Wt. W3253/ P 511. 27/2. H. & K., Ltd. (E. 2634).

"C" Form.

Army Form C. 2123.
(In books of 100.)

MESSAGES AND SIGNALS.

No. of Message

Prefix .... Code .... Words ....

£ s. d.

Charges to Collect

Service Instructions

Received. From .... By ....

Sent, or sent out. At .... m. To .... By ....

Office Stamp

App Gef

246

Handed in at ... Ile Rear ... Office ... m. Received ... 10.26 ... m.

TO Gef

*Sender's Number.	Day of Month.	In reply to Number.	AAA
G 131	18		

9th	Glosters	will	come
under	command	of	199
Bde	forthwith	aaa	added
9th	Glosters	and	199
Bde	repeated	CRE	and
[illegible]A	Bde		

FROM
TIME & PLACE
Mese

*This line should be erased if not required.

100,000.—John Bleson, Ltd.—8/17.—8141. Forms C2123.

"C" FORM.
MESSAGES AND SIGNALS.

Army Form C. 2123.
(In books of 100.)
No. of Message............

Prefix...... Code...... Words......	Received.	Sent, or sent out.	Office Stamp.
£ s. d.	From......	At......m.	253
Charges to Collect	By......	To......	
Service Instructions Pty 2adds		By......	

Handed in at [illegible] Office 1617 m. Received 1644 m.

TO [illegible]

* Sender's Number	Day of Month.	In reply to Number	AAA
G137	18		

Ref	my	G136	aaa
SA	Bde	will	not
be	relieved	by	199
Bde	until	it	is
definite	that	former	has
completely	gained	and	secured
line	K36A1.9	– K23C13	which
will	be	reported	to
DHQ	by	'phone	aaa
Add	SA	and	199
Bdes			

FROM
PLACE & TIME 66 Div

* This line should be erased if not required.

(3557.) Wt. W528—M1970. 25m., 100 lvs. 5/17. J. H., Ltd. (E.)

"C" Form.

Army Form C. 2123.
(In books of 100.)

MESSAGES AND SIGNALS.

No. of Message ______

Prefix ____ Code ____ Words ____	Received.	Sent, or sent out.	Office Stamp.
£ s. d.	From YFF	At ____ m.	254
Charges to Collect	By ____	To ____	
Service Instructions		By ____	

Handed in at YFF Office ____ m. Received ____ m.

TO ____

* Sender's Number	Day of Month.	In reply to Number	AAA
	15		

FROM ____

PLACE & TIME ____

* This line should be erased if not required.

[illegible]—W ____—100,000—[illegible]—S.P.Co.—[illegible]

256

Army Form C. 2123.
(In books of 100.)

"C" Form.

MESSAGES AND SIGNALS.

No. of Message ______

Prefix ____ Code ____ Words ____	Received.	Sent, or sent out.	Office Stamp.
£ s. d.	From YFF	At ____ m.	[illegible]
Charges to Collect	By [illegible]	To ____	
Service Instructions		By ____	

Handed in at YFF Office ____ m. Received [illegible] m.

TO JEFE

* Sender's Number	Day of Month.	In reply to Number	AAA
514 D	18		

7th	Bde	will	establish
its	HQ	about	R 3 a D
central	when	accommodation	here
has	been	made	aaa
Owing	to	change	of
[illegible]	order	SA	? Bde
HQ	must	move	[illegible]
0276	before	0200	[illegible]
19th			

FROM [illegible]
PLACE & TIME

* This line should be erased if not required.

[illegible]—W. [illegible]—E.P.Co.—[illegible]

257

"C" Form.

MESSAGES AND SIGNALS.

Army Form C. 2123. (In books of 100.)

No. of Message 866

Prefix SB Code 2010 Words 81 T

Received. From YFF By Fisher

Sent, or sent out. At ... To ... By Rob

Office Stamp.

Charges to Collect YFF

Service Instructions 3 adds Bty

Handed in at YFF Office 2010 m. Received 2100 m.

TO S/A BDE ~~198~~ ~~199~~

* Sender's Number.	Day of Month.	In reply to Number.	AAA
G 146	18		

Reports	from	air	and
ground	indicate	that	enemy
is	retiring	aaa	Leading
BDES	will	push	out at
once strong	patrols	and	maintain
touch	with	enemy	aaa
troops	not	to	advance
east	of	RICHEMONT river	
aaa	artillery	SOS	line
will	raised	to	line
of	RICHEMONT river		until
further	information	is	received
from	BDES	concerning	Location
of	enemy	aaa	added
Infy	BDES	and	18 DA
who	will	inform	artillery

~~and~~ units concerned repted Corps

FROM

PLACE & TIME

* This line should be erased if not required.

(19629) W1528/M1970. 300,000 Pads. 4/17. McC. & Co. Ltd. (E1213).

"C" Form.

MESSAGES AND SIGNALS. App 69(a)

Army Form C. 2123. (In books of 100.)

No. of Message ______

Prefix SO Code ____ Words 73	Received. From GFE By A6	Sent, or sent out. At ____ m. To 255 By ____	Office Stamp. SZA 8/x/18
Charges to Collect £ s. d.			
Service Instructions			

Handed in at GFF Office 2035 m. Received 2123 m.

TO Urgent Operation Pty
Gfe

*Sender's Number	Day of Month.	In reply to Number	AAA
G147	18		

Your	BMX109	received	aaa
relief	of	your	sector
by	199	Bde	is
cancelled	199	Bde	will
take	over	left	of
198	Bde	sector	as
ordered	aaa	will	retain
one	Battalion	concentrated	west
of	SELLE	and	on
BN	about	Q7B	aaa
199	Bde	will	be
prepared	to	advance	through
198	&	SA	Bde
tomorrow	if	enemy	has
retired	aaa	Addsd	SA Bde
reptd	199	& 198 Bde	

FROM
PLACE & TIME 66th Division 2030

* This line should be erased if not required.

3110—W.528—100,000—19/5/17—E.P.Co.

SECRET.

Copy No.........

258/10

App 68(8)

66th DIVISION ORDER NO.110.

19th October 1918.

1. 66th Division (less Divl. Artillery, 9th Glouc. R.(Pioneers), 3 F. Coys, R.E.) will be relieved from the line by 18th Division night 20/21st October, in accordance with attached Tables.
Relief to be complete by 06.00 21st October.
Details will be arranged between Brigades concerned.

2. Squadron Northumberland Hussars and Coy 13th Cyclist Battalion will be transferred on relief and will report to 18th Division for orders at 18.00, 20th October.

3. Field Ambulances will move under orders of A.D.M.S.

4. Distances in accordance with S.S.724 will be strictly observed.
Troops on halting must immediately clear road.
Weather permitting, Transport will use avoiding road via P.17.a. and L'EPINETTE during same hours as allotted to Brigades in Table 1.
Any Transport using Roman Road must march through without halting.

5. Brigades will hand over all dumps of ammunition and R.E.material on relief. Locations and approximate contents will be wired to Division "Q" by 12.00, 21st October.

6. 66th Div .H.Q.,(less Forward Echelon) will open at SERAIN, at 16.00, 20th October. Forward Echelon will remain at REUMONT BREWER till 21 October.

7. Command of the sector will pass from G.O.C. 66th Division to G.O.C. 18th Division on completion of the relief of the two Brigades in the line. Completion of these reliefs will be reported to D.H.Q. by wiring Code Word "COMPLETE".

8. ACKNOWLEDGE.

Walter Guinness

Lieut.-Colonel.
General Staff.
66th Division.

DISTRIBUTION.

Copy No. 1. War Diary.
2 " "
3 File.
4. A & Q.
5. Signals.
6. 18th Div.Arty.
7. CRE.
8. 198 Inf. Bde.
9. 199th do.
10. S.A. Bde.
11. 9th Glouc.R.(Pioneers)
12. Train, A.S.C.
13. A.D.M.S.
14. D.A.D.V.S.
15. D.A.P.M.
16. D.A.D.O.S.
17. 100th Bn.M.G.C.
18. [illegible]th Bn. M.G.C.
19. D.G.O.
20. Camp Commdt.
21. 25th Division.
22. 38th Division.
23. 35th Squadron R.A.F.
24. XIII Corps.
25. A.D.C.

---

26. A.P.M.XIII Corps.
27. Squad.North'd Hrs.
28. Coy. XIII Cyclist Bn.
29. Area Commdt.MAUROIS.

259

Tables to accompany 66th Division Order No. 110.

T A B L E 1.

Locations of 66th Division for nights during relief.

	19/20th	20/21st.	21/22nd.	
S.A.Bde.	REUMONT etc.	SERAIN.	SERAIN.	Head to pass road Jun[illegible] P.17.c.8.6. at 1030.21[illegible]
198th Bde.	Line Right.	MAUROIS.	PREMONT	Head to pass Road Juncti[illegible] P.22.b.1.1. at 10.00 21st[illegible]
199th Bde.	Line Left.	MAUROIS.	ELINCOURT.	Head to pass Road Junct[illegible] P.22.b.1.1.11.30 21st Oc[illegible]
100th Bn. M.G.C.	REUMONT & MAUROIS.	PREMONT.	PREMONT.	Head to pass Road Junct[illegible] P.22.b.1.1 at 12.30 20[illegible] To leave Roman Rd at MAR[illegible]
Div.Train A.S.C.	AVELU.	SERAIN. Sth. end.	SERAIN.	
Div.H.Q.	REUMONT.	SERAIN. (less Forward Ech)	SERAIN.	

T A B L E II

Locations of 18th Division for nights furing reliefs.

	19th/20th	20th/21st	21st/22nd.
53rd Bde.	1 Bn MAUROIS. 2 Bns PREMONT. Bde.H.Q.PREMONT.	Line right.	Line Right.
54th Bde.	2 Bns MAUROIS. 1 Bn SERAIN. Bde.HQ. PREMONT.	Line Left.	Line Left.
55th Bde.	ELINCOURT.	ELINCOURT.	MAUROIS.
18th Bn M.G.C.	Bn.H.Q. REUMONT. 4 Coys in Line.	Bn H.Q. REUMONT. 4 Coys in Line.	Bn H.Q.REUMONT. 4 Coys in Line.
18th D.H.Q.	SERAIN.	REUMONT.	REUMONT.

C Form. Army Form C. 2123.
(In books of 100.)

MESSAGES AND SIGNALS.

No. of Message

Prefix ___ Code ___ Words ___	Received.	Sent, or sent out	Office Stamp.
£ s. d.	From	At ___ m.	App 69 (03)
Charges to Collect	By	To	SIGNALS
Service Instructions		By	

Handed in at [illegible] YFF Office 0128 m. Received ___ m.

TO ~~[illegible]~~ SA Bde

* Sender's Number	Day of Month.	In reply to Number	AAA
9	19		

~~25~~ Div are tonight taking over front to K36d60 aaa 197 Bde will take over remainder of Divl front with 1 Battn from Divl northern boundary to road K29d1.7 inclusive and one battn from K29d1.7 exclusive to K36d6.0 exclusive 3rd Battn in support aaa On Relief 198 Bde will move 1 battn to REUMONT 2 battns to Q7 and Q2 aaa Remaining moves on 20th and 21st as in DO 110 aaa 198 Bde will not enter REUMONT before 11 00 on 20th ack aaa Head of Column SA Bde will pass P17c8.6 at 1000 20th aaa ack aaa added 3 Bdes Repts 18 DA Q Signals CRE 25 Div 15 Corps & 16 Bn MGC

FROM 66 Div
PLACE & TIME 0040

* This line should be erased if not required.

9310—W.14633—200,000—2/17—E.P.Co.—(E930.)

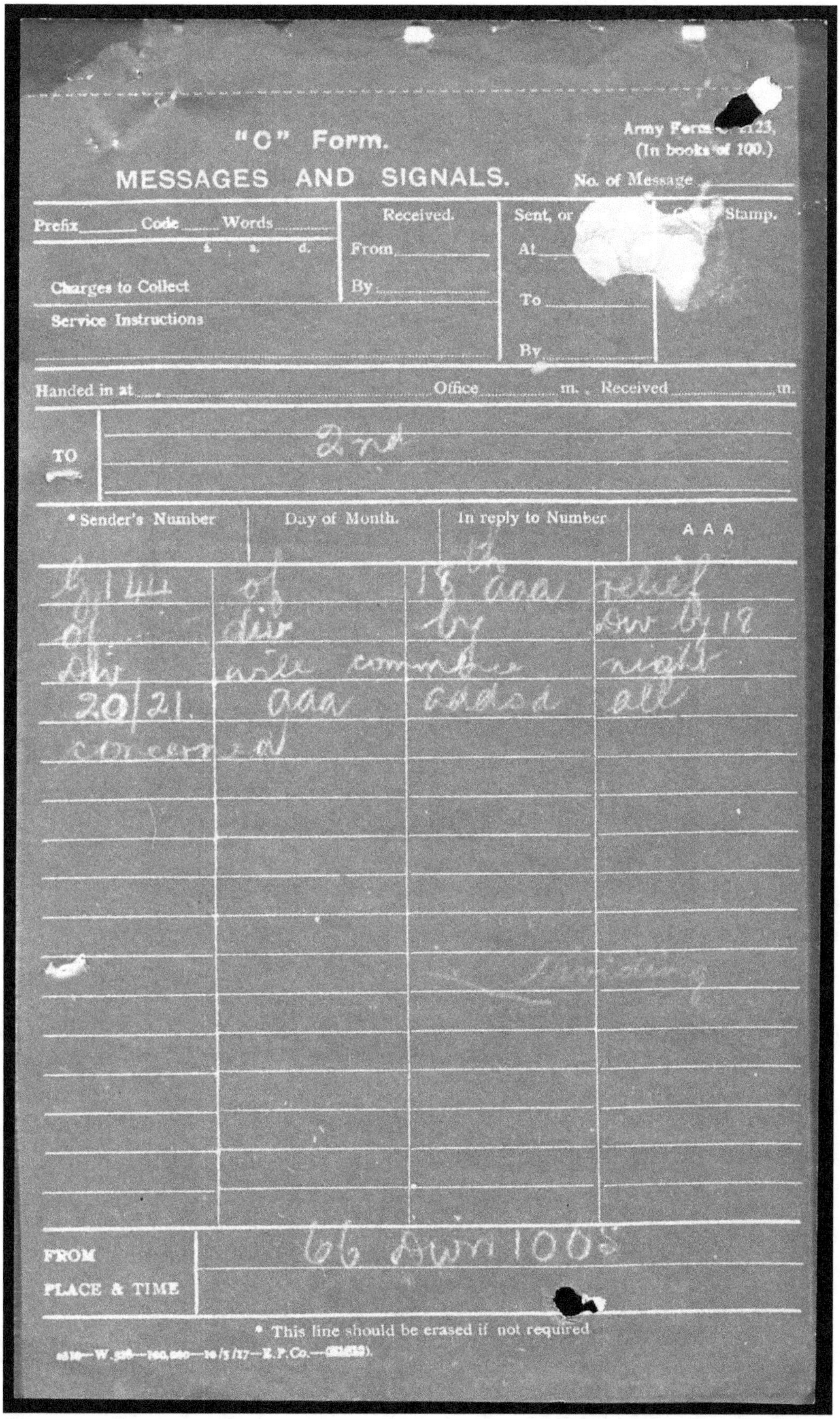

"C" Form.

MESSAGES AND SIGNALS.

Army Form C. 2123.
(In books of 100.)

No. of Message

Prefix ______ Code ______ Words ______

£ s. d.

Charges to Collect

Service Instructions

Received. From ______ By ______

Sent, or At ______ To ______ By ______

Stamp.

Handed in at ______ Office ______ m. Received ______ m.

TO 2nd

*Sender's Number	Day of Month.	In reply to Number	AAA
G/144	of	18th aaa	relief
of	div	by	Div by 18
Div	will	commence	night
20/21.	aaa	addsd	all
concerned			

FROM PLACE & TIME 66 Div 1005

* This line should be erased if not required

6510—W. 536—100,000—10/5/17—E.P.Co.—(E1512).

"C" Form. 250 Army Form C. 2123. (In books of 100.)

MESSAGES AND SIGNALS. No. of Message ______

Prefix ____ Code ____ Words ____ £ s. d. Charges to Collect	Received. From ____ By ____	Sent, or sent out. At ____ m. To ____ By ____	Office Stamp.
Service Instructions			

Handed in at ______ Office ______ m. Received ______ m.

TO [illegible]

*Sender's Number	Day of Month.	In reply to Number	AAA
[illegible]	19		

[illegible]	4 C.I.F.	[illegible]	197
Bde	54	Bde	[illegible]
[illegible]	[illegible]	[illegible]	[illegible]
4114	[illegible]	Bn	[illegible]
[illegible]	of	BELLE	[illegible]
[illegible]	[illegible]	4AA	H6
[illegible]	2	[illegible]	ROUMONT
[illegible]	[illegible]	G134	[illegible]
[illegible]	accordingly		

K 32 d Central

FROM 66 Div
PLACE & TIME

* This line should be erased if not required.

(1810—W. 528—100,000—10/5/17—E.P.Co.—(E1212).

Sheet 2

"C" FORM.

MESSAGES AND SIGNALS.

Army Form C. 2123.
(In books of 100.)

No. of Message ....

Prefix........Code......Words..........	Received.	Sent, or sent out.	Office Stamp.
£ s. d. Charges to Collect	From.......... By..........	At..........m.	249
Service Instructions		To.......... By..........	

Handed in at..........Office..........m. Received..........m.

TO	

* Sender's Number.	Day of Month.	In reply to Number.	AAA

and	flank	divisions	

FROM	66 DIV
PLACE & TIME	20·00

* This line should be erased if not required.

(19629) Wt528/M1970. 300,000 Pads. 4/17. McC. & Co., Ltd. **(E1213).**

"C" Form.

MESSAGES AND SIGNALS.

Army Form C. 2123.
(In books of 100.)

No. of Message

Prefix	Code	Words 105	Received. From YFFR By HG	Sent or sent out. At m. To By	Office Stamp. SA Bde 19.10.18

Charges to Collect

Service Instructions

Handed in at YFF Office 1025 m. Received 1144 m.

TO Bde by fullerphone
SA Bde

*Sender's Number	Day of Month	In reply to Number	AAA
G152	19		

Following	moves	today	aaa
Div	HQ	to	REUMONT
opening	at	P17b43	at
1200	aaa	198	Bde
HQ	to	K32D	central
199	Bde	HQ	to
LE CATEAU	SA Bde	HQ	to
Q7a74	by	1800	aaa
after	dusk	199	Bde
will	relieve	SA Bde	in
line	aaa	dividing	
line	between	198	and
199	Bdes	road	K35c93
K38D70	—	GARDE MILL	incl
to	199	Bde	aaa
Command	post	to	be
established	at	K35c93	aaa

FROM
PLACE & TIME

on relief SA Bde will be disposed as ordered in my

* This line should be erased if not required.

326—100,000—10/5/17—E.P.Co.—(E1323).

251

Instructions regarding War Diaries and Intelligence Summaries are contained in F. S. Regs., Part II. and the Staff Manual respectively. Title pages will be prepared in manuscript.

WAR DIARY
or
INTELLIGENCE SUMMARY.
(Erase heading not required.)

1.

Army Form C. 2118.

November, 1918.

Place	Date	Hour	Summary of Events and Information	Remarks and references to Appendices
SERAIN	1st.		66th Div. Prelim. Order 111 received. Orders for forthcoming operations	App 1. (O)
			SA Bde Order 249 issued. Re forthcoming operations	App 2.
			66th Div. Order 112 received. Moves on 2/11/18	App 3. (O)
			S.A. Bde Order 250 issued. Bde to move to REUMONT on 2/11/18	App 4
	2nd		S.A. Bde moved to REUMONT.	
REUMONT			66th Div Order 113 received. Moves on 3/11/18	App 5 (O)
	3rd.		Bde remained at REUMONT.	
REUMONT	4th		66th Div. G.173 received. Moves on 4/11/18.	App 6 (O)
			S.A. Bde Order 251 issued. Bde to move to LE CATEAU today	App 7.
			Bde moved to LE CATEAU.	
LE CATEAU			Bde H.Q. moved to a different building in LE CATEAU owing to outbreak of fire in quarters occupied.	
			66th Div. G.B.124 received. Moves on Nov. 5th	App 7A (O)
			66th Div G.B.127 received. One troop 12th Lancers to report to S.A. Bde at POMMEREUIL on 5th.	App 8. (O)
	5th		66th Div Order 114 received, also Add. A. and Amend. 1. Orders for operations on 5/11/18.	App 9. (O)
			S.A. Bde Order 252 issued. Bde to move to POMMEREUIL today	App 10.
			66th Div G.B.128 received. Moves to take place forthwith	App 11. (O)
			S.A. Bde Order 255 issued also Amend. 1. Plan of operations by Divn for 5/11/18	App 12.
			S.A. Bde moved to POMMEREUIL	
			(N.B. Documents wrongly numbered BO. 253/4 not assigned for this Diary)	

(A6086) Wt W5300/P714 250,000 2/18 Sch. 52 Forms/C2118/16

260

Instructions regarding War Diaries and Intelligence Summaries are contained in F. S. Regs., Part II. and the Staff Manual respectively. Title pages will be prepared in manuscript.

WAR DIARY or INTELLIGENCE SUMMARY.

(Erase heading not required.)

2. November, 1918

Army Form C. 2118.

Place	Date	Hour	Summary of Events and Information	Remarks and references to Appendices
POMMEREUIL	6th		66th Div. Order 115 received. Bde Group, including 9th Gloucester R. and portion of 100th Bn. M.G.C. to be prepared to move to LANDRECIES from 10 am on 6/11/18.	App. 13. (O)
			66th Div G.B. 44 received. S.A. Bde Group to move to LANDRECIES immediately	App. 14 (O)
			S.A. Bde Order 256 issued. Bde Group to move to LANDRECIES this afternoon.	App. 15.
			Brigade Group moved to LANDRECIES.	
LANDRECIES	7th		66th Div ~~B~~ Order 117 received. Action of Divn. on 7th if required.	App. 16 (O)
			66th Div G.C. 199 received Bde Group to move to BASSE NOYELLES at 14.00 hours	App. 17 (O)
			S.A. Bde Order 257 issued. Bde Group to move to BASSE NOYELLES this afternoon.	App. 18
			Bde. Group moved to BASSE NOYELLES.	
			66th Div. G.C. 200, G.B. 90 and G.B. 91 received. Relief in line of 25th Divn by 66th Divn. 198th & 199th Bdes to continue the advance tomorrow	App. 19. (O).
			S.A Bde B.S. 168 issued, ~~[illegible]~~ ~~[illegible]~~ Extract of Divn G.C. 200.	App. 20.
			66th Div. Order 118 and G.C. 208 received. Operations on 8/11/18. (Extracts of Div. Order sent out to Units). S.A. Bde in Divisional Reserve and to move to DOMPIERRE	App. 21 (O)
			S.A. Bde. Order 258 issued. Bde. to move DOMPIERRE. tomorrow, 8th.	App. 22.
	8th		Bde. Group moved to DOMPIERRE.	

D. D. & L., London, E.C. (A10266) Wt W5300/P713 750,000 2/18 Sch. 52 Forms/C2118/16

3

Army Form C. 2118.

WAR DIARY
or
INTELLIGENCE SUMMARY. November, 1918
(Erase heading not required.)

Instructions regarding War Diaries and Intelligence Summaries are contained in F. S. Regs., Part II. and the Staff Manual respectively. Title pages will be prepared in manuscript.

Place	Date	Hour	Summary of Events and Information	Remarks and references to Appendices
DOMPIERRE	8th		~~Verbal orders received for Bde to move to Road from J.18.d.5.0. to K.7. central~~	
			66th Div. Order 119 received. 198th & 199th Bdes to continue advance on objectives laid down in Order 118.	App 23(0)
			~~S.A. Bde Order 259 issued. Bde Group to move to and concentrate on road~~	
	9th		Verbal orders received for Bde to move forward at once.	
			S.A. Bde Order 259 issued. Bde to move to and concentrate on road from J.18.d.5.0. to K.Y. central today.	
			Amend 1 to O. 259 issued amending destination to BEUGNIES.	App 24
			66th Div. G.2 received. Formation of Mobile Column under Brig. Gen. TANNER composed of S.A. Bde. and Bde. Signal Section, 1 Batty. R.F.A., 1 Section 4.5" Hows., 430th Fld. Coy. R.E., 1 Coy, 100th Bn. M.G.C., S.A. Fld. Amb., 2 platoons Corps Cyclists and possibly 2 Armoured Cars. Column to move to and concentrate in BEUGNIES.	App 25(0)
			66th Div. G.B.96 received. 431st and 432nd Fld. Coys. R.E. to join Mobile Column under Brig. Gen. TANNER and report at SOLRE LE CHATEAU.	App 26(0)
			Verbal instructions received from Div. that Column is to move on to SOLRE LE CHATEAU.	
			SA Bde BMY 21 issued. Column to rest an hour at BEUGNIES before moving on to SOLRE LE CHATEAU.	App 27
			66th Div O. 120 received. Formation & constitution of Mobile Force under command of G.O.C. 66th Div. and ~~the~~ action to be taken by it.	App 28(0)
			Column moved to BEUGNIES and then on to SOLRE LE CHATEAU.	

262

D. D. & L., London, E.C. (A10066) Wt W5300/P713 750,000 2/18 Sch. 52 Forms/C2118/16

Instructions regarding War Diaries and Intelligence Summaries are contained in F. S. Regs., Part II. and the Staff Manual respectively. Title pages will be prepared in manuscript.

WAR DIARY
or
INTELLIGENCE SUMMARY.
(Erase heading not required.)

4th November, 1918

Army Form C. 2118.

Place	Date	Hour	Summary of Events and Information	Remarks and references to Appendices
SOLRE LE CHATEAU.	10th.		Verbal orders received from 66th Div later conveyed in 66th Div Order 121.	
			Mobile Column Order 1 issued. S.A. Bde (less 4th SAI to remain at SOLRE LE CHATEAU) to move on BEAUMONT in pursuit of the enemy. Scots Greys and 12th Lancers to cover the advance. Movement of 1st Cav. Bde H.Q. and XIII Corps Cyclists. The enemy, if encountered, to be vigorously engaged. Order of advance of mobile Column.	app. 29
			66th Div Order 121 received. Pursuit of enemy to be continued on 10/11/18 with objective - River line BEAUMONT - SOLRE ST. CERY - RENLIES - FROIDCHAPELLE. 2 Armoured Cars attached to S.A. Bde	app. 29 (0)
			66th Div G.13 received. Moves of 199th Bde. etc.	app. 30 (0)
			Bde H.Q. established at HESTRUD	
HESTRUD			1st SAI. AX 6 (timed 12.20) received. Left held up by M.G. high ground and white house. Centre Coy making slow progress. No news from right but were on high ground when last seen. Enemy has evidently (opened) sluice gates and river is now unfordable for transport.	app. 31. (0)
			1st SAI AX 7 (timed 14.20) received. Have just returned from Coys. They are pushing on slowly. Have instructed them they must make progress. Left are near white house. M.G. fire very heavy. Low flying planes gave considerable trouble. Stream is now fordable again. Right are on the high ground on right. All Coys. are in touch.	app 31A (0)
			1st SAI. AX 15 (timed 14.20) received. No change in situation. Outposts now digging in. Bridge across stream complete for infantry in fours, transport and Field Guns.	app. 32 (0)

263

D. D. & L., London, E.C.
(A10266) Wt W5300/P713 750,000 2/18 Sch. 52 Forms/C2118/16.

WAR DIARY
or
INTELLIGENCE SUMMARY.
(Erase heading not required.)

Army Form C. 2118.

5.

November, 1918.

Instructions regarding War Diaries and Intelligence Summaries are contained in F. S. Regs., Part II. and the Staff Manual respectively. Title pages will be prepared in manuscript.

Place	Date	Hour	Summary of Events and Information	Remarks and references to Appendices
HESTRUD	10th		4th Army Adv. Guard GX 83 received. 4th S.A.I. to detail one Coy. for outpost duty, north of SOLRE LE CHATEAU	App. 33 (0)
			Mobile Column Order 2 issued. Line at dusk on 10/11/18. On the right, high ground at point 240x immediately W of VIVERIAUX. In centre approaching village of GRANDIEU. On left, high ground immediately N. of A in GRANDIEU. 1st SAI to continue the advance tomorrow 11th. Remainder of Mobile Column to be prepared to move forward at 07.00 tomorrow but to await orders to move.	App. 34
			66th Div Order 122 received. 199th and S.A. Bdes responsible for protection of front during night 10/11th Novr. Advance to be continued tomorrow. 12th Lancers co-operating with S.A. Bde. 9th and 13th Corps Cyclists and 2 Sections Field Coy. R.E. withdrawn from S. A. Bde.	App. 35 (0)
	11th		1st SAI AX14 (timed 06.45) received. Right Coy. report cannot make progress. No report from Left or Centre Coy. yet. From personal observation during night enemy are holding yesterdays line strongly. Artillery very active.	App. 36 (0)
			1st SAI AX19 (timed 04.10) received. Reports received from left and centre Coys stating they cannot get forward owing to heavy M.G. fire. I am therefore leaving outpost line as last night. I see no chance of getting forward unless we get good artillery support.	App. 37 (0)

264

D. D. & L., London, E.C.
(A10266) Wt W5300/P713 750,000 2/18 Sch. 52 Forms/C2118/16

Instructions regarding War Diaries and Intelligence Summaries are contained in F. S. Regs., Part II. and the Staff Manual respectively. Title pages will be prepared in manuscript.

WAR DIARY
or
INTELLIGENCE SUMMARY.
(Erase heading not required.)

Army Form C. 2118.

6.

November, 1918

Place	Date	Hour	Summary of Events and Information	Remarks and references to Appendices
HESTRUD	11th		4th Army Adv. Guard GX 41 received. Hostilities will cease at 11th hour today, Nov. 11th. Troops will stand fast on line reached at that hour which will be reported by wire. Defensive precautions to be ~~taken~~ maintained. There will be no intercourse of any description with enemy until receipt of instructions.	app. 38 (o)
			Mobile Column Special Order issued, repeating above	app. 39.
			Bde H.Q. moved to Chateau N.W. of H in HESTRUD	
Outskirts NW of HESTRUD			4th Army Adv. Guard G.B. 14, 15, G.18 and G.C. 22. received. Line on cessation of hostilities. Units to concentrate on repair of roads and construction of bridges.	app. 40 (o)
			Mobile Column Order 3 issued. 2nd SAI to relieve 1st SAI in line at 19.00 hours, tomorrow, 12/11/18. 4th S.A.I. returns to S.A. Bde command.	app. 41
			66th Div G.B. 16 received. 4th SAI to move forthwith to BEAURIEU	app. 42 (o)
			66th Div G.B. 16 received. Move of 4th S.A.I. ordered above to take place tomorrow, 12/11/18	app. 43 (o)
do.	12th		Fourth Army Adv Guard G. 21. received. Coys 100th Bn. M.G.C. ~~[illegible]~~ withdrawn from S A Bde & to join Battn at MOULARD	app. 44 (o)
			Mobile Column Order 4 issued. 4th S.A.I. to move to ~~GR~~ GRANDRIEU tomorrow, 13/11/18. 3 Coys detailed for work on roads etc under CRE on 13/11/18.	app. 45

265

D. D. & L., London, E.C.
(A10266) Wt W3300/P713 750,000 2/18 Sch. 82 Forms/C2118/16

Instructions regarding War Diaries and Intelligence Summaries are contained in F. S. Regs., Part II. and the Staff Manual respectively. Title pages will be prepared in manuscript.

WAR DIARY
or
INTELLIGENCE SUMMARY.
(*Erase heading not required.*)

Army Form C. 2118.

4

November 1918

Place	Date	Hour	Summary of Events and Information	Remarks and references to Appendices
N.W. Outskirts of HESTRUD	12		SA Bde BS. 175 sent 66th Div and 198th Bde. Our line has been slightly altered today and now runs as follows - Ref Map NAMUR Sheet 1/100,000 from a point in S fringe of large wood N of A in GRANDRIEU SE to the road junction immediately E. of U in GRANDRIEU thence through the outskirts of GRANDRIEU village at the point N of first V in VIVERIAUX thence S to the nearest road junction E. of VIVERIAUX thence to a point about 300 yards N of the road junction E. of FRASIES where we have established touch with left flank of 199 Bde.	App 46 (0)
			Narrative of operations of Bde from 1/11/18 attached as an Appendix	App 47.
do	13		–	
do	14		66th Div A. 987 received. Field Ambulance to come under orders of Brigade from this date.	App 48 (0)
			66th Div G.48 received. 66th Div and attached troops transferred to 9th Corps from 12 noon today.	App 49 (0)
			The Corps Commander visited the 66th Divn. A guard of honour ~~for~~ consisting of 3 Officers and 46. O.R. from each Battalion in the Division was detailed to receive him. The portion of the Guard from the S. A. Bde was commanded by Lt. Col. JENKINS, 1st S.A.I. and was particularly well turned out. The smartness and physique of the men was very noticeable in the march past. The ceremony was held in the square at SOLRE LE CHATEAU and was a very impressive sight.	

D. D. & L., London, E.C.
(A10266) Wt W5300/P713 750,000 2/18 Sch. 52 Forms/C2118/16

266

Instructions regarding War Diaries and Intelligence Summaries are contained in F. S. Regs., Part II. and the Staff Manual respectively. Title pages will be prepared in manuscript.

WAR DIARY
or
INTELLIGENCE SUMMARY.
(Erase heading not required.)

8

Army Form C. 2118.

November, 1918.

Place	Date	Hour	Summary of Events and Information	Remarks and references to Appendices
N.W. Outskirts of HESTRUD	15		The Brig. General Commanding held a conference with Unit Commanders at 10 am to discuss the various points ~~– connection with the~~ gone into the previous day at the Divl. Conference in connection with the march to the RHINE. The most important point was the amount of baggage to be carried on the Transport and on the man, and it was finally decided as follows –	
			On the Transport	
			Greatcoat, 1 Blanket per man (second blanket), 100 prs Boots (if available), 1 pr. Socks per man, Cleaning material, Officers kits, Officers Messes.	
			On the Man	
			1 Blanket, 2 prs Socks (not including pair worn) 1 set clean clothes, 1 Iron Ration, 1 Emergency Ration (hard) Unconsumed portion of days ration, Cleaning material, etc.	
			All instructions issued and received in connection with the March to the RHINE are attached in Appendix 50	App 50. (O)
			At 5 pm warning order was received and issued for the S.A. Bde to move from GRANDRIEU and HESTRUD to SIVRY. The actual order (vide Appendix 51) for the move was received at 9 pm	App 51 (O)
	16		The Bde marched to SIVRY Area in accordance with Bde Order 261 and was billeted as follows :–	App 52
			Bde H.Q. } SIVRY 1st S.A.I. } SIVRY 2nd S.A.I. } SIVRY 4th S.A.I. BEAURIEUX SALTMB. SIVRY	
SIVRY	17		The day was taken up by the usual Church services and in completing arrangements for the March to the RHINE. Units had to sort out all baggage and despatch what was not required to the Divl. Dump at AVESNES.	

267

D. D. & L., London, E.C.
(A10266) Wt W5300/P713 750,000 2/18 Sch. 52 Forms/C2118/16

Instructions regarding War Diaries and Intelligence Summaries are contained in F. S. Regs., Part II. and the Staff Manual respectively. Title pages will be prepared in manuscript.

WAR DIARY
or
INTELLIGENCE SUMMARY.
(Erase heading not required.)

November, 1918.

Army Form C. 2118.

Place	Date	Hour	Summary of Events and Information	Remarks and references to Appendices
SIVRY	17 (Contd)		Boots and repairing material which had been on indent for some time past and which were very urgently ~~required~~ needed were drawn from DADOS.	
			The 4 extra G.S. wagons per Battn. reported to Units in accordance with 66th Divn Q.Y948/8/Q.	
do	18.		The 66th Divn commenced the march to the RHINE. (66th Div. Order 124)	App. 53 (0)
			The 199th Inf. Bde was the leading Brigade followed by the 198th Inf. Bde and Divl. H.Q. Group. The S.A. Bde Group was only required to concentrate in the SIVRY – MONTBLIART Area. (S.A. Bde Order 262). This was done by bringing the 4th S.A.I. from BEAURIEUX and the S.A.F.A. and 542nd Coy A.S.C. from SOLRE LE CHATEAU to SIVRY, and the 430th Fld. Coy. R.E. from SOLRE LE CHATEAU to MONTBLIART. The concentration was completed by 16 hours.	App. 54
			At 14.30 the B.G.C. inspected the 1st S.A.I. and took the opportunity of thanking them for the gallant work they had done in the closing stages of the war, particularly at BEAUREVOIR on the 8th and LE CATEAU on the 17th October.	
			Divl. Order 125 for the move of the Bde. Group to SENZEILLE Area received	App. 55 (0)
			Bde. Order 263 issued.	App. 56.
do	19		The 66th Div. continued the march, the S.A. Bde. Group moving to SENZEILLE Area. The march was a long one – some 16 miles – and was rendered more difficult by the sticky nature of the roads and continual halts. In spite of this the men marched particularly well and not a man fell out. The move was completed by 18.00 hours.	
SENZEILLE	20		There was no move on the 20th. Parties for work on roads were supplied by 2nd S.A.I. and 4th S.A.I. The B.G.C. inspected the 4th S.A.I. and 2nd S.A.I. at 11.30 and 14.30 respectively.	
do	21		Still no move owing to difficulties of supply. Football match played between 4th S.A.I. and S.A. Fld. Amb. resulting in a win for the latter by 6 to nil.	
do	22		66th Div. Order 126 and G.123. Moves to take place on 23.11.18	App. 57 (0)
			S.A. Bde Order 264 + Amend. 1 issued. S.A. Bde Group, less 2nd S.A.I. to move to PHILIPPEVILLE and ROSEE on 23.11.18	App. 58

D. D. & L., London, E.C. (A10266) Wt W5300/P713 750,000 2/16 Sch. 82 Forms/C2118/16

Instructions regarding War Diaries and Intelligence Summaries are contained in F. S. Regs., Part II. and the Staff Manual respectively. Title pages will be prepared in manuscript.

WAR DIARY
or
INTELLIGENCE SUMMARY.
(Erase heading not required.)

Army Form C. 2118.

November, 1918.

10.

Place	Date	Hour	Summary of Events and Information	Remarks and references to Appendices
PHILIPPEVILLE	23.		The S.A. Infy. Bde. Group (less 2nd S.A. Infy.) marched to PHILIPPEVILLE and ROSEE preparatory to marching to the MEUSE	
BAC du PRINCE.	24		The Brigade Group marched to the MEUSE and was billeted as follows:- Bde HQ. and Signal Sec. — BAC du PRINCE. 1st SAI. — do 2nd SAI — AGIMONT. 4th SAI, SALTMB., 542 Coy A.S.C. — HERMETON S.A. Fld. Ambulance — GOCHENEE 430 Fld. Co. R.E. — AGIMONT. See 66th Div. Order 124 and G.134 and S.A. Bde Order 265 The march was a long one but the weather conditions were perfect for marching and not a single man fell out.	App 59(0) App 60.
do	25		Training under Battalion arrangements.	
do	26		do do do Particular attention paid to Ceremonial, Handling of arms and Detail.	
do	24/29		Usual Battalion and Coy. Training 66 Div. transferred from IX Corps to X Corps at 23.59 hours on 28.11.18 (66 Div G.S. 3/9 - 27/11/18)	App 61(0)
do	30		Inspection of 1st line Transport of 1st S.A.I. by B.G.C. S.Afr. Scottish held interplatoon competition S.Afr. Scottish gave a dinner to celebrate St. Andrew's Day.	

[signature] Brig. General
Commanding S. African Infantry Bde

269

D. D. & L., London, E.C.
(A10260) Wt W5300/P713 750,000 2/18 Sch. 52 Forms/C2118/16

Opp 1 (o)

SECRET. CopyNo. 10.

410

66th DIVISION PRELIMINARY ORDER No. 111.

31st October 1918.

Ref Map 57A1/40000

1. GENERAL PLAN.

At a date and hour to be notified later a major operation will be carried out by First, Third and Fourth Armies, and by First French Army with a view to breaking down the enemy's defence. The front involved is approximately 50 miles.

2. OBJECTIVES AND BOUNDARIES.

The objectives allotted to the XIII Corps and the Inter-Corps and Inter-Divisional boundaries are shown on the attached map.
The IX Corps will attack on the Right of the XIII Corps and the V Corps on the Left.

3. CORPS PLAN AND TROOPS EMPLOYED.

The attack will be carried out on a three Division front as follows :-

1st Phase (Up to GREEN Line).

25th Division on the Right.
50th Division in the Centre.
18th Division on the Left.
66th Division in Corps Reserve.

During this phase the 25th Division will force the crossing of the Canal and operate on the Southern bank up to the GREEN Line, the 50th and 18th Divisions operating North of the Canal.

2nd Phase. (Up to Final objective).

66th Division on the Right.
50th Division in the Centre.
18th Division on the Left.
25th Division in Corps Reserve.

During this phase the 66th Division will pass through the 25th Division and will become the Southern Division in the Corps. The 50th Division will cross the Canal and operate on the Southern bank. The 18th Division will continue to operate North of the Canal.

/4. Divisional....

4. DIVISIONAL PLAN OF ATTACK.

(a) 66th Division will carry out the attack with 199th Inf. Bde on Right, 198th Inf. Bde on Left and South African Bde in Divisional Reserve.

411

(b) Inter-Brigade boundary will be grid line between H.4.d.0.0. and J.2.c.0.0.

(c) South African Bde will be prepared to exploit the high ground in J.2.b. and d., J.8.b., and J.3.a.and c. or to seize and hold the high ground in I.21.central, I.28.central, I.30.c.0.0., J.25.c.0.0., J.19.c.5.0. in order to cover the Right flank of the Division.

(d) Affiliated Troops.
One Battery of Field Artillery, One Section of 4.5" Hows., One Section Cyclists, One troop 12th Lancers, and One Section 100th Bn M.G.Corps, will be attached to each Brigade.

(e) C.R.E. will be prepared to bridge the GRAND HELPE River for Infantry and Field Artillery in addition to making good the MAROILLES - MARBAIX Road and the MAROILLES - NOYELLES Road.

(f) Further instructions will be issued later on Preliminary moves, Artillery & M.G. Arrangements, Communications, Aircraft, etc.

5. Artillery supporting 66th Division will be as follows :-

66th Divisional Artillery. Brig-Genl.A. BIRTWISTLE, C.M.G.,D.S.O.

330th	Bde. R.F.A.	66th	Divisional	Artillery.
331st	" "	"	"	"
110th	" "	25th	"	"
112th	" "	"	"	"
150th Army Bde. R.F.A.				

27th Bde. R.G.A.

6. BRIDGING IN FIRST PHASE OF OPERATIONS.

(a) The C.E. XIII Corps is arranging for the construction

/of.....

412

of heavy bridges at LANDRECIES (to carry Tanks) and at HACHETTE, B.27. (to carry M.T.)

431st Fld. Co. R.E. is placed at the disposal of C.E. XIII Corps to assist in the construction of those bridges.

(b) The Pontoon Equipment of the 66th Division will be located in a position of readiness to be selected by G.O.C. 25th Division by 06.00 on 'Z' day, and will be at the disposal of that Division if required.

(c) Arrangements will be made with 25th Division to relieve the Field Company working under C.E. XIII Corps as soon as that Division is withdrawn into Corps Reserve.

7. ACKNOWLEDGE.

done

Walter Guinness
Lieut-Colonel,
General Staff,
66th Division.

DISTRIBUTION.

Copy No. 1	War Diary.	* 10.	South African Bde.
2	" "	* 11	100th Bn. M.G.Corps.
3	File.	12	9th Bn Glouc.R.(Pioneers).
4	'A' & 'Q'.	13	A.D.M.S.
* 5	Signals.	14	D.A.P.M.
* 6	C.R.A.	15	XIII Corps.
* 7	C.R.E.	16	25th Division.
* 8	198th Inf. Bde.	17	50th Division.
* 9	199th Inf. Bde.	18	A.D.C.

* Copies of map sent only to those marked with asterisk.

Secret.

Copy No. 7.

SOUTH AFRICAN INFANTRY BRIGADE.
PRELIMINARY
OPERATION ORDER No. 249.

App 2

1.11.18.

413

Ref. Map:,
57A - 1/40,000

1. At a date and hour to be notified later a major operation will be carried out by the Fourth Army with a view to breaking down the enemy's defences.

2. Objectives alloted to XIII corps and the Inter- corps and Inter-divisional boundaries are shown on the attached map.

The IX Corps will attack on the right of the XIII Corps, and the V Corps on the Left.

3. The attack will be carried out on a three-divn. front, as follows:

1st. Phase (up to GREEN line).
25 Div. on Right
50 Div. in Centre
18 Div. on Left
66 Div. in Corps Reserve

During this phase the 25th. Div. will force the crossing of the canal and operate on the Southern bank up to the GREEN Line, the 50 and 18 Divns. operating North of the canal.

2nd. Phase (up to Final objective)
66 Div. on Right
50 Div. in Centre
18 Div. on Left
25 Div. in Corps Reserve.

During this phase the 66th. Div. will pass through the 25th. Div. and will become the Southern Div. in the Corps. The 50th. Div. will cross the Canal and operate on the Southern bank. The 18th. Div. will continue to operate North of the Canal.

4. DIVISIONAL PLAN OF ATTACK.

(a) 66th. Div. will carry out the attack with 199 Bde. on Right, 198 Bde. on Left, and S.Afr.Bde. in Divl. Reserve.

(b) Inter-Bde. Boundary will be prepared to exploit the high ground in J.2.c.6.6.

(c) S.Afr. Bde. will be prepared to exploit the high ground in J.2.b. and d. J.8.b. and J.3.a. and c. or to seize and hold the high ground in I.21. central, I.28. central, I.30.c.0.0., J.25.c.0.0., J.19.c.5.0. in order to cover the R. flank of the Divn..

(d) Affliated troops:
Each BN. will probably be alloted a section of Field Artillery and a sub-section of Machine-guns..

5. Further instructions will be issued later on Preliminary move, Artillery and MG. arrangements, Communications, Aircraft, etc.

6. ACKNOWLEDGE.

Issued at 11.30 thro' Signals to :
x 1. 1st. S.A.I. x 2. 2.S.A.I.
x 3. 4th. S.A.I. 4. SALTMB&
5. Bde. Signal Officer. 6. 66 Div.
Copy of map sent only those marked. x

(Signed) E. BARLOW.
Major,
Brigade Major,
South Afr. Inf. Bde.

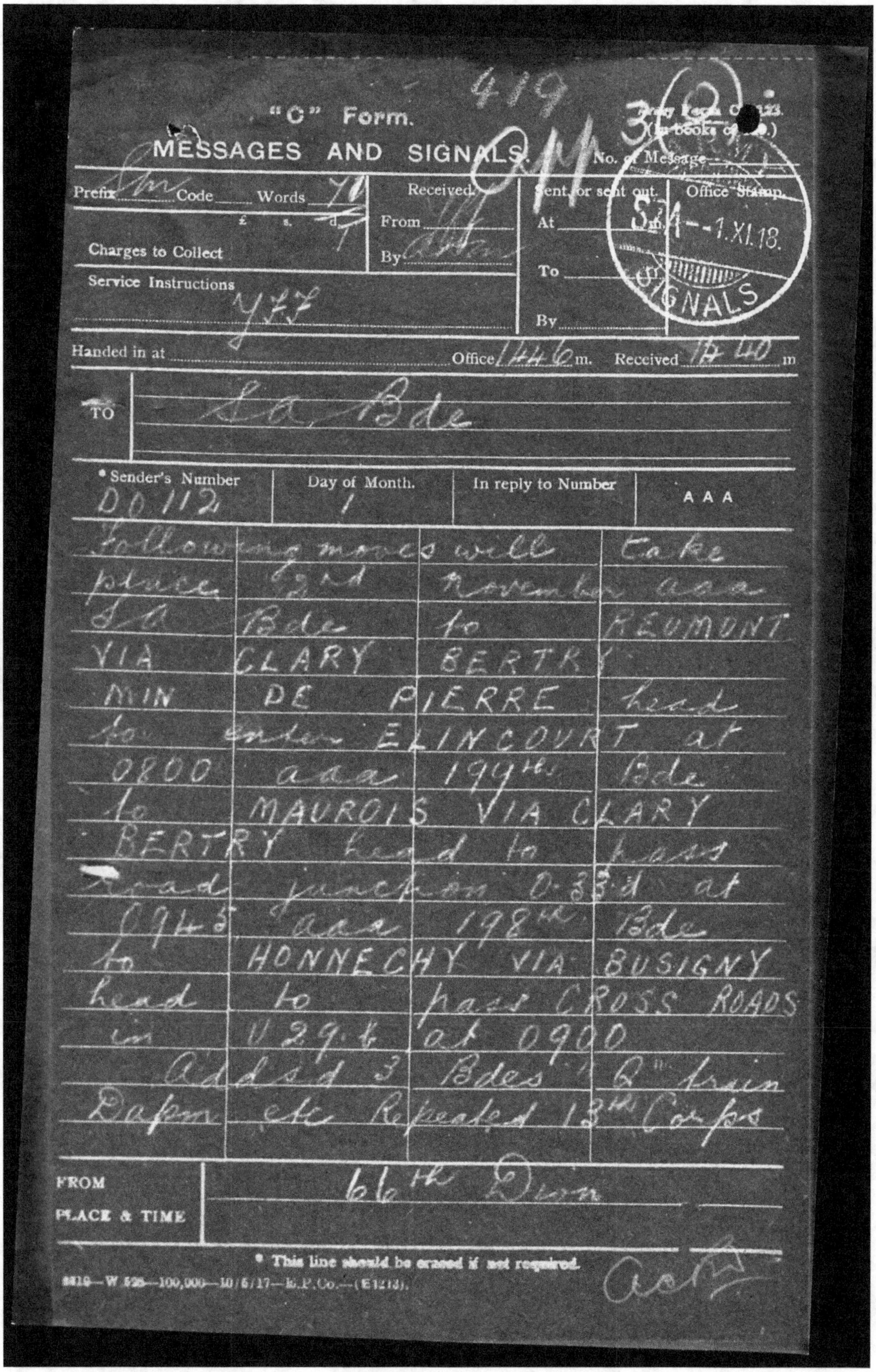
419

"C" Form.
MESSAGES AND SIGNALS.

Army Form C. 2123. (In books of 100.)

No. of Message ___

QM 3

Prefix SM Code ___ Words 70	Received.	Sent, or sent out.	Office Stamp.
£ s. d.	From U/J	At ___ m.	SM - 1.XI.18. SIGNALS
Charges to Collect	By [illegible]	To ___	
Service Instructions Y77		By ___	

Handed in at ___ Office 1446 m. Received 1440 m.

TO Sa Bde

* Sender's Number	Day of Month.	In reply to Number	AAA
DO 112	1		

Following moves will take place 2nd November aaa SA Bde to REUMONT VIA CLARY BERTRY MIN DE PIERRE head to enter ELINCOURT at 0800 aaa 199th Bde to MAUROIS VIA CLARY BERTRY head to pass road junction O.33.d at 0945 aaa 198th Bde to HONNECHY VIA BUSIGNY head to pass CROSS ROADS in V 29.b at 0900 Added 3 Bdes "Q" train Dafm etc Repeated 13th Corps

FROM PLACE & TIME 66th Dvn

* This line should be erased if not required.

8819—W 525—100,000—10/5/17—B.P.Co.—(E1213).

acb

Secret app 4

SOUTH AFRICAN INFANTRY BRIGADE

Map Reference -
Sheet 57B : 1/40,000

ORDER No. 250

Copy No. 17

1-11-18

1. The South Afr. Inf. Bde. will move tomorrow, Nov. 2nd., 1918, to billets in REUMONT, in accordance with the attached March Table.

2. 1st.-Line Transport will accompany Units.

3. Staff Captain to make all billeting and administrative arrangements.

4. Bde. Units will notify Bde. HQ. of location of their HQ. on arrival.

5. Bde. HQ. will close at SERAIN at 09.00, and open at REUMONT on arrival.

6. ACKNOWLEDGE.

[signature]
Major,
Brigade Major,
South Afr. Inf. Bde..

Issued at 18.30 thro' Signals
to - 1. 1st. SAI
2. 2nd. SAI
3. 4th. SAI
4. SALTM Bty.
5. 542 Co., ASC.
6. 66 Divn.
7. Area Comdt., SERAIN
8. do. , REUMONT
9. 198 Inf. Bde.
10. 199 Inf. Bde.
11. Bde. Sig. Officer,
12. Staff Captain,
13. Bde. Major,
14/17. War Diary.

MARCH TABLE

Serial No.	UNIT	Starting Point Place	Starting Point Time	ROUTE	REMARKS
1.	1st. S.A.I.	MILL in U.14.b. central.	07.40	ELINCOURT - CLARY - BERTRY - Mn. DE PIERRE.	Distances as usual. (Fourth Army Standing Order.)
2.	2nd. S.A.I.		08.05		
3.	4th. S.A.I.		08.20		
4.	S.A.L.T.M. Bty.		08.35		
5.	Bde.HQ.& Signal Section.		08.40		

App

"C" Form.

MESSAGES AND SIGNALS.

Army Form C. 2123. (In books of 100.)

No. of Message 56

Prefix ___ Code ___ Words ___	Received	Sent, or sent out.	Office Stamp.
£ s. d.	From	At ___ m.	
Charges to Collect	By	To	
Service Instructions		By	

Handed in at ___ Office ___ m. Received ___ m.

TO La Bde

*Sender's Number	Day of Month	In reply to Number	AAA
G 113	2nd		

Following moves to LE CATEAU will take place 3rd Nov. 198 Bde VIA HONNECHY STATION and QLC aaa 199 Bde VIA REUMONT aaa Heads of column to enter LE CATEAU at 1700 aaa Div HQrs will close at SERAIN and open at LE CATEAU STATION BUILDINGS Q.10 b 5.5 at 1700 aaa ack

done

FROM 66th Division

PLACE & TIME

* This line should be erased if not required.

"C" Form. 415 Army Form C. 2123
(In books of 100.)

MESSAGES AND SIGNALS. App 6(a) No. of Message

Prefix SM Code 2315 Words 77	Received From 447 By ...	Sent, or sent out. At ... To ... By ...	Office Stamp. 4 XI 18 SIGNALS
Charges to Collect			
Service Instructions By DR			

Handed in at 447 Office 2315 m. Received 2315 m.

TO SA Bde.

* Sender's Number	Day of Month	In reply to Number	AAA
G 173	3		

Following moves will take place Nov. 4th aaa 100 Bn. MGC to concentrate in POMMEREUIL by 12 noon aaa 198th Brigade to POMMEREUIL head of column to enter POMMEREUIL at 12 noon aaa SA Brigade to LE CATEAU by 1300 not to enter before 11 00 aaa Accomodation in POMMEREUIL to be arranged by 66th Div Q aaa addsd SA 198th Bdes and 100th Bn MGC to acknowledge aaa Reptd all concerned

FROM 66th Div

PLACE & TIME 2330

* This line should be erased if not required.

Army Form C. 2121
(In pads of 100.)

"A" Form
MESSAGES AND SIGNALS.

App 1

No. of Message..........

Prefix..........Code..........m. Office of Origin and Service Instructions	Words / Charge. Sent At ....m. To By	This message is on a/c of: ....Service. 417 (Signature of "Franking Officer")	Recd. at......m. Date...... From ...... By......

TO			
	1st S A I	SALTMB	66 Div.
	2nd S A I	Bde Sig Off	
	4th S A I	542 Coy ASC	

Sender's Number.	Day of Month.	In reply to Number.	AAA
BO 251	4		

S. African Bde will move today to LE CATEAU in following order 2nd SAI 10 am 4th SAI 10.12 am 1st SAI 10.24 am SALTMB 10.36 am Bde HQ and Signals 10.40 am Starting point Road East edge of REUMONT P.18.a.3.9. AAA First line transport with units aaa Addsd all concerned repts 66. Div. aaa Acknowledge

From S A Bde
Place
Time 02.30

The above may be forwarded as now corrected. (Z) (Sgd) E Barlow Major

Censor. Signature of Addressor or person authorised to telegraph in his name

* This line should be erased if not required. Bde Major.

Order No. 1625. Wt. W3253/ 511. 27/2 H. & K., Ltd. (E. 2634)

"A" Form. Army Form C. 2121.
(In pads of 100.)

MESSAGES AND SIGNALS. No. of Message............

Prefix.........Code..........m.	Words.	Charge.	This message is on a/c of:	Recd. at..........m.
Office of Origin and Service Instructions.	Sent At..........m. To.......... By..........		App 4A (0) ....Service. (Signature of "Franking Officer.")	Date.......... From.......... By 418

TO ~~198 Bde~~ 199 Bde S A Bde — ~~CRA~~ CRE Q — ~~Signals~~ 25 Division ~~50 Division~~ — ~~33 Div~~ 13 Corps APM BA?

Sender's Number.	Day of Month.	In reply to Number.	AAA
100 Bn M G C / CB 124	4th		

Following moves will take place Novemb 5th aaa 198 Bde to valley G 9a and c via L 29a 34 L 18a 88 G 8d central AAA To clear POMMEREUIL by ~~0945~~ aaa 199 Bde to ~~G~~ Valley G 14 c G 20a via POMMEREUIL and G 20 c 51 AAA To enter POMMEREUIL at 0845 AAA SA Bde to POMMEREUIL ~~at~~ leaving Le CATEAU 0930 aaa Affiliated Fd Coys ~~[illegible]~~ ~~[illegible]~~ to join respective Brigades in time to march at tails of Columns aaa 100th Bn M Gun less Coys which have been attached to 18th & 25th Division will accompany

From 199th Bde to G 14 c & G 20a & will march
Place under their orders.
Time

The above may be forwarded as now corrected. (Z)
Censor. Signature of Addressor or person authorised to telegraph in his name.

* This line should be erased if not required.

(3796.) Wt. W492/M1647. 650,000 Pads. 5/17. H. W. & V., Ld. (E. 1167.)

"O" Form. 420 Army Form C. 2121. (In books of 100.)

MESSAGES AND SIGNALS.

No. of Message

Prefix SM Code ___ Words 72	Received From VFF By [illegible]	Sent, or sent out. At 8.9 To By	Office Stamp. SIGNALS
Charges to Collect £ s. d.			
Service Instructions	[illegible]		

Handed in at VFF Office 00[illegible] m. Received 0030 m.

TO SA Bde

* Sender's Number	Day of Month.	In reply to Number	AAA
G B127	4		
[illegible]	RH	Corps	[illegible]
Ho 10	Series	D	please
detail	one	troop	to
report	at	1100	Hrs
[illegible]	to	each	of
following	AAA	198	Bde
[illegible]	Valley	G9a	and
[illegible]	AAA	199	Bde
[illegible]	Valley	G14c	and
G20a	AAA	South	African
Bde	in	POMMEREUIL	AAA
Div	troop	to	report
to	GL	[illegible]	[illegible]
Coy	at	HAPPEGARBES	about
G21a 99	at	1200	AAA
12th	Lancers	to	ack
addsd	12th Lancers	Repd 198	199 &

FROM SA Bde & 13th Corps

PLACE & TIME [illegible]

* This line should be erased if not required.

[illegible]—W [illegible]—[illegible]—E.P.Co.—[illegible]

app 9(o)

SECRET.

Copy No 10..

421

66th DIVISION ORDER No. 114.

4th November 1918.

1. SITUATION. (a) 32nd Division were at 18.30 on general line M.22.a. - G.32.central. 14th and 96th Infantry Brigades are continuing operations to gain RED LINE (M.17.central - G.29.central) before 08.00 on November 5th.

(b) 25th Division have 74th Infantry Brigade on line H.25.b.8.2. - H.20.central - H.14.a.2.8. with patrols attempting to seize crossings over PETITE HELPE River. 75th Inf. Bde. form a defensive flank to South along line H.25.b.8.2. - H.29.a.0.0. 7th Inf. Bde. in support with one battalion in RED LINE and 2 battalions about G.16.

(c) 50th Division and 18th Division are on GREEN LINE (B.27.d.7.6. - B.8.central).

2. GENERAL PLAN OF ATTACK. The advance will be continued November 5th at 06.00.

32nd Division will advance with 97th Inf. Bde. to road I.24., I.30., I.36.

25th Division will capture GREEN LINE (H.17.d.7.6. - H.11.d.0.2. - H.4.central - B.27.d.7.3.) with 74th and 7th Inf. Bdes. and will exploit Eastwards if opportunity arises.

50th Division will complete capture of area North of Canal within Divisional boundaries and will make preparations for crossing Canal about B.27.central. 50th Division infantry will not cross Canal until high ground in H.6. - 10.- 11.- and 12. is secured.

66th Division will keep in close touch with 25th Division and will be ready to pass through when ordered.

422

3. DIVISIONAL PLAN OF ATTACK. On capture of GREEN LINE by 25th Division, 66th Division will carry on the pursuit in accordance with instructions laid down in Preliminary Order No. 111 of 31st October. (copy herewith for 32nd Div. and 12 R. Lancers)

By 12.00, November 5th, 198th and 199th Bdes will be concentrated near G.9. and G.14. respectively in accordance with instructions already issued.

Routes of advance forward of these areas will be detailed later, but it is probable that 199th Bde. will advance through LANDRECIES and along LANDRECIES - MAROILLES Road, while 198th Bde will advance by road through G.9., 10., 11., and 12., and cross CANAL by bridge to be constructed by 50th Division at G.13.a.5.5. H

4. OBJECTIVES. In addition to the final objective (BROWN LINE - J.19.a.0.2. - J.2.c.0.0. - D.26.c.5.0.) an intermediate objective (BLUE LINE - Road I.15.c.0.0. to I.3.d.0.0. - thence along GRANDE HELPE Rau to I.2.b.9.9. - thence C.26.d.2.2.) will be made good by 199th and 198th Bdes.

5. LIGHT SIGNALS. Success signals will be employed by attacking troops as follows :-

On arrival at BLUE LINE :- Two RED VEREY Lights fired in quick succession.

" " " BROWN LINE:- Three RED VERY Lights fired in quick successio

6. CONTACT PLANES. Will call for Flares at 16.00 and about dusk.

7. MACHINE GUNS. In addition to the sections allotted to each Inf. Bde., 100th Bn M.G.C. will detail one Company to follow up the advance of 199th Inf. Bde. and to establish itself along the high ground J.17. - I.21., with a view to assisting advance of 32nd Division or forming a defensive flank against counter-attack from S.E.

100th Bn M.G.C. (less above detachments) will be retained in Divisional Reserve and will accompany Adv. D.H.Q.

423

8. **R.E. and PIONEERS.** In addition to repair of roads, and bridging of GRANDE HELPE R^au as already ordered, C.R.E. will arrange for clearing two horse transport tracks to run as follows :-

(a) H.5.central - J.2.central.
(b) H.16.d.2.7. - H.18.central - I.7.d.5.2. - I.17.b.- DOMPIERRE.

9. **COMMUNICATIONS AND HEADQUARTERS.** The Division Axial Line of Communications will runs as follows :-

Adv. D.H.Q. (G.17.) - Fme de CATILLON (H.14.a.1.7.) - H.11.b.4.3. - I.8.b.1.6. - I.5.c.3.6.

Adv. D.H.Q. will move along this line as the advance proceeds.

Headquarters of leading Inf. Bdes will be established successively as follows :-

199th Bde.	198th Bde.
H.14.a.1.7.	H.14.a.1.7.
H.16.b.3.0.	H.4.c.6.3.
H.12.d.3.5.	H.6.c.central.
I.9.b.0.9.	I.2.c.8.3.
I.4.d.5.3.	I.4.d.2.7.

10. ACKNOWLEDGE.

F.P. Nosworthy

Lieut-Colonel,
General Staff,
66th Division.

done 30 5.11.18

DISTRIBUTION.

Copy No.		Copy No.	
1	War Diary.	12	9th Bn Glouc.R.(Pioneers)
2	" "	13	A.D.M.S.
3	File.	14	D.A.P.M.
4	'A' and 'Q'.	15	XIII Corps.
5	Signals.	16	25th Division.
6	C.R.A.	17	50th Division.
7	C.R.E.	18	35th Squad. R.A.F.
8	198th Inf. Bde.	19	4th Tank Bde.
9	199th Inf. Bde.	20	32nd Division.
10	S.African Bde.	21	12th Royal Lancers (thro' 198th Bde.).
11	100th Bn M.G.C.	22	A.D.C.

****

424

APPENDIX 'A' to DIVISION ORDER No. 114.

COMMUNICATIONS.

I. GENERAL.

1. The main Division chain of Communications will run along the line G.17. - H.14.a.1.7. - H.11.b.4.3. - I.8.b.1.6. - I.5.c.3.6.

2. Signal Offices will be established at each of these points to form Divl. Report Centres with Code Calls as follows :-

(a)

G. 17.	J Q R
H.14.a.1.7.	C.T.N.
H.11.b.4.3.	M R L
I.8.b.1.6.	T S N
I.5.c.3.6.	H A T

3. Artillery and Inf. Bde. H.Qrs., and Machine Guns will keep themselves in touch with these offices as necessary, and liaison between all arms will be carried on through this channel.

4. Certain intermediate offices will be closed and moved forward if it is required to extend this chain.

5. Each successive bound of any H.Q. will be laid down beforehand as far as possible and all concerned informed.

6. Messages may be sent in "Clear" and earth return lines used throughout.

II. WIRES.

1. Two cables will be laid, one to each of the successive leading Inf. Bde. HQrs. coming together again at each Divl. Report Centre.

2. One cable detachment will be at the disposal of the C.R.A. for keeping Artillery Bdes in touch with the axis of communications.

3. No other lines except Artillery wires will be laid until troops are on their final objectives.

425

III WIRELESS.

1. Spark Wireless Sets will be established at the following offices :-

J Q R
M R L
T S N
H M T

2. Loop wireless sets will be established connecting each Bde. Hqrs. to its Report Centre.

3. Continuous wave wireless and Power Buzzers will not be employed.

4. Accumulators will be recharged at Adv. Div. H.Q.

IV VISUAL.

1. The country is unsuitable for visual communication.

2. Where possible Infantry Coys will keep in touch with Bn H.Q. and the latter with Bde. Report Centres by lamp and shutter.

V DESPATCH CARRIERS.

1. Motor cyclists.

One will remain with Div. H.Q. rear echelon, one with each Inf. Bde. and two with C.R.A. Two will be sent to each Divl. Report Centre.

The remainder will move with Adv. Div. H.Q.

2. Push cyclists.

These will be used as possible by Brigades, none are available for the Divisional chain.

3. Mounted Orderlies.

Each Bn will have two, one found from the unit and one attached from the Divl. Train.

Each Brigade will have six, four found within the formation and two attached from the Cavalry Signal Troop.

Each Divl. Report Centre will have two, detailed from the Signal Troop.

The remainder will be retained for use at Adv. Div.H.Q.

4. Runners.

Runners will be held at Artillery Bde, Infantry Bdo, Battery and Bn H.Q. as required, the Artillery and Machine Guns providing their own runners.

426

V 5. All units keeping touch with the Divl. Report Centres will send two runners to remain at that Signal Office with which they are keeping touch at the time.

VI AEROPLANES. 1. The Divl. Dropping Station will be near C T N at H.8.c.8.1.

2. Both contact and counter-attack aeroplanes will be prepared to accept messages by Popham Panel, these will be immediately dropped at the Divisional Dropping Ground.

Lieut-Colonel,
General Staff,
66th Division.

D.H.Q.,
4.11.18.

DISTRIBUTION.

198th Inf.Bde.	(2)	C.R.E.	(2)
199th " "	(2)	"G".	(2)
S. A. Bde.	(2)	XIII Corps.	(1)
Signals.	(6)	25th Divn.	(1)
C.R.A.	(8)	32nd Divn.	(1)
		50th Divn.	(1)

****

app 9(o)

66th Divn.

427

Amendment No. 1. to 66th Division Order

No. 114.

No. 9 :-

Headquarters of 199th Bde. will be amended to read as follows :-

(a) H.14.a.3.8. (FERME DE CATILLON).
(b) H.16.b.3.0. (MAROILLES).
(c) H.12.d.3.5. (VALLEZ).
(d) I.8.b.3.8. (House, western entrance of TAISNIERES).
(e) I.12.a.9.9. (Chateau).

In each case the advance report centre will be one bound in advance of Bde. H.Q.

Lieut-Colonel,
General Staff,
66th Division.

D. H. Q.
5.11.18.

Copies to :-

Signals.
C.R.A.
C.R.E.
198th Inf. Bde.
199th Inf. Bde.
S. African Bde.
100th Bn. M.G.C.
9th Bn. Glouc. R.
35th Squad. R.A.F.

SOUTH AFRICAN INFANTRY BRIGADE Secret. 428

BRIGADE ORDER No. 255. CopyNo.
5.11.18.

---

1. Situation: (a) The 32nd. Div. were at 18.30. 4Nov. on general line M.22.a. - G.32. central. 14th. and 96th. INF. Bdes. are continuing operations to gain RED LINE (N.17. central) before 08.00 to-day.
(b) The 25th.Div. have 74th. Inf. Bde. on line H.25.b.8.2. - H.20.central - H.14.a.2.8. with patrols attempting to seize crossings over PETITE HELPE river. 75th. Inf. Bde. form a defensive flank to South along line H.25.b.2.2. - H.29.a.0.0.7th. Inf. Bde. in support with one BN. in RED LINE and 2 BNs. about G.16..
(c) 50th. Div. and 18th. Div. are on GREEN LINE (B.27.d.5. - B.8.central.)

2. GENERAL PLAN OF ATTACK.
The advance continued at 06.00 to-day.
32nd. Div. will advance with 97th. Inf. Bde. to road I.24., I.30., I.36.,
25th. Div. will capture GREEN LINE (H.17.d.7.a. - H.11.d.0.2. H.4.central - B.27.d.7.3.) with 74 and 7 Inf. Bdes. and will exploit Eastwards if opportunity arises.
50th. Div. will complete capture of area N. of canal within Divl. boundaries, and will make preparations for crossing canal about B.27.central. 50th. Div. Infabtry will not cross canal until high ground in H.6. - 10. 11. and 12. is secured.
66th. Div. will keep in close touch with 25th. Div., and will be ready to pass through when ordered.

3. DIVL. PLAN OF ATTACK.
On capture of GREEN LINE by 25th. Div., 66th. Div. will carry on the pursuit in accordance with instructions laid down in Prelmn. Order 111 of Oct. 31st..

4. OBJECTIVES.
In addition to the final objective (BROWN LINE) J.19.a.0.2. J.2.c.0.0. D.26.c.5.0.) and Intermediate objectives (BLUE LINE, Road. I.15.c.0.0. to I.3.d.0.0.- thence along GRANDE HELPE Rau to I.1.b.9.9.- thence C.26.d.2.2.) will be made good by 199 and 198Bdes.

5. LIGHT SIGNALS.
Success signals will be employed by attacking troops as follows:
On arrival at BLUE LINE - Two RED Very lights fired in quick succession.
do. BROWN LINE- Three RED Very lights fired in quick succession.

6. R.E. AND POINEERS:
In addition to repair of roads and bridging of GRANDE HELPE Rau as already ordered, CRE. will arrange for clearing two horse-transport tracks to run:
(a) H.5.central - J.2.central
(b) H.18.d.2.7. - H.18.central - I.7.d.5.2. - I.17.b. -DOMPEIRRE.

7. COMMUNICATIONS AND HEADQUARTERS;
Divl. Axial line of communications will run as follows; Adv.DHQ. (G.17.) - Fme. de CATALION (H.14.a.1.7.) H.11.b.4.3. I.8.b.1.6. I.5.c.3.6.
Adv. DHQ. will move along this line as the advance proceeds.

8. ACKNOWLEDGE.
Issued through signals at 07.00 to
1. 1st.SAI 2. 2nd.SAI
3. 4th.SAI 4. SALTMB. B.S.Off.

Major,
Brigade Major,
South Afr.Bde.

Amendment to Order No.255. of to- day.
In para 3 for Prelmn. Order. 111
Read Prelmn. Order No. 249.

429

App. 12

:Copy of Telegram:

Addsd. Recipients Bde. Order 255 aaa BO.255/1 5

Amendment to B.O. 255 of today aaa In para. 3 for Prelim. Order 111 read Prelim. Order 249

S.A. Bde.. (sd) E. BARLOW,
Major,
Bde. Major.

430

S E C R E T. Copy No. 11

app 12(0)

66th DIVISION ORDER No. 115.

5th November 1918.

1. On ~~October~~ November 6th 32nd Division, 25th Division and 50th Division are continuing the advance with present boundaries continued Eastwards and objectives main MAUBEUGE - AVESNES Road.

2. If the advance continues successfully 66th Division will move as under with a view to concentrating in area MAROILLES - TAISNIERES - MARBAIX.

   (a) S.A. Bde Group including 9th Glouc. R. and portion of 100th Bn M.G.C., now at POMMEREUIL, to LANDRECIES. To be prepared to move ~~after~~ from 10.00.

   (b) 198th Bde Group to TAISNIERES. To be prepared to move from 12.00.

   (c) 199th Bde Group to MARBAIX. To be prepared to move from 12.00.

   (d) Advanced D.H.Q. to MAROILLES. Rear D.H.Q. will be established in LANDRECIES by 12.00.

   Note.- Brigade Groups will include attached Artillery.

3. The Squadron of 12th Lancers at present attached to 66th Division will concentrate ~~at~~ by 08.00 at Fme du CATILLON (H.14.a.). O.C. Squadron will get into touch forthwith with O.C. 12th Lancers with a view to rejoining Regiment.

4. ACKNOWLEDGE.

Done

Lieut-Colonel,
General Staff,
66th Division.

DISTRIBUTION.

Copy No 1.	War Diary.	12	9th Glouc. R. (Pioneers).
2	" "	13	Train A.S.C.
3	File.	14	A.D.M.S.
4	'A' and 'Q'.	15	D.A.P.M.
5	Signals.	16	XIII Corps.
6	C.R.A.	17	A.P.M. XIII Corps.
7	C.R.E.	18	25th Division.
8	198th Inf. Bde.	19	50th Division.
9	199th Inf. Bde.	20	32nd Division.
10	S. A. Bde.	21	2nd Tank Bde.
11	100th Bn M.G.C.	22	Squad. 12th Lancers.
		23.	A.D.C.

431

"A" Form.

MESSAGES AND SIGNALS.

Army Form C. 2121.
(In pads of 100.)

No. of Message ......

Prefix ...... Code ...... m	Words. Charge.	This message is on a/c of:	Recd. at ...... m
Office of Origin and Service Instructions.	Sent At ...... m. To ...... By	Service. App 14 (0) (Signature of "Franking Officer.")	Date ...... From ...... By ......

TO { SABde

Sender's Number.	Day of Month.	In reply to Number.	AAA
* GB77	6th		

SABde Group will move up to LANDRECIES immediately & will be billetted East of the Canal aaa 9th Glosters & [illegible] 2 Coys of 100th Bn M.G. Corps will march under your orders aaa Acknowledge.

From 66th Div

Place

Time 13.45

The above may be forwarded as now corrected. (Z) [signature] Lt Col

Censor. Signature of Addressor or person authorised to telegraph in his name.

* This line should be erased if not required.

(3198.) Wt. W 12952/M1294. 375,000 Pads. 1/17. H. W. & V., Ld. (E. 818.)

Secret.

432

SOUTH AFRICAN BRIGADE
ORDER No. 25[illegible]

Ref. Map-
Sheets 57A and 57B- 1/40,000

Copy No.
6.11.18. App 15

1. The S.Afr. Bde. Group will move by March Route this afternoon to LANDRECIES, and will be billeted E. of the Canal.

2. Starting point - Road Junction in L.27.c.9.8. Order of March -

Bde. HQ. and Signal Section	-	16.00
1st. SAI	-	16.05
2nd. SAI	-	16.20
4th. SAI	-	16.35
SALTMB.		16.48
9th. Gloucesters	-	17.05
Two coys. 100 MG.BN.	-	17.20

3. 1st. Line Transport will march with Units.

4. Billeting parties will report forthwith to Staff Captain at the Church at LANDRECIES.

5. Units will report Location of their HQ. to this Office immediately on arrival.

6. Bde. HQ. will close at POMMEREUIL at 16.00 and open at LANDRECIES. on arrival.

7. ACKNOWLEDGE.

(Signed) E.BARLOW.

Issued through Signals at 15.10

Major,
Brigade Major,
South Afr. Inf. Bde.

App 16(a)

S E C R E T.

Copy No 10

433
END

66TH DIVISION ORDER NO. 117.

6th November 1918.

1. The present line (18.30) appears to be MARBAIX - TAISNIERES (both inclusive) thence road through G.22. central to railway crossing G.24.c - thence approximately due North.

2. 25th Division are continuing the advance with final objectives MAUBEUGE - AVESNES Road from J.12.d.5.0 to D.30.c.2.4.

3. It is improbable that the 66th Division will be used tomorrow November 7th, but in the eventuality of its being ordered to pass through 25th Division and take up the pursuit the Division will advance on a two Brigade front with 199th Brigade on right and 198th Brigade on left. Divisional and inter-Brigade boundaries as before produced eastwards.

4. Field Companies R.E. at present attached to 198th and 199th Infantry Brigade s (less 1 section from each Field Company) will revert to disposal of C.R.E. from 06.00 November 7th.

5. Brigades and C.R.E. to acknowledge.

Lieut Colonel.
Generl Staff, 66th Division.

DISTRIBUTION.

No. 1	War Diary.	Copy No. 11	100th M.G.C.
2	" "	12	9th Bn. Glouc. R.
3	File.	13	Train A.S.C.
4	A. & Q.	14	A.D.M.S.
5	Signals.	15	D.A.P.M.
6	C.R.A.	16	XIII Corps.
7	C.R.E.	17	25th Division.
8	198th Bde.	18	50th Division.
9	199th Bde.	19	32nd Division.
10	S.A. Bde.	20	A.D.C.

appx 21 (o)
351

SECRET.

Copy No. 10

66TH DIVISION ORDER NO. 116.

1. **SITUATION.** According to last reports received 19.15 our line now runs from cross roads on Southern Corps boundary J.21.b.5.5 – J.16.central – J.10.central – J.5 central – D.29.d.0.0 with an advanced post established East of the River in J.16.d.
The enemy is occupying the East bank of stream in advance of that line.

2. **INTENTION.** The 66th Division will continue the pursuit tomorrow November 8th at 07.30 with the utmost vigour.
199th Brigade will be on the right and 198th Brigade on the left. Divisional and inter-Brigade boundaries as shewn on attached map.*
32nd Division (97th Brigade) are advancing on the right.
50th Division (150th Brigade) are advancing on the left.
12th Lancers are operating in advance covering the Corps front.

3. **OBJECTIVES.** The Divisional objective will be the general line K.16.a.5.0., K.4.d.8.0., E.25.c.0.1.
On securing this line Infantry patrols will clear the ground 500 yards East of objective whilst Cavalry will ascertain whether FELLERIES and BEUGNIES are held by the enemy or not.
Liaison posts will be established with 50th Division on the North side of the stream at E.28.b.1.5.

4. **ARTILLERY.** In addition to the Batteries at present attached for the close support of Infantry Brigades, 112th Brigade R.F.A. (H.Q. J.7.a.9.2.) will support the advance of 199th Brigade;
150th Brigade R.F.A. (H.Q. J.7.a.8.2.) will support the advance of the 198th Brigade.
C.R.A. will arrange for two 60 Pdr guns to enfilade the SARS POTERIES-SOIRE le CHATEAU Road east of the final objective with bursts of fire during the night and from Zero onwards.
The 6" How. Battery attached to the Division will stand by in Divisional reserve.

352

(2)

5. MACHINE GUNS. The Coys of 25th BN. M.G.C. at present affiliated to leading Brigades of the 25th Division will remain affiliated to the 198th and 199th Brigades and will co-operate in the advance under their orders.
O.C. 100th Bn. M.G.C. will detail 2 Coys to move from NOYELLES at 07.30 to secure the Divisional objective when captured. Details to be arranged by O.C. Coys direct with Brigadiers concerned.
On arrival of these 2 Coys of 100th Bn. M.G.C. the Coys of 25th Bn. M.G.C. will be withdrawn to MARBAIX.
H.Q. 100th Bn. M.G.C. with remaining Company will move to DOMPIERRE in Divisional reserve.

6. S.A.BRIGADE. S.A. Brigade Group will remain in Divisional Reserve and will move at 08.00 on DOMPIERRE.

7. R.Es and PIONEERS. (a) 1 Section R.E. is allotted to each of 198th and 199th Brigades; remainder of Field Coys R.E. will be employed under C.R.E. on repair of roads and bridges.

(b) 9th Bn. Glouc. R. (Pioneer Bn.) will move to DOMPIERRE starting at 07.30 and will construct a cross country track to link up the road junction E.25.d.9.2 through J.5 and 6 to road in J.4.d. Work to be done from east to west.

8. COMMUNICATIONS. (a) Divisional axial line of communication will be the grid line from J.1.d.0.0 to K.5.c.0.0. Brigades will select their Headquarters and Report Centres as near as possible to this line.

(b) C.R.A. will arrange for 1 mounted R.A. Officer and 2 mounted R.A. orderlies to report to each of 198th Brigade and 199th Brigade by 07.30 for liaison purposes.

MESSAGES AND SIGNALS. No. of Message ....

Prefix ...... Code ...... m.	Words	Charge	This message is on a/c of	Recd. at ...... m.
Office of Origin and Service Instructions	Sent		O.H.M.S. Service.	Date
	At ...... m.			From
	To			By 373
	By		(Signature of "Franking Officer.")	

TO S A Bde

Sender's Number.	Day of Month.	In reply to Number.	AAA
G 6208	7		

Re BO 118 para 10 for LA CROISETTE J.15.c read LA TUILERIE J.10.a.5.4

From 66 Bde
Place
Time 2350

The above may be forwarded as now corrected. (Z)

Censor. (Sgd.) J Monmouth Capt.
Signature of Addressor or person authorised to telegraph in his name.

* This line should be erased if not required.

Order No 1625. Wt. W3253/ P 511 27/2 H. & K., Ltd. (E. 2634)

387

"A" Form
MESSAGES AND SIGNALS.

Army Form C. 2121 (In pads of 100.)

No. of Message ....

Prefix .... Code .... m.	Words	Charge	This message is on a/c of:	Recd. at ......m.
Office of Origin and Service Instructions	Sent		App 10	Date ....
Copy	At .... m.		..........Service.	From ....
	To			By ....
	By		(Signature of "Franking Officer")	

TO
1st SAI | Bde Sig Off.
2nd SAI | SALTMB.
4th SAI. | 542 Coy ASC.

Sender's Number.	Day of Month.	In reply to Number.	AAA
BO. 252	5.		

SA Bde moves to POMMEREUIL today. Order of march Bde HQ and Signal Coy 09.30 SALTMB 09.35 4th SAI 09.40 1st SAI 10.02 2nd SAI 10.14 Starting point Cross Roads in K.35.c.2.5. AAA. Transport to move with Units AAA Billeting parties to meet Staff Captain at Area Comdt. POMMEREUIL at 10.00 AAA. B teams are to be left at LE CATEAU Billets will be notified later. aaa Acknowledge.

From S. A. Bde
Place
Time

The above may be forwarded as now corrected. (Z)

(Sgd) E Barlow Major Bde Major.

Censor. Signature of Addressor or person authorised to telegraph in his name

* This line should be erased if not required.

Order No. 1625. Wt. W3253/ P 511. 27/2 H. & K.. Ltd. (E. 2634)

388

"C" Form.

Army Form C. 2123. (In books of 100.)

MESSAGES AND SIGNALS.

No. of Message ___

Prefix ___ Code ___ Words 46	Received.	Sent, or sent out.	Office Stamp.
£ s. d.	From [illegible]	At ___ m.	[illegible]
Charges to Collect	By [illegible]	To ___	5/11/18
Service Instructions		By ___	

Handed in at [illegible] Office [illegible] m. Received [illegible] m.

TO: 66 Bde

*Sender's Number	Day of Month.	In reply to Number	AAA
G.13 128	5		

Following	moves	will take	place
aaa	[illegible]	[illegible]	199
Bde	group	to	LANDRECIES
aaa	198	Bde	group
to	FAUBOURG	SOYERS	and
LES	ETOQUIES	aaa	Adv
Div	HQ	to	[illegible]
opens	at	1500	aaa
Standard	precautions	to be	
taken	to	keep	roads
clear.			

[illegible signature]

FROM: 66 Div
PLACE & TIME

* This line should be erased if not required.

[illegible printer's line] E. P. Co.

"A" Form

Army Form C. 2121
(In pads of 100.)

MESSAGES AND SIGNALS.

No. of Message..........

Prefix.......Code.......m. Office of Origin and Service Instructions	Words / Charge. Sent At ......m. To ...... By	This message is on a/c of: ......Service. (Signature of "Franking Officer")	Recd. at ......m. Date ...... From ...... By 368
		app 1(o)	

TO { 198 } Bdes / 199 } / SA } — Rear HQ

Sender's Number.	Day of Month.	In reply to Number.	AAA
G.199	7.		

Bde groups will move at 1400 as follows AAA. 199 Bde MAROILLES to MARBAIX AAA 198 Bde BASSE NOYELLES to DOMPIERRE AAA SA Bde LANDRECIES to BASSE NOYELLES AAA Pioneers and Fld Coys concentrate in TANNIERES AAA DHQ TANNIERES ~~[illegible]~~ AAA. Rear DHQ will be prepared to move to TANNIERES 0800 Nov. 8th. AAA
ACK

From

Place

Time 1245.

The above may be forwarded as now corrected. (Z) [illegible signature] Capt.

Censor. Signature of Addressor or person authorised to telegraph in his name

* This line should be erased if not required.

66 D.W.

Order No. 1625 Wt. W3253/ P 511. 27/2 H. & K., Ltd. (E. 2634).

"A" Form
MESSAGES AND SIGNALS.

Army Form C. 2121
(In pads of 100.)

No. of Message..........

Prefix.......... Code.......... m. | Words | Charge.
Office of Origin and Service Instructions

Copy

Sent
At..........m.
To..........
By..........

This message is on a/c of:
App 18
..........Service.
(Signature of "Franking Officer")

Recd. at.....m.
Date..........
From 367
By..........

TO			
	1st SAI	SALTMB	C Coy 100 M G Bn
	2nd SAI	Bde Sig Off	
	4th SAI	MG Sec	

Sender's Number.	Day of Month.	In reply to Number.	AAA
BO 257	7		

SA Bde Group will move to BASSENOYELLES this afternoon AAA Order of march Bde HQ and Signal Sec 14·15 2nd S.A.I. 14·20 4th SAI 14·32 1st SAI 14·44 SALTMB 15·10 MG Sec 15·20 AAA Starting point Road Junction G·23.d 1.8. AAA Billeting parties to report to Staff Captain forthwith at Church BASSENOYELLES AAA First line transport march with units Completion of moves to be reported on arrival.

From SA Bde
Place
Time

The above may be forwarded as now corrected. (Z)

(Sgd) E Barlow
Major

Censor. Signature of Addressor or person authorised to telegraph in his name

* This line should be erased if not required.

Bde Major

Order No. 1625. Wt. W3253/ P 511. 27/2 H. & K. Ltd. (E. 2634)

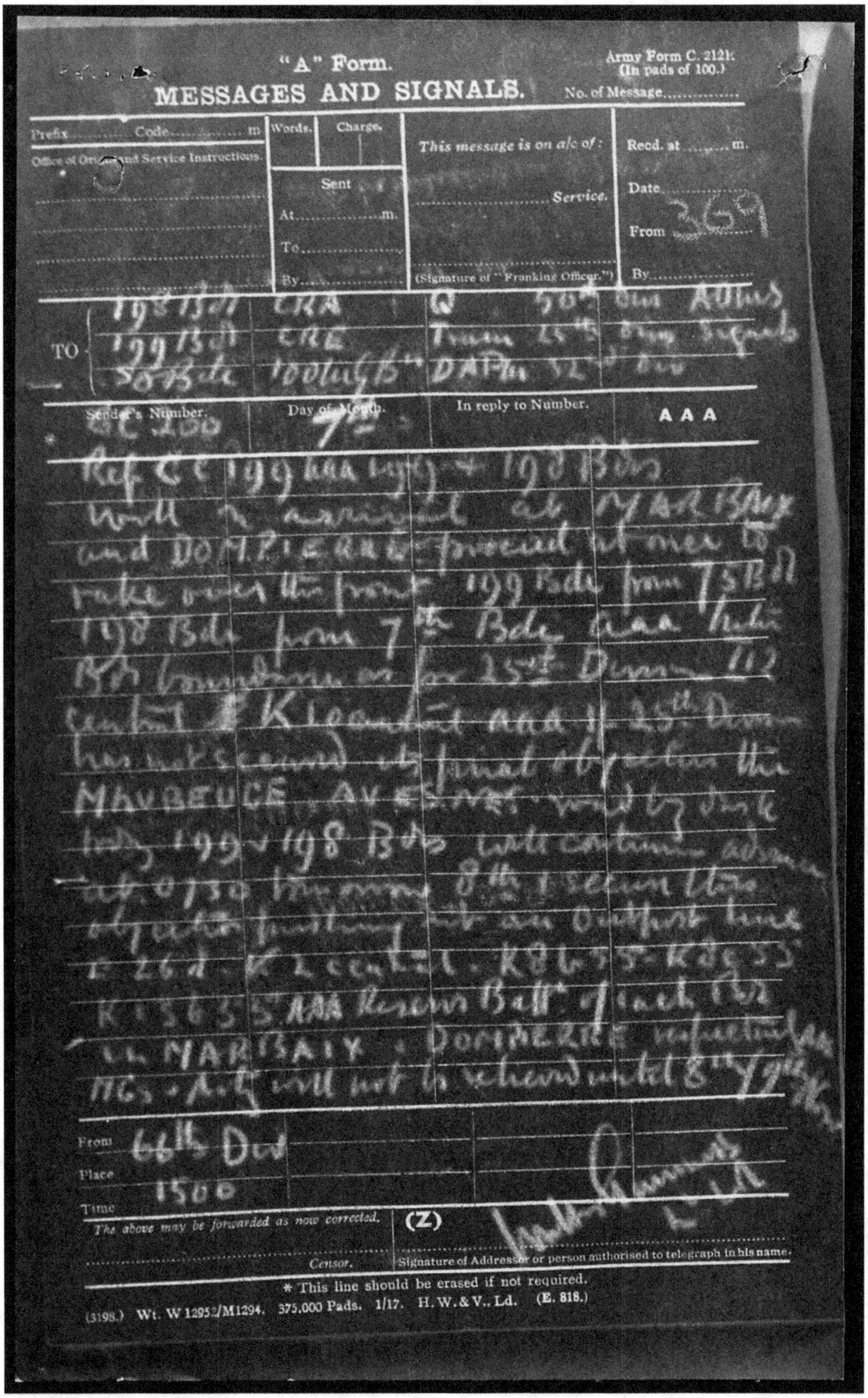
"A" Form.

MESSAGES AND SIGNALS.

Army Form C. 2121.
(In pads of 100.)

No. of Message..............

Prefix...... Code...... m	Words.	Charge.	This message is on a/c of:	Recd. at ...... m.
Office of Origin and Service Instructions.	Sent		...... Service.	Date
	At...... m.			From 369
	To......			
	By......		(Signature of "Franking Officer.")	By......

TO: 198 Bde, CRA, Q, 50th Div Arty; 199 Bde, CRE, Train, 25th Div Signals; 50 Bde, 100 [illegible] Bn, DAPM, 52nd Div

Sender's Number.	Day of Month.	In reply to Number.	AAA
GC 200	7th		

Ref CC 199 aaa 199 + 198 Bdes will on arrival at MARBAIX and DOMPIERRE proceed at once to take over the front 199 Bde from 75 Bde 198 Bde from 7th Bde aaa Inter Bde boundaries as for 25th Divn 112 central K10 central aaa If 25th Divn has not secured its final objective the MAUBEUGE – AVESNES road by dusk today 199 + 198 Bdes will continue advance at 0730 tomorrow 8th + secure this objective pushing out an Outpost line E26d – K2 central – K8655 – K8655 – K1565 aaa Reserve Battn of each Bde in MARBAIX + DOMPIERRE respectively aaa MGs + Arty will not be relieved until 8th [illegible]

From 66th Div
Place
Time 1500

The above may be forwarded as now corrected. (Z)

Censor. Signature of Addressor or person authorised to telegraph in his name.

* This line should be erased if not required.

(3198.) Wt. W 12952/M1294. 375,000 Pads. 1/17. H. W. & V., Ld. (E. 818.)

"A" Form. Army Form C. 2121. (In pads of 100.)

MESSAGES AND SIGNALS.

371 No. of Message

Prefix .... Code .... m. | Words | Charge

Office of Origin and Service Instructions.

Sent At .... m. To .... By ....

This message is on a/c of: .... Service. app

(Signature of "Franking Officer.")

Recd. at .... m. Date 19(U) From .... By ....

TO { ~~198th Bde~~ ~~199th Bde~~ S.A. Bde } Q Train

Sender's Number.	Day of Month.	In reply to Number.	AAA
* GB91	7th		

Reference GC200 of today owing to continuing of advance tomorrow orders for Reserve Battalions (of 198th 199th Bdes) to go to MARBAIX and DOMPIERRE is cancelled

From 66th Div

Place

Time 1950

The above may be forwarded as now corrected. (Z)

Censor. Signature of Addressor or person authorised to telegraph in his name. [illegible] Lt Col

* This line should be erased if not required.

(3796.) Wt. W 492/M1647. 650,000 Pads. 5/17. H.W. & V., Ld. (E. 1187.)

"C" FORM.
MESSAGES AND SIGNALS.

Army Form C. 2123.
(In books of 100.)

No. of Message

Prefix ... Code 2015 Words 46 | Received. From ... By ... | Sent, or sent out. At ... m. To ... By ... | Office Stamp. TELEGRAPHS 372

£ s. d.

Charges to Collect

Service Instructions

Handed in at YFF Office 2015 m. Received 2042 m.

TO SA Bde

* Sender's Number.	Day of Month.	In reply to Number.	AAA
GB 90	7		

Ref	GC 200	of	today
Command	of	sector	will
pass	from	GOC	25
Div	to	GOC	66
Div.	at	0001	Nov.
8th	at	which	time
Command	of	artillery	covering
div	front	will	pass
from	CRA	25	Div.
to	CRA	66	Div

FROM 66 Div
PLACE & TIME 1900

* This line should be erased if not required.

(19629) Wt528/M1970. 300,000 Pads. 4/17. McC. & Co., Ltd. (E1213).

370

"A" Form

Army Form C. 2121
(In pads of 100.)

MESSAGES AND SIGNALS.

No. of Message ....

Prefix ..... Code ..... m.	Words	Charge	This message is on a/c of:	Recd. at ......m.
Office of Origin and Service Instructions				Date ....
Copy	Sent At ....m. To .... By		App 2 ....Service. (Signature of "Franking Officer")	From .... By ....

TO		
	1st S A I	S A L T M B
	2nd S A I	Bde Sig Off
	4th S A I	

Sender's Number	Day of Month	In reply to Number	AAA
BS 168	8		

Following received from Division is forwarded for information AAA 199 & 198 Bdes will on arrival at MARBAIX and DOMPIERRE proceed at once to take over the front 199 Bde from 75 Bde 198 Bde from 7 Bde AAA Inter Bde boundaries as for 25th Division 1.12. central K.10. central AAA If 25th Division has not secured its final objective the MAUBEUGE - AVESNES road by dusk today 199 & 198 Bdes will continue advance at 07 30 tomorrow 8th & secure this objective pushing out an outpost line ~~E.4~~ E.26.d. - K.2. central - K.8 b. 5. 5. - K.8.c. 5. 5. - K.13. b. 5. 5.

From S. A. Bde.

Place

Time

The above may be forwarded as now corrected. (Z) Sgd E Barlow Maj

.... Censor. Signature of Addressor or person authorised to telegraph in his name

SECRET

278

Extracts from 66th. Div. Order No. 118

1. Situation: According to last reports received 19.15 our line now runs from cross roads on Southern Corps boundary J.21.b.5.5 - J.16.central - J.10.central - J.5.central - D.29.d.0.0. with an advanced post established East of the river in J.16.d.. The enemy is occupying the E. bank of stream in advance of that line.

2. Intention: The 66th. Div. will continue the pursuit tomorrow Nov. 8th. at 07.30 with the utmost vigour. 198 Bde. will be on the Rt. and 199 Bde. on the left.
Northern Divisional Boundary: D.27.c.0.2. - E.25.a.9.2. - E.28.a.7.5 - E.23.c.0.2..
Southern Divisional Boundary: J.21.b.8.5. - J.18.d.9.1. - K.14d.3.8. - K.14.b.4.1. - K.16.a.4.0.
Inter-Bde. Boundary: Grid line J.3.c.0.0. - K.4.d.8.0..
32nd. Divn. (97 Bde.) are advancing on the right.
50th. Divn. (150 Bde.) are advancing on the left.
12th. Lancers are operating in advance covering the Corps front.

3. Objectives: The Divl. objective will be the general line K.16.a.5.0. - K.4.d.8.0 - E.23.c.0.1..
On securing this line infantry patrols will clear the ground 500x. E. of objective whilst Cavalry will ascertain whether FELLERIES and BEUGNIES are held by the enemy or not.
Liaison posts will be established with 50 Div. on the North side of the stream at E.28.b.1.5..

6. S.A. Brigade: S.A. Bde. Group will remain in Divl. reserve and will move at 08.00 on DOMPIERRE.

7. REs. and Pioneers:
(b) 9th. Glouc. R. (Pioneer BN.) will move to DOMPIERRE, starting at 17.30 and will construct a cross-country track to link up the road junction E.25.d.9.2. through J.5. and 6. to road in J.4.d.. Work to be done from east to west.

8. Communications:
(a) Divl. axial line of communication will be the grid line from J.1.d.0.0. to K.5.c.0.0.. Bdes. will select their HQ. and Report centres as near as possible to this line.

(sd) E. BARLOW,
Major,
Bde. Major,
S. Afr. Inf. Bde..

7th. Nov., '18

[MES]SAGES AND SIGNALS.

No. of Message..........

Prefix.......... Code..........m. Office of Origin and Service Instructions.	Words. Charge. Sent At..........m. To.......... By..........	This message is on a/c of: ....Service. (Signature of "Franking Officer.")	Recd. at..........m. Date.......... From.......... By..........

TO | 2 | 363

* Sender's Number.	Day of Month.	In reply to Number.	AAA
GB124			

above 2 Coys MGC. will stand fast at POMMEREUIL aaa 9th Glouc R to POMMEREUIL following S A Bde aaa Advanced D H Q. will be prepared to move to neighbourhood of G17 after 10.00 aaa Bdes CRE 100 MG Bn Q & Signals W acknowledge

done

From 66th Div
Place
Time

The above may be forwarded as now corrected.
Censor.

(Z) [illegible] Lt Col
Signature of Addressor or person authorised to telegraph in his name.

* This line should be erased if not required.

(3796.) Wt. W 492/M1647. 650,000 Pads. 5/17. H. W. & V., Ld. (E. 1187.)

SIGNALS. No. of Message

App 23 (0)

383

TO [illegible]

Sender's Number.	Day of Month.	In reply to Number.	AAA
Div Order 119	8th		

[illegible]

198 & 199th Bdes will be withdrawn for protection of Division (?) and will continue the attack early tomorrow morning with a view to obtaining objectives as laid down in DO 118 of 7th Nov AAA Objectives of Flank Divisions will be notified later AAA Ack AAA

Addsd 198 & 199th Bdes CRA 100 Bn MG Corps – repeated all concerned

From 66th Div

Place

Time 2000

The above may be forwarded as now corrected. (Z)

Censor. Signature of Addressor or person authorised to telegraph in his name.

* This line should be erased if not required.

(3796.) Wt. W492/M1647. 650,000 Pads. 5/17. H. W. & V., Ld. (E. 1187.)

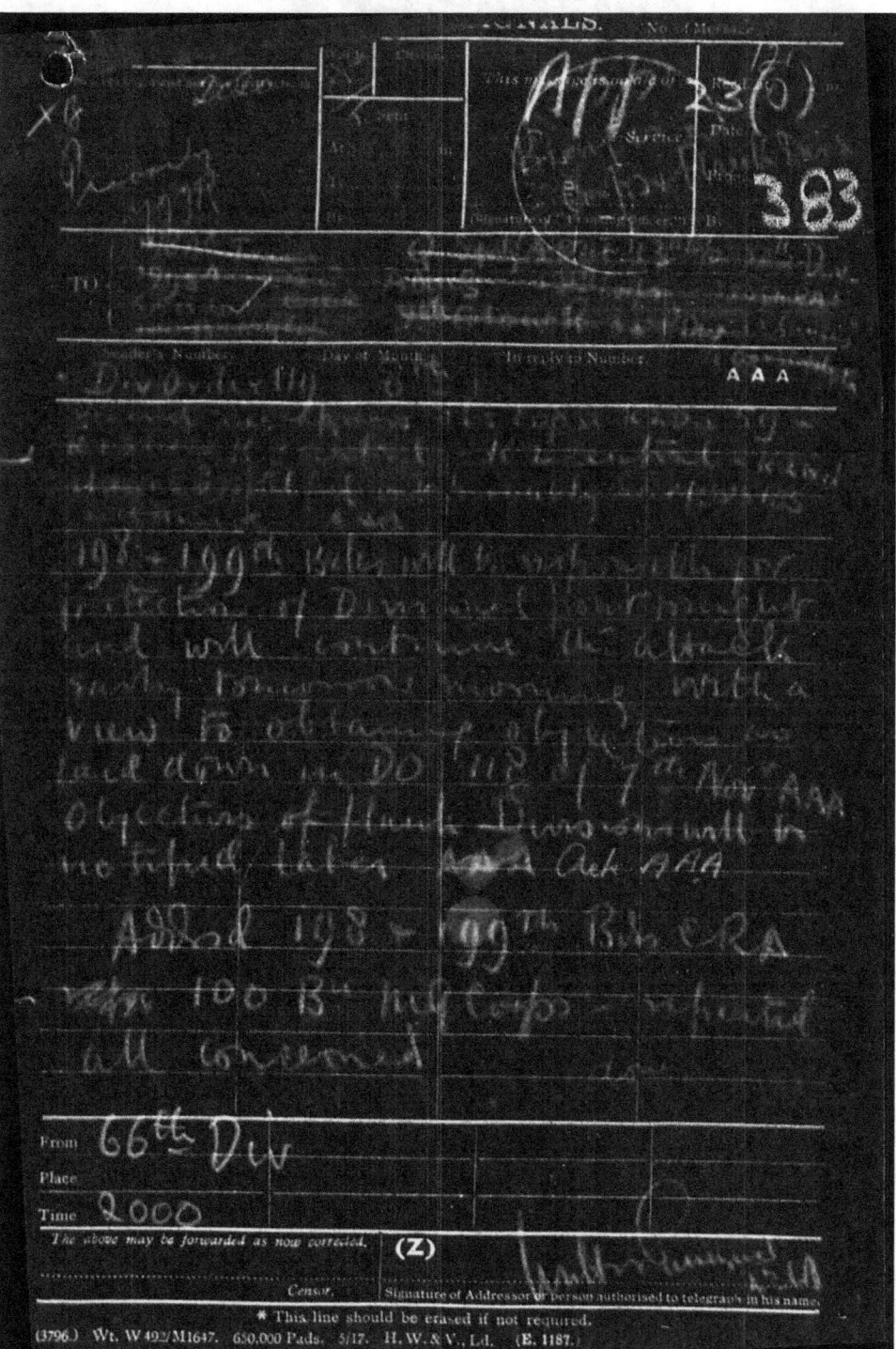

App. 24

Copy of Telegram:

A.1 to BO.259 9

Amend starting point to read road junction in J.7.a.5.9. and Route to read road junctn. in J.2.a.2.5. LA TUILERIE thence 2nd. class road K.6.c.4.5. thence if road finished by engineers from LA CENSE FOTELLE FME. LA JONQUIERE destination BEUGNIES aaa St_rting time one hour later.

S.A. Bde.

(sd) E. BARLOW
Major,
Bde. Major.

Copy of telegram.   App. 24.

1st S.A.I.   S.A.L.T.M.B.   Lt. JOHNSTON.
2nd S.A.I.   Bde. Sig. Off.
4th S.A.I.   Section 100 M.G.Bn.

B.O. 259.   9

S.A.Bde will move by march route and concentrate on road running from J.18.d.5.0. to K.7.central today AAA Order of march Bde H.Q. & Signal Section 12.00 1st S.A.I. 12.05. 4th S.A.I. 12.17. 2nd S.A.I. 12.29. S.A.L.T.M.B. 12.41. Section M.G.Bn 12.45. AAA Starting Point Road Junction in J.7.a.7.3. Route Passetemps LE Gd.PUCHAU thence road junction in J.9.c.8.2. road junction XXZEXEXSXXXXRaaX XmnXXXaM J.16.a.6.1. Railway crossing J.16.d.8.7. Road junction J.17.b.2.2. AAA Transport will be brigaded and move under orders of Lt.JOHNSTON in rear of column and will be concentrated on road running J.7.a.0.0. to J.7.a.7.3. AAA Head of column will be in K.7.central and all troops on arrival on road of concentration will get well clear to the South of this road AAA Dress Fighting Order.

S.A.Bde.   (Sd). E.BARLOW.
                                                Major,
                                                Bde Major.

386

26th Inf. Bde.	D.A.D.V.S.
27th Inf. Bde.	D.A.D.O.S.
S.A. Inf. Bde.	A.P.M.
C.R.A.	Camp Comdt.
C.R.E.	XV Corps.
9th Signals.	XV Corps H.A.
9th Seaforth Highrs.	XV Corps R.A.
9th Bn. M.G. Corps.	1st Aust. Division.
'Q'.	38th Division.
9th Div. Train.	'E' Special Coy. R.E.
A.D.M.S.	

G.S.1/234. 10th July 1918.

Para. 5 of 9th Division Order No. 246 is cancelled.

T. C. Mudie

Lieut-Colonel.
General Staff.
9th (Scottish) Division.

"A" Form.
MESSAGES AND SIGNALS.

Army Form C. 2121 (In pads of 100)

No. of Message

Prefix	Code 1250 m.	Words	Charge	This message is on a/c of:	Recd. at m.
Office of Origin and Service Instructions.		Sent		Service.	Date
4998		At m.		app 2	From
		To			By
		By		(Signature of "Franking Officer.")	

366

TO [illegible] S.A. Bde [illegible] A Coy [illegible]

Sender's Number.	Day of Month.	In reply to Number.	AAA
G. 2.	9th		

The enemy appears to be retiring and 12th Lancers have been ordered forward to keep in touch AAA A mobile column constituted as follows will be organised at once under command of Brig-Gen. W. TANNER AAA S.A. Bde plus Bde Signal Section AAA 1 Battery [illegible] and one section 4.5" hows to be detailed by C.R.A. AAA 430th F. Co. R.E. AAA one Machine Gun Coy to be detailed by 1[illegible]th [illegible] M.G.C. AAA S.A. Bde Field Ambulance AAA Possibly 2 armoured cars AAA 2 platoons XIII Corps [illegible] now attached [illegible] and 199th Bdes will report to G.O.C. mobile column by 3.0 pm AAA Column will move forthwith via [illegible] (J.10.d.) and [illegible] FAVRIL (D.26.d.) with a view to concentrating in [illegible] this afternoon AAA

From

Place

Time

The above may be forwarded as now corrected. (Z)

Censor. Signature of Addressor or person authorised to telegraph in his name.

* This line, except AAA, should be erased if not required.

Wt. W [illegible] 200,000 Pads. [illegible] B. & S. Ltd. (E2389.)

"A" Form.

MESSAGES AND SIGNALS.

No. of Message

Prefix	Code	m.	Words	Charge

Office of Origin and Service Instructions

Sent At m. To By

This message is on a/c of: Service.

(Signature of "Franking Officer.")

Recd. at m. Date From By

TO

364

Sender's Number.	Day of Month.	In reply to Number.	AAA

Arrangements are being made to provide 3 days rations AAA G.O.C. Mobile Column will get into touch with G.O.C. of similar column from 50th Division (Brig-Gen ROLLO) at LASAVATTE (E.18.c.0.0) AAA Touch will also be obtained with O.C. 12th Lancers who is at present in communication with 198th Bde (H.[illegible].K.1.b.5.8.) AAA Added all concerned

Recd 1645 at BERGNIES 9.11.18

From 66th Div
Place
Time

The above may be forwarded as now corrected. (Z)

Censor. Signature of Addressor or person authorised to telegraph in his name.

* This line, except AAA, should be erased if not required.

W.D. W 3253/P511. 250,000 Pads. 1/18. B. & S. Ltd. (E2389.)

MESSAGES AND SIGNALS.

No. of Message ......

Prefix ...... Code ...... m.	Words ...... Charge	This message is on a/c of:	Recd. at ...... m.
Office of Origin and Service Instructions.	Sent		Date ......
	At ...... m.		From ......
	To		By ......
	By	(Signature of "Franking Officer.")	

TO [illegible] 365

Sender's Number.	Day of Month.	In reply to Number.	AAA
[illegible]	9		

[illegible]

From [illegible] Div

Place

Time

The above may be forwarded as now corrected. (Z)

Censor. Signature of Addressor or person authorised to telegraph in his name.

* This line should be erased if not required.

"A" Form
MESSAGES AND SIGNALS.

Army Form C. 2121
(In pads of 100.)

No. of Message ...

Prefix ... Code ... m.	Words	Charge	This message is on a/c of:	Recd. at ... m.
Office of Origin and Service Instructions. Copy	Sent At ... m. To ... By ...		App 7 ... Service. (Signature of "Franking Officer.")	Date ... From 374 By ...

TO 1st SAI SALTMB B 331 RFA
2nd SAI MGCy Sec How Batty
4th SAI 9th Cy RE

Sender's Number.	Day of Month.	In reply to Number.	AAA
BMY 21.	9		

Column will rest at BEUGNIES for one hour before moving on to SOLRE LE CHATEAU Route for transport to SOLRE LE CHATEAU via SARS POTERIES and LEZ FONTAINE to road junction in F.10.d.1.2. thence through F.17 to destination. Guides will meet column at entrance to village.

From S A Bde
Place
Time 1645

The above may be forwarded as now corrected. (Z)

Censor. Signature of Addressor or person authorised to telegraph in his name
* This line should be erased if not required.

Wt. W3253/ P 511 27.2 H & K Ltd (E. 2634)

SECRET. Recd Op. 15 10/11/18 [handwritten initials] app 28(O)

Copy No. 6 395 Kentrary

66TH DIVISION ORDER NO. 120.

9th November 1918.

1. **GENERAL SITUATION.** The enemy is still retiring towards the MEUSE. Main bodies of Divisions will remain for the present approximately on and west of the LA CAPELLE - AVESNES - MAUBEUGE Road. They will be distributed in depth with a view to easing as far as possible the situation as regards supply and communication.

2. **COMPOSITION OF MOBILE FORCE.** A mobile column will be formed tomorrow, 10th November, to act in advance of the outpost line. Composition as under:-

Commander. - G.O.C. 66th Division. (H.Q. SARS POTERIES).

Troops.

66th Divisional Signal Coy. (with 12 additional D.Rs and 1 box car).
5th Cavalry Brigade.
No. 17 Armoured Car Battalion.
One Infantry Brigade of 66th Division.
Two Batteries R.F.A. 66th Division.
Two Sections 4.5" Hows.
One Company 100th Bn. M.G.C.
430th Field Company R.E. with bridging equipp.
431st " " " " " "
432nd " " " to" join on completion of present bridging work.
One Company 9th Bn. Glouc. R. (Pioneers).
Eight light ambulances will be detailed by A.D.M.S. (to be attached to 1st S.A. Fld. Ambulance).
IX Corps Cyclist Battalion.
XIII Corps Cyclist Battalion.
One Section Anti-aircraft.
Two squadrons R.A.F.

S E C R E T.

Copy No. 5

66TH DIVISION ORDER NO. 121.

9th Novr 1918.

Ref. VALENCIENNES & NAMUR
Sheets 1/100,000.

1.
SITUATION.

The enemy continues to retire, our Cavalry were in touch with him this evening along the Frontier east of HESTRUD, through the F of CLAIRFAYTS, thence due south. The main bodies of Divisions are remaining for the present approximately on and west of, the LA CAPELLE - AVESNES - MAUBEUGE Road where they will be distributed in depth with a view to easing as far as possible the situation as regards supplies and communications.

2.

The pursuit of the enemy on the Fourth Army front will be taken over tomorrow, November 10th, at 07.00, by the column detailed below. Its duty will be to keep touch with the enemy rearguard, and with any advanced troops, sent out by the First French Army on the right, and by the Third British Army on the left.

Commander. - Major General H.K. BETHELL, CMG., DSO.,
(Commanding 66th Division).
H.Q. SARS POTERIES 5 miles N.E. of AVESNES.

Troops.

66th Divisional Signal Coy (1 box car and 12 D.Rs in addition).
5th Cavalry Brigade.
No. 17 Armoured Car Battalion.
1X Corps Cyclist Battalion.
X111 Corps Cyclist Battalion.
S. A. Infantry Brigade Group (66th Divn).
A/331 and B/331 Btys RFA (66th Div. Arty).
1 Sect. Anti-Aircraft.
1 Coy 100th Bn. M.G.C. (66th Divn).
430th Field Coy. R.E. " "
431st Field Coy. R.E. " "
432nd Field Coy. R.E. (to join later).
1 Coy 9th Bn. Glouc. R. (Pioneers).
2 Squadrons R.A.F.
2 Sections D/331 (4.5" Hows) 66th D[illegible]
1st S.A. Fld.Amb. with 4 light & 3 [illegible]
abms of 2/2nd & 2/3rd (E.L.) Fld.[illegible]
(66th Divn).

3. The above force will be disposed at 06.00 on 10th Novr. as follows:-

S.A. Inf. Bde. with its affiliated M.G.Coy, Bty RFA., and section 4.5" Hows.	SOLRE LE CHATEAU.
12th Lancers.	- do -
1 Coy 9th Bn.Glouc.R. (Pioneers).	- do -
XIII Corps Cyclist Battalion.	- do -

Column, less above assembled or assembling at SARS POTERIES and BEUGNIES.

Divl H.Q. eastern end of SARS POTERIES.

4. The pursuit will be continued at 07.00, 10th Novr., the objective being the River line BEAUMONT - SOLRE ST. GERY - RENLIES - FROIDCHAPELLE.

5th CAV. BDE. The 5th Cavalry Brigade, with 1 Bty R.H.A., will cover the advance, one Regiment working in the area from Army northern boundary to SOLRE LE CHATEAU - BEAUMONT Road exclusive, one Regiment the area SOLRE LE CHATEAU - BEAUMONT Road inclusive to LIESSIES - SIVRY - RENLIES Road exclusive, one Regiment LIESSIES - SIVRY - RENLIES Road inclusive to Army Southern boundary. The Regiments operating in the northern and southern sectons will pay particular attention to their flanks in the eventuality of advanced troops of the Armies on either side not being up, without however allowing such a situation in any way to effect the pace of their own advance. 5th Cavalry Brigade H.Q. and 1 Battery artillery will move along SOLRE - CLAIRFAYTS - SIVRY - RENLIES Road.

XIII Corps Cyc. Bn. XIII Corps Cyclist Battalion (less 1 platoon) will advance along the SOLRE - CLAIRFAYTS - SIVRY Station - RENLIES Road and will be affiliated to the Cavalry Regiment operating in centre sector with the object of crossing at RENLIES and securing itself in RENLIES for night 10th/11th Novr.

IX Corps Cyc. Bn. The IX Corps Cyclist Battalion (less 1 platoon) will advance along the LIESSIES - EPPE SAUVAGE-RANCE - FROIDCHAPELLE Road, with the object of securing itself in FROIDCHAPELLE for night Novr. 10th/11th, in addition to a bridgehead across the River east of the town.

ARMOURED CARS. A pair of armoured cars will be attached to each Cyclist Bn. and to S.A. Brigade H.Q. These cars will not be used in advance of Cavalry screen, but to mop up any M.Gs that may have been located and engaged with fire by Cavalry or Infantry.

S.A. Bde. The South African Bde (less 1 Bn. in column reserve - which will remain at SOLRE LE CHATEAU under column orders) will move on BEAUMONT with the object of crossing the River and securing itself in BEAUMONT for night 10th/11th Novr.

1 Platoon each from 9th and 13th Corps Cyclist Bns. will report to O.C. 66th Division Signals at column H.Q. (SARS POTERIES) by 10.00 on 10th Novr.

Column advanced report centre will be established at SOLRE LE CHATEAU at Zero and will move later to GRANDRIEU.

5. C.R.E. will make good the road SOLRE LE CHATEAU (exclusive) - BEAUMONT. He will detail 1 Field Coy to move with the 5th Cav. Bde.

198th and 199th Inf. Bdes. with 9th Glouc. R. (Pioneers) (less 1 Coy) have been allotted tasks on road from DOMPIERRE through J.8.b. and c and K.1.a and b - LES TROIS PAVES - SOLRE LE CHATEAU inclusive.

6. COMMUNICATIONS. Particular attention will be paid by all ranks of the column to co-operate with R.A.F. who will of necessity be our main means of communication, though wireless, visual, cyclist and mounted orderlies will be employed to the maximum to supplement the former. O.C. Column Signals has already a line working from SARS POTERIES to DOMPIERRE, this line will be extended to BEAUMONT and will be the only line maintained by column signals. XIII Corps have undertaken to maintain this line from LES TROIS PAVES westwards from 07.00 tomorrow 10th Novr.

7. The enemy on many portions of the front is thoroughly demoralised and is disintegrating rapidly. It has been impossible to get into touch with the H.Q. of several units of our column, notwithstanding this any unit herein referred to and to which the contents of this order have been communicated by any other formation will at once proceed to carry out its allotted role.

8. ACKNOWLEDGE.

Lieut. Colonel.
General Staff, 66th Division.

Issued at 23.00.

For distribution see over.

386

6. Mines have burst at BEUGNIES, E.24.d.6.4., 500 yards west and in middle of village, making road impassable for wheeled traffic. Road is however passable from MONT DOURLERS E.14. central, through LA SAVATE - SARS POTERIES and LEZFONTAINE to cross roads F.16.d. and thence to SOLRE LE CHATEAU.

Lieut Colonel.
General Staff, 66th Division.

DISTRIBUTION.

Noz 1	War Diary.	No. 14	A.D.M.S.
2	" "	15	A Coy X111 Corps Cyclists.
3	File.	16	12th Lancers.
4	198th Bde.	17	A.P.M. X111 Corps.
5	199th Bde.	18	9th Bn. Glouc R.
6	S.A. Bde.	19	5th Cavalry Brigade.
7	C.R.A.	20	17th Bn. Armoured Cars.
8	C.R.E.	21	Sect.A.A.
9	Signals.	22	Squadron R.A.F.
10	A & Q.	23	X111 Corps
11	Train A.S.C.	24	X111 Corps.
12	100th Bn.M.G.C.	25	50th Division.
13	D.A.P.M.	26	32nd Division.
27	A.D.C.		

DISTRIBUTION.

Copy No. 1 War Diary.
2 " "
3 File.
4 198th Bde.
5 S.A. Bde. @
6 C.R.A.
7 C.R.E.
8 Signals. @
9 A & Q.
10 Train A.S.C.
11 100th Bn.M.G.C.
12 D.A.P.M.
13 A.D.M.S.
14 12th Lancers. @
15 A.P.M. X111 Corps.

No. 16 7th Bn.Glouc.R.
17 5th Cav. Brigade.@
18 17th Bn.Armoured Cars.@
19 Section A.A.
20 Squadron R.A.F. @
21 Squadron R.A.F. @
22 Fourth Army @
23 X111 Corps @.
24 50th Division.
25 32nd Division.
26 1X Corps.
27 1X Corps Cyclist Bn.
28 X111 Corps Cyclist Bn.
29 199th Brigade.
30 A.D.C.

Map sent to those marked @.

381

App. 22

Copy of Telegram:

BO.258 - 7 AAA

SA Bde. will move by March Route tomorrow 8th. inst. to DOMPIERRE as follows: 4th. SAI 08.00 1st. SAI 08.12 2nd. SAI 08.24 Bde. HQ. Sig. Sectn. 08.36 SALTM Bty. 08.40 MG.Sec. 08.45 aaa Starting point road junctn. in C.25.d.2.7. aaa Billeting parties to meet Staff Capt. at Church DOMPIERRE at 08.00 aaa 1st. line transport moves with Units aaa Units to report completion of move on arrival aaa Bde. HQ. closes 08.00 at BASSE NOYELLES and opens at DOMPIERRE on arrival aaa Acknowledge

S.A. Bde.

(sd) E. BARLOW

Major,
Bde. Major.

(3)

9. **CYCLISTS.** 'A' Company XIII Corps Cyclists will detail 1 section to report to 198th Brigade and 199th Brigade by 07.30. Remainder of Company will accompany Adv. D.H.Q.

10. **HEADQUARTERS.** Adv. D.H.Q. report centre will be established at Zero at present 198th Brigade H.Q. (J.1.c.8.1.) and will move to ~~LA CROISETTE FME~~ (J.5.c.) at a later hour. Rear D.H.Q. will move from LANDRECIES to TAISNIERES starting at 07.30 8th November.

11. ACKNOWLEDGE.

LA TOILERIE (J.10.d.5.4.)

[signature]

Lieut Colonel.
General Staff, 66th Division.

DISTRIBUTION.

Copy No. 1	War Diary.	Copy 13	25th Bn. M.G.C.
2	" "	14	A.D.V.S.
3	File.	15	9th Bn. Glouc. R.
4	A. & Q.	16	D.A.P.M.
5	Signals.	17	A.P.M. XIII Corps.
6	C.R.A.	18	XIII Corps.
7	C.R.E.	19	25th Division.
8	198th Bde.	20	32nd Division.
9	199th Bde.	21	50th Division.
10	S.A. Bde.	22	35th Squadron R.A.F.
11	Train A.S.C.	23	12th Lancers.
12	100th Bn. M.G.C.	24	A Coy XIII Corps Cycli
25	A.D.C.		

* Issued to Inf. Brigades, C.R.A & 100th Bn. M.G.C. only

Copy.   SECRET.

279

MOBILE COLUMN ORDER No. 1.

10/11/18.

Ref. Map NAMUR 1/100,000.

1. INFORMATION.

(a) The enemy is reported to be retiring rapidly destroying communications as he withdraws. There are signs of demoralisation and disintegration among many of his formations.

(b) Our mounted ~~formations~~ troops hold the frontier from a point E. of HESTRUD to the F of CLAIRFAYT - thence due S.

2. INTENTION.

The S.A.Bde (less one Battalion, the 4th S.A.I.) which will remain at SOLRE LE CHATEAU under Divisional orders) will move on BEAUMONT with the object of crossing the river and securing itself in BEAUMONT for the night 10-11 Nov.

The advance of the infantry will be covered by mounted troops as follows -

In Southern Area	-	Scots Greys.
Centre "	-	XII Lancers.
Northern "	-	XX Hussars.

The boundaries of these areas are -

Southern - LIESSIES - SIVRY - RENLIES - Road (inl) to Army S. boundary (SAINS - EPPE SAUVAGE - FROIDCHAPELLE - NERVILLE)

Central - SOLRE LE CHATEAU - BEAUMONT road (inc) to LIESSIES - SIVRY - RENLIES road (incl).

Northern - From Army N, boundary (WATTIGINIES - COUSOLRE - N. of THIRMONT - STREE - COUR SUR HEURE) to SOLRE LE CHATEAU - BEAUMONT road (incl).

The pursuit will continue at 07.00 hours today - the objective being the river line BEAUMONT - SOLRE ST CERY - RENLIES - FROIDCHAPPELLE.

The 1st Cavalry Bde H.Q. with one Batty R.F.A. will move along SOLRE LE CHATEAU - CLAIRFAYTS - SIVRY - RENLIES road. Cyclists XIII Corps (less 1 platoon) will advance along SOLRE LE CHATEAU - CLAIRFAYTS - SIVRY - RENLIES road and will be affiliated to the cavalry regiment operating in the central area - with the object of crossing the river ar RENLIES and securing itself in RENLIES on the night of 10-11 Nov.

The Cyclists Bn IX Corps (less one platoon) will advance along the LIESSIES - EPPE SAUVAGE - RANCE - FROIDCHAPELLE road with the object of securing itseld in FROIDCHAPELLE for the night 10-11 Nov.

One platoon each IX and XII Corps Cyclists will report to Signals at H.Q. 66th Division (Advanced H.Q.) at 14.00 hours today (at SOLRE LE CHATEAU)

The enemy, if encountered will be vigorously engaged.

3. DEATIL of MOBILE COLUMN.

Van Guard.	1 Coy. 1st S.A.I.
	1 Section 430th Field Coy. R.E.
	1 Section C Coy 100th Bn. M.G.C.
	1 Bearer Section S.A.F.A.
(Advance Guard	Commander - Lieut Col H.H.JENKINS, 1st S.A.I.
MAIN Guard.	1st S.A.I. (less 3 Coys.
	1 Section B.Bty 331st F.A.B.
FLANK Guard.	2 Coys. 1st S.A.I.
MAIN BODY.	H.Q. S.A.Bde.
	2 Armoured Cars.
	2nd S.A.I. (less 1 platoon)
	C Coy. 100th Bn. M.G.C. (less 1 section.)
	S.A.L.T.M.B.
	B Bty. 431st F.A.B. (less 1 section).
	1 Section D Baty. 431st F.A.B.
	430th Field Co. R.E. (less 1 section)
	S. A.F.A. (less 1 bearer section)
	Baggage including rations in order of units

280

under command of Major BROWNE, M.C., 4th S.A.I.. Pack Animals, Lewis Gun Limbers of Infantry, Fighting limbers of M.G's, Technical vehicles of Field Coy. R.E. will march with units. Field Kitchens and mess carts will move in rear of main body.
1 platoon 2nd S.A.I..

4. COMMUNICATIONS.
Particular attention will be paid by all ranks of Mobile Column to cooperation with R. A.F. which will of necessity be the principal medium of communication. Wireless, visual, cyclists and mounted orderlies will be employed to maximum extent to supplement R.A.F. communications.

5. All troops will march in battle order, one days ration - (and the iron ration) will be carried on the person and 3 days rations on the transport.

6. REPORTS.
To the head of the Main body.

7. MARCH TABLE. Annexed.

(Sgd) JAMES R. LEISK.
Major,
A/Bde. Major, S.A.Bde.

Issued at 0 .15 hours by runner.

Copy No.1 1st S.A.I.
2 2nd S.A.I.
3 4th S.A.I.
4 B Batty. 431st F.A.B.
5 D " "
6 430th Field Co. R.E.
7 432 Field Co. R.E.
8 C Coy 100th Bn. M.G.C.
9 S.A.F.A.
10 S.A.L.T.M.B.
11 Cyclists (2platoons) XIII Corps
12/15 War Diary.
16 6 Division.

"A" Form. Army Form C. 2121

MESSAGES AND SIGNALS.

No. of Message

Prefix ... Code ... m. Office of Origin and Service Instructions.	Words	Charge	This message is on a/c of:	Recd. at ... m.
Urgent Operation Priority			OM ... Service. (Signature of "Franking Officer.")	Date 30 (O)
	Sent At ... m. To ... By ...			From ... By ... 282

TO { 198 } Bdes / 199 } — S.A. Bde — Cyclists — Signals — ~~Rear Div H.Q.~~

Sender's Number	Day of Month	In reply to Number	
G 13			AAA

199 Bde move at once on RENLIES via SOLRE - LE - CHAU — CLAIRFAYTS — SIVRY road AAA 198 Bde. will at once take over Divl. front at present held by 2 Bns 199 Bde with one Bn. and one M.G. Coy AAA Units of 199 Bde to move irrespective of relief by 198 Bde. AAA No ~~change~~ change in ~~disposition~~ of Two rear Bns + H.Q. 198 Bde. will not move AAA O.C. 100 M.G. Bn M.G.C. will detail one ~~the~~ Coy. for affiliation to 199 Bde AAA A/331 Bty R.F.A. + one Sec. D/331 Bty. R.F.A. will report to 199 Bde H.Q. on arrival of latter in SOLRE-LE-CHAU AAA

From 66 Div.

Place SOLRE-LE-CHAU

Time 12.20

The above may be forwarded as now corrected. (Z) [illegible signature]

Censor. Signature of Addressor or person authorised to telegraph in his name.

* This line should be erased if not required.

W. & S. L. M. Ltd. London. W 14042/M44. 75,000 12/15. Forms C 2121/10.

283

"A" Form
MESSAGES AND SIGNALS.

Army Form C. 2121
(in pads of 100).

No. of Message.................

Prefix..........Code..........m. Office of Origin and Service Instructions.	Words.	Charge.	This message is on a/c of: ....Service. (Signature of "Franking Officer.")	Recd. at..........m. Date.......... From.......... By..........
	Sent At..........m. To.......... By..........			

31 (6)

TO: 5 H Bde

* Sender's Number.	Day of Month.	In reply to Number.	AAA
AX 6	16/4		

Left held up by
MG high ground and
white house (three white
chimneys) one [illegible] Centre [illegible]
making [illegible] slow progress [illegible]
the [illegible] from right
the [illegible] on high
ground where last seen
[illegible] enemy has evidently
[illegible] [illegible] and [illegible]

From
Place
Time

The above may be forwarded as now corrected. (Z)
.... *Censor.* Signature of Addressor or person authorised to telegraph in his name.

* This line should be erased if not required.

(18965.) Wt. W12952/M1294. 187,500 Pads. 1/17 McC. & Co., Ltd. (E. 818.)

284

"A" Form
MESSAGES AND SIGNALS.

Army Form C. 2121
(in pads of 100).

No. of Message..................

Prefix........ Code.......... m.	Words.	Charge.	This message is on a/c of:	Recd. at.......... m.
Office of Origin and Service Instructions.	Sent		..........................Service.	Date ....
	At..................m.			From ....
	To....................			By ....
	By....................		(Signature of "Franking Officer.")	

TO

* Sender's Number.	Day of Month.	In reply to Number.	AAA

An [illegible] gun unfortunately
from Transport [illegible] have
worked actually to [illegible]
as house are [illegible]
so a small [illegible]
bridge about 200 yds
N of where troops [illegible]
[illegible].

13.30 [illegible]

From 1st S.A. Inf
Place
Time 1720

[illegible signature]

The above may be forwarded as now corrected. (Z)

.... Censor.

Signature of Addressor or person authorised to telegraph in his name.

* This line should be erased if not required.

(18965.) Wt. W12952/M1294. 187,500 Pads. 1/17 McC. & Co., Ltd. (E. 818.)

[illegible]

MESSAGES AND SIGNALS. No. of Message..............

A (0)

Prefix......Code......m.	Words. Charge.	This message is on a/c of:	Recd. at......m.
Office of Origin and Service Instructions.	Sent	285 Service.	Date
	At......m.	App 34	From
	To......		
	By......	(Signature of "Franking Officer.")	By......

TO S. A Bde. [illegible]

Sender's Number.	Day of Month.	In reply to Number.	AAA
A-X-Y	10	BMY. 27	

Have	just	returned	from
Coys	they	are	pushing
on	slowly	AAA	Have
instructed	them	they	must
make	progress	AAA	Left
are	near	white	House
[illegible]	white	chimneys)	AAA
MG	fire	very	heavy
low	flying	plane	some

From			
Place			
Time			

The above may be forwarded as now corrected. (Z)

Censor. Signature of Addressor or person authorised to telegraph in his name.

* This line should be erased if not required.

(18965.) Wt. W12952/M1294. 187,500 Pads. 1/17 McC. & Co., Ltd. (E. 818.)

(in pads of 100).

MESSAGES AND SIGNALS.

No. of Message..............

Prefix..........Code..........m.	Words. / Charge.	*This message is on a/c of:* 286 ....Service.	Recd. at..........m.
Office of Origin and Service Instructions.	Sent At..........m. To.......... By..........	(Signature of "Franking Officer.")	Date.......... From.......... By..........

TO

*Sender's Number.	Day of Month.	In reply to Number.	AAA

Considerable trouble before guns arrived AAA heavy [illegible] [illegible] [illegible] [illegible] [illegible]

END

From 1st S.A.I.

Place

Time [illegible]

The above may be forwarded as now corrected. (Z)

Censor. Signature of Addressor or person authorised to telegraph in his name.

* This line should be erased if not required.

(18965.) Wt. W12952/M1294. 187,500 Pads. 1/17 McC. & Co., Ltd. (E. 818.)

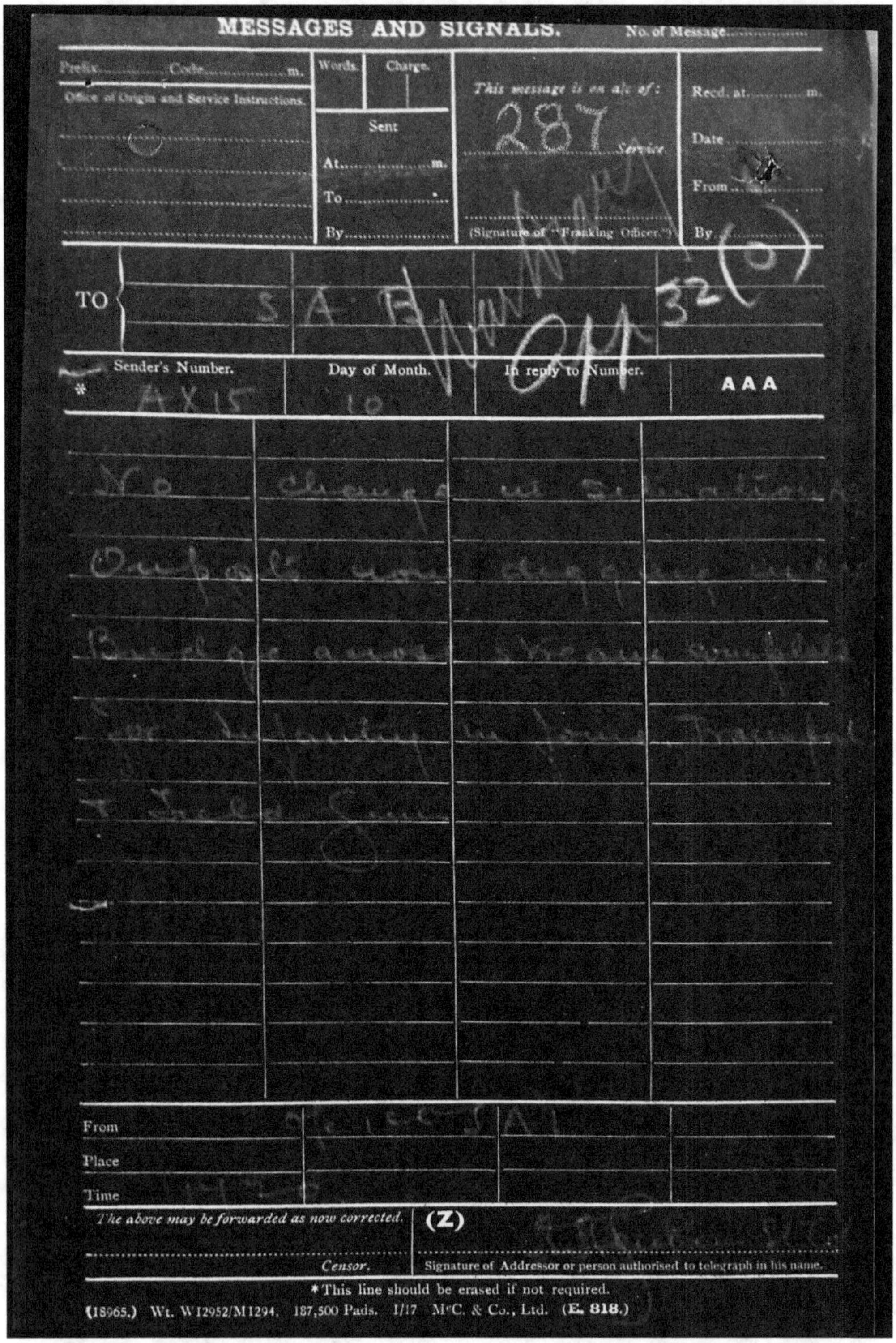

MESSAGES AND SIGNALS. No. of Message..............

Prefix........ Code........m. | Words. | Charge. | This message is on a/c of: 287 Service | Recd. at........m.

Office of Origin and Service Instructions.

Sent At........m. To........ By........

(Signature of "Franking Officer.")

Date........ From........ By........

TO: S A B

Sender's Number. AX15 | Day of Month. 10 | In reply to Number. | AAA

No change in situation. Outposts now digging in. Bridge across stream complete for Infantry in [illegible] Transport & Field Guns

From: [illegible] SA1

Place

Time

The above may be forwarded as now corrected. (Z)

Censor. Signature of Addressor or person authorised to telegraph in his name.

*This line should be erased if not required.

(18965.) Wt. W12952/M1294. 187,500 Pads. 1/17 McC. & Co., Ltd. (E. 818.)

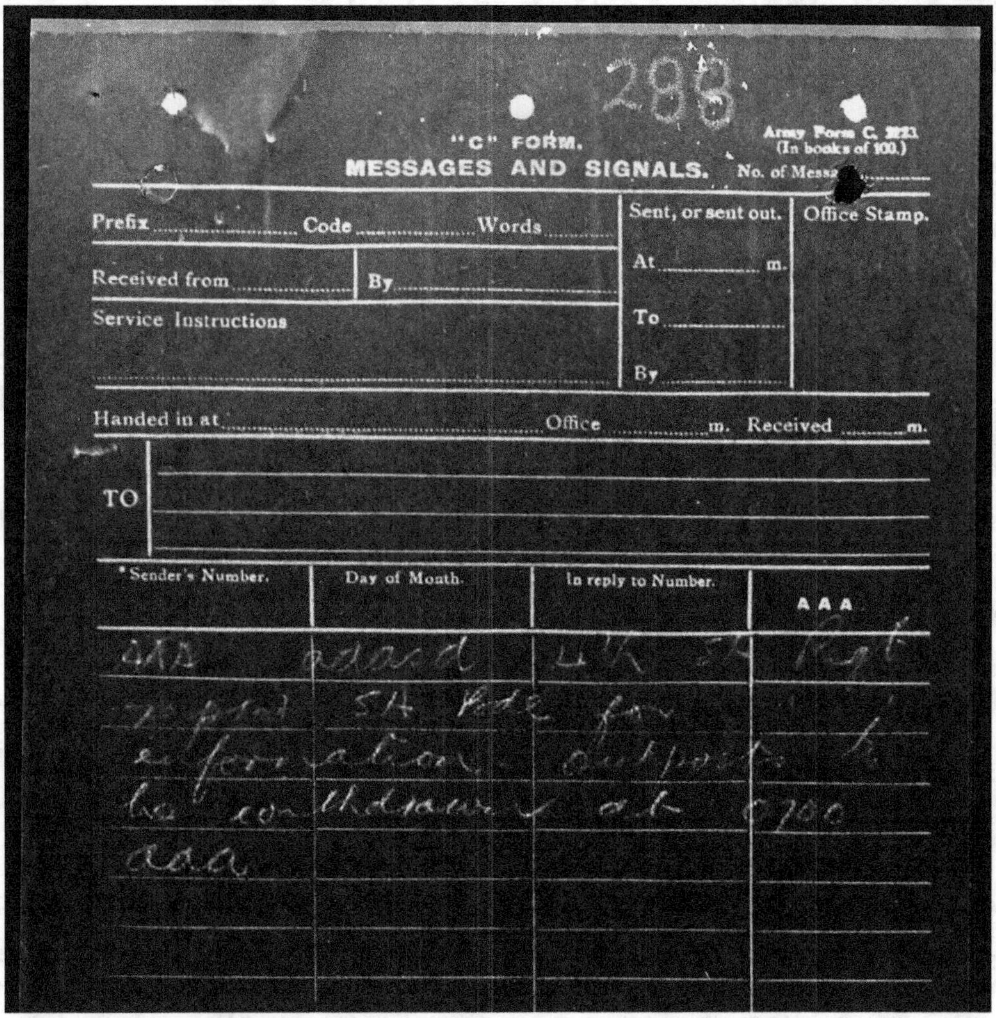

288

"C" FORM.
MESSAGES AND SIGNALS.

Army Form C. 2123.
(In books of 100.)

No. of Message

Prefix .... Code .... Words ....

Received from .... By ....

Service Instructions

Sent, or sent out.
At .... m.
To ....
By ....

Office Stamp.

Handed in at .... Office .... m. Received .... m.

TO

*Sender's Number.	Day of Month.	In reply to Number.	AAA

aaa addsd 4th 5th Regt
report 5th Bde for
information outposts to
be withdrawn at 0700
aaa

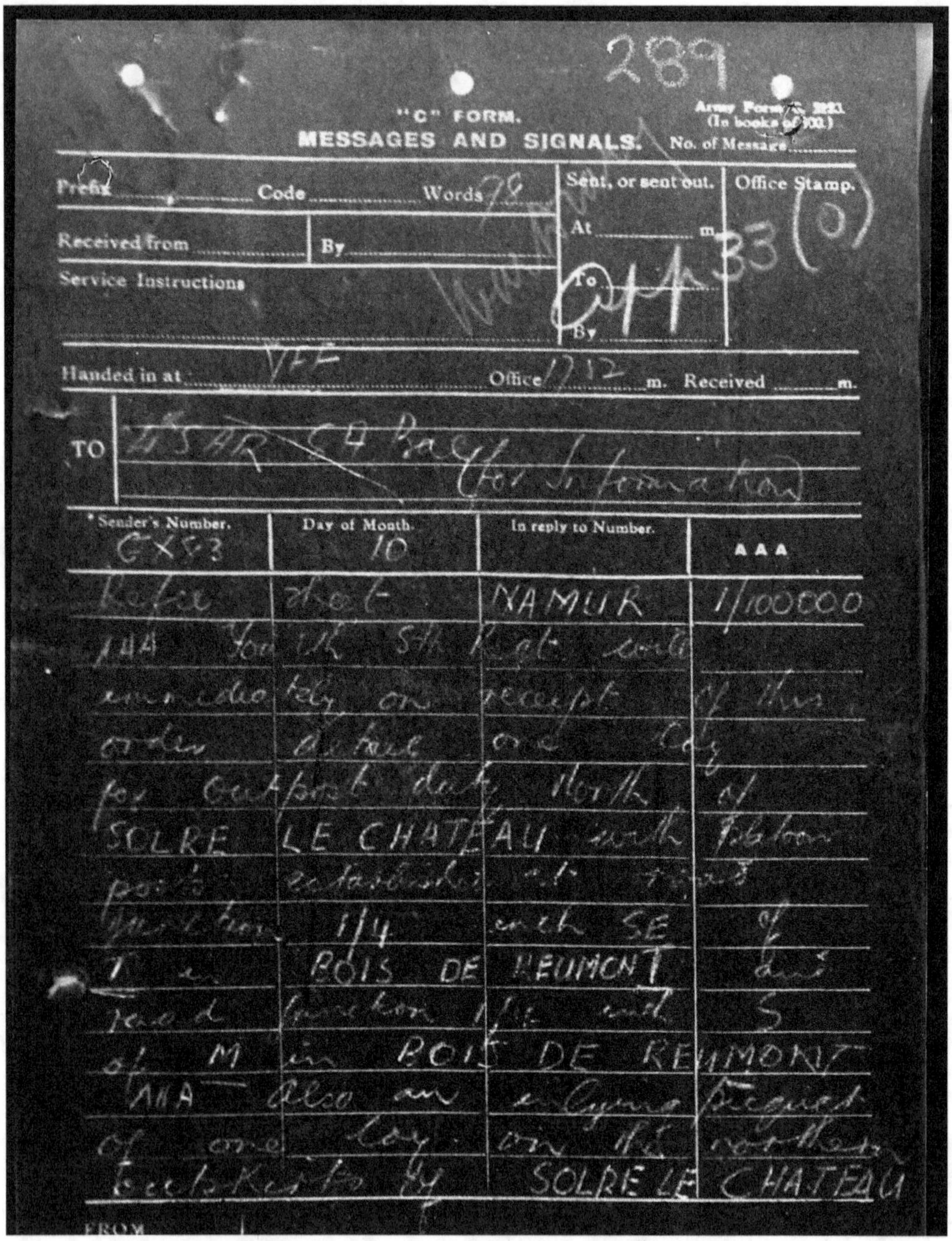

289

"C" FORM.

MESSAGES AND SIGNALS.

Army Form C. 2121 (In books of 100.)

No. of Message

Prefix ... Code ... Words 78	Sent, or sent out. At ... m. To 0114 By	Office Stamp. 33 (0)
Received from ... By ...		
Service Instructions		

Handed in at VFF Office 1712 m. Received ... m.

TO 4 SAR 5 Bde (For Information)

Sender's Number.	Day of Month.	In reply to Number.	AAA
GX53	10		

Refer sheet NAMUR 1/100000 AAA You with 5th Regt will immediately on receipt of this order detail one Coy for outpost duty North of SOLRE LE CHATEAU with platoon posts established at road junction 1/4 inch SE of T in BOIS DE REUMONT and road junction 1/4 inch S of M in BOIS DE REUMONT AAA Also an outlying picquet of one Coy on the northern outskirts of SOLRE LE CHATEAU

FROM

Copy. APP. 34 290

SECRET.

MOBILE COLUMN ORDER NO. 2.

10/11/18.

Ref. Map
NAMUR, 1/100,000.

1. Information.
(1) The enemy is offering a stubborn resistance to the Column's advance but is being steadily pressed back.
(2) At dusk this evening the line of our advanced troops was roughly as follows - On the right they occupied the high ground at point 240 immediately X of VIVERIAUX. In the centre they were approaching the village of GRANDIEU. On the left they were checked on the crest of the high ground immediately N of A in GRANDIEU. The 199th Bde was ordered today to move on RENLIES via SOLRE LE CHATEAU - CLAIRFAYTS - SIVRY.

2. INTENTION.
The 1st S.AFRICAN INF. will continue the advance at daybreak tomorrow and report progress. All other units of the Mobile Column will be prepared to move forward at 07.00 hours tomorrow - but will not necessarily form up in column of route until ordered to move.

3. DETAIL.

As in head 3 of Mobile Column Order No. 1, with the exception (a) that only one section of the 430th Field Coy. R.E. will move with vanguard - the Field Coy (less this section) marching with MAIN BODY in rear of 2nd S.African Inf. (b) that the Artillery will remain in present firing positions until it has been ascertained that the forward area is sufficiently clear for the advance to be resumed.

4. REPORTS.
To H.Q., S.A.Bde. in HESTRUD until Column again advances when reports will be to head of MAIN BODY.

(Sgd) JAMES R. LEISK.
Major,
A/Bde Major.

Issued at 21.30 hours by runner.

Copy No. 1. 1st S.A.I.
2. 2nd S.A.I.
3. 4th S.A.I.
4. B Bty. 331 F.A.B.
5. D " "
6. 530th Fld Co. R.E.
7. C Coy 100 Bn M.G.C.
8. S.A.F.A.
9. S.A.L.T.M.B.
10. Major BROWNIE.M.C.
11. O.C. XII Lancers.
12 66th Division.
13/16 War Diary.

294

SECRET.

Copy No. 5

66th DIVISION ORDER No. 122.

1. PROTECTION OF ARMY FRONT. 198th and S.A. Bdes will be responsible for the protection of the Army front during the night 10th/11th November. Dividing line between Brigades :-

A Line drawn from Northern outskirts of CLAIRFAYTS to COURTTOURNANT Road junction.

2. INTENTION. The advance will be continued at 07.00 on 11th November, objective being the same as for today, the 12th Lancers co-operating with South African Bde Group and 20th Hussars with 199th Brigade Group.

3. CAVALRY. So long as close touch, as at present, is maintained with the enemy, the Cavalry will only be used to clear up the situation on the flanks; the main bodies of each Regiment being retained in reserve and rested with a view to its operating intensively immediately the enemy resistance has been broken again by the Infantry.

4. 5th CAV. BDE. 5th Cavalry Brigade, less 12th Lancers and 20th Hussars, will concentrate in SOLRE LE CHATEAU by 15.00 11th November.

5. CYCLISTS. 13th Corps Cyclists will be withdrawn during night 10th/11th November into Divisional Reserve to SOLRE LE CHATEAU.

9th Corps Cyclists are placed under command of B.G.C. 199th Bde.

6. R.E's. Two sections of each Field Co. R.E. at present affiliated to Inf. Bdes will be withdrawn and be at disposal of C.R.E. from 07.00 November 11th.

7. A.A. PROTECTION. Units will pay immediate attention to the rapid engagement of all low-flying hostile aeroplanes, also utilising to the full existing cover, e.g., hedges and woods for bodies of troops and transport when parked.

The necessity for this would seem to have been overlooked in many cases today.

295

8.
HEADQUARTERS.

The present locations are :-

199th Bde. H.Q.	CLAIRFAYTS.
S. A. Bde H.Q.	HESTRUD.
Adv. Div. H.Q.	SOLRE LE CHATEAU. (200 yards West of Church).
198th Bde. H.Q.	DOMPIERRE.
Rear Div. H.Q.	DOMPIERRE.

9. ACKNOWLEDGE.

[signature]

Lieut-Colonel,
General Staff,
66th Division.

DISTRIBUTION.

Copy No. 1	War Diary.	14	12th Lancers.
2.	" "	15	9th Glouc. R.
3	File.	16	5th Cav. Bde.
4	198th Inf. Bde.	17	Section A.A.
5	S.A. Bde.	18	35th Squad. R.A.F.
6	C.R.A.	19	80th Squad. R.A.F.
7	Lt-Col. ADAMS.	20	Fourth Army.
8	C.R.E.	21	XIII Corps.
9	Signals.	22	IX Corps.
10	A & Q.	23	9th Corps Cyclistx Bn
11	Train A.S.C.	24	13th Corps Cyclist Bn.
12	100th Bn M.G.C.	25	199th Inf. Bde.
13	A.D.M.S.	26	A.D.C.

Army Form C. 2121
(in pads of 100).

"A" Form

MESSAGES AND SIGNALS.

No. of Message............

Prefix.......Code.......m. Office of Origin and Service Instructions.	Words. Charge. Sent At.......m. To....... By.......	This message is on a/c of: 291 ....Service. (Signature of "Franking Officer.")	Recd. at.......m. Date....... From 36 By.......

TO S A B... Off

Sender's Number.	Day of Month.	In reply to Number.	AAA
* AX 7	11		

Right coy reports ... the progress AAA No ...

From

Place

Time

The above may be forwarded as now corrected. **(Z)**

Censor. Signature of Addressor or person authorised to telegraph in his name.

* This line should be erased if not required.

(13965.) Wt. W12932 M1294. 187,500 Pads. 1/17. McC. & Co., Ltd. **(E. 818.)**

"A" Form

MESSAGES AND SIGNALS.

292

Army Form C. 2121
(in pads of 100).

No. of Message..................

Prefix.........Code.........m.	Words.	Charge.	This message is on a/c of:	Recd. at.........m.
Office of Origin and Service Instructions.	Sent		...............Service.	Date............
	At...........m.			From............
	To............			By............
	By............		(Signature of "Franking Officer.")	

37(o)

TO { S A Bde App

Sender's Number.	Day of Month.	In reply to Number.	AAA
* AX 19	11		

Report received from left and centre Coys stating they cannot get forward owing to enemy M G fire AAA Patrols last night failed in attempt AAA I am therefore remaining [illegible] as last night AAA I see no chance of getting forward unless line get a good artillery support [illegible]

Recd 0500 [illegible] 11/11

From	OC 1st S A I	
Place		
Time	0410	

The above may be forwarded as now corrected. (Z)

Censor.

[illegible] Lt Col
OC 1st S A I

Signature of Addressor or person authorised to telegraph in his name.

*This line should be erased if not required.

(18965.) Wt. W12952/M1294. 187,500 Pads. 1/17 McC. & Co., Ltd. (E. 818.)

"A" Form. Army Form C. 2121.
(In pads of 100.)

MESSAGES AND SIGNALS.

No. of Message ......

Prefix SO Code ...... m. | Words. | Charge.

Office of Origin and Service Instructions.

Priority

BFR

Sent
At ...... m.
To ......
By ......

This message is on a/c of: A/Bde ...... Service.

App 38(c)

(Signature of "Franking Officer.")

Recd. at ...... m.
Date ......
From ......
By ......

TO 9th Corps and 13th Corps Cyclists Bns.
Q. Sigs. CRA CRE 198th Bde. 199th Bde S.A.
Bde. Train ASC 100th Bn MGC 9th Glouc.R.
ADMS DADVS DAPM 12th Lancers 5th Cav.Bde
17th Arm.Car Bn 35th & 80th Squadn RAF

Sender's Number.	Day of Month.	In reply to Number.	AAA
* G.X. 91	11		

Hostilities will cease at 11th hour today Nov. 11th AAA Troops will stand fast on line reached at that hour which will be reported by wire to H.Q. 4th Army Adv. Guard AAA Defensive precautions will be maintained AAA There will be no intercourse of any description with enemy until receipt of instructions AAA

SOLRE LE CHATEAU

From
Place 4th Army Adv. Guard.
Time

The above may be forwarded as now corrected. (Z)

Censor. Signature of Addressor or person authorised to telegraph in his name.

* This line should be erased if not required.

(3796.) Wt. W492/M1647. 650,000 Pads. 5/17. H. W. & V., Ld. (E. 1187.)

296

app 39

Copy.

MOBILE COLUMN SPECIAL ORDER.

Ref. Map NAMUR Sheet,
1/100,000.

11/11/18.

Following from 66th Division is repeated for information of all concerned :-

Begins "Hostilities will cease at 11th hour Novr. 11th. Troops will stand fast on line reached at that hour which will be reported by wire to H.Q. 4th Army Advanced Guard, SOLRE LE CATEAU. Defensive precautions will be maintained. There will be no intercourse of any description with enemy until futther instructions" Ends.

Any dispositions of units of the Mobile Column consequent upon the foregoing information will be notified later.

(Sgd) JAMES R. LEISK.
Major,
A/Bde. Major,

Issued at 11.30 hours by runner.

Copy No. 1. 1st S.A.I.
2. 2nd S.A.I.
3. B. Bty 331 F.A.B.
4. 430 Fld Co R.E.
5. C Coy, 100 Bn. M.G.C.
6. S.A.F.A.
7 S.A.L.T.M.B.
8 66th Division.
9 O.C. XII Lancers.
10/23 War Diary.

297

Reference Sheet:-
NAMUR 1/100,000.

By Aeroplane Post.

G.B. 14.

Fourth Army.
5th Brigade R.A.F.
XIII Corps.

Your G.609 of today concerning the cessation of hostilities received by aeroplane post. The order reached all units in touch with the enemy in sufficient time. At 11.00 today 11th November 1918, our line ran from COUSOLRE along the western banks of the LA THURE River tox the PONT DE LA REPUBLIQUE where river crosses the frontier; along small stream to a point on road ½ inch N. of N of GRANDRIEU (HILL 246 (incl.); along ~~western~~ Eastern edge of GRANDRIEU to first V of VIVERIAUX (HILL 240 incl.); first R of R de GRANDRIEU along rivers southern bank to point where SIVRY - COURT TOURNANT road crosses it; to a post on the SIVRY Station road 300 yards N.E. of cross roads at S.W. corner of BOIS DE MATTINSART; cross roads ¼ inch N. of S of VIEUX SART; due south along road to LA FROMONS River; along road to M of MONTBLIART, (MONTBLIART incl.); South along road to MONTBLIART River.

IV Army Adv. Guard G.X. 106 of 12-11-18

Dispositions as follows:-

12th Lancers. H.Q. BERELLES, holding front from Army northern boundary to PONT DE LA REPUBLIQUE (incl.).

South African Brigade. H.Q. HESTRUD Chateau, holding front from PONT DE LA REPUBLIQUE to northern bank of GRANDRIEU River.

199th Brigade. H.Q. SIVRY, holding front from northern bank of GRANDRIEU River (excl.) to MONTBLIART River.

Fourth Army Advanced Guard H.Q. SOLRE LE CHATEAU.

In touch on north with 3rd Hussars at COUSOLRE.

In touch on South with French at EPPE SAUVAGE where line runs EPPE SAUVAGE along west bank of River MOUSTIER inclusive.

Staff Officers were sent at midday with our situation to French Unit Headquarters at TRELON.

(Sgd) A. R. Bethell

Major General.
Commanding, Fourth British Army Advanced Guard.

11th November 1918.

Copies to:-

198th Brigade.	199th Brigade.	S.A. Brigade.
C.R.A.	C.R.E.	12th Lancers.

298

G.B.15.

~~198th Brigade.~~ ~~199th Brigade.~~
S.A. Brigade. ~~12th Lancers.~~
~~C.R.A.~~ ~~C.R.E.~~

---

1. With reference to G.B.14 sent by aerial post to Fourth Army, copy of which has been sent to you.

O.C. 12th Lancers and B.Gs.C. 199th and S.A. Brigade Groups will be responsible for defensive precautions on their respective fronts. It must be distinctly understood by all that no advance whatsoever is permitted beyond this line until further orders, whether the enemy have gone or not. No intercourse of any description will take place with the enemy until receipt of further instructions. Aeroplanes of either side will not cross the line.

2. The following units at present affiliated to each Brigade Group will remain:-

1 Bty R.F.A.
1 Section 4.5" Hows.
1 Company M.G.Bn.

and (in case of 199th Brigade) 1 Company X111 Corps Cyclists.
Divisional Artillery, less A/331, B/331 and D/331 will remain concentrated in DOMPIERRE Area.
X111 Corps Cyclists (less 1 Company) will remain in Divisional Reserve at SOLRE LE CHATEAU.

3. The following moves will be completed by 12.00 tomorrow 12th Nov.

198th Brigade H.Q. and 1 Battalion.	BEUGNIES.
1 Battalion.	SARS POTERIES.
1 Battalion.	BAS LIEU.

ST. HILAIRE will be available for 5th Cavalry Brigade in lieu of BAS LIEU.
9th Bn. Glouc. R. will concentrate in SOLRE LE CHATEAU by 12.00 12th November.

4. C.R.E. will at once arrange to construct a bridge to take lorry traffic over the River at HESTRUD. The existing bridge for light wheeled traffic may be taken down after 09.00 tomorrow.

A bridge will at once be constructed over the stream on SOLRE - ECCLES Road, in BOIS DE REUMONT, for light wheeled traffic.

The following roads will be made fit for lorry traffic:-

(i) BAS LIEU - LA TROIS PAVES - BEUGNIES - SOLRE LE CHATEAU - GRANDRIEU Road.
(ii) The SOLRE LE CHATEAU - CLAIRFAYTS - SIVRY - SIVRY Station Road.
(iii) The LIESSIES - SIVRY Road.

5. All units will concentrate on repair of main roads, construction of bridges to take lorry traffic, also search for and removal of delay action mines.

198th Brigade will be responsible for the road from BAS LIEU (inclusive) - SOLRE LE CHATEAU (exclusive).

S.A. Brigade for the road from SOLRE LE CHATEAU to GRANDRIEU both exclusive.

199th Brigade for the CLAIRFAYTS - SIVRY Station road.

All Field Coys and Pioneer Battalion will be at the disposal of C.R.E. for bridging, road repair &c.

Walter Guinness
Lieut Colonel.
General Staff, BETHELL's FORCE.

11th November 1918.

appx. 299

SECRET

Copy No. 12

11-11-18

SOUTH AFRICAN INFANTRY BRIGADE

MOBILE COLUMN ORDER - No. 3

1. The 2nd. SAI will relieve the 1st. SAI in the line at 19.00 hours tomorrow, 12th. Nov.. The relief will be carried out as if active operations had not been ceased. Blankets, however, may be carried.

2. Strict attention will be paid by all ranks to the Divl. Order to the effect that there shall be no intercourse with the enemy; (Mobile Column Special Order, 11.11.18).

3. Units of the Mobile Column will render as soon as possible to HQ., S. Afr. Bde., Casualty Returns covering the operations of the 10th. and 11th. insts..

4. Any Officers sent over to our lines by the enemy as envoys will be blindfolded & taken to Bde. HQ..

5. So far as may be possible without interfering with dispositions in and for the line, Units of the Mobile Column will concentrate their detachments, transport, etc., in one billeting area, for convenience of administration and control.

6. The 4th. SAI has returned to S. Afr. Bde. Command from its period in Divl. Reserve.

7. ACKNOWLEDGE.

Issued thro' Signals at 20.00 to -
1. 1st. SAI ✓
2. 2nd. SAI ✓
3. 4th. SAI ✓
4. S. Afr. Fld. Ambulance ✓
5. SALTM Bty. ✓
6. 'B' Bty. 331 F.A. Bde.. ✓
7. 430 Fld. Co., RE ✓
8. 'C' Coy., 100 BN., MGC.. ✓
9. 66th. Divn. ✓
10. Staff Captain
11. Bde. Major
12/16. War Diary.

[signature]
Major,
Brigade Major,
South African In. Bde..

"A" Form
Army Form C. [illegible]
(In pads of 100.)

MESSAGES AND SIGNALS.

No. of Message........

Prefix........Code........m.	Words	Charge.	This message is on a/c of:	Recd. at........m.
Office of Origin and Service Instructions	Sent		........Service.	Date........
	At........m.		[illegible] 4	From........
	To........			By........ 302
	By........		(Signature of "Franking Officer.")	

TO: 5 SA Bde

Sender's Number.	Day of Month.	In reply to Number.	AAA
[illegible] 816	11		

Move forthwith to [illegible]
aaa [illegible] aaa [illegible]
4th SA Regt reports [illegible]
for information

From: SA [illegible]
Place
Time

The above may be forwarded as now corrected. (Z)
....
Censor.
Signature of Addressor or person authorised to telegraph in his name

"C" FORM.

Army Form C. 2121
(In books of 100.)

MESSAGES AND SIGNALS. No. of Message ....

Prefix SM Code 2219 Words 43

Received from YEF By WM

Service Instructions
BFR

Sent, or sent out. At .... To .... By ....

Office Stamp. SZA - 1?.XI.18 SIGNALS

Handed in at .... Office 2259 m. Received 2350 m.

TO 29 Bde. OH 4-(C) 301

*Sender's Number.	Day of Month.	In reply to Number.	AAA
GB16	11		
Move	of	4th	SAI
to	BEAURIEU	ordered	by
G16	of	today	will
take	place	tomorrow	12th
November	aaa	4th	SAI
will	be	clear	of
SOLRE	LE	CHATEAU	by
0900	aaa	addressed	4th
SAI	repeated	SA	Bde.

FROM 66 Div

PLACE & TIME

* This line, except AAA, should be erased, if not required.

(2287) Wt. W54/P738 691,000 Pads 3/18. A. P. Ltd. (E3013)

"C" Form.

MESSAGES AND SIGNALS.

No. of Message

Prefix ___ Code ___ Words ___	Received.	Sent, or sent out.	Office Stamp.
£ s. d.	From Of	At ___ m.	
Charges to Collect	By ab	To	
Service Instructions RLR		By	

Handed in at ___ Office 1703 m. Received 2000 m.

TO SA Bde 300

* Sender's Number	Day of Month.	In reply to Number	AAA
G 21	12		

Two Coys MGC at present affiliated to 199th and SA Brigades will be withdrawn and whole of your battalion concentrated in MOULARD by 12 noon Nov 13th aaa Addsd 100 K Bn MGC to acknowledge reptd 199th and SA Bdes Q and Signals

FROM
PLACE & TIME

Fourth Army Advance
[illegible] 1650

* This line should be erased if not required.

8910—W 548—100,000—10/5/17—E.P.Co.—(E1213)

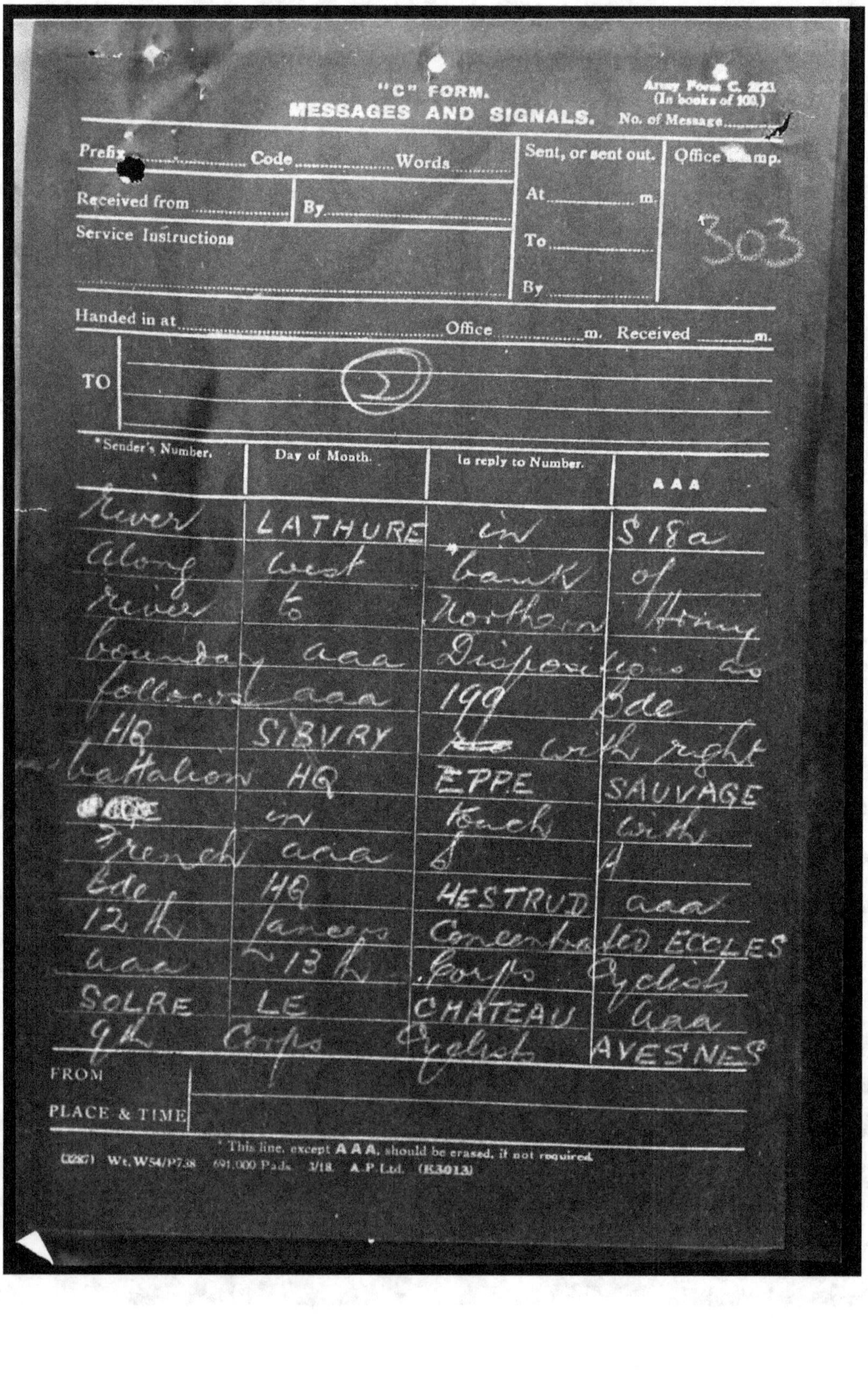

"C" FORM.
MESSAGES AND SIGNALS.

Army Form C. 2121
(In books of 100.)

No. of Message

Prefix .... Code .... Words ....

Received from .... By ....

Service Instructions

Sent, or sent out.
At .... m.
To ....
By ....

Office Stamp.
303

Handed in at .... Office .... m. Received .... m.

TO

*Sender's Number.	Day of Month.	In reply to Number.	AAA
River	LATHURE	in	S18a
along	west	bank	of
river	to	Northern	Army
boundary	aaa	Dispositions	as
follows	aaa	199	Bde
HQ	SIBVRY	with	right
battalion	HQ	EPPE	SAUVAGE
[illegible]	in	touch	with
French	aaa	8	H
Bde	HQ	HESTRUD	aaa
12th	Lancers	Concentrated	ECCLES
aaa	13th	Corps	Cyclists
SOLRE	LE	CHATEAU	aaa
9th	Corps	Cyclists	AVESNES

FROM

PLACE & TIME

* This line, except AAA, should be erased, if not required.

(3287) Wt. W54/P7.38 691,000 Pads. 3/18. A.P.Ltd. (E3013)

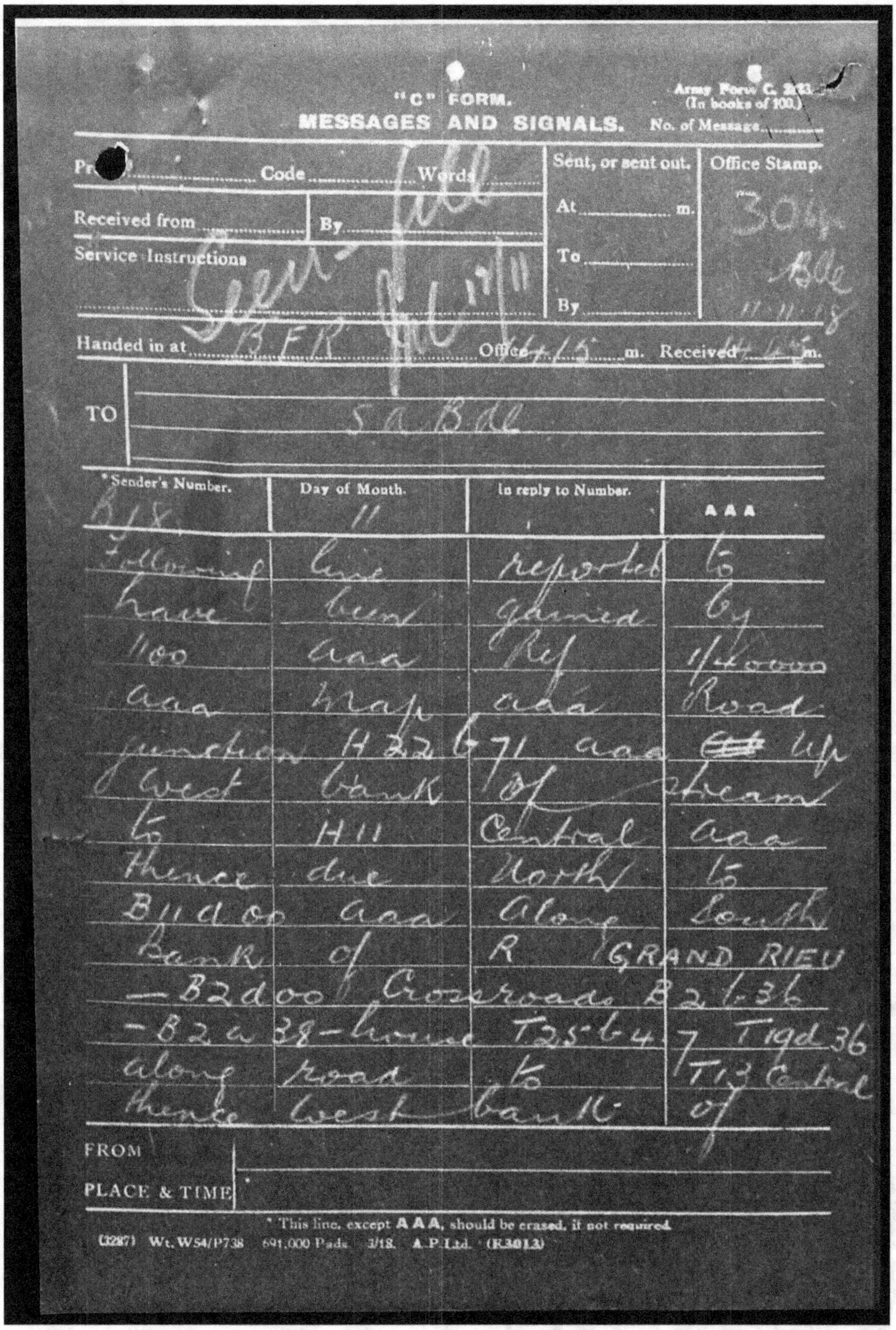

"C" FORM.
MESSAGES AND SIGNALS.

Army Form C. 2123.
(In books of 100.)
No. of Message

Prefix Code Words
Received from By
Service Instructions
Gen. Staff [illegible]

Sent, or sent out.
At m.
To
By

Office Stamp.
30th Bde
11.11.18

Handed in at BFR Office 14.15 m. Received 14.45 m.

TO SA Bde

*Sender's Number.	Day of Month.	In reply to Number.	AAA
B18	11		
Following	line	reported	to
have	been	gained	by
1100	aaa	Ref	1/40000
aaa	Map	aaa	Road
junction	H22b71	aaa	Up
West	bank	of	stream
to	H11	Central	aaa
Thence	due	North	to
B11d00	aaa	Along	South
bank	of	R	GRAND RIEU
— B2d00	Crossroads	B2b36	
— B2a38 — house		T25b47	T19d36
along	road	to	T13 Central
thence	West	bank	of

FROM
PLACE & TIME

* This line, except AAA, should be erased, if not required.
(3287) Wt. W54/P738 691,000 Pads 3/18. A.P.Ltd. (E3013)

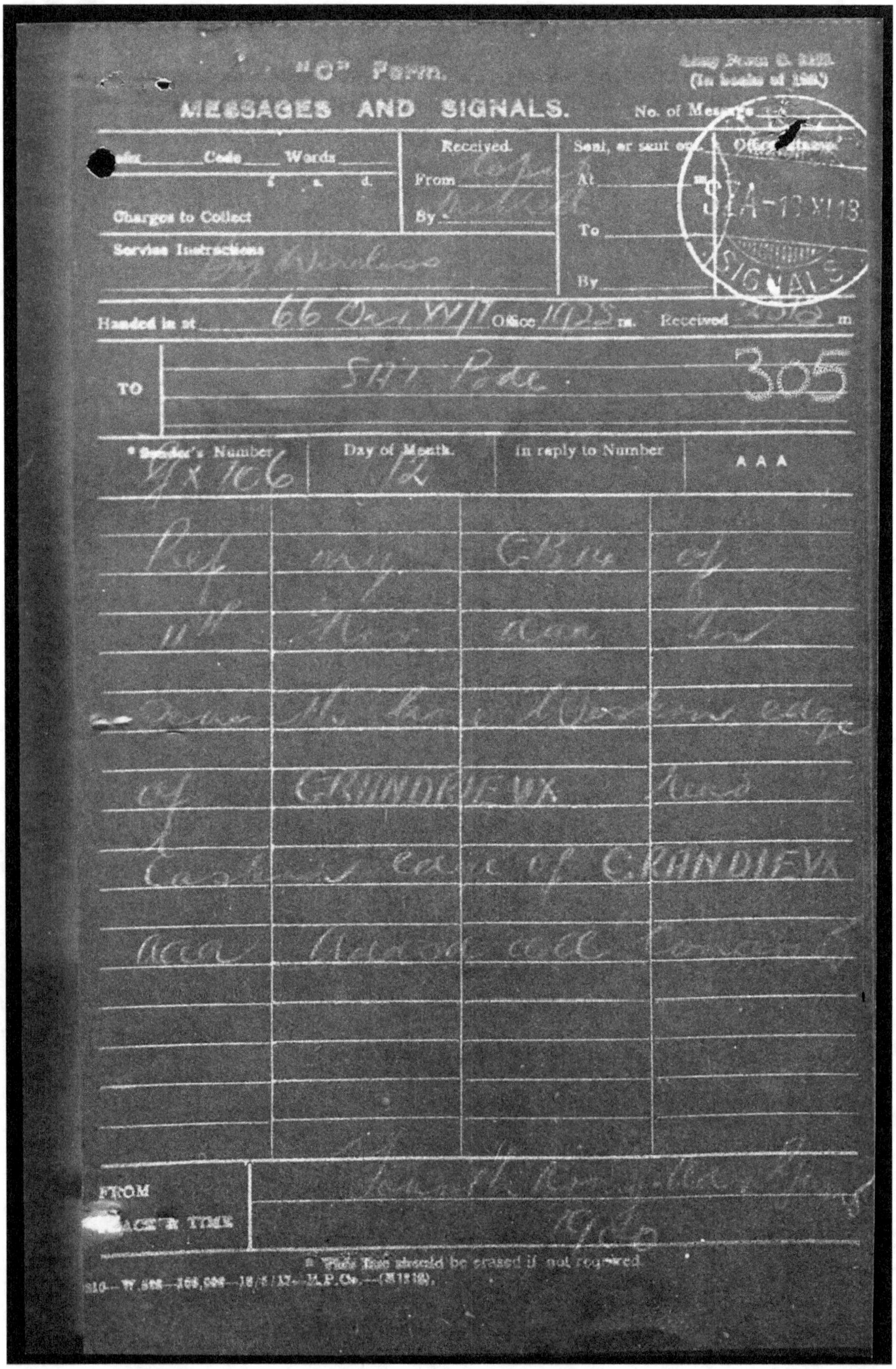

"C" Form.

MESSAGES AND SIGNALS.

Army Form C. 2121. (In books of 100.)

No. of Message [illegible]

Prefix ___ Code ___ Words ___ £ s. d.	Received. From [illegible] By [illegible]	Sent, or sent out. At ___ m. To ___ By ___
Charges to Collect		
Service Instructions By Wireless		

Office Stamp: SIGNALS [illegible] 12 XI 18.

Handed in at 66 Div W/T Office 1025 m. Received [illegible] m.

TO SHT Pode. 305

*Sender's Number	Day of Month.	In reply to Number	AAA
G/X 106	12		

Ref	my	CB14	of
11th	Nov	aaa	[illegible]
[illegible]	[illegible]	[illegible]	[illegible] edge
of	GRANDRIEUX		[illegible]
Eastern	edge	of	GRANDIEUX
aaa	[illegible]	[illegible]	[illegible]

FROM	[illegible]
PLACE & TIME	1030

* This line should be erased if not required.

[illegible] W. [illegible] 100,000 [illegible] H.P. Co. [illegible]

"C" FORM.
MESSAGES AND SIGNALS.

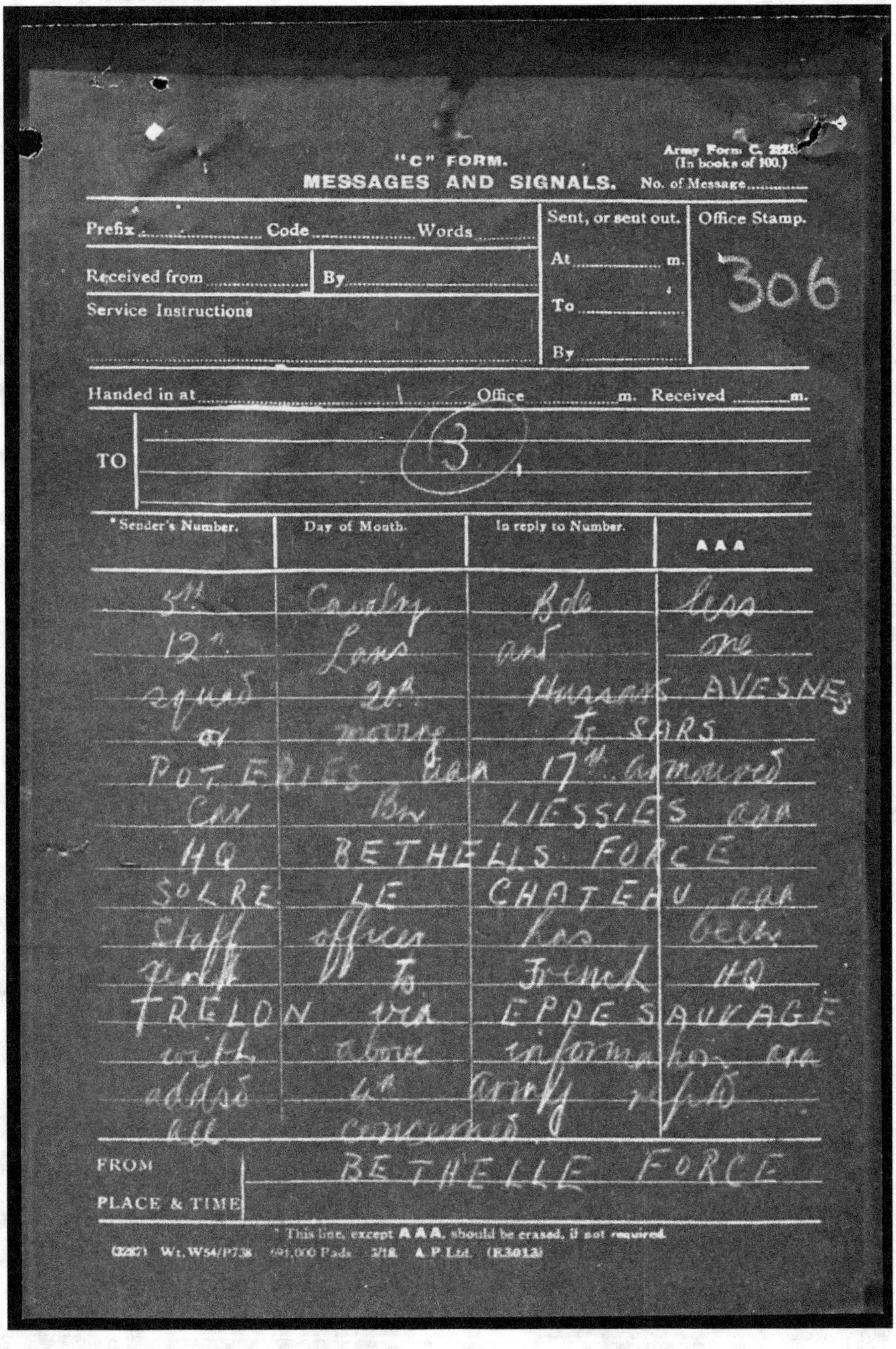

Army Form C. 2123
(In books of 100.)
No. of Message ....

Prefix .... Code .... Words ....
Received from .... By ....
Service Instructions

Sent, or sent out. | Office Stamp.
At .... m.
To ....
By ....

306

Handed in at .... Office .... m. Received .... m.

TO ③

*Sender's Number.	Day of Month.	In reply to Number.	A A A

5th Cavalry Bde less 12th Lans and one squad 20th Hussars AVESNES & moving to SARS POTERIES aaa 17th Armoured Car Bn LIESSIES aaa HQ BETHELLS FORCE SOLRE LE CHATEAU aaa Staff officer has been sent to French HQ TRELON via EPPE SAUVAGE with above information aaa addsd 4th army rpld all concerned

FROM: BETHELLE FORCE
PLACE & TIME:

"A" Form.

Army Form C. 2121.
(In pads of 100.)

MESSAGES AND SIGNALS.

No. of Message ....

Prefix .... Code 1910 m. | Words | Charge.

Office of Origin and Service Instructions.

BJR

Sent
At .... m.
To ....
By ....

This message is on a/c of:
.... Service.
(Signature of "Franking Officer.")

Recd. at .... m.
Date ....
From ....
By ....

TO	~~174~~	S A.	12 ~~Corps~~	307

Sender's Number.	Day of Month.	In reply to Number.	AAA
* SC22	11		

Reference my S18 of date NAMUR sheet 1/100000 ~~[illegible]~~ correct line should have read COUSOLRE along N. Bank of river to POINT where LATHURE RIVER crosses at E along stream to a POINT ¼ of mile N of N in GRANDRIEU. W edge of GRANDRIEU just W of VINERIEU as before to cross roads ½ N of S in VIEUX SART thence S along roads to PLAUMONT. RIVER along road to M of MONTBLIART thence S along road to MONTBLIART RIVER thence S along road to FORGENT FARM on Montbliart River. It is to be distinctly understood that no advance is permitted E of this line whether enemy is there or not.

From 46 Divn

Place

Time 1815

* The above may be forwarded as now corrected. (Z)

.... Censor. | J. Buttrum[?]
Signature of Addressor or person authorised to telegraph in his name.

~~1. (a) The 4th. SAI (less 3 coys.) will move by March Route tomorrow from BEAURIEUX to GRANDRIEU~~

app 45

308

SECRET 12.

Copy No.

12-11-18

SOUTH AFRICAN INFANTRY BRIGADE

MOBILE COLUMN ORDER No. 4 -

1.(a) The 4th. SAI. (less 3 coys.) will move from BEAURIEUX to GRANDRIEU by March Route tomorrow, 13th. inst., at 10.00 hours. Billeting party (for whole Bn.) will meet Staff Captain at Church in GRANDRIEU at 09.30 hours tomorrow.

First-line transport will march with the Bn..

(b) Three coys. 4th. SAI will be at the disposal of the C.R.E. tomorrow for road parties. At 09.30 hours tomorrow these coys. will be at the following points respectively:- (Ref. Map Sheet 57,1/40,000)

I coy. at Rd. junction, A.9.c.9.7.,
do. " , at L'HORTWISSE
do. large Farm on top of hill at A.4.d.7.8.

They will be met at these points by guides detailed under orders of the C.R.E., who will indicate the required tasks. Shovels will be carried.

(c) The tasks allotted will be upon estimated duration of 6 hours, and coys. will proceed to billets in GRANDRIEU whenever their respective tasks, as indicated, have been completed.

(d) If desired travelling kitchens may accompany these coys..

2. One coy. of the 1st. SAI will be at the disposal of the C.R.E. as a road party tomorrow, 13th. inst.. This coy. will rendezvous at the School, HESTRUD, at 09.30 hours tomorrow, when a guide detailed under orders of C.R.E. will indicate the task, on completion of which the coy. will return to billets

3. O.Cs. Units will take steps to ensure that discipline is not in any way relaxed by reason of the cessation of hostilities.

On the contrary, discipline should be everywhere tightened up - a special point being made of guard-mounting.

Strict orders should be issued that no firing is to take place by individuals or Units.

4. The following wire has been received from Corps:-

Begins aaa There is to be no unauthorised intercourse or fraternising of any description with the enemy aaa He will NOT be permitted to approach our lines and any attempt to do so will be immediately stopped if necessary by fire aaa Any parties of the enemy coming over to our lines under white flag will be made prisoners and report sent to Divl. HQ. aaa Enemy aircraft will NOT be permitted to cross ~~them~~ the line aaa Should any attempt to do so they will be attacked by fire from ground and air aaa No civilians will be permitted to cross our line in either direction aaa Ends

James [signature]
Major, Brigade Major,
South Afr. Inf. Bde..

Issued thro' Signals at 22.30 to:

1. 1st.SAI
2. 2nd. SAI
3. 4th. SAI
4. S. Afr. Fld.Amb.
5. SALTM Bty.
6. Bde. Sig. Off..
7. "B" Bty. 331 FA Bde.
8. 430 Fld. Co., RE
9. 66th. Divn.
10. Staff Captain
11. Brigade Major,
12/16. War Diary. ✓

app 47

309

SOUTH AFRICAN

INFANTRY BRIGADE

---*---

NARRATIVE of the Operations carried out by the Brigade during the period 1st. Nov. - 14th. Nov., 1918.

Nov.1 1st. Nov. found the Bde. still at SERAIN. On the 2nd. of the month, however, the Bde. was once more moving forward. By a succession of daily marches the Bde. moved successively to REUMONT, LE CATEAU, POMMEREUIL, LANDRECIES, and BASSE NOYELLES.

Nov.8 On the morning of the 8th. the Bde. moved from BASSE NOYELLES to DOMPIERRE, via TAISNIERES.. Bde. HQ. was established in the CHATEAU HUGEMENT, Units of the Bde. being billeted in DOMPIERRE village and its outskirts.

Nov.9 The following day, the Bde. marched via BEUGNIES to SOLRE LE CHATEAU, where Bde. HQ. opened at 19.00. This march was somewhat arduous owing to roads and bridges having been destroyed by the enemy on his withdrawal. Field tracks had to be resorted to, which involved long detours and heavy haulage for transport and supply wagons, etc.. Accordingly it was late in the day before the marching troops reached their billets in SOLRE LE CHATEAU.

As Bde. HQ. was leaving DOMPIERRE verbal orders were received from the Divl. Commander that in order to deal with the situation created by the rapid retirement of the enemy on the Fourth Army front it had been decided to create a Mobile Column under the command of the S. Afr. Inf. Bde. Commander. This force would concentrate at SOLRE LE CHATEAU immediately, and push on with the utmost rapidity. Definite orders would be issued later in the day, but the general intention was that the Mobile Column, comprising the S. Afr. Inf. Bde. and artillery, machine-guns and engineer and cyclist units, should move from SOLRE LE CHATEAU at daybreak on Nov. 10 and push on the same day to BEAUMONT.

The enemy was reported to be retiring rapidly; indeed, so little opposition was anticipated that two further bounds, each of a full day's marching, were scheduled for the column's progress. As will be seen later, however, the column met with a most determined enemy resistance shortly after leaving SOLRE LE CHATEAU.

Nov.10 At ~~03.00~~ 0030 on Nov. 10 verbal orders arrived at Bde. HQ. at SOLRE LE CHATEAU (afterwards confirmed in writing) for the organisation, composition, and operations of the Mobile Column. It was stated that the column, which was being placed under the command of Brig.-General W.E.C. TANNER, CMG., DSO., would consist of:

S. Afr. Inf. Bde. (less 4th. SAI. in Divl. Reserve.)
B/331 Bde. RFA. (6 18.pdrs.)
D/331 Bde. RFA. (1 Sec. 4.5" hows.)
430 Field Co., RE.,
"C" Coy., 100 MGC. Bn.
2 Armoured cars.
2 Platoons XIII Corps Cyclists.

Moreover, the general scheme was that at daylight that morning the pursuit of the enemy on the Fourth Army front would be vigorously taken up by the Mobile Column, covered by the 12th. Lancers, whilst the remainder of the 5th. Cav. Bde. was to operate on the Southern flank. The first bound was to be the river line BEAUMONT - SOLRE St. GERY - RENLIES - FROIDCHAPELLE. The Mobile Column was to move on the main road from SOLRE LE CHATEAU to BEAUMONT with the object of crossing the river and securing itself in BEAUMONT for the night 10/11 Nov..

DO. 121, 9-11-18

Mobile Column Order 1, 9-11-18

At 07.00 on Nov. 10., in accordance with orders, the Mobile Column moved out from SOLRE LE CHATEAU on the BEAUMONT road, the advance being covered by the 12th. Lancers. The advance guard, under the command of Lt.Col. H.H. JENKINS, 1st. SAI., consisted of the 1st. SAI., 1 section 430 Fld. Co., RE., 1 section "C" Coy. 100 BN. MGC., 1 bearer sub-section S. Afr. Field Amb., and 1 section B/331 Bde., RFA.. It had previously been reported ~~that~~ that the road had been blown up at a culvert some 1500x. E. of SOLRE LE CHATEAU., and an RE. party were accordingly despatched at dawn to effect the necessary repairs. But the damage proved more considerable than was expected, and the progress of the column was checked for about an hour. It was therefore about 09.30 when the advance guard reached HESTRUD. This village was found to be occupied by the 12th. Lancers, whose commander reported that the enemy was in considerable force on the high ground N. and S. of GRANDRIEU. Accordingly the main body of the column was halted under cover in the neighbourhood of the BOIS DE MADAME, HQ. of the column being established in the W. edge of HESTRUD.. After a brief reconnaissance of the ground and general situation, the 1st. SAI. was ordered to deploy for the attack, in order to break down the enemy resistance and clear the way for the further progress of the column.. The enemy position was an extremely strong one, and proved to be held by troops of the Prussian Guard Reserve. The difficulties were not lessened by the fact that contact had not been established with any of the co-operating units on either flank. The attack by the 1st. SAI. opened at about 10.30.. It was organized on a 3-coy. front (D, B, and A coys.) with C coy. in support.

The assaulting troops had first to cross the River THURE, the road bridge at HESTRUD having been blown up. The crossing was not difficult, but shortly after it became quite unfordable, evidently owing to the enemy opening sluice-gates of a reservoir further up the stream. Possibly the enemy miscalculated the rapidity of our attack, as otherwise there was no object in creating such a barrier after the assaulting troops had passed over. By 14.00 the water had again reached normal and fordable level.

During the afternoon a message from 66th. Div. timed 12.30 was received stating that the 199 Inf. Bde. had been ordered to move up on the Right of the S. Afr. Inf. Bde. to SIVRY, with the object of pushing on to RENLIES. The movement of this Bde. was made consequent upon the absence of the 5th. Cav. Bde., which was some way behind, and had been unable to reach its allotted position in the time available.

The progress of the attacking coys. was now very slow, and in parts completely held up by heavy MG. fire from houses and prepared positions. Artillery fire from field-guns and 4.2"s added to the difficulties of the situation, while low-flying enemy aeroplanes were very active. This was the situation at nightfall, and orders were given to dig in and prepare for a resumption of the attack on the following morning.

Reference must be made to the work done by "C" Coy., 100 BN., MGC.. When the attack opened up at HESTRUD a section of this Coy. took up a position near the river crossing E. of the village, engaging direct targets where possible. A second section formed part of the defence of the left flank, bringing fire to bear on the SE. corner of the BOIS du PRINCE de LIGNE, and with orders to open up rapid fire on any target that appeared in that direction, for the purpose of protecting the northern flank. At night this section slightly altered its positions in order to defend the valley running N. and S. from the wood. The remainder of the coy., one section, was kept in reserve.

<u>Nov.11</u> At 06.00 on the 11th. Nov., reports were received that the situation had not materially altered since the previous evening, the line running: (Map NAMUR 8, 1/100,000) - from the crest of the high ground N. of the 'N' in GRANDRIEU, Southwards through the valley slightly E. of the Belgian frontier, thence in a SE. direction to the high ground some 400x. W. of the junction of the GRANDRIEU - FRASIES rd. and the HESTRUD - VIVERIAUX rd..

In the meantime the river bridge at HESTRUD had been rebuilt by 430 Field Co., RE., and was capable of carrying transport and field guns. This work was most expeditiously carried out, notwithstanding heavy artillery fire, which also searched the back areas of the column, causing some casualties to men and animals.

312

At 10.00 telephonic advice was received at column HQ. that an armistice had been signed and that hostilities would cease at 11.00.. The news reached the enemy's lines before it reached the column, and he signalised the occasion by a considerable increase in his bombardment, which at times was most severe. Evidently he was determined not to have much surplus ammunition when the fateful hour arrived.

The terms of the original Divl. Order on the subject were as follows:-

> "Hostilities will cease at 11.00 today Nov. 11 aaa Troops will stand fast on line reached at that time which will be reported immediately by wire to HQ. Fourth Army Advance Guardaaa Defensive precautions will be maintained aaa There will be no intercourse of any description with the enemy until receipt of instructions."

At 11.00 exactly the firing on both sides suddenly ceased, and was followedby a silence no less dramatic. Combatants on both sides came out of their trenches and protected positions, and walked about in full view of each other, but there were no further hostilities, and of course no intercourse.

The total casualties for the two days' operations were 3 Officers and 70 other ranks, made up as follows:

Unit.	Killed		Wounded		Missing		TOTAL	
	O.	OR.	O.	OR.	O.	OR.	O.	OR.
Bde. HQ.	-			-	-		-	
Sig. Sectn.	-			2	-			2
1st. Rgt.		5	1	28	-		1	33
2nd. Rgt.		1		6	-			7
4th. Rgt.		2		-	-			2
331 Bde.RFA.	-			5	-			5
100 Bn. MGC.	1	2		4		1	1	7
S.Afr.Fld.Amb.		5	1*	9	-		1	14
	1	13	2	56		1	3	70

* At duty.

On the afternoon of Nov. 11 Column HQ. closed at HESTRUD and opened at the CHATEAU in the NW. outskirts of the village. 1st.SAI. remained in the line that night, maintaining full active-service precautions, and securing touch with 199 Inf. Bde. on the Right. At midday two Prussian Guard Reserve Officers came over to our line to discuss the best means of preventing their men from mixing with our troops, and were informed that the best way to overcome this difficulty was for them to remove their men to a safe distance. They quite agreed that this was the best means, and the following morning the last of them was seen disappearing over the high ground towards BEAUMONT.

On Nov. 12, 2nd. SAI. which, on the previous day had moved up to billets in HESTRUD, relieved the 1st. SAI. in the line, 1st. SAI returning to billets in HESTRUD; and on Nov. 14, 4th. SAI. which had been released from Div. Reserve, moved up to billets in GRANDRIEU, that village having been included in our outpost chain. During the morning the enemy withdrew from the E. side of GRANDRIEU to the vicinity of BEAUMONT.

On Nov. 14 a Guard of Honour of 5 Officers and 126 Other Ranks, dr drawn from all three BNs. of the Bde., and under the command of Lt.-Col. H.H. JENKINS, 1st. SAI., proceeded to SOLRE LE CHATEAU, the occasion being the visit of the Army Commander to Div. HQ..

* * * * *

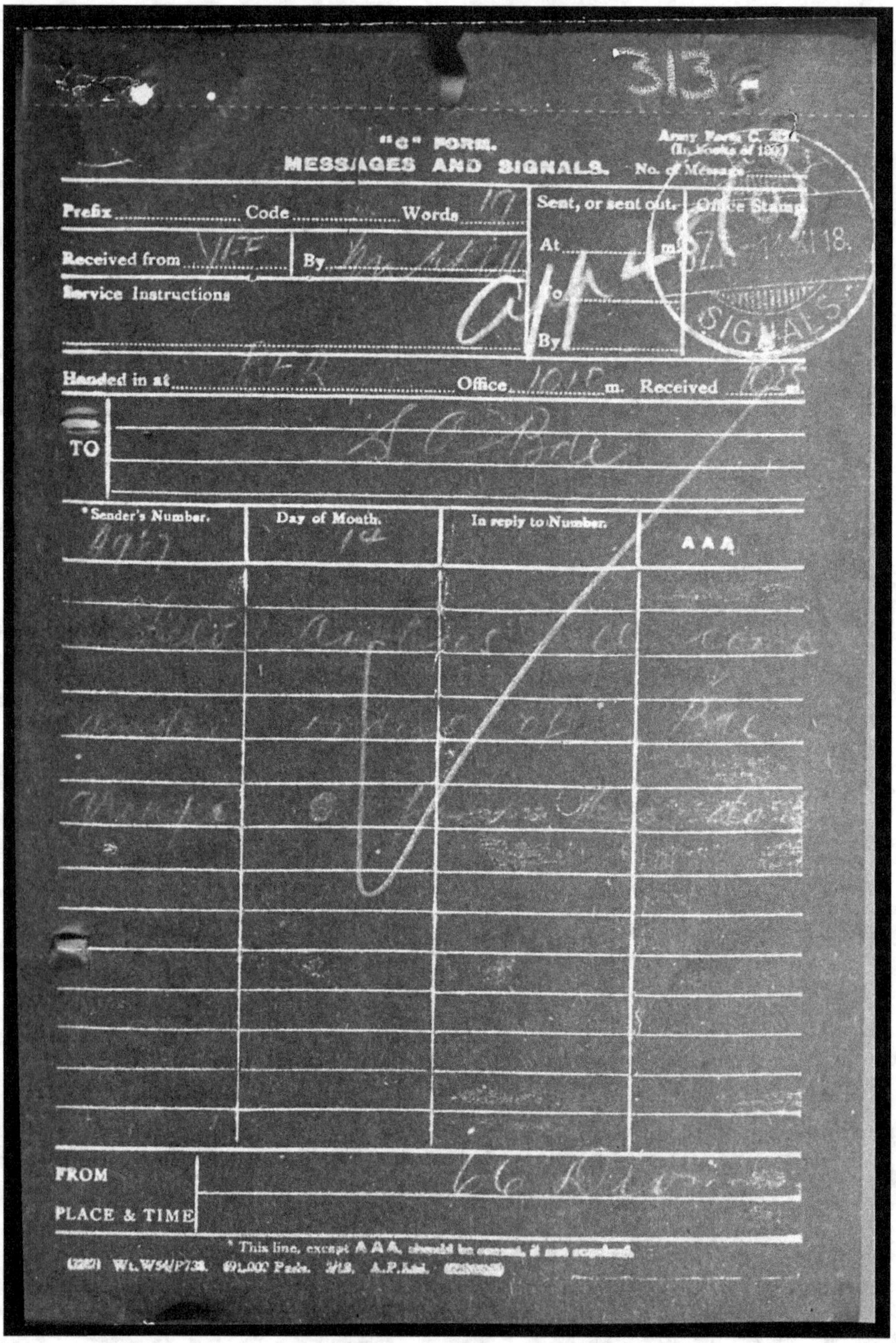

313

"C" FORM.
MESSAGES AND SIGNALS.

Army Form C. 2121. (In books of 100.)
No. of Message

Prefix ……… Code ……… Words 19	Sent, or sent out.
Received from YEF	By
Service Instructions	At ……… m.
	To
	By
	Office Stamp. SIGNALS 18.

Handed in at ……… Office 1015 m. Received 1025 m.

TO

*Sender's Number.	Day of Month.	In reply to Number.	AAA
4917	12		

FROM 66 Div
PLACE & TIME

* This line, except AAA, should be erased, if not required.

(282) Wt.W54/P738. 691,000 Pads. 3/18. A.P.Ltd.

"C" FORM.

MESSAGES AND SIGNALS.

Army Form C. 2123. (In books of 100.)

No. of Message ......

Prefix SM Code 2015 Words 23	Sent, or sent out.	Office Stamp.
Received from BM By [illegible]	At	
Service Instructions	To	
	By	

Handed in at ...... Office 2015 m. Received 2023 m.

TO: 2 A Bde

*Sender's Number.	Day of Month.	In reply to Number.	AAA
B 48	14		
66	Division	and	attached
troops	are	transferred	
to	7th	[illegible]	[illegible]
12	noon	today	aaa
Added	[illegible]	[illegible]	

FROM 66 Div

PLACE & TIME [illegible] 14/10/18

* This line, except A A A, should be erased, if not required.

(5287) Wt. W54/P733. 691,000 Pads. 3/18. A.P.Ltd. (E.1613)

314

SOUTH AFRICAN INFANTRY BRIGADE

SO.A.

315

1st. SAI
2nd. SAI
4th. SAI
SALTM Bty.
S.A.Fld. Amb.,
Bde. HQ..

The following information regarding Administrative Arrangements for the March to the Rhine is availableup to the present, and is forwarded to enable Units to make any adjustments necessary:-

Railways
Railhead for the present will remain at ANDIGNY, and will be pushed on as rapidly as possible. In the meantime a lorrly convoy will be used for bringing supplies forward from Railhead to Lorryhead, from which point the Divl. Supply Columns will function in the usual way. In order to avoid congestion, no lorries will move by day in the area occupied by advancing troops

Baggage & Dumps
4 extra GS. wagons will be at the disposal of each BN.. It will therefore be necessary to cut down stores to a minimum. Further instructions will be issued regarding stores which can be dispensed with. All surplus stores will be dumped at VAUX ANDIGNY. No other dumps can be permitted.

Transport
The greatest care will have to be taken with animals in order to reduce wastage to a minimum. A certain number of spares will probably be available for each Unit, but beyond these it will be impossible to replace. The country is very hilly, and wagons must not be overloaded. Frostcogs must be drawn from DADOS. at once, and care taken that the cogs fit the shoes.

Unfit Men
Any men unfit to march 10 miles daily will be sent to VAUX ANDIGNY under Divl. arrangements. Further instructions will follo

Accommodation
Accommodation is reported to be NIL, and approx. 100 trench shelters will be carried forward by each BN..

Clean Clothing
An attempt is being made to supply each man with a spare change of underclothing, to be carried by Unit.

Leave
Leave will continue as usual, use being made of returning lorrie for sending men back to railhead.

Rations
Each man will carry 1 Ixxxx Iron Ration and 1 spare ration (hard in addition to unconsumed portion of day's ration.

(sd) S.W.E. STYLE, Capt.,
Staff Captain,
South Afr. Inf. Bde..

14-11-18

Copy.

316

SOUTH AFRICAN INFANTRY BRIGADE.

SC.A.

1st S.A.I.
2nd S.A.I.
4th S.A.I.
S.A.L.T.M.B.
S, Afr. Fld. Amb.
Bde. H.Q.

In continuation of my No. SC.A. of 14th inst., the following stores will be carried .-

On the Transport.

Greatcoats.
1 Blanket per man (second blanket).
100 prs. Boots (if available).
1 pr. Socks per man.
Cleaning material.
Officers' kits.
Officers' Messes.

On the Man.

1 Blanket.
2 prs. Socks. (not including pair worn.)
1 set clean clothes.
1 Iron Ration.
1 Emergency Ration (hard).
Unconsumed portion of day's ration.
Cleaning Material, etc.

The following stores will be left at the Divl. Dump, AVESNES :-

Cup for firing grenades.
Wire-cutters, large.
Reserve of SBR. and containers.
Horse Respirators.
Bomb Carriers.
Vigilant Periscopes.
A.A.Lewis Guns.

Binoculars will be issued to and carried by Section Leaders, who will be responsible for them.

The Brigadier General Commanding wishes particular attention to be paid to men's packs in order to see that they are not overlooked.

Mobile reserve of S.A.A. and picks and shovels must be carried forward.

Officers should endeavour to cut their valises down to within reasonable limits.

Canteen stores must be left behind.

(Sgd) S.W.E.STYLE.
Captain,
Staff Captain,
South Afr. Inf. Bde.

16.11.18.

Secret   Fourth Army 293/3 (G)   317

NOTES FOR STAFFS REGARDING MARCH AND HALT ORDERS

Divisions will be marched by Bde. Groups - three Inf. Bdes. and on e Div. Arty. Group. The composition of these groups will, it is presumed, be left more or less to divns., but in forming them it is important to remember -

(a) The water question, i.e., if you put the whole of the Div. Arty. in the Div. Arty. Group it might be difficult to find sufficient water in one Group Area.

(b) A certain amount of artillery will have to be in the advance guard.

(c) So as to equalise the work of Commanders and Staffs, groups should be as near equal as possible in size.

Although Divns. are divided into four Bde. Groups it must be remembered that Staffs of Bde. Groups will be small; therefore everything it is possible for Divl. Staffs to do should be done by them and not handed over to the Bde. Groups. For instance, in making out march orders, the Div. Staff should lay down the starting point and time for the Bde. Groups.

Starts should not be made too early in the morning, so as to ensure the men get properly fed before they move off, and that vehicles have not to be packed in the dark. The Div. should allot the starting point for each Bde. Group near the head or in front of the Bde. Group area, so that no unit in the Bde. has to march back to reach its starting point. There will be no 10 minutes' halt on the way to the starting point, but the 10 minutes' halt will be rigidly adhered to once units have reached the main line of march.

Orders for the halt and for billets for the night must be issued in good time so as to reach Bde. Group HQ. some time before the leading Units of the Group reach the billeting area allotted to them. A form is attached showing a convenient way of issuing these orders. These forms can be printed or waxed and kept ready at Divl. HQ..

It is most important in these orders to put in the meeting point for the train where the Offices i/c of the various sections of the train, both baggage and supply, will find guides from units to lead wagons to the billets of their Units. The meeting point should be as near the entrance to the Bde. Group area as possible, and at a good road centre.

It is also important in the halt orders to fix a report centre for each Bde. Groupnto which all orders can be sent and all which all reports can be received from subordinate Units, until a permanent Bde. Group HQ. has been fixed for the night. As soon as this permanent HQ. has been selected it must be notified to Div. HQ. and subordinate units.

Billeting parties should start at the head of each Bde. Group, and should be as far as possible mounted on bicycles or horses. They can then go ahead, and on arrival at the entrance to their Bde. Group area they will be met by the Staff Captain of the Bde. Group, who will then allot them their billets.

At a certain hour, to be laid down by Corps, before which the march will have been completed, all roads will be kept clear for the advance of the supply column. No guns or transport must be parked on roads which can in any way interfere with the forward and backward movement of these lorries to and from refilling points. All supply lorries will be clear of the roads by a certain hour in the morning which will be laid down by Corps. That is to say, during the day roads will be employed for the marching troops, and during the night will be kept clear for the advance and return of supply lorries.

Advance parties of the leading Divns. or Corps can be sent forward with the cavalry to arrange billets, and have everything out and dried in plenty of time for the arrival of the troops in their new billeting area. Similarly the advance parties of the rear divs. can be sent forward with the leading divs. of each corps so as to find out all details as regards billets, water, etc..

Its duty will be to keep in touch with the enemy rearguard on the whole Army front, and to keep in touch with any troops sent out by Third Army on left, and First French Army on the right.

In the event of further support being required it will be found from 66th Division.

Major General H.K. BETHELL, C.M.G.,D.S.O. will take over command of this force at 12.00 10th Novr.

3. Mobile force (less S.A. Brigade, SOLRE LE CHATEAU, 12th Lancers, HESTRUD, and 5th Cavalry Brigade) will be concentrated about BEUGNIES at 10.00 10th Novr.

4. 66th Division will be disposed as follows by 12.00
<u>66TH DIV.</u> 10th November:-

199th Brigade - Brigade H.Q. BEUGNIES.
1 Battalion SARS POTERIES.
2 Battalions & 1 Coy 100th Bn.M.G.C. disposed in depth on the Divisional front E.23.c.0.0. K.10.d.0.0.

198th Brigade - Brigade H.Q. DOMPIERRE.
(Brig.Genl. A.J.HUNTER,DSO., MC, taking over command of 66th Divn. less Mobile force above detailed).
1 Battalion in houses along road through J.18., J.12., J.6.
1 Battalion ST. HILAIRE.
1 Battalion J.2.
9th Bn. Glouc. R. (less 1 Company BEUGNIES).
100th Bn. M.G.C. (less 2 Coys) BAS - LIEU.

Rear Divl H.Q. to move to DOMPIERRE at 08.00 10th November.
Artillery as at present excepting that 1 Brigade only will cover Divisional front, remainder being withdrawn to their wagon lines at DOMPIERRE.

5. XIII Corps are taking over all communications as far east as LES TROIS PAVES.
<u>COMMUNICATIONS.</u>

"A" is arranging for the strengthening of all Divl. and Corps police to deal with stragglers and unauthorised persons in the areas occupied by Corps and Divns. during the march. In every case stragglers posts should be detailed to follow up formations during the march. ~~In every case etc~~ It must be remembered that APM's duties are traffic control and maintenance of discipline. March discipline of Units is the duty of Staff and Regimental Officers, and is no part of the APM's duty.

When advance parties report any obstacles or steep hills on the road, divns. must be ready at once to send forward working parties to deal with them and to remain there until the whole divn. has passed through.

Divns. and Corps must make full use of all Staff Officers to ensure that there are no blocks at road junctions or other difficult places.

Arrangements will be made for the position of all HQ. to be clearly marked. All sentries, traffic control posts, and police will be instructed as to the position of and route to all HQ. in the vicinity.

In order to give space on the road, bands will march in sections of threes, and not in sections of fours.

As soon as possible after the arrival in a billeting area all Units will send an Orderly who knows the position of the Unit's HQ., to report himself at Bde. HQ..

(sd) -----------
Major-General,
General Staff,
Fourth Army.

13-11-18

320

Copy. 66th Division 7948/Q.

SECRET.

ADMINISTRATIVE INSTRUCTIONS No. 1.

in connection with 66th Div. Preliminary Order No. 123 dated 15.11.18.

1. AMMUNITION.
Horsed Echelons will move full, with the exception that grenades will not be carried.

2. SUPPLIES.
In addition to the Iron Rations, one day's preserved ration will be carried by units.
On the line of march each echelon will move full.
Supply Section, 66th Div. M.T.Coy will leave lorry head in order of march of formations.
Units will ensure that guides are left to meet their supply wagons, these guides will be posted at the appraoches to billets.

3. ORDNANCE.
Ordnance Stores will as far as possible be delivered to Refilling Points. Units will attach to their affiliated Train Coy a representative to take over Ordnance Stores at Refilling Point, and deliver the same by Supply Wagon to the Unit.

4. TRANSPORT.
Extra Transport for the conveyance of blankets and great coats will be provided. In addition, it is hoped to allot 1 Motor Lorry to each Brigade Group for conveyance of stores etc.
Horse Transport will be underloaded as roads will be met with of difficult gradients. Replacement of broken down vehicles will not be possible. The replacing of animals will be extremely difficult.
All units will be in possession of horse shoes tapped for frost cogs, and will satisfy themselves that the thread of the cogs received fit the sockets. The D.A.D.O.S. will carry a reserve of both of these.

5. PROVOST ARRANGEMENTS.
(a) Police will be strengthened in Formations and Units, great care will be taken in selecting men for this duty.
(b) Group Commanders will be responsible for the adequate picqueting of their areas, and for taking the necessary precautions against fire.
(c) Necessary steps will be taken by all concerned to prevent damage to property. The tying of animals to trees is prohibited.
(d) Groups Commanders will be responsible for the collection of stragglers of their respective Groups.

6. BILLETING.
The Division will be billeted in four groups: Three Infantry Brigade Groups, and one Div. Hd.Qr.Groups.
Groups Areas will be allotted in Divisional Orders, Group Commanders will then send on Billeting Parties mounted on bicycles ahead of the Division to make detailed arrangements for billeting and meeting troops on arrival.
C.R.A. in conjunction with an Officer to be detailed by Camp Commandant will be responsible for billeting Div. Hd.Qr Group.
The following Units of Div. HD.QR Group will send Billeting Parties in accordance with instructions to be issued to them by C.R.A.

Camp Commandant.
100th Bn. M.G.C.
Div. Train for Hd.Qrs. and No. 1 Coy.
Mob. Vet. Section.

323

7. TRAFFIC.

(a) No Mechanical Transport other than Motor Cars and Motor Cycleswill be allowed to proceed along the line of March until the day's march has been completed by troops.

(b) Lorries and Wagons will not be loaded or unloaded on any main traffic route.

(c) Broken down vehicles will be moved clear of the road by the first troops to discover them.

8. LEAVE.

All ranks due to proceed on leave up to and including 25th November, and desirous of so proceeding, will be despatched to Divisional Reception Camp, VAUX ANDIGNY, and will not proceed on the march.

9. MEDICAL.

Sick will be collected by Field Ambulances from their respective Brigade Groups. Those of Div. Hd. Qrs. Group will be collected under arrangements to be made by A.D.M.S.

Cases will be evacuated to C.C.S. through the Field Ambulance with the Rear Brigade Group.

10. SANITATION.

(a) Latrines will invariably be dug immediately troops reach billets or Camp, and also during prolonged halts.

All Latrines must be filled in before troops move off, and the site marked.

(b) Water for drinking purposes will only be drawn from xxxxx water carts.

Group Commanders will make the necessary arrangements to ensure that water is tested before it is passed fit for drinking, and that xxxxx the amount of chloride of lime necessary for sterilisation is clearly indicated.

(c) Camphor Powder for the feet should be freely used during the march. Supplies can be obtained by units from the Field Ambulance collecting their sick.

(Sgd)

Lieut-Colonel,
A.A. & Q.M.G.
66th Division.

16.11.18.

"A" Form
Army Form C. 2121
(In pads of 100.)

MESSAGES AND SIGNALS.

No. of Message..........

Prefix.......Code.......m. Office of Origin and Service Instructions	Words / Charge. Sent At.......m. To....... By.......	This message is on a/c of: ....Service. (Signature of "Franking Officer")	Recd. at......m. Date....... From....... By....... 321

TO	Sender's Number.	Day of Month.	In reply to Number.	AAA
		2		

of	VIVERIAUX	thence	to
a	point	about	three
hundred	yards	N	of
the	road	junction	E
of	FRASIES	where	we
have	established	touch	with
left	flank	of	199th
Bde	AAA	Addsd	66
Div	repld	199	Bde.

From S A Bde
Place
Time

The above may be forwarded as now corrected.

Censor.

[signature] Major
Bde Major
Signature of Addressor or person authorised to telegraph in his name

* This line should be erased if not required.

Order No. 1625. Wt. W3253/ P 511. 27/2. H. & K., Ltd. (E. 2634).

A Form (In pads of 100.)

MESSAGES AND SIGNALS.

No. of Message............

Prefix............Code.........m. Office of Origin and Service Instructions	Words	Charge.	This message is on a/c of:	Recd. at......m.
	Sent At ....m. To .... By		......Service. appx 6(c) (Signature of "Franking Officer.")	Date...... From ...... By......

TO 66 Div
198 Inf Bde
322

Sender's Number.	Day of Month.	In reply to Number.	AAA
BS. 145	12.		

Our	line	has	been
slightly	altered	today	and
now	runs	as	follows
AAA	Ref	Map	NAMUR
Sheet	1/100,000	AAA	from
a	point	~~x~~ in	S
fringe	of	large	wood
N	of	A	in
GRANDRIEU	SE	to	the
road	junction	immediately	E
of	U	in	GRANDRIEU
thence	through	the	outskirts
of	GRANDRIEU	village	at
the	point	N	of
first	V	in	VIVERIAUX
thence	S	to	the
nearest	road	junction	E.

From
Place
Time

The above may be forwarded as now corrected. (Z)

Censor. Signature of Addressor or person authorised to telegraph in his name

* This line should be erased if not required.

Order No. 1625. Wt. W3252/ P 511. 27/2 H. & K., Ltd. (E. 2634).

326 app 5

SOUTH AFRICAN INFANTRY BRIGADE

SECRET
Copy No.

ORDER No. 210

15-11-18

Ref. Map -
NAMUR 1/100,000

MARCH TO THE RHINE

1. In accordance with the terms of the armistice, occupied portions of FRANCE, BELGIUM, and LUXEMBURG, are to be evacuated by the enemy by Nov. 26th..

A further withdrawal to east of the RHINE will take place at a later date.

2. The advance of the Allied forces will commence on Nov. 17th..

3. 66th. Div. will lead the advance on the Right of the British Army. 169th. French Divn. will be on its Right, and 1st. (British) Divn. on its left.

66th. Divn. will be preceded by the 2nd. Cav. Divn., which will cover the front of the Fourth Army.

32nd. Divn. will follow 66th.Divn. 1 day's march in its rear.

4. Divl. boundary to the MEUSE will be as follows:
(a) Northern boundary:- L'ECREVISSE (excl.) - ~~xxxxx~~ FRASIES (excl.) - SIVRY Station (incl.) - RAMLIES - SILENRIEUX - FONTAINE - FLORENNES - JUSAINES (all excl.) ROSEE (incl.) - ROSEE-DINANT road (excl.)..
(b) Southern boundary:- EPPE SAUVAGE (incl.) - through 'DE' of FORET DE RANCE - railway crossing ¼ inch. S. of 'C' of CERFONTAINE - SAMART (excl.) - VILLERS-le-GAMBON (incl.) - ~~xxxxx~~ SURICE (incl.) - road junctn. ¾ inch. W. of 'H' of HEER.

5. Preliminary Moves:
(a) On Nov. 16th., 1st. Divn. will take over the portion of front from FRASIES (incl.) to E. Army boundary. Relief to be completed by 12.00. Dividing line between 66 and 1 Divns. -
FRASIES - BOIS de BEAURIEUX - L'ECREVISSE all incl. to 1st. Divn..
(b) On Nov. 17th., 2nd. Cav, Div. will pass through our present outpost line. The Cavalry will be followed by billeting parties to be detailed by 66th. Divn 'Q' and by working parties to be detailed by the leading Bde. Group; reconnaissance will be carried out to ascertain whether state of roads will permit a full day's march on the 18th..

(6) On Nov. 18, the Divn. will advance in Bde. Groups with 199 Bde. Group leading along the road RANCE - FROIDCHAPELLE - CERFONTAINE - PHILIPPEVILLE - ROSEE. Should the road be sufficiently good it is intended that the march on 18th. should be to the line of L'EAU D'HEURE.

7. Military precautions will be observed during the march as follows:-
(a) Leading Inf. Bde. Group will detail an escort and covering party of 2 coys. to accompany the billeting and working parties which will be moving a day in advance of the main body of the Div..
Working parties will consist of:- 1 Fld. Co., Rs.,
1 Sec. Tunnelling Co., Rs.,
Proportion of Pioneer Bn.)
and additional working parties will be held in readiness at the head of the Bde. Group in case they should be required.
(b) Leading Bde. Group will march with an advance Guard including 1 Battery, RFA..
(c) In billets the leading Bde. will picquet the roads leading from front and flanks to their billets.
(d) Troops will be distributed in sufficient depth to facilitate supply, but arrangements will be made to ensure that a sufficient force can be available at 48 hrs.' notice to overcome the resistance of the enemy should any attempt be made to oppose our advance.

325

66th Divn. 7948/8/Q.

S.A.Bde.

1. The following G.S.wagons will be allotted for the march to the RHINE.

Div. H.Q.		2
R.E. H.Q.		1
Each Inf. Bn. 4		40
100th Bn.M.G.C.		2
Each Field Co.1		3
Each Field Ambce.1		3
Total		51

These wagons will report to respective formations Headquarters on evening of 17th.

Instructions as to wagons for 2 battalions of 198th Brigade are being issued separately.

The above transport is to be used primarily ~~for the carriage~~ for the carriage of blankets and greatcoats.

2. Lorries for move are allotted as under, and will report to formations on evening of 17th

1.	Div. H.Q.		6
2.	Signal Co.		1
3.	D.A.D.O.S.		4
4.	Post		2
5.	Each Inf. Bde Group	3	9
6.	Div. Batchs Officer		2
7.	" Canteen Offr.		1
8.	R.A. H.Q.		1
9.	R.E. H.Q. & Pnr. Bn.		1

Serial Nos. 1. 7, 8 & 9 will march with Divisional Headquarters Group.

Serial Nos. 2, 3, 5 & 6 will march with 66th Divl. M.T.Coy.

The above lorries are primarily to be used for the carriage of trench shelters, but are available for other stores as space p permits.

The normal daily procedure will be as follows. Lorries will park under Brigade Group arrangements during the night and no lorries will start to rejoin Groups until all troops have completed their day's march.

3. Infantry Brigades will indent on 66th Div. Train for the necessary petrol. This will be sent up on supply wagons of the Train as required.

4. Under no circumstances will any transport be loaded with more than 80% of the normal load.

N.B. 1 lorry carries 150 Trench Shelters loose.
or 200 " " in bales.

5. A supply of trench shelters will be distributed. It is not known how many can be made available, but it is hoped to send a supply to formations on the lorries referred to, on 17th.

(Sd.) R.E.OTTER, Major,
D.A.Q.M.G.
66th Division.

16.11.18.

327

8. (a) Subject to above, the comfort of the troops will be the principal object in the conduct of the march. Bands will be, and colours may be, taken on the march.

(b) Bde. Group Commanders will be responsible that the strictest march discipline is maintained by all units in their respective groups.

(c) DRESS: Full marching order: 1 blanket in lieu of greatcoat; 70 rounds SAA. to be carried by each man in lieu of 120 rounds. 1 day's hard ration to be carried by each man in addition to emergency ration and unexpended portion of day's ration.

9. COMMUNICATIONS.

During the march communications will be maintained entirely by wireless, visual, DRs., and orderlies.

10. Orders for the relief in the line indicated in para. 5 will be issued later.

11. The S. Afr. Bde. Group will be composed as follows:

Bde. HQ. & Signal Section
1st. SAI
2nd. SAI
4th. SAI
430 Fld. Co., RE
No. 2 Co., Divl. Train, ASC.,
SA Field Ambulance.

12. ACKNOWLEDGE.

R. Saunders Lt

for Captain,
A/Bde. Major,
South Afr. Inf. Bde.

1. 1st. SAI
2. 2nd. SAI
3. 4th. SAI
4. SALTM Bty.
5. Bde. Sig. Off.
6. S. Afr. Fld. Amb.
7. 430 Fld. Co., RE
8. 2 Co., Div. Train, ASC.
9. 66 Divn.
10. 198 Inf. Bde.
11. 199 Inf. Bde.
12. Bde. Major
13. Staff Captain
14/18. War Diary.

APPENDIX "A".

COMPOSITION OF BRIGADE GROUPS & DISPOSITIONS OF DIVISION BY 18.00 November 17th.

	LOCATION.
Divisional H.Q. Group. (Brig. Genl. A. BIRTWISTLE, CMG., DSO.)	
Divl H.Q. and H.Q. Troops.	SOLRE LE CHATEAU.
H.Q. Group, Divl Signal Company.	" " "
1 Troop 13th Aust. Light Horse.	" " "
Detachment IX Corps Cyclists.	" " "
"B.T." Cable Section.	" " "
Div. R.A. (less 1 Battery). 14th Brigade A.F.A. D.A.C.	LIESSIES, WILLIES, TOUVENT, RAMOUSIES Area.
H.Q. Div. R.E.	SOLRE LE CHATEAU.
@ 567th A.T. Company R.E.	FELLERIES.
@ 1st Aust. T. Company R.E. (less 2 Sects).	FELLERIES.
100th Bn. M.G.C.	SIVRY.
H.Q. & No. 1 Coy. Divl. Train A.S.C.	SOLRE LE CHATEAU.
1/1st East. Lancs. Mobile Vet: Section.	" " "

South African Brigade Group. (Brig. Genl. W.E.C. TANNER, CMG., DSO.)	
Brigade H.Q. & Signal Section. 1st Bn. S.A. Regiment. 2nd Bn. S.A. Regiment. 4th Bn. S.A. Regiment.	SIVRY. MOULARD. BEAURIEUX.
430th Field Company R.E.	SOLRE LE CHATEAU.
No. 2 Coy. Divl Train A.S.C.	" " "
S.A. Field Ambulance.	" " "

......

P.T.O.

329

(2)

LOCATION.

198th Brigade Group.
(Brig. Genl. A.J. HUNTER, D.S.O.,M.C.)

Brigade H.Q. & Signal Section.	BEAURIEUX.
6th Bn. Lancashire Fusiliers.	RANCE.
5th Bn. R. Innis: Fusiliers.	CLAIRFAYTS.
6th Bn. R. Dublin Fusiliers.	RANCE.
431st Field Company R.E.	SOLRE LE CHATEAU.
No. 3 Coy. Divl. Train A.S.C.	" " "
2/2nd East Lancs. Field Ambulance.	" " "

199th Brigade Group.
(Brig. Genl. G.C. WILLIAMS, D.S.O.).

Brigade H.Q. & Signal Section. 18th Bn. (LHY) Kings L'pool R. 9th Bn. Manchester Regt. 5th Bn. Connaught Rangers. 432nd Field Company R.E. 2/3rd East Lancs. Field Ambulance.	Covering Divisional front and in area - MONTBLIART - VIEUX SART - TRES BOUCHAUX.
No. 4 Coy. Divl. Train A.S.C.	SOLRE LE CHATEAU.
*9th Bn. Glouc. R. (Pioneers).	RANCE.
*1 Battery R.F.A. (for protection of Divisional front).	
*1 Section 1st Aust. T. Coy. R.E.	RANCE.

---

*Temporarily attached only.
@Will march in rear of Divisional Column.

D.H.Q.
18th Nov. 1918.

330

APPENDIX 'H'

COMPOSITION OF BRIGADE GROUPS & DISPOSITIONS OF DIVISION
by 18,00 November 16th.

GROUP,	LOCATION.
South African Brigade Group. (Brig. Genl. W.E.C. TANNER, C.M.G., D.S.O.),	
Brigade H.Q. & Signal Section. 1st Bn. S.A. Regiment. 2nd Bn. S.A. Regiment. 4th Bn. S.A. Regiment.	SIVRY. MOULARD. BEAURIEUX.
430th Field Company R.E. No. 2 Coy, Divl Train A.S.C. S.A. Field Ambulance.	SOLRE LE CHATEAU. " " " " " "
198th Brigade Group. (Brig. Genl. A.J. HUNTER, D.S.O., M.C.)	
Brigade H.Q. & Signal Section. 6th Bn. Lancs. Fusiliers. 5th R. Inniskillin Fusiliers. 6th R. Dublin Fusiliers.	BEAURIEUX. SOLRE LE CHATEAU. CLAIRFAYTS. SOLRE LE CHATEAU.
431st Field Company R.E. No. 3 Coy. Divl Train A.S.C. 2/2nd E. Lancs. Field Ambulance.	SOLRE LE CHATEAU. " " " " " "
199th Brigade Group. (Brig. Genl G.C. WILLIAMS, D.S.O.)	
Brigade H.Q. & Signal Section. 18th (LHY) Kings L'pool R. 9th Bn. Manch. R. 5th Bn. Conn. Rang. 432nd Field Company R.E. 2/3rd E. Lancs. Field Amb.	Covering Divisional front and in area EPPE SAUVAGE - RUE D'on HAUT - MONTBLIART - VIEUX SART.

P.T.O.

331

G R O U P.	L O C A T I O N.
199th Brigade Group. (Contd).	
No. 4 Coy., Divl Train A.S.C.	SOLRE LE CHATEAU.
1 Battery R.F.A. (Temporarily attached to 199th Bde for protection of Divisional front).	
Divisional H.Q. Group.	
D.H.Q. and H.Q. Troops.	SOLRE LE CHATEAU.
H.Q. Group Divl Signal Coy.	" " "
Div. R.A. (less 1 Battery) plus 14th Bde. A.F.A., plus D.A.C.	LIESSIES, WILLIES, TOUVENT Area.
H.Q. Div. R.E.	SOLRE LE CHATEAU.
1/1st E. Lancs. Mob. Vet. Sect.	" " "
100th Bn. M.G.C.	SIVRY.
9th Bn. Glouc. R. (Pioneers).	SOLRE LE CHATEAU.
H.Q. & No. 1 Coy. Divl. Train A.S.C.	" " "

D.H.Q.
15th Novr 1918.

324

Copy. 66th Div 7948/8/Q.

APP 50

To All recipients of 66th Div. No. 7948/8/Q of 16/11/18.

This Office No. 7948/8/Q para. 2 is amended.

Serial Nos. will accompany Formations as under :-

Nos.	1,2,8 & 9	D.H.Q. Group.
"	3,4,6,7,	Divl. M.T.Coy.
No.	5	Respective Infantry Brigade Groups.

(Sgd) R.E.OTTER,
Major,
D.A.Q.M.G.
66th Division.

17.11.18

app 51 (o)

332

S E C R E T.   Copy No. 6

66th DIVISION PRELIMINARY ORDER No. 123.

Map Reference:-
1/100,000 NAMUR Sheet.   15th November 1918.

MARCH TO THE RHINE.

1. In accordance with terms of the armistice, occupied portions of FRANCE, BELGIUM and LUXEMBURG are to be evacuated by enemy by November 26th.
A further withdrawal to east of RHINE will take p lace at a later date.

2. The advance of the Allied Forces will commence on Nov. 17th.

3. 66th Division will lead the advance on the right of the British Army.
169th French Division will be on its right, and 1st (British) Division on its left.
66th Division will be preceded by the 2nd Cavalry Division, which will cover the front of the Fourth Army.
32nd Division will follow 66th Division 1 day's march in rear.

4. Divisional boundary to the Meuse will be as follows:-

(a) Northern boundary:-
L'ECREVISSE (excl.) - FRASIES (excl.) - SIVRY Station (incl.) - RENLIES - SILENRIEUX - FONTAINE - FLORENNES - JUSAINE (all excl.), - ROSEE (incl.) - ROSEE - DINANT Road (excl.).

(b) Southern boundary:-
EPPE SAUVAGE (incl.) - through DE of FORET DE RANCE - Railway crossing ¼ inch south of C of CERFONTAINE - SAMART (excl.) - VILLERS-LE-GAMBON (incl.) - SURICE (incl.) - Road junction ¼ inch W. of H of HEER.

5. Preliminary Moves.
(a) On November 16th, 1st Division will take over the portion of front from FRASIES (incl.) to N. Army boundary. Relief to be complete by 12.00.
Dividing line between 66th and 1st Divisions:-
FRASIES - BOIS de BEAURIEUX - l'ECREVISSE all inclusive to 1st Division.

333

(b) By 18.00 November 16th, 66th Division will be disposed as shewn in Appendix 'A'.

Necessary moves to be carried out under orders of Brigade Group Commanders concerned.

Moves of 12th Royal Lancers subsequent to relief by units of 1st Division will be notified direct to 12th Royal Lancers by 5th Cavalry Brigade.

(c) On November 17th, 2nd Cavalry Division will pass through our present outpost line. The Cavalry will be followed by billeting parties to be detailed by 66th Division 'Q', and by working parties to be detailed by the leading Brigade Group; reconnaissance will be carried out to ascertain whether state of roads will permit a full day's march on the 18th.

6. On November 18th, the Division will advance in Brigade Groups (Composition as in Appendix 'A') with 199th Brigade Group leading along the road, RANCE - FROIDCHAPELLE - CERFONTAINE - PHILLIPEVILLE - ROSEE.

Should the road be sufficiently good it is intended that the march on 18th should be to the line of L'EAU D'HEURE.

7. Military precautions will be observed during the march as follows:-

(i) Leading Infantry Brigade Group will detail an escort and covering party of 2 Coys to accompany the billeting and working parties which will be moving a day in advance of the main body of the Division.
Working parties will consist of:-
1 Field Company R.E.
1 Section Tunnelling Company R.E.
Proportion of Pioneer Battalion.
and additional working parties will be held in readiness at the head of the Brigade Group in case they should be required.

(ii) Leading Brigade Group will march with an advance guard including 1 Battery R.F.A.

(iii) In billets the leading Brigade will picquet the roads leading from front and flanks to their billets.

(iv) Troops will be distributed in sufficient depth to facilitate supply, but arrangements will be made to ensure that a sufficient force can be available at 48 hours notice to overcome the resistance of the enemy should he attempt to oppose our advance.

8. (a) Subject to the above, the comfort of the troops will be the principal object in the conduct of the march.
Bands will be, and colours may be, taken on the march.

(3)

8\. (b) Brigade Group Commanders will be responsible that the strictest march discipline is maintained by all units in their respective groups.

(c) DRESS:-

Full marching order; 1 blanket in lieu of greatcoat; Helmet worn in lieu of cap; 70 rounds S.A.A. carried by each man in lieu of 120 rounds; 1 day's hard ration to be carried by each man in addition to emergency ration and unexpended portion of day's ration.

9\. COMMUNICATIONS.

During the march communications will be maintained entirely by wireless, visual, D.Rs and orderlies.

1 Officer and 15 other ranks from IX Corps Cyclists have been attached to Divisional Signal Company.

1 Troop Australian Light Horse may be subsequently attached to the Division.

10\. ACKNOWLEDGE.

F.P. [signature]
Lieut Colonel,
General Staff,
66th Division.

Issued at 1630

DISTRIBUTION.

Copy No. 1 War Diary.
2 " "
3 File.
4 198th Brigade.
5 199th Brigade.
6 [illegible] Brigade.
7 C.R.A.
8 C.R.E.
9 Signals.
10 A & Q.
11 Train A.S.C.
No. 12 100th Bn. M.G.C.
13 A.D.M.S.
14 12th Lancers.
15 9th Bn. Glouc.R. (Pioneer
16 5th Cavalry Brigade.
17 IX Corps.
18 IX Corps Cyclist Bn.
19 1st Division.
20 169th French Division.
21 2nd Cavalry Division.
22 32nd Division.
23\. A.D.C.

335

SECRET.

Copy No. 6

Reference 66th Division Order No. 123 of 15th November 1918.

Cancel Appendix 'A' and substitute Appendix forwarded herewith.

F.P. [signature]

Lieut Colonel.
General Staff.
66th Division.

Issued at 23.30.

Issued to:- All Recipients of D.O. 123.

app 82 336

SECRET.
Copy No.

SOUTH AFRICAN INFANTRY BRIGADE.

Ref. Map -
NAMUR. 1/100,000

ORDER No. 261.

15-11-18.

1. On 16th November the 1st Division will take over the portion of the front FRASIES (incl.) to N. Army boundary, relief to be complete by 13.00

Dividing line between 66th Division and 1st Division FRASIES - BOIS de BEAURIEUX - l'ECREVISSE all inclusive to 1st Division.

2. All details of relief of the outpost line will be arranged by O's. C. Battalions concerned. Particulars regarding relieving Battalion will be notified later.

3. The South African Infantry Brigade will move in accordance with attached march table and will be located as follows :-

Brigade H.Q.	SIVRY.
1st S.A.I.	do
2nd S.A.I.	do
4th S.A.I.	BEAURIEUX.
S.A.L.T.M.B.	SIVRY.

4. Billeting parties of the 1st S.A.I. and 2nd S.A.I. will meet Lt. R. O. SAUNDERS at the Church, SIVRY, at 11.00 hours.

4th S.A.I. will arrange their own billets in BEAURIEUX, the whole village being at its disposal except portion occupied by 198th Bde. H.Q.

5. 1st Line Transport will move with Unit.

6. Flares, S.O.S. very lights and bombs surplus to establishment may be dumped before moving. Location of dumps to be reported to Bde. H.Q. by 19.00 hours.

7. Brigade H.Q. will close at HESTRUD CHATEAU at 14.00 hours and open at SIVRY on arrival.

8. Acknowledge.

[signature]
Captain,
A/Brigade Major,
S.African Inf. Bde.

1. 1st S.A.I.
2. 2nd S.A.I.
3. 4th S.A.I.
4. S.A.L.T.M.B.
5. S.A.Fld. Amb.
6. Bde Sig. Officer.
7. 5XX th Fld Co. R.E.
8. 2nd Co., Div. Train, A.S.C.
9. 66th Division.
10. 198th Inf. Bde.
11. 199th Inf. Bde.
12. Bde. Major.
13. Staff Captain.
14/18. War Diary.

338

Guideswill always meet Units on the road of advance at the W. end of the village in which they are billeted.

6. Traffic

(a) No mechanical transport, other than motor-cars and motor-cycles, will be allowed to proceed along the line of march until the day's march has been completed by troops.

(b) Throughout the march the main road along which the Bde. advances will be kept absolutely clear of all troops and vehicles from 1..00 till 06.00 in order to allow free passage for supply convoys.

(c) Lorries and wagons will not be loaded or unloaded on any main traffic route.

(d) Any obstructions will be moved clear of the road by the first troops to discover them.

7. Notice Boards....

All HQ. of Units must be clearly marked by notice boards.

8. Sanitation

(a) Latrines will invariably be dug immediately troops reach Camp, and also during prolonged halts. All latrines must be filled in before troops move off, and sites marked. This is very necessary owing to the number of troops moving up behind.

(b) Water for drinking purposes will only be drawn from water-carts. Medical Officers must test water before it is passed as fit for drinking.

9. Report Centres

A Report Centre will be detailed for each Unit in the March Table issued with the Bde. Order for the move to a new area. These Report Centres will remain open until HQs. Units have been definitely decided upon and reported to Bde. HQ. immediately by Orderly. Likewise the Bde. Report Centre will be notified to Units.

10. Rendezvous

nA rendezvous, where Units' guides will meet baggage and supply wagons, will also be notified in March Table issued with Bde. Order.

11. Halts

The usual 10-min. halt will not be observed when marching to the starting point, but will be rigidly adhered to once Units have reached main line of march.

12. Bands

In order to give space on roads, all bands will march in sections of threes, and not sections of fours.

13. Canteen

A lorry with canteen goods will follow closely behind the Bde. Group, and Units will be notified from time to time when they can draw.

14. Feet

Feet must be rubbed daily. Supplies of camphor powder can be obtained from S. Afr. Fld. Ambulance.

15. Medical

S.A.F. Amb. will collect the sick of the Bde. Group.

16. Protection of Property.

Units will take steps to prevent damage to property. The tying of animals to trees is prohibited. Usual precautions will be taken against fire.

17. Synchronisation: Bde. Sig. Off. will arrange to synchronise watches at 08.00 and 20.00 with Div. daily. Units will synchronise at 09.00 daily.

18. Reports on Line of March: Bde. HQ. will close 30 mins. before head of column is due to pass starting point, and from then on reports will be sent to head of column.

19. Standing Orders: Usual standing orders will be observed on line of march.

(sd) S.W.E. STYLE, Captain,
Staff Captain,
South Afr. Inf. Bde..

MARCH TABLE TO ACCOMPANY BDE. ORDER 271

Unit	Starting Point...	Time	From	To	ROUTE	REMARKS
4th. SAI	Where track crosses 2nd.- class rd. W. of VIVERIAUX	13.00	GRANDRIEU	BEAURIEUX	FRASIES - BEAURIEUX	
2nd. SAI	do.	13.15	do.	SIVRY	FRASIES - SIVRY	
1st S.A.I.	Main X-rds. in GRANDRIEU immediately S. of ~~[illegible]~~ 'R' in GRANDRIEU	13.15	HESTRUD	SIVRY	GRANDRIEU - FRASIES - SIVRY	
SALTER Bty.	do.	13.25	do.	do.	do.	

337

Secret

SOUTH AFRICAN INFANTRY BRIGADE

INSTRUCTIONS IN CONNECTION WITH THE MARCH TO THE RHINE - No. 1.

17-11-18 339

1. Rations
Each man will carry 1 iron ration, 1 emergency ration, and unconsumed portion of day's ration. Rations will be issued daily in the usual way. Any surplus rations on hand will be handed in to Bde. HQ. by 16.00 on 18th. inst..

2. Transport
(a) The following additional transport will be available for Units:

For each BN	- 4	GS. wagons
Field Co., RE	- 1	do.
Fld. Amb.	- 1	do.

These wagons will report to HQ. of Units on evening of 17th. inst.. Units will report by 09.00 18th. if they have not arrived.

(b) Position of Transport on line of March
First-line transport will move with Units.
Second-line transport (plus extra GS. wagons) will move with No. 2 Co., Div. Train, in same order of march as detailed for Units.

3. Baggage
The following stores will be carried:

On the Transport
- 1 blanket per man (second blanket)
- Greatcoats
- 100 prs. boots (if available)
- 1 pr. socks per man
- Cleaning material
- Officers' Kits
- Officers' Messes.

On the Man
- 1 blanket
- 2 prs. socks (not including pr. worn)
- 1 iron ration
- 1 emergency ration (hard)
- Unconsumed portion of day's ration.
- Cleaning material, etc..

SALTM Bty. will only carry 6 Stokes Mortars on the move; the remaining two will be dumped. All wagons must be underloaded in order to save both animals and vehicles. The Div. Dump for surplus stores is established in AVESNES.

4. Ordnance
Ordnance stores will as far as possible be delivered to Refilling Points. Each Unit will send a Representative to report to No. 2 Co., Div. Train, ASC, at SIVRY at 16.00 tomorrow, 18th. inst., to take over Ordnance Stores at Refilling Point and deliver same by supply-wagon to Unit.

5. Billeting
Each Unit will detail permanent billeting parties as follows:

	Off.	NCOs.
Bde. HQ.	1	2
Each Bn.	1	6
Field Co. RE	1	1
Fld. Amb.	1	1
No. 2 Co., Train	1	1

These parties will be mounted on bicycles or horses, and will report to Lt. R.O. Saunders, Bde. Billeting Officer, at 11.00 tomorrow, 18th.. They must carry with them rations for 19th. inst..

Billeting parties will always move on a day ahead of Units, ie., they will push on to next area immediately their Units are in their billets; and will, from 11.00 tomorrow, receive instructions direct from the Bde. Billeting Officer. It will be necessary for 4th. SAI, 430 Co., RE, No. 2 Co., ASC., and S.A.Fld. Amb., to detail two billeting parties tomorrow - one to report to Staff Captain at 09.30 in accordance with Bde. Order 261 of today, and the other to report to Bde. Billeting Off. at 11.00.

S E C R E T.   Copy No. 6

App 53(0)

66TH DIVISION ORDER NO. 124.

17th November 1918.   340

MARCH TO THE RHINE.

1. On November 18th, the Division will march by Brigade Groups in accordance with attached table.
   Groups, composition as in Appendix 'A' of D.O.123, will march under orders of Brigade Group Commanders therein detailed.

2. During the march and night November 18th/19th, B.G.C. 199 Brigade Group will be responsible for the protection of the Division.

3. Following distances will be maintained during march:=

In rear of Infantry Company.	10	yards.
" " " Battery or other similar formation.	25	"
" " " Bde R.A. or Infantry Bn.	50	"
Between units and their transport.	20	"

4. Any Germans encountered will be made prisoners and sent in to Divisional Headquarters at the end of day's march.

5. Divisional Headquarters will close at SOLRE LE CHATEAU and open FROIDCHAPELLE at 11.00.
   A Divisional Report Centre will also be maintained at head of Div. H.Q. Group during march.

6. ACKNOWLEDGE.

F.P. [signature]

Lieut Colonel.
General Staff,
66th Division.

Issued at 13.00.

DISTRIBUTION.

Copy No. 1	War Diary.	No. 13	A.D.M.S.
2	" "	14	12th Lancers.
3	File.	15	9th Bn.Glouc.R.(Pioneers)
4	198th Brigade.	16	5th Cavalry Brigade.
5	199th Brigade.	17	IX Corps.
6	S.A. Brigade.	18	IX Corps Cyclist Bn.
7	C.R.A.	19	1st Division.
8	C.R.E.	20	169th French Division.
9	Signals.	21	2nd Cavalry Division.
10	A. & Q.	22	32nd Division.
11	Train A.S.C.	23	D.A.P.M.
12	100th Bn.M.G.C.	24	A.D.C.

347.

MARCH TABLE

Serial No.	Group.	From.	To.	Route.	Remarks.
1.	199th Bde Group.	VIEUX SART. Area.	CERFONTAINE.	RANCE - FROID-CHAPELLE.	To clear Railway at RANCE by 09.00.
2.	198th Bde Group.	BEAURIEUX, &c.	RANCE and TRES BOUCHAUX.	SIVRY.	TRES BOUCHAUX - RANCE Sta. Road to be clear by 10.30.
3.	D.H.Q. Group.	SOLRE LE CHATEAU and WILLIES Areas.	FROIDCHAPELLE and FOURBECHIES.	RANCE.	Road to pass road junction TRES BOUCHAUX at 11.00.
4.	S.A. Brigade Group.	BEAURIEUX & SOLRE LE CHATEAU.	SIVRY and MONTBLIART.	SIVRY.	Not to move before 11.00.

.H.Q.,
7/11/18.

NOTE. All units in SOLRE LE CHATEAU will march via CLAIRFAYTS.

app 54
342

SECRET
17-11-18
Copy No. 14

SOUTH AFRICAN INFANTRY BRIGADE

ORDER No. 302

Ref. Map -
NAMUR, 1/100,000

1. On Nov. 18th. the 66th. Divn. will continue the march to the RHINE by Bde. Groups.
The 199 Inf. Bde. Group will lead, followed by the 198 Inf. Bde. Group and the DHQ. Group.

2. The South African Inf. Bde. Group will concentrate in the SIVRY - MONTBLIART Area, in accordance with the attached March Table.

3. The following distances will be maintained during the march:

In rear of Infantry Coy.	...	10 yards
" Infantry Bn.	...	50 yards
Between Units and their Transport	...	50 yards

4. First-line transport and baggage wagons will move with Units.

5. Billeting parties from the 430th. Field CO., RE., 4th. SAI., S. Afr. Fld. Amb., and No. 2 Co., Div. Train, ASC., will report to the Staff Captain at Bde. HQ. in SIVRY at 09.30 hours, 18th. inst..

6. Bde. HQ. will remain at the CHATEAU in SIVRY.

7. ACKNOWLEDGE.

Issued at 17.30 thro' Signals
to:-
1. 1st. SAI
2. 2nd. SAI
3. 4th. SAI
4. SALT. Bty.
5. SA Fld. Amb.
6. Bde. Sig. Off.
7. 430 Fld. CO., RE.
8. No. 2 Co., Div. Train ASC.
9. 66 Divn.
10. Bde. Major
11. Staff Captain
12. 198 Inf. Bde.
13. 199 Inf. Bde.
14/18. War Diary.

[signature]
Captain,
Brigade Major,
South Afr. Inf. Bde..

MARCH TABLE ISSUED WITH SOUTH AFR. BDE. ORDER No. 262

Unit	Starting Point	Time	Area Allotted	ROUTE	Report Centre until HQ. is established.	Meeting Pt. for supply Wagons.	REMARKS
Bde. HQ. & Sig. Section.	—	—	SIVRY	—	—	—	
1st. SAI	—	—	do	—	—	—	
2nd. SAI	—	—	do	—	—	—	
4th. SAI	where stream crosses BEAURIEUX – MOULARD Rd. at X in BEAURIEUX	14.00	SIVRY	MOULARD-SIVRY	—	—	
S.A.H.A. Bty.	—	—	—	—	—	—	
S. Afr. F. Amb.	X Roads due South of G in SORLE-LE CHATEAU	13.00	SIVRY	CLAIRFAYTS-SIVRY	—	—	
4[illegible] Co., R.E.	do	12.30	MONTBLAIRT	CLAIRFAYTS-SIVRY-MONT-JUMONT	—	—	
5c. 2 Co., Div. Train, ASC.	do	13.30	SIVRY	CLAIRFAYTS-SIVRY	—	—	

MARCH TABLE.

Serial No.	Group.	From.	To.	Route.	Remarks.
1.	199th Bde Group. 9th Glouc.R. 1 Sect. 1st Aus. T.Coy. R.E. 1 Bty RFA.	RANCE.	PHILIPPEVILLE. HEMPTINNE. JAMAGNE	FROID-CHAPELLE, CERFONTAINE, SENZEILLE.	Head of column to pass RANCE Sta. at 09.00. 9th Glouc.R. & 1 Sec. 1st Aust. T.Coy and 1 Bty R.F.A. to join column at CERFONTAINE.
2	D.H.Q. Group.	FROID-CHAPELLE area.	PHILIPPEVILLE, JAMIOLLE and DAUSSOIS.	CERFONTAINE.	Head to pass road crossing 1½ miles east of S of FOURBECHIES at 11.00.
3.	S.A. Bde Group.	SIVRY area.	SENZEILLE, VILLERS DEUX EGLISES, SOUMOY.	RANCE, CERFONTAINE.	Head to pass TREUBOUCHAUX 11.00.

app 55(0)

345

S E C R E T.

Copy No. 16

66TH DIVISION ORDER NO. 125.

18th November 1918.

MARCH TO THE RHINE.

1. On November 19th, the Division will continue the march in accordance with attached table.

2. B.G.C. Div. H.Q. Group will ensure that FROIDCHAPELLE - CERFONTAINE Road is kept clear for passage of 198th Brigade Group.

3. The midday halt will be from ~~[illegible]~~ 11.50 to 13.00.

4. 567th A.T. Coy. R.E. and 1st Aust. T. Coy. R.E. (less 2 sections) will billet for night 19th/20th Novr in CERFONTAINE.

5. Responsibility for the protection of the Division will pass from B.G.C. 199th Brigade Group to B.G.C. 198th Brigade Group at 11.00 Novr 19th.

6. Divl H.Q. will close FROIDCHAPELLE and open PHILIPPEVILLE at 14.00 Novr 19th.
A Divisional Report Centre will also be maintained at head of Div. H.Q. Group during march.

7. ACKNOWLEDGE.

[signature]
Lieut Colonel.
General Staff.
66th Division.

Issued at 17.50

DISTRIBUTION.

No. 1 War Diary.	No. 2 War Diary.	No. 3 File.
4 198th Bde.	5 199th Bde.	6 S.A. Bde.
7 C.R.A.	8 C.R.E.	9 Signals.
10 A & Q.	11 Train ASC.	12 100th Bn. MGC.
13 A.D.M.S.	14 9th Glouc. R.	15 5th Cav. Bde.
16 IX Corps.	17 IX Corps [illegible]	18 1st Division.
19 169th French Div.	20 2nd Cav. Div.	21 32nd Divn.
22 D.A.P.M.	23 66th M.T. Coy.	24 D.A.D.O.S.
25 A.D.C.		

SECRET app 56

Copy No. 14

346

SOUTH AFRICAN INFANTRY BRIGADE

Ref. Map:-
NAMUR, 1/100,000

ORDER No. 263

18-11-18

MARCH TO THE RHINE

1. On Nov. 19, 66th. Div. will continue the march. 198 Inf. Bde. are leading and will be responsible for the protection of the Divn. DHQ. Group follows 198 Inf. Bde. Group.

2. S. Afr. Inf. Bde. Group will march in accordance with attached March-Table.

3. The midday halt will be from 11.30 to 13.00.

4. Baggage wagons will join 548 Co., ASC., at 09.00.

5. Bde. HQ. will close at SIVRY at 09.40 and open at head of column at 10.10.

6. ACKNOWLEDGE.

Issued at 21.00 thro' Signals to:-
1. 1st. SAI
2. 2nd. SAI
3. 4th. SAI
4. SALTM Bty.
5. S.A. FD. Amb.
6. 4X Fld. Co., RE.
7. 3n. Co., Div. Tn., ASC.
8. Bde. Signal Off..
9. 66th. Div.
10. 198 Bde.
11. 199 Bde.
12. Bde. Major
13. Staff Captain
14/18. War Diary.

Captain, Brigade Major,
South Afr. Inf. Brigade.

NOTE:- Bde. Order 261 of 17th. inst. should have been numbered '262'.

MARCH TABLE ISSUED WITH SOUTH AFR. BDE. ORDER No. 26

Serial No.	Unit	Starting Point	Time	Area Allotted	ROUTE	Report Centre until HQ. is established.	Meeting Pt. for supply Wagons.	REMARKS
1	Bde. HQ. & Sig. Section.	X roads due North of S in VIEUX SART	10 10	SENZEILLE	TRIEU BOUCHAUX - RANCE - FROIDCHAPELLE - CERFONTAINE	Where Soumoy & joins CERFONTAINE SENZEILLE Rd	As details for Report Centre	SALTMB will move with Bde HQ
2	1st. SAI	do	10 12	SOUMOY		CHURCH at SOUMOY		
3	2nd. SAI	do	10 23	VILLERS deux EGLISES	SENZEILLE	WESTERN entrance to village point S of Second E in EGLISES		
4	4th. SAI	do	10 33	SENZEILLE		As for Serial No 1		
5	SALTM Bty.	do	10 16	do		do		
6	S. Afr.F.Amb.	do	10 50	do		do		
7	4th Co., RE.	Road Junction N of E in TRIEU BOUCHAUX	11 10	VILLERS deux EGLISES	SENZEILLE	As for Serial No 3		4.30th Fld Coy RE to march in rear of 1st S.A.I.
8	HQ. & 2 Co., Div.Train, ASC.	X roads due N of S in VIEUX SART	10 44	SOUMOY		As for Serial No 2		

347

MARCH TABLE TO ACCOMPANY D.O. 126.

Serial No.	UNIT.	From.	TO.	REMARKS.
1.	9th Bn. Glouc.R.	VILLERS-LE-GAMBON.	MORVILLE.	To clear cross roads 1½ miles North of VILLERS Church by 09.45. Accommodation in MORVILLE to be arranged with 198th Brigade.
2.	198th Bdo Group	PHILIPPE-VILLE &c.	ROSEE & MORVILLE.	Head to pass cross roads 1½ miles North of VILLERS Church by 09.00.
3.	S.A. Bde Group.	SENZEILLE &c.	PHILIPPE-VILLE. VILLERS-LE-GAMBON ROSEE (1 Bn.) VILLERS-DEUX-EGLISES. (1 Bn.)	Head to enter PHILIPPEVILLE at 10.00.
4.	330 Bde R.F.A. 331 Bde R.F.A. 66th DAC.	DAUSSOIS.	JAMIOLLE JAMAGNE & HEMPTINNE.	Move to be complete by 15.00
5.	1st Aus. T.Coy RE. [illegible] A.T. Coy. [illegible]	CERFON-TAINE & FALE-PRI[illegible].	PHILIPPE-VILLE.	Under orders from [illegible] Div. R.A. Group. Head of column to enter PHILIPPEVILLE at 11.30.

app 57(0)

348

SECRET.

Copy No. 6

66TH DIVISION ORDER NO. 126.

1. On November 23rd 1918, moves of Groups and units will take place in accordance with attached march table.

2. ACKNOWLEDGE.

F.P. Lisemothy

Lieut Colonel.
General Staff.
66th Division.

Issued at 23.55

21st November 1918.

DISTRIBUTION.

Copy No.		No.	
1	War Diary.	15	1st Division.
2	" "	16	32nd Division.
3	File.	17	D.A.P.M.
4	198th Brigade.	18	66th M.T. Coy.
5	199th Brigade.	19	D.A.D.O.S.
6	S.A. Brigade.	20	A.D.C.
7	C.R.A.		
8	C.R.E.		
9	Signals.		
10	A. & Q.		
11	Train A.S.C.		
12	A.D.M.S.		
13	9th Bn. Glouc. R.		
14	IX Corps.		

*** *********

360

Army Form C. 2123.
(In books of 100.)

"C" FORM.
MESSAGES AND SIGNALS. No. of Message

Prefix SB Code .... Words 66

Sent, or sent out. Office Stamp.

At .... m.

To ....

By ....

Received from .... By ....

Service Instructions

[illegible]

Handed in at Y[illegible] Office 2220 m. Received 2328 m.

TO SA Bde

*Sender's Number.	Day of Month.	In reply to Number.	AAA
G123	22		
Div	areas	have	been
altered	as	follows	aaa
66th	Div	order	no
126	dated	21/11/18	is
amended	aaa	Serial	no
1	cancelled	aaa	Serial
no	2	stands	except
100th	Bn	MGC	[illegible]
[illegible]	[illegible]	[illegible]	198
Bde	group	aaa	Serial
no	3	[illegible]	Bn
ROSEE	in	lieu	of

VILLERS-LE-GAMBON aaa Serial no
4 and 5 cancelled aaa Acknowledge

FROM
PLACE & TIME 66 Div 2310

* This line, except A A A, should be erased, if not received.

(2337) Wt. W5[illegible]/P738. 691,000 Pads. 2/18. A.P.Ltd. [illegible]

app 58

SECRET

Copy No. 353

SOUTH AFRICAN INFANTRY BRIGADE

Ref. Map:
NAMUR 8. 1/100,000

ORDER No. 304

22-11-18

1. The South Afr. Inf. Bde. Group (less 2nd. SAI.) will move on the 23rd. Nov. in accordance with the attached March Table.

Order of March:-

4th. SAI
Bde. HQ.)
Signal Section)
SALTM Bty.)
1st. SAI
430 Fld. Co., RE.
South Afr. Fld. Amb.
542 Co., ASC.

2. 2nd. SAI. will remain in VILLERS deux EGLISES.

3. 1st.-Line Transport will move with Units. Baggage wagons of 1st. SAI. will report to 542 Co., ASC., at SOUMOY, at 08.00; those of 4th. SAI. and S. Afr. Fld. Amb. will join 542 Co., ASC., at the Church in SENZEILLE and will be drawn up along road running from 4th. SAI. HQ. to Bde. HQ. by 09.00, leaving main road clear.

4. Bde. HQ. will close at SENZEILLE at 09.30, and open at PHILIPPEVILLE on arrival.

5. ACKNOWLEDGE.

Captain,
Brigade Major,
South Afr. Inf. Bde..

Issued at 18.00 through Sigs.
to:-
1. 1st. SAI
2. 2nd. SAI
3. 4th. SAI
4. SALTM Bty.
5. Bde. Sig. Off..
6. S. Afr. Fld. Amb.
7. 542 Co., ASC.
8. 430 Fld. Co., RE.
9. 66 Divn.
10. 198 Inf. Bde.
11. 199 do.
12. Staff Captain
13. Bde. Major
14/18. War Diary.

MARCH TABLE ISSUED WITH SOUTH AFR. BDE. ORDER No. ____

Serial No.	Unit	Starting Point	Time	Area Allotted	ROUTE	Report Centre until HQ. is established.	Meeting Pt. for supply Wagons.	REMARKS
1	Bde. HQ. & Sig. Section.	[illegible] cross road due N of S in SENZEILLE	08.55	PHILIPPEVILLE	SENZEILLE - VILLER deux EGLISES - PHILIPPEVILLE - VILLERS le GAMBON	Square in PHILIPPEVILLE	Same as Report Centre. Units must send guides back as early as possible so as not to keep Baggage Wagons [illegible]	(a) Head of Column to enter PHILIPPEVILLE at 10.00
2	1st. SAI	do	08.57	do		do		(b) 1930 the Coy RE to march in rear of 1st S.A.I.
3	2nd. SAI	—	—	—		—		(c) S.A.L.T.M.B to march with B.H.Q.
4	4th. SAI	do	08.45	VILLERS le GAMBON		Church at VILLERS le GAMBON		(d) Units must maintain distances laid down in Bde. Order 262
5	S.A.L.T.M. Bty.	do	08.55	PHILIPPEVILLE		As for Serial No 1		(e) Halt from 08.50 to 09.00 will not be observed.
6	S. Afr.F.Amb.	do	09.10	do		do		
7	4th Co., RE.	X roads S.E. of S in EGLISES	09.25	do		do		
8	No. 2 Co., Div.Train, ASC.	As for Serial No 1	09.15	do		do		

356

"A" Form
MESSAGES AND SIGNALS.

Army Form C. 2121
(In pads of 100.)

No. of Message...........

Prefix..........Code..........m. Office of Origin and Service Instructions Copy	Words / Charge. Sent At ....m. To .... By	This message is on a/c of: OM Service. (Signature of "Franking Officer") Recd. at......m. Date.......... From .... By..........

TO			
	1st SAI	Bde Sig Off	66 Div
	2nd SAI	SAFA	
	4th SAI	542 Coy ASC	

Sender's Number.	Day of Month.	In reply to Number.	AAA
A 1/0264	22		

Serial	No 4	of	March
Table	AAA	Under	Area
allotted	read	ROSEE	AAA
Under	Route	and	Report
Centre	For	VILLERS	LE
GAMBON	read	ROSEE	AAA.
Billeting	Party	4th	SAI
to	be	at	Church
at	ROSEE	09.30	hours
tomorrow.			

From S. A. Bde
Place
Time

The above may be forwarded as now corrected. (Z) (Sd) W T Jacobs Capt for Bde Major

Censor. Signature of Addressor or person authorised to telegraph in his name

* This line should be erased if not required.

Order No. 1625. Wt. W3253/ P 511. 27/2 H. & K. Ltd. (E. 2634)

app 59 (?)

SECRET.

Copy No. 6 355

66TH DIVISION ORDER NO. 127.

23rd November 1918.

1. On November 24th, the march of the Division will be continued in accordance with attached table.
On completion of march, the Division will probably halt until November 27th.

2. During the halt, responsibility for protection of Divisional front will be allotted as follows:-

S.A. Brigade Group.	From Southern Divisional Boundary to ~~HASTIERE LAVAUX~~ HERMETON (inclusive).
198th Brigade Group.	From ~~HASTIERE LAVAUX~~ HERMETON to Northern Divisional Boundary.

3. Responsibility for the repair and maintenance of roads is allotted as follows:-

R.A. Units. 9th Bn. Glouc. R. 567 A.T. Coy R.E. 1st Aus. T. Coy R.E.	PHILIPPEVILLE - NORVILLE Road from road junction 2 miles east of PHILIPPEVILLE to 25 kilo stone west of NORVILLE.
S.A. Brigade Group.	GOCHENEE - AGIMONT - HERMETON Road from stream east of SOULME to HASTIERE LAVAUX (exclusive).
198th Brigade Group.	HASTIERE (inclusive) - WAULSORT - ANSEREMME Road to northern Divisional Boundary. Also to MAURENNE (exclusive).
199th Brigade Group.	MAURENNE (inclusive) - ROSEE Road to 25 kilo stone, and NORVILLE - SOULME Road to stream east of SOULME.

4. Divisional Headquarters will close PHILIPPEVILLE and open WAULSORT at 15.00 November 24th.

5. ACKNOWLEDGE.
done

Issued through Signals at 15.00

Y Brittains Lieut
for Lieut Colonel.
General Staff,
66th Division.

DISTRIBUTION.

Copy No. 1	War Diary.	No. 11 Train A.S.C.
2	" "	12 A.D.M.S.
3	File.	13 9th Bn. Glouc.R.
4	198th Brigade.	14 IX Corps.
5	199th Brigade.	15 1st Division.
6	S.A. Brigade.	16 32nd Division.
7	C.R.A.	17 169th French Division.
8	C.R.E.	18 D.A.P.M.
9	Signals.	19 66th M.T. Coy.
10	A & Q.	20 D.A.D.O.S.
		21 A.D.C.

MARCH TABLE TO ACCOMPANY D.O. 127.

Serial No.	Unit.	From.	To.	Route.	Remarks.
1.	D.H.Q. Group (less R.A. Units).	PHILIPPEVILLE.	VAULSORT.	ROSEE - ANTHEE - HASTIERE.	By lorry, to start Philippville 09.00.
2.	S.A. Brigade Group.	PHILIPPEVILLE, ROSEE, VILLERS DEUX EGLISES.	HERMETON. BAC du PRINCE, AGIMONT, GOCHENEE, SOULME.	ROSEE - GOCHENEE and VILLERS - LE-GAMBON - ROMEDENNE Roads.	To clear PHILIPPEVILLE and ROSEE by 09.00. Heavy transport to proceed via main PHILIPEVILLE - GIVET Road.
3.	198th Brigade Group (less M.G. Bn & A/331 Bty R.I.A.)	ROSEE and MORVILLE.	ANSEREMME, LENNE, HASTIERE LAVAUX.	ANTHEE - HASTIERE.	To clear ANTHEE by 10.30.
4.	199th Brigade Group.	CERFONTAINE.	MAURENNE, MAVOYE, MORVILLE.	PHILIPPEVILLE - ROSEE.	Head to pass cross roads north of C of CERFONTAINE at 07.00.
5.	R.A. Units.	DAUSSOIS. JAMIOLLE. JAMAGNE.	ROSEE, VILLERS-LE-GAMBON, VODECEE, HEMTINNE, JAMAGNE.	PHILIPPEVILLE.	Not to enter PHILIPPEVILLE before 10.45.

P.T.O.

357

Serial No.	Unit.	From.	To.	Route.	Remarks.
6.	100th Bn. M.G.C.	JAMIOLLE.	VAULSORT.	PHILIPPEVILLE - ROSEE.	Head to pass cross roads south of LL of PHILIPPEVILLE, at 10.00 To stage night 24th/25th in ROSEE.
7.	9th Bn. Glouc R.	VILLERS-LE-GAMBON.	Chateau 1 mile N. of ROSEE.	ROSEE.	Head to pass cross roads 1½ miles N. of VILLERS Church at 11.45.
8.	567 A.T. Coy R.E. 1st Aus. T. Coy. R.E.	CERFONTAINE and FALEMPRISE.	CHANMONT.		To march in rear of 199th Brigade Group column under orders from B.G.C. 199th Brigade.

358

359

"C" FORM.

MESSAGES AND SIGNALS.

Army Form C. 2121 (In books of 100). No. of Message ....

Prefix Am Code 0934 Words 33

Received from [illegible] By [illegible]

Service Instructions [illegible]

Sent, or sent out. At ....m. To .... By ....

Office Stamp. [illegible] SIGNALS

Handed in at [illegible] Office 0934 m. Received 1702 m.

TO S A Bde

*Sender's Number.	Day of Month.	In reply to Number.	AAA
G 134	24		
Ref	para	2	of
Div	order	No	127
AAA	For	HASTIERE	LAVAUX
Substitute	HERMETON	AAA	Gaa
S A	and	198	Bdes
to	ack	repeated	199
Bde	and	CRA	

FROM 66 Div

PLACE & TIME 0935

* This line, except A A A, should be erased, if not required.

(2287) Wt. W54/P728. 691,000 Pads. 2/18. A.P.Ltd. [illegible]

Ref. Map. NAMUR. 1/100,000.

SOUTH AFRICAN INFANTRY BRIGADE — SECRET — app 60 — 360

ORDER No. 265 — Copy No. 13

MARCH TO THE RHINE.... — 22-11-18

1. 66th. Div. will continue the march to the RHINE tomorrow, Nov. 24th.

2. S. Afr. Inf. Bde. Group will move in accordance with the attached March Table. Order of March:

Bde. HQ.
Signal Section
SALTM. Bty.
1st. SAI
430 Fld. Co., RE.
2nd. SAI
S. Afr. Field Amb..

3. Owing to the hilly nature of the country over which the Infantry will march, all 1st. and 2nd. Line Transport will be brigaded and move with 548 Co., ASC., along main PHILIPPEVILLE - GIVET road. These will report to 548 Co., ASC., on main road just N. of VILLERS le GAMBON, by 10.00. 548 Co., ASC. will halt there until transport from all Units except 4th. SAI. joins up.

4. A lorry will be placed at the disposal of 4th. SAI. to carry the mens second blanket. Baggage wagons will be loaded as lightly as possible, as there are several very steep hills between ROSEE and AGIMONT. This lorry will be at the Church, ROSEE, at 10.00..

5. Bde. HQ. will close at PHILIPPEVILLE at 09.00 and open at BAC du PRINCE on arrival.

6. ACKNOWLEDGE.

Issued at 18.00 through signals to -
1. 1st. SAI
2. 2nd. SAI
3. 4th. SAI
4. SALTM Bty.
5. Bde. Sig. Offr.
6. S. Afr. Fld. Amb.
7. 430 Fld. Co., RE
8. 548 Co., ASC.
9. 66 Div.
10. 198 Inf. Bde.
11. 199 Inf. Bde.
12. Staff Captain.
13. Bde. Major
14/18. War Diary.

[signature]
Captain,
Brigade Major,
South Afr. Inf. Bde..

361

MARCH TABLE ISSUED WITH SOUTH AFR. BDE. ORDER No. 265

Serial No.	Unit	Starting Point	Time	Area Allotted	ROUTE	Report Centre until HQ. is established.	Meeting Pt. for supply Wagons.	REMARKS
1	Bde. HQ. & Sig. Section.	X roads S of O in VODECEE	08 48	BAC du PRINCE	VILLERS le GAMBON ROMEDENNE - VODELEE - AGIMONT	at Southern entrance to Village	As for Report Centre	(1) 2nd SAI will clear PHILIPPEVILLE before halting at 08 50 hrs. (2) Halt will be observed at 08 50 hrs
2	1st. SAI	do	09 00	do	do	do		
3	2nd. SAI	do	09 15	AGIMONT	do	CHATEAU AGIMONT		
4	4th. SAI	X roads between points 17 MS on ROSEE-GOCHENEE Rd	09 00	HERMETON	AGIMONT - BAC du PRINCE	CHURCH in HERMETON		
5	S.A.L.T.M. Bty.	As for Serial No 1	08 48	do	As for Serial No 1	do		
6	S. Afr.F.Amb.	do	09 25	GOCHENE	do	CHURCH in GOCHENE		
7	4th Co., R.E.	do	09 10	AGIMONT	do	CHURCH in AGIMONT		
8	No. 2 Co., Div.Train, ASC.	do	08 30	HERMETON	MAIN PHILIPPEVILLE GIVET Rd to Point 19 - BAC du PRINCE	CHURCH in HERMETON		

362

Bul 1009

66th Division.

G.S. 3/9

App 6.(

C.R.A.	'Q'.
198th Brigade.	9th Glouc. R.
199th Brigade.	D.A.P.M.
S.A. Brigade.	Signals.
C.R.E.	Train.
A.D.M.S.	567 A.T. Coy. R.E.
1st Aus. T. Company R.E.	

On November 28th the following transfers will take place:-

(a) 66th Division from 1X Corps to X Corps at 23.59 hours.

(b) 567 A.T. Company R.E. in situ (CHANMONT) from 66th Division to 1st Division at 12.00 hours.

(c) 1st Australian Tunnelling Company R.E. from 1X Corps to Australian Corps at 23.59 hours.

J. Marris Capt

for Lieut Colonel.
General Staff,
66th Division.

D.H.Q.
27/11/18.

Instructions regarding War Diaries and Intelligence Summaries are contained in F. S. Regs., Part II. and the Staff Manual respectively. Title pages will be prepared in manuscript.

WAR DIARY

or

~~INTELLIGENCE SUMMARY.~~

(Erase heading not required.)

Army Form C. 2118.

Place	Date	Hour	Summary of Events and Information	Remarks and references to Appendices
ROCHEFORT AREA.	15th.		Move of the Brigade Group continued by march route. Second days stage - ROCHEFORT area - reached by 15.00 hours. Units of Brigade Group billeted as follows:.	
			Brigade Headquarters,) Signal Section,) 1st. SAI,) 2nd. SAI,) ROCHEFORT. SALTMB.,) S.A.F.Amb.) 542 Coy. ASC.)	
			4th. SAI.) 4[illegible]0 Field Co. RE.) JEMELLE.	
			Brigadier General Commanding proceeded by Motor to Divisional Headquarters to attend meeting with Commander-in-Chief.	
MARCHE AREA,	16th		Move of the Brigade Group continued by march route. Third (and final) days stage - MARCHE area - reached by 12.15 hours. Units of Brigade Group billeted as follows:,	
			Brigade Headquarters,) Signal Section,) 1st. SAI,) 2nd. SAI,) MARCHE. SALTMB.,) SAF Amb.) 542 Co. ASC.	
			4th. SAI. AYE,	
			4[illegible]0 Field Co. RE. WAHA.	

390

D. D. & L., London, E.C.
(20340) Wt W5300/P713 750,000 3/15 E 2688 Forms/C2118/13.

Instructions regarding War Diaries and Intelligence Summaries are contained in F. S. Regs., Part II. and the Staff Manual respectively. Title pages will be prepared in manuscript.

24

WAR DIARY
or
~~INTELLIGENCE SUMMARY~~
(Erase heading not required.)

Army Form C. 2118. 66

DECEMBER, 1918. S. AFRICAN INFANTRY BRIGADE.

VR 33

Place	Date	Hour	Summary of Events and Information	Remarks and references to Appendices
BAC DE PRINCE.	1st.- 13th December.		Training continued under Battalion arrangements.	
"	4th.		66th. Division preliminary Order No. 128 received - Division to move on 10Th. December.	App. 1,(o)
"	6th.		66th. Division G 206 received, Move notified in Division Order No. 128 of 4th. Dec. postponed for at least four days	App. 2.(o)
	10 th.		66th. Division Order No. 129 received - Move of Division notified in Divisional Order No. 128 of 4Th. Dec. to commence on 13th. Dec. and to be completed on 16th. Dec. Move of S.A. Brigade Group to commence on 14th. Dec. and be completed by 16th. Dec.	App. 3.(o)
"	13th.		S.A.Brigade Order No. 266 issued - Orders for movement of Brigade Group on 14th. 15th- & 16th. December	App. 4.4
HOUYET AREA.	14th.		The Brigade Group moved by march route as per S.A.Brigade Order No. 266, Brigade Headquarters, Signal Section, 1st. SAI, 2nd. SAI, S.A.Field Amb., 542 CO, ASC. and 430th. Field Co.RE. via GIVET. 4th. SAI and SALTM Bty. via HASTIERE. First days stage - HOUYET area - reached by 15.00 hours. Units of Brigade Group billetted as follows:-	
			Brigade Headquarters, Signal Section, 4th. SAI, SALTM Bty. SAF Amb.) HOUYET.	
			1st. SAI. FERAGE.	
			2nd. SAI. MESNIL EGLISE.	
			430th. Field Co.RE. HERHET.	
			542nd. Co. ASC, SANZINNE.	

D. D. & L., London, E.C. (10340) Wt W5300/P713 750,000 3/18 1688 Forms/C2118/15.

389

Army Form C. 2118.

Instructions regarding War Diaries and Intelligence Summaries are contained in F. S. Regs., Part II. and the Staff Manual respectively. Title pages will be prepared in manuscript.

WAR DIARY
or
~~INTELLIGENCE SUMMARY.~~
(Erase heading not required.)

Place	Date	Hour	Summary of Events and Information	Remarks and references to Appendices
	18th		Division Commander arrived in MARCHE (12.00 hours) and saw Column march in (less 4th. SAI and 430 Field Co. RE. which had been directed to their respective billeting areas). Division Commander informed Brigadier General Commanding, a large reinforcement draft for S.African Brigade had just detrained at Haversin, that from reports received, some train looting had been done by this Draft and that the whole draft seemed to be in an unsatisfactory state. BM,- 30 issued instructing Major T.G.McEwan, 1st. SAI, to proceed at once to Haversin to take command of Draft, taking with him 2 Officers and 4 selected NCOs. from each Regiment (1st. 2nd. & 4th. SAI,)	App. 5.
MARCHE AREA.	17th to 19th		All Units settling into Billets and cleaning up. Reinforcement Draft arrived (on 17th. Dec.) from Haversin, and taken over by respective Units. 66th. Divisional letter. Confidential 8271/A dated 18/12/18 received. Report required by G.O.C. as to condition and behaviour of Draft which arrived at Haversin on 16.12.18. S.A. Brigade BM 1086 issued (19.12.18) - Assembly of Court of Enquiry.	App. 6(a) App. 7
MARCHE AREA.	20th to 24th		Training resumed under Battalion arrangements. Message received (23.12.18) by telephone from 66th. Division that Brigade would be visited on 26th. December by H.R.H. The Prince of Wales.	
	25th		Christmas Day. Successful arrangements for dinners and entertainment of all Brigade Units (less 4th. SAI which celebrated 1st. January instead of Christmas Day) S.A.Brigade Order 267 issued - orders for ceremonial parade on 26th. December.	App. 8.
	26th		Boxing Day. H.R.H. The Prince of Wales visited the Brigade, attended by Capt. Lord Claude Hamilton (Grenadier Guards); Commanders of X Corps and 66th. Division were present. Order of inspection was:-	
MARCHE.			2nd. SAI, SALTM Bty., and SAF Amb. formed up in close column of companies. 1st. SAI, formed up in line.	
AYE.			4th. SAI formed up in close column of Companies.	

391

D. D. & L., London, E.C.
(10340) Wt W5300/P713 750,000 3/18 Sch. 52a Forms/C2118/15.

Army

Instructions regarding War Diaries and Intelligence Summaries are contained in F. S. Regs., Part II. and the Staff Manual respectively. Title pages will be prepared in manuscript.

WAR DIARY
or
~~INTELLIGENCE~~ ~~SUMMARY~~.

(Erase heading not required.)

Place	Date	Hour	Summary of Events and Information	Remarks and references to Appendices
	26th.		At the conclusion of each inspection H.R.H. addressed the parade, congratulating all ranks on their fine performances in action and on their high standard of discipline at all times: he wished them the best of luck on their return to South Africa. H.R.H. afterwards visited a few of the men's billets in Marche and inspected a Cook house. H.R.H. and the other visitors lunched at the Brigade Headquarters Mess, and at 14.30 hours left Marche by Motor car for ROCHEFORT.	
	27th to 31st		Training resumed under Battalion arrangements.	

F. J. Thackeray
Lieut. Colonel,
Commanding,
S.Afr.Inf.Bde.

392

App. 1 (b)
393

S E C R E T.   Copy No. 6

66TH DIVISION ORDER NO. 128.

4th December 1918.

1. Attached tracing shows the area allotted to the Division for the Winter.

Proposed Sub-division of the area into Div.H.Q., Brigade and Artillery Groups is shown in red.

2. The Division will march to the new area in accordance with attached table.

All marches will be completed daily by 15.00.

3. Div. R.A. and Brigades will reconnoitre their respective routes and areas forthwith and will arrange with 66th Division 'Q' for the early dispatch of billeting parties.

4. ACKNOWLEDGE.

F.P. Nosworthy
Lieut Colonel.
General Staff.
66th Division.

Issued through
Signals at 0900

DISTRIBUTION:-

No. 1	War Diary.	No. 12	Train A.S.C.
2	" "	13	A.D.M.S.
3	File.	14	9th Glouc.R. (Pioneers).
4	198th Brigade.	15	X Corps.
5	199th Brigade.	16	~~32nd Division~~.
6	S.A. Brigade.	17	~~34th Division~~.
7	C.R.A.	18	.
8	C.R.E.	19	D.A.P.M.
9	Signals.	20	66th M.T. Company.
10	A & Q.	21	D.A.D.O.S.
11	100th Bn. M.G.C.	22	Camp Comdt.

23. A.D.C.

394

MARCH TABLE TO ACCOMPANY 66TH DIVISION ORDER NO. 128.

Serial No.	Date.	Unit.	From.	To.	Route.	Remarks.
1.	Dec. 9th.	199th Brigade Group plus 100th Bn. M.G.C.	MORVILLE Area.	DINANT - BOUVIGNIES, ONHAYE.	ONHAYE.	To be clear of MORVILLE by 10.00. 100th Bn. M.G.C. to march under orders from 199th Brigade.
2.	" "	Div. R.A. Group.	PHILIPPE-VILLE Area.	MORVILLE & ROSEE.		
3.	Dec. 10th.	Serial No. 1.	DINANT Area.	CINEY - EMPTINNE - HAMOIS Area.	ACHENE.	To clear DINANT by 10.00. Billets in CINEY to be allotted by 66th Div. 'Q'.
4.	" "	D.H.Q. Group plus 431 Fld.Coy.R.E.	WAULSORT.	CINEY.	DINANT.	Head to cross DINANT Bridge at 10.00. M.T. via CELLES and CONNEUX.
5.	" "	R.A. Group.	MORVILLE area.	DINANT - BOUVIGNIES.	ONHAYE.	Not to cross DINANT Bridge before 11.30.
6.	" "	S.A. Brigade Group.	BAC DU PRINCE &c.	HOUVET Area.	HASTIERE.	
7.	Dec. 11th.	199th Brigade Group.	EMPTINNE Area.	HUY Area.	Any.	
8.	" "	R.A. Group.	DINANT Area.	LEIGNON &c.	ACHENE	
9.	" "	S.A. Brigade Group.	HOUVET Area.	ROCHEFORT Area.	CIERGNON.	
10.	" "	198th Brigade Group. (less 431 Fld.Coy. RE)	HASTIERE &c.	HOUVET Area.	Any.	

Serial No.	Date.	Unit.	From.	To.	Route.	Remarks.
11.	Dec. 12th.	S.A. Brigade Group.	ROCHEFORT Area.	MARCHE Area.	Any.	To be clear of ROCHEFORT Sub. area by 11.00.
12.	" "	Serial No. 10.	HOUVET Area.	ROCHEFORT Area.	Any.	

D.H.Q.
4th December 1918.

395

396

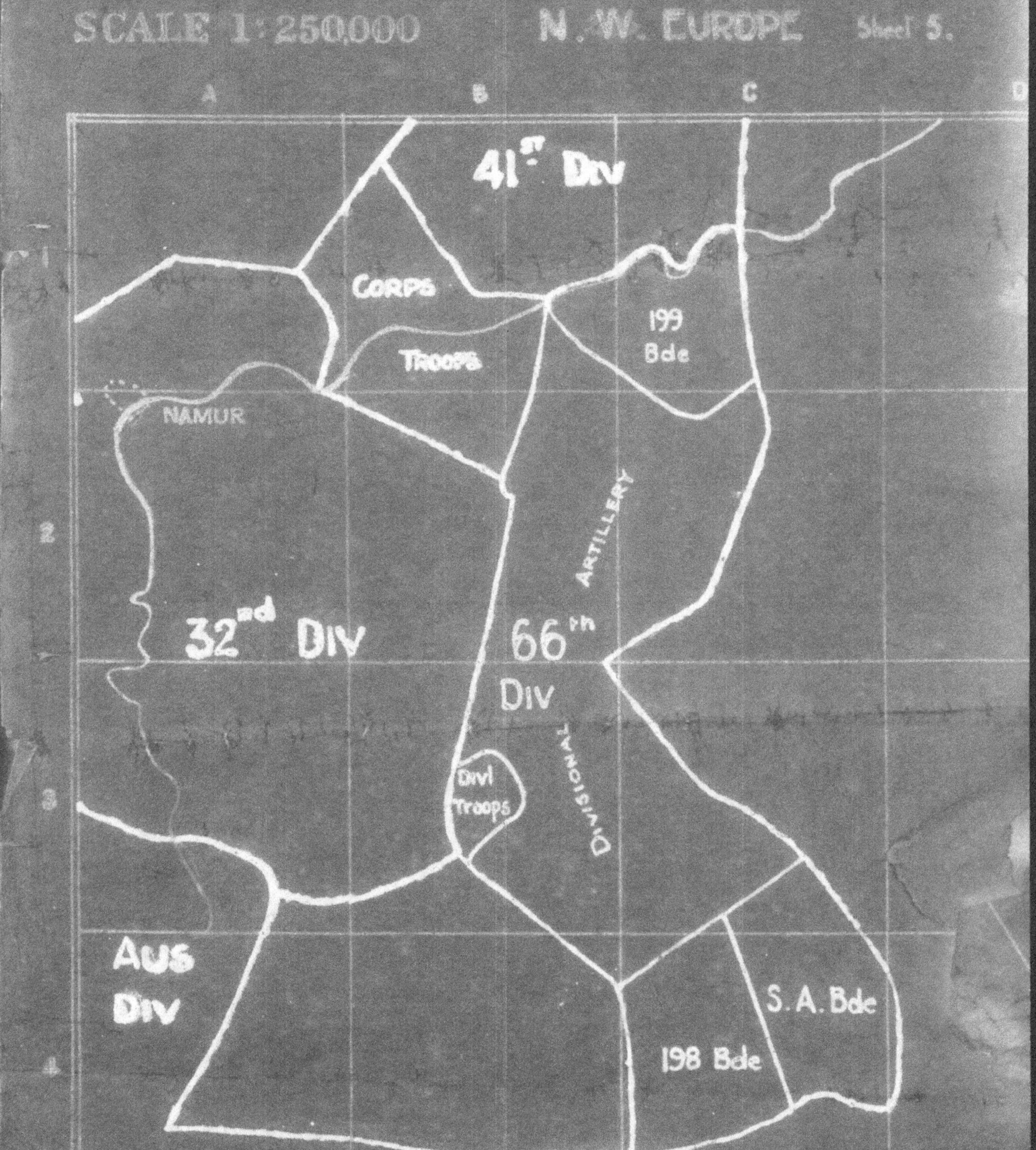

SCALE 1:250,000
N.W. EUROPE
Sheet 5.
A
B
C
D
41st Div
CORPS
TROOPS
199
Bde
NAMUR
ARTILLERY
32nd DIV
66th
Div
DIVISIONAL
Divl
Troops
AUS
DIV
S.A. Bde
198 Bde

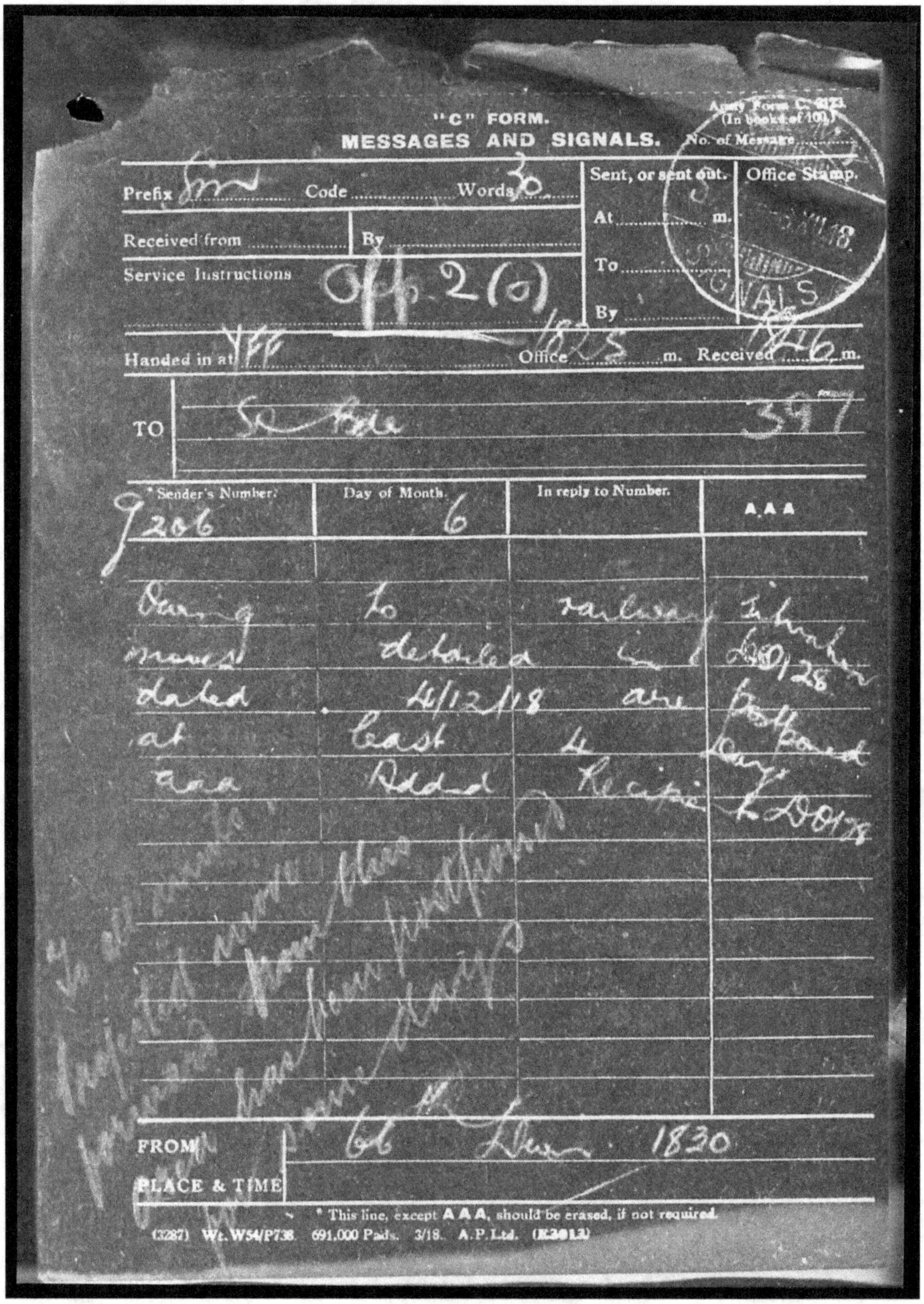

Army Form C. 2121.
(In books of 100.)

"C" FORM.
MESSAGES AND SIGNALS.

No. of Message

Prefix SM Code .... Words 30	Sent, or sent out. At .... m. To .... By	Office Stamp. 6 XII 18 SIGNALS
Received from .... By		
Service Instructions Off 2(0)		
Handed in at YFF Office 1825 m.	Received 1846 m.	

TO 5th Bde 397

* Sender's Number.	Day of Month.	In reply to Number.	A A A
G206	6		

Owing to railway situation moves detailed in LDO/128 dated 4/12/18 are postponed at least 4 days aaa Added Recipients LDO/128

to all recipients projected moves from there forward have been postponed for four days

FROM PLACE & TIME: 6th [illegible] 1830

* This line, except A A A, should be erased, if not required.

(3287) Wt. W54/P738. 691,000 Pads. 3/18. A.P.Ltd. (E3013)

~~full~~ 13/12 Off. 3 (a)

SECRET.

Copy No. 6

398

66TH DIVISION ORDER NO. 129.

10th December 1918.

1. Division will march to new area in accordance with attached table.

Division Order No. 128 of 4th December will be amended accordingly.

2. ACKNOWLEDGE.

F.P. Crosthwaite

Lieut Colonel.
General Staff,
66th Division.

Issued through
Signals at 1300

DISTRIBUTION.

No. 1	War Diary.	No. 12	Train A.S.C.
2	" "	13	A.D.M.S.
3	File.	14	9th Glouc. R. (Pioneers).
4	198th Brigade.	15	X Corps.
5	199th Brigade.	16	32nd Division.
6	S.A. Brigade.	17	D.A.P.M.
7	C.R.A.	18	66th M.T. Company.
8	C.R.E.	19	D.A.D.O.S.
9	Signals.	20	Camp Comdt.
10	A & Q.	21	A.D.C.
11	100th Bn.M.G.C.		

****

MARCH TABLE TO ACCOMPANY 66TH DIVISION ORDER NO. 128.

Serial No.	Date.	Unit.	FROM.	TO.	ROUTE.	REMARKS.
1.	Dec. 13th.	199th Brigade Group.	MORVILLE Area.	DINANT Area.	ONHAYE.	To clear MORVILLE by 10.00.
2.	" "	330 Brigade RFA. D.A.C. 541 Coy A.S.C.	VILLERS-LE-GAMBON, FRANCHIMONT.	MORVILLE.	-	Under orders to be issued by C.R.A.
3.	Dec. 14th.	199th Brigade Group.	DINANT Area.	HAMOIS - EMPTINNE area.	ACHENE.	To be clear of SORINNE by 11.30.
4.	" "	D.H.Q. Group.	WAULSORT.	CINEY.	DINANT.	Tail of column to be clear of WAULSORT at 08.30 and of GEMMECHENNE by 11.50. M.T. via CELLES and CONNEUX, to cross DINANT Bridge between 11.00 and 12.00.
5.	" "	Div. R.A. Group plus 100th Bn. M.G.C.	MORVILLE Area.	ACHENE, SORINNE, DINANT.	DINANT.	H.Q. R.A. & one Bde R.F.A. to LEIGNON, head of column to crpss DINANT Bridge at 12.15. 100th Bn. M.G.C. to march under orders of C.R.A.
6.	" "	S.A. Brigado Group.	BAC DU PRINCE &c.	HOUYET Area.	HASTIERE.	

399

Serial No.	Date.	Unit.	FROM.	TO.	ROUTE.	REMARKS.
7.	Dec. 15th.	199th Brigade Group.	HAMOIS – EMPTINNE Area.	HUY Area.	Any.	
8.	" "	Serial No. 5.	SORINNE &c.	LEIGNON &c.	ACHENE.	Billets for 100th Bn. M.G.C. in CINEY from 66th Division 'Q'.
9.	" "	S.A. Brigade Group.	HOUYET Area.	ROCHEFORT Area.	CIERGNON.	
10.	" "	198th Bde Group. (less 431 Fld Coy. R.E.)	HASTIERE &c.	HOUYET Area.	Any.	
11.	Dec. 16th.	S.A. Brigade Group.	ROCHEFORT Area.	MARCHE Area.	Any.	To be clear of ROCHEFORT Area by 11.00.
12.	" "	Serial No. 10.	HOUYET Area.	ROCHEFORT Area.	Any.	

D.H.Q.
10th Dec. 1918.

400

app. 4.

401

Secret

SOUTH AFRICAN INFANTRY BRIGADE

Ref. Maps:-
NAMUR)
MARCHE) - 1/100,000

Copy No. ......

ORDER No. 206.

13-12-18

1. MOVE
(a) The 66th. Divn. is continuing its forward move.
(b) S. Afr. Inf. Bde. Group will move on the 14th., 15th., and 16th. Dec. in accordance with the attached March Tables.

2. TRANSPORT & SUPPLIES
(a) First-line transport and baggage wagons will move with Units. Baggage wagons will be lightly loaded.
(b) Orders regarding Supplies, and allotment and movement of lorries are being issued separately.

3. BILLETING PARTIES
(a) Billeting parties for night of 14th. Dec. have alrwady been detailed by Staff Captain.
(b) Billeting parties for succeeding nights will be as detailed later from the same source.

4. SICK
The S. Afr. Field Ambulance will detail an Ambulance Car to move in rear of the column.

5. BRIGADE HEADQUARTERS
Bde. HQ. will close and open as follows:-

	Close	Open
BAC du PRINCE	08.00	On arrival.
HOUYET	08.00	
ROCHEFORT	08.00	

6. ACKNOWLEDGE.

James K. Leisk (?)
Major,
A/Brigade Major,
South Afr. Inf. Bde..

Issued at 11.30 through Sigs. to
1. 1st. SAI
2. 2nd. SAI
3. 4th. SAI
4. SALTM Bty.
5. Bde. Sig. Off.
6. S. Afr. Fld. Amb..
7. 542 Co., ASC.
8. 430 Fld. Co., RE.
9. 66 Divn.
10. 198 Inf. Bde..
11. 199 Inf. Bde..
12. Staff Captain
13. Brigade Major
14/18. War Diary.

MARCH TABLE.

ADVANCE GUARD.

Unit in order or march.	Starting Pt.	Time.	Route	Remarks.
1 Coy. 1st S.A.I.	X Roads due N of E in SOLRE LE CHATEAU.	06.15	HESTRUD-GRANDIEU - BEAUMONT.	Advance Guard to be in position by 06.45. Distance between Main Gd. and head of Main Body 700 yards.
430 Fld Co R.E.		06.18.		
1 section C Coy 100 BN M.G.C.		06.23		
1 Bearer Section		06.25.		Technical vehicles to move with Units Remainder of transport to be brigaded under Major C.M.BROWNE. 4th S.A.I.
1st S.A.I. (less 1 Coy)		06.30.		
1 section, 431st Batty R.F.A.		06.35		
S.A.Bde H.Q.)		07.00		
2 Armoured Cars)				
2nd S.A.I. (less 1 platoon.		07.02.		
C Coy. 100 M.G.C. (less 1 section.		07.10.		
S.A.L.T.M.B.		07.15.		
"B" Bty. 431 R.F.A.		07.17.		
1 sect. "D" Bty. 431st A.F.A.Bde.		07.25.		
[illegible].				
432nd Flf Co. R.E.		07.28.		
S.A.F.A. (less 1 bearer section)		07.38.		
[illegible]. Rear Guard.				
2nd S.A.I.		08.00.		

MARCH TABLE ISSUED WITH SOUTH AFR. INF. BDE. ORDER No. [illegible]

December 14th., 1918.

Serial No.	Unit	Starting Point	Time	Area Allotted	ROUTE	Report Centre until HQ. is established.	Meeting Point for Supply Wagons	REMARKS
1.	Bde. HQ. & Sig.Section	River Bridge, GIVET	08.40	HOUYET	E. side of River Br., GIVET - PETIT CAPORAL INN - FESCHAUX	Southern entrance to village.	SAME AS FOR REPORT CENTRE	Units proceeding via GIVET will observe midday halt from 11.[illegible] to 1[illegible]. Units proceeding via HASTIERE will observe midday halt when head of column reaches X-rds. S. of Point [illegible].
2.	1st. SAI	do.	09.20	FERAGE	Same as in Serial 1- to rd. junctn. S. of F in FERAGE	CHATEAU		
3.	2nd. SAI	do.	09.35	MESNIL EGLISE	Same as in Serial 1.	CHURCH		
4.	4th. SAI	River Bridge, HASTIERE	09.10	HOUYET	River Br., HASTIERE - MESNIL St.BLAISE - X. rds. S of Point 2[illegible]	Southern entrance to Village		
5.	SALTM Bty.	do.	09.25	do.	Same as in Serial 4.	do.		
6.	S.A.F.Amb.	River Bridge, GIVET	08.48	do.	Same as in Serial 1.	do.		
7.	4?0 Co.,RE.	do.	09.10	HERHET	Same as in Serial 2.	do.		
8.	542 Co.ASC.	do.	08.30	SANZINNE	Same as in Serial 1.	do.		

MARCH TABLE ISSUED WITH SOUTH AFR. INF. BDE. ORDER No. 266.

15th. December, 1918

Serial No.	UNIT	Starting Point.	Time.	Area Allotted	ROUTE	Report Centre Until HQ. is established.	Meeting Point for Supply Wagons.	REMARKS
9.	Bde. HQ. & Sig. Section	River Br. E. of Level Crossing in HOUYET	08.48	ROCHEFORT	CIERGNON	Road crossing over railway in centre of village	SAME AS FOR REPORT CENTRE	Midday halt to be observed from 11.50 to 12.00
10.	1st. SAI	do.	09.15	do.	HOUYET and CIERGNON	do.		
11.	2nd. SAI	do.	09.30	do.	do.	do.		
12.	4th. SAI	do.	08.30	JEMELLE	CIERGNON	Level Crossing.		
13.	SALTM Bty.	do.	09.10	ROCHEFORT	do.	Same as Serial 9		
14.	S.A.F.Amb.	do.	09.45	do.	do.	do.		
15.	430 Co. RE	do.	08.45	JEMELLE	HOUYET and CIERGNON	Level Crossing		
16.	542 Co. ASC	Rd. junction Sb. of SANZINNE	09.10	ROCHEFORT	CIERGNON	Same as Serial 9		

MARCH TABLE ISSUED WITH SOUTH AFR. INF. BDE. ORDER No. [illegible]

14th. December, 1918

Serial No.	UNIT	Starting Point.	Time.	Area Allotted	ROUTE	Report Centre until HQ. is established.	Meeting point for Supply Wagons.	REMARKS.
17.	Bde. HQ. & Sig. Section	Level Crossing S. of First R in ROCHEFORT	09.05	MARCHE	HARGIMONT	Hotel de la Cloche	SAME AS FOR REPORT CENTRE	There will be no midday halt for Units billeting in MARCHE and WAHA. Units billeting beyond MARCHE (4th.SAI and possibly 1st.SAI) will observe midday halt on clearing X-rds. N. of R in MARCHE.
18.	1st. SAI	do.	08.40	To be notified later	To be notified later	To be notified later		
19.	2nd. SAI	do.	09.10	MARCHE	HARGIMONT	Same as Serial 17		
20.	4th. SAI	Eastern end of JEMELLE village	09.15	AYE	HARGIMONT (thence forward to be reconnoitred by Unit)	Rd. crossing over railway		
21.	SALTM Bty.	Same as Serial 17	09.35	MARCHE	HARGIMONT	Same as Serial 17		
22.	S.A.F. Amb.	do.	09.25	do.	do.	do.		
23.	4?? Co. ASC	Same as Serial 17	09.01	WAHA	do.	W. entrance to village		
24.	542 Co. ASC	Same as Serial 17	08.30	MARCHE	do.	Same as Serial 17		

App 5
406

SOUTH AFRICAN INFANTRY BRIGADE.

BM 30

1st. SAI,
2nd. SAI,
4th. SAI.

Reference MARCHE SHEET 1/100,000.

Reinforcements for the Brigade have arrived at HAVERSIN STATION - on railway about 8 miles W. of MARCHE. They will join up with Brigade tomorrow. Meantime you will please detail 2 officers and 4 NCOs. (selected) to proceed at once to HAVERSIN to assist in tomorrows move.

Motor transport for this Officer and NCO. party is being provided from MARCHE - it will pick up 4th. SAI party en route.

The party will remain overnight at HAVERSIN.

The party will be under the command of Major McEWEN (1st. SAI) who will be one of the two officers detailed by 1st. SAI, and who on arrival at HAVERSIN will assume command of all reinforcements. He will move the reinforcements from HAVERSIN tomorrow so as to reach MARCHE by 12.00 hours - 4th. SAI reinforcements being dropped at AYE.

Officers and NCOs. of 1st. and 2nd. SAI parties will report at Brigade Headquarters at once.

Acknowledge.

(Sgd) JAMES R. LEISK,

Major,
A/Brigade Major,

Issued through
Sigs. 12.00.
B.H.Q.,
16/12/18

COPY.

App. 6 (c)
405

CONFIDENTIAL.

66th. Division.
8271/A.

Headquarters,
South African Infantry Brigade.

The GOC. this morning saw some 1400 men of your Brigade who had just detrained at HAVERSIN, where they were being met by a detraining Officer of the 9th. Bn. Glousestershire Regt.

The Draft for the 4th. Regiment, and the Company of the BEF. men, considering the conditions from which they had come, and the difficult circumstances (i.e. great shortage of both Officers and NCOs.) called for no remarks.

The Draft of the 1st. and 2nd. Regiments degenerated into mobs of men. The Officer in Charge told the GOC. that a ration train had been broken into, and the men had presumably filled their waterbottles with rum.

The GOC. has already spoken to you of this, and is aware that you have taken the necessary steps, at the same time he directs that a full report be rendered as to how, and what train or canteen was wrecked.

(Sgd) ....

Major,
for A.A. & Q.M.G.
66th. Division.

16/12/18

COPY.

App 7

407

SOUTH AFRICAN INFANTRY BRIGADE.

BM 1086.

1st. SAI,
2nd. SAI,
4th. SAI,
SAF. Amb.

Court of enquiry.

A Court of Enquiry, composed as under, will assemble at Brigade Headquarters Office, at 11.30, 21st. December 1918,

To enquire into , and report upon the condition in which the reinforcement Draft for Brigade Units arrived at HAVERSIN on 16th. December 1918, and the behaviour of the Drafts in the journey from the Divisional Reception Camp, with special reference to the statements contained in 66th Division Confidential letter No. 2271/A of 16/12/18, of which a copy is appended, marked "A".
And further to enquire into and report upon the causes which contributed to the Drafts being in such a condition and behaving in such manner.

PRESIDENT.

Major C.R.HEENAN, D.S.O.,
Commanding 2nd. SAI.

MEMBERS.

Capt. T. ROFFE, MC., 1st. SAI.
Capt. A.M.D.CAMERON, 4th. SAI.

All available witnesses will be warnedto attend.

(Sgd) JAMES R. LEISK,

Major,
A/Brigade Major,
S. Afr. Inf. Bde.

19/12/18.

app. 8

SOUTH AFRICAN INFANTRY BRIGADE

Copy No. 13

408

BRIGADE ORDER No. 267

Ref. MARCHE sheet, 1/100,000

25-12-18

---

1. Inspection by H.R.H. the Prince of Wales:
H.R.H. the Prince of Wales has intimated his intention to visit t[illegible] S.Afr. Inf. B e. on 26th. Dec..

2. Guard of Honour:
A Guard of Honour, under the command of Captain F.L. MARILLIER, 2nd. SAI., will be detailed to receive HRH. on arrival at Bde. HQ.. The Guard will consist of one ~~xxxxxx~~ subaltern Officer and thirty-three ORs. from each of the three BNs.. The detachments from each B[illegible] will report to the Commander of the Guard at the Church, MARCHE, at 10.00 on 26th. Dec.. The Guard will be formed up at Bde. HQ. by 10.[illegible] to receive HRH.. The Band of the 1st. SAI. will parade with the Gua[illegible] of Honour. After inspection by HRH. the Guard of Honour will return to billets, and the Band, 1st. SAI., will rejoin its BN. for inspection parade. Men will be specially selected for their smartness a[illegible] bearing.

3. Units to be inspected, and Sites:
Bde. Units - less transport and transport personnel - will parade for inspection by HRH. on t e sites, in the respective BN. areas, w[illegible] have already been pointed out to BN. Commanders.

4. Hour of Inspection and Formations:
Bde. Uni s will be inspected in the following order and formations:
2nd. SAI (with whom will be S.A.F.A., SALTM Bty., Bde. HQ., and Sig. Section.) at 11.00 - formed up in close column of coys..
1st. SAI at 11.45 - formed up in line.
4th. SAI at 12.30 - formed up in close column of coys..

5. Dress Order:
The Dress Order will be fighting order (without mess-tins), that i[illegible] to say - haversacks on back with waterproof sheets under the flaps; entrenching tools and water-bottles. Officers will wear gloves and [illegible] NOT carry sticks.

6. Ceremonial:
Notes on Ceremonial have been issued to Units in order to secure uniformity.

7. March past:
The usual ceremonial march-past will not take place, but after inspection, each BN. (and Units attached as indicated in para. 4), wil[illegible] march past in column of route (in fours.) This march past will take place on the road - the saluting bases being at the points already pointed out to BN. Comdrs. Bayonets will remain fixed for th[illegible] March Past.

8. Bands:
Bands will lead BNs. (and attached Units) off the field, and on to the road. Bands will then turn out from the road and take station on the opposite side from the saluting Base - at a sufficient distance (before reaching saluting base) to be able to play BNs. past without drowning words of command. Bands will then fall in at the tail of their respective columns.

9. Salute - Marching past:
The Salute, in marching past, will be by platoons.

10. Return to Billets:
After marching past BNs. (and attached Units) will return to billets - 2nd. and 1st. SAI (and attached Units) by routes as pointed out.

11. Transport Personnel:
Transport personnel will not parade for inspection with their Units. They will however parade (under their respective transport Officers) in rear of their bands when troops are marching past in column of route. Bde. HQ. transport personnel will parade with transport personnel of 1st. SAI. - under T.O., 1st. SAI.

12. Road Police Duties:
30 ORs. from 1st. SAI. and 2nd. SAI (60 in all) including a suitable proportion of NCOs., will be detailed to report at the Church, MARCHE, to Lieut. INGARFIELD, at 10.00 on 28th. Dec., for duty as road police, etc..

Major,
A/Brigade Major,
South Afr. Inf. Bde..

Issued through Signals at
13.00 to

1. 1ST. SAI
2. 2nd. SAI
3. 4th. SAI
4. SALTM Bty.
5. S.A.F.A.
6. Bde. Sig. Off.
7. Bde. Transport Officer
8. 430 Fld. Co., RE.
9. 542 Co., ASC.
10. Staff Captain
11. 66th. Division. (3)
12. Bde. Major,
13/16, War Diary.

66TH DIVISION

STH AFRICAN INFY BRIGADE

(0) 1

BRIGADE HEADQUARTERS

JAN - FEB 1919

(COPY No. 1)

Army Form C. 2118.

WAR DIARY
or
~~INTELLIGENCE SUMMARY.~~
(Erase heading not required.)

(1)

Instructions regarding War Diaries and Intelligence Summaries are contained in F. S. Regs., Part II. and the Staff Manual respectively. Title pages will be prepared in manuscript.

SOUTH AFRICAN INF. BRIGADE.

JANUARY, 1919.

Vol. 34

Place	Date	Hour	Summary of Events and Information	Remarks and references to Appendices
MARCHE	1st.		Training continued during month under Battalion arrangements.	
AREA.	2nd.		Sport within the Brigade being organised. Men entering for Brigade and Divisional Competitions excused duties during training, Brigade Football teams being specially accommodated-	
	3rd.		Church Parades as usual.	
	7th.		Brig. General W.E.C.Tanner, CMG., DSO., left under instructions from War Office to attend meeting of reorganisation Committee in LONDON. Lt. Col. E. THACKERAY, CMG., DSO., appointed to command South African Brigade during temporary absence of Brig. General TANNER.	
	8th.		Rugby Match between 13th. Australian Infantry Brigade and South African Brigade at MARCHE, S.A.Brigade - 14. Australian Brigade - nil.	
	9th.		Under instructions Fourth Army AX/54 (66th. Division D/58) 108 other ranks despatched to South African Demobilization centre in England (Perham Downs, Salisbury Plain) i/c of 2 officers. These men belong to the Mechanical Staff of the South African Railways, and their release from Military Service had been expidited at the request of the South African Government.	
	11th.		Rugby Match between officers of 14th. Infantry Brigade and Officers of South African Bde. at GODINNE. Result - 14th. Infantry Brigade 15. S. A. Brigade - 3.	
			66th. Division 8493/1/Q received, calling for volunteers from Brigade to fill vacancies in Divisional Artillery caused by demobilization of Artillery Drivers.	
	12th.		Church Parades as usual.	
	13th.		On instructions from 66th. Division (8578/A) Guard of three officers and 45 men detailed to reportat SPA Railway station to relieve Guard of 2nd. Cavalry Division.	2

D. D. & L., London, E.C.
(10340) Wt W5300/P713 750,000 3/18 & 2688 Forms/C2118/15.

Instructions regarding War Diaries and Intelligence Summaries are contained in F. S. Regs., Part II. and the Staff Manual respectively. Title pages will be prepared in manuscript.

WAR DIARY
or
~~INTELLIGENCE SUMMARY.~~
(Erase heading not required.)

(2)

Army Form C. 2118.

JANUARY, 1919.

Place	Date	Hour	Summary of Events and Information	Remarks and references to Appendices
MARCHE AREA.	14th.		Brigade Commander and Brigade Major attended at Fourth Army Headquarters, NAMUR, to be present at meeting with Archbishop of Canterbury and Bishop Gwynne.	
	16th.		Brigade Canteen and recreation-room opened in Cinema Hall, Rue de la Cloche, MARCHE. Brigade BS. 438 issued. Brigade Transport to be inspected by Divisional Commander on 17th.	App.1.
	17th.		66th. Division G. 616 received, postponing inspection of transport by Divisional Commander.	App.2. (o)
	19th.		66th. Division Warning Order (GS. 3/17 of 18/1/19) received. One Battalion of South African Brigade to go to SEILLES and take over administration of X Corps Concentration Camp. Remainder of Brigade Group to move to HUY on or about Jan. 31. 199 Inf. Brigade to take over MARCHE area.	App.3. (o)
			Brigade Warning Order issued.	App.4
	20th.		1st. South African Infantry detailed to move to SEILLES.	App.4a.
			66th. Division D/98 received. Instructions re move of South African Brigade Group to HUY.	App.5 (o)
	21st.		Brigade Order 288 issued. Move of 1st. South African Infantry from MARCHE to SEILLES in 3 stages.	App.6.
			Transport Competition held by 1st. SA. Infantry; judged by Brigade Commander. Party of 60 men (20 from each Battalion) detailed for 14th. F. A. Brigade as Drivers (Division 8493/1/Q)	
	22nd.		66th. Division G 687 received. Divisional Commander to inspect Brigade Group transport on 23rd BS. 508 sent to Division. Programme of inspection submitted for approval.	App.7 (o) App.8
			Brigade Rugby team played team of South African Heavy Artillery. Brigade - 6 S.A.H.A. - 3.	
	23rd.		66th. Division Order 130 received. Exchange of areas between South African Brigade Group and 199 Brigade Group to be completed by 1st. February.	App 8a. (o)

4

2

D. D. & L., London, E.C.
(16340) Wt W5300/P713 750,000 3/18 S 2688 Forms/C2118/15.

Army Form C. 2118.

Instructions regarding War Diaries and Intelligence Summaries are contained in F. S. Regs., Part II. and the Staff Manual respectively. Title pages will be prepared in manuscript.

WAR DIARY
or
~~INTELLIGENCE SUMMARY~~. (3) January, 1919.

(Erase heading not required.)

Place	Date	Hour	Summary of Events and Information	Remarks and references to Appendices
MARCHE	24th.		On instructions from 66th. Division (A 832) R.A. drivers employed with Trench Mortar Battery returned to D.A.C.	
AREA.	25th.		Platoon competition held by 4th. South African Infantry; judged by Brigade Major. Further 29 men despatched to 14th. F.A.Brigade as Drivers.	
	26th.		Route March by 2nd. South African Infantry. Brigade Rugby team sent to Cologne to play against New Zealanders.	
	27th.		Brigade Order 269 issued. Move of Brigade Group (less 1st. South African Infantry & 430 Field Co. RE.) to HUY, via MAFFE, MEAN, and CHARDENEUX, on Jan. 30, 31, and Feb. 1.	App. 9.
			66th. Division G 742 received, cancelling orders for move of Brigade to HUY area. 1st. South African Infantry to move from SEILLES to CINEY. Brigade BS. 536 issued, cancelling Brigade Order 269.	App. 10 (o) App. 11
	28th.		66th. Division Order 131 received. Details of cancellation of move orders and despatch of 1st South African Infantry to CINEY	App. 12
			On instructions from 66th. Division, party of 4 officers, 14 NCOs. 11 cooks., and 83 other ranks despatched to 2nd. Cavalry Division Headquarters, VERVIERS west, to run a Halte Repas under orders of Cavalry Corps.	
	29th.		Brigade Rugby team played against New Zealand team at Cologne. Result New Zealanders 21. South African Brigade - Nil.	

Brig. General Commanding
S. Afr. Inf. Bde

5

3

D. D. & L., London, E.C.
(10340) Wt W5300/P713 750,000 3/18 & 2688 Forms/C2118/15.

"A" Form
Army Form C. 2121
(In pads of 100.) 4

MESSAGES AND SIGNALS.

No. of Message..........

Prefix.......Code.......m. Office of Origin and Service Instructions	Words / Charge. Sent At ....m. To .... By	This message is on a/c of: ....Service. Opp. 1 (Signature of "Franking Officer")	Recd. at......m. Date.... 36 From .... By........

TO: 1st SAI 2nd SAI 542 Co ASC
4th SAI SALTMBty
SAF amb 430 Fwd? Co RE

Sender's Number.	Day of Month.	In reply to Number.	AAA
BS 438	16	—	

Inspection of transport by Divisional Commander will take place tomorrow Jan 17 commencing 10 AM [illegible]

Time table giving order in which units will be inspected will be issued later aaa Forwarding? addresses? to all units in Bde. [illegible] Group

From: S A Bde
Place:
Time:

The above may be forwarded as now corrected. (Z) .... Censor.

Signature of Addressor or person authorised to telegraph in his name: [signature] Maj? Sig. Offr?

* This line should be erased if not required.

Order No. 1625. Wt. W3253/ P 511. 27/2. H. & K., Ltd. (E. 2634).

20A

"C" Form.

Army Form C. 2123. 4

(In books of 100.)

MESSAGES AND SIGNALS.

No. of Message ________

Prefix ____ Code ____ Words 105

£ s. d.

Charges to Collect

Service Instructions

Received. From 7H By

Sent, or sent out. At ____ m. To ____ By ____

Office Stamp. S A 1.19 SIGNALS

App. 2 (c)

Handed in at 7H Office 3.05 m. Received ____ m.

TO 2 Bde

*Sender's Number	Day of Month.	In reply to Number	AAA
G 66	16		

Cancel	my	G609	of
today	aaa	There	will
be	no	inspection	on
17th	aaa	On	18th
Div	Commander	will	inspect
A/331	Bty	RFA	at
PAILHE	commencing	10.00	and
afterwards	D/331	at	HAVELANGE
aaa	Addsd	all	recipients
of	G609		

FROM 66th Div

PLACE & TIME

* This line should be erased if not required.

9810—W.526—100,000—10/5/17—E.P.Co.—(E1213).

4

SECRET. App. 3(c) 66th Divn. G.S. 3/17. 35

66th DIVISION.

Copy No. 4

W A R N I N G   O R D E R.

18th January 1919.

1. Under instructions to be issued by 66th Division 'G', the S.A. Brigade will detail one Battalion to move to SEILLES about 21st January to take over and administer the X Corps Concentration Camp at that place.

2. About 31st January, S.A. Brigade Group (less one Battalion) will move to HUY and 199th Brigade Group to MARCHE.

F.P. Nosworthy

Lieut-Colonel,
General Staff, 66th Division.

DISTRIBUTION.

Copy No.	1.	War Diary.	9	Signals.
	2	" "	10	'A' and 'Q'.
	3	File.	11	Train A.S.C.
	4	S.A. Bde.	12	A.D.M.S.
	5	198th Inf. Bde.	13	X Corps.
	6	199th Inf. Bde.	14	D.A.P.M.
	7	C.R.A.	15	Camp Commandant.
	8	C.R.E.	16	A.D.C.

SOUTH AFRICAN INFANTRY BRIGADE. Secret.
Copy No.
19/1/19. 34

App. 4

WARNING ORDER.

Ref. Maps:
MARCHE SHEET 1/100,000
LIEGE SHEET 1/100,000.

1. Under WARNING ORDER (GS 3/17 dated 18/1/19) received from 66th. Division, 1st. S.A.Infantry will move by March Route from MARCHE to SEILLES probably on 22nd. 23rd. and 24th. January; on road MAFFE - OHEY - ANDENNE. On arrival at SEILLES, 1st. S.AFRICAN INFANTRY will take over and administer the X Corps Concentration Camp at that place.

2. 1st. SA INFANTRY will detail two officers, one of them being of Captain's rank, to report at SEILLES on 20th. January to learn the work of the Concentration Camp. They will take batmen. Transport for party to be arranged with Staff Captain.

3. Staff Captain will arrange with billeting parties for staging the move of 1st. SOUTH AFRICAN INFANTRY to SEILLES.

4. About 31st January SOUTH AFRICAN BRIGADE GROUP (less 1st. SOUTH AFRICAN INFANTRY) will move from MARCHE area to HUY, and the 199th BRIGADE GROUP from HUY to MARCHE area.

James K Levin(?)
Major,
A/Brigade Major,
S.Afr.Inf.Bde.

Issued through Signals, at 20.30 hours:

Copy No.	1.	1st. SAI,		
	2	2nd. SAI.	9.	430 Field CO. RE.
	3	4th. SAI.	10	542 CO. ASC.
	4	SALTMB.,	11	66th. DIVISION.
	5	STAFF CAPT.,	12	198 INFANTRY BDE.
	6	BDE. SIG. OFF.	13.	199 " "
	7	BDE. TRANSPORT OFF.	14	War Diary
	8	S.A.F.AMB.	15	" "

5

"A" Form App. 4A. Army Form C. 2121 (in pads of 100).

MESSAGES AND SIGNALS.

No. of Message..................

Prefix..........Code..........m. | Words. | Charge. | This message is on a/c of: ....Service. | Recd. at. 33 ...m.

Office of Origin and Service Instructions.

Sent At......m. To...... By......

(Signature of "Franking Officer.") Date...... From...... By......

TO 66th Div

Sender's Number.	Day of Month.	In reply to Number.	AAA
*B.S. 492	20	Q 839	

Batter selected is 1st SAI aaa Two officers despatched to report today at Senlis as instructed

From Sa Bde
Place
Time

The above may be forwarded as now corrected. (Z)

Censor.

Signature of Addressor or person authorised to telegraph in his name. [signature] Capt Major

* This line should be erased if not required.

(18965.) Wt. W12952/M1294. 187,500 Pads. 1/17 McC. & Co., Ltd. (E. 818.)

App. 5 (o) 5

66th Divn.
D/98.

31

SECRET.

(3) Headquarters,
S.African Infantry Bde.

Reference 66th Division Warning Order No. GS.3/17 of 18.1.19, para 1.

1. The Battalion of the South African Brigade will move to SEILLES as follows :-

Janry. 22nd: to area SOMME-LODZE - MEAN-MAFFE.

Janry. 23rd: to area HAILLON - OHEY.

Janry. 24th: to SEILLES.

2. Billeting parties will meet Area Commandants concerned at the Burgomaster's House, at MAFFE and OHEY, at 10.00 hours on Janry. 21st and 22nd respectively.

3. During the move, supply arrangements will be as under:-

Janry. 22nd: Supplies for consumption 23rd will be delivered by M.T. at MAFFE.

Janry. 23 rd: Supplies for consumption 24th will be delivered by M.T. at OHEY.

O.C. 66th Div.Train will notify all concerned time and place of drawing.

Supplies for consumption 25th and onwards will be under Corps arrangements.

4. Six lorries, for carriage of blankets and extra stores, will report at South African Brigade Headqrs. at 16.00 hours on Janry.21st, and will remain with the Battalion throughout the move.

On completion of the move, these lorries will return to park.

5. All area stores will be handed in to Area Commandant or Town Major concerned, and copies of receipts forwarded to this office.

6. South African Infantry Brigade to acknowledge.

[signature]

Lt.Colonel,
A/A.A.& Q.M.G.
66th Division.

20.1.19.

Copies to:-

X Corps G.	199 Inf.Bde.	Area Comdt.	MAFFE
G.	D.A.P.M.	-do-	HEURE
Camp Commdt.	A.D.M.S.	-do-	OSSOGNE Sub-Area
C.R.A.	D.A.D.O.S.		
C.R.E.	Div.Train.	Town Major	MARCHE.
Signal Co.	D.A.D.V.S.		
198 Inf.Bde.			

6

SOUTH AFRICAN INFANTRY BRIGADE.

Order No. 268.

Secret.
Copy No.
21/1/19.

Reference Maps:-

App. 6

30

MARCHE } 1/100,000.
LIEGE }

---

1. MOVE. (a) With reference to Brigade WARNING ORDER of 19/1/19, the 1st. SAI. will move by march route from MARCHE to SEILLES as follows:-

Jan. 22. to MAFFE area - including villages of MEAN-VERLEE and SOMME LODZE, selection of last mentioned three villages to be made on receipt of reports from billeting party this evening.

Jan. 23. to area OHEY - HAILLON.

Jan. 24. to SEILLES.

(b) Each day's move to be completed by 15.00 hours.

2. DRESS. (a) Full marching order, one blanket on man, two blankets and greatcoat on lorries.

(b) Jerkins to be worn or carried according to orders of O.C.Unit.

3. MARCH DISCIPLINE. An interval of 20 yards will be observed between Platoons.

4. TRANSPORT. (a) First Line transport and baggage wagons will move with Units.

(b) Six lorries for carriage of blankets greatcoats and extra stor are available. These will remain with Battalion throughout the move. On completion of move lorries will return to park.

5. SUPPLIES. During move, supply arrangements will be as follows:-

Jan.22. Supplies for consumption on 23rd. will be delivered by MT. at MAFFE.

Jan.23. Supplies for consumption on 24 th. will be delivered at OHEY by MT.

These supplies will be available for drawing on each day by 12.00 hours.

Supplies for consumption on 25th. and onwards will be under Corps arrangements.

6. AREA STORES MARCHE. These will be handed in to Town Major and copies of receipts forwarded to this office.

7. BILLETS. Special care will be taken to see that all billets are properly cleaned on leaving.

8. MEDICAL. Under orders from ADMS. 66th. Division, O.C. 1st. S.A. Field Ambulance, details one horsed ambulance wagon (with wagon orderly) and one large motor ambulance car (with orderly) to accompany 1st. SAI. on the move. These vehicles will be at the disposal of officer in medical charge of unit.

9. BILLETING PARTIES. Parties will meet Burgomaster at OHEY at 10.00 hours on 22nd. January.

10. Completion of move to be notified to this office by wire.

11. Officers and other ranks on educational Courses in MARCHE area or detailed for recreational contests will be temporarily attached to 2nd. SAI.

12. ACKNOWLEDGE.

                              Major,
                              A/Brigade Major,
                              S.Afr.Inf. Bde.

Issued through Signals at 17.00 hours
to :-

No.		No.	
1.	1st. SAI,		
2.	2nd. SAI,	11.	4?? Field Oc. RE.
3.	4th. SAI,	12.	542 Oc. RASC.
4.	SALTMB.	13.	66th. Division.
5.	Bde. Education Off.	14.	198 Infantry Brigade.
6.	Staff Capt.	15.	199 " "
7.	Bde. Sig. Off.	16.	Area Commandant, MARCHE.
8.	Bde. Transport Off.	17.	Town Major, MARCHE,
9.	Bde. Major,	18.	War Diary.
10.	S.A.F. Amb.	19.	War Diary.

32 Army Form C. 2123.
(In books of 100.)

"C" Form.

MESSAGES AND SIGNALS.

No. of Message

Prefix SG Code Words 23	Received.	Sent, or sent out.	Office Stamp.
£ s. d.	From Y77	At m.	
Charges to Collect	By 82	To	
Service Instructions Priority App. 7 (0)		By	

Handed in at Y77 Office 1544 m. Received 1550 m.

TO 66 Bde

*Sender's Number	Day of Month.	In reply to Number	AAA
G687	22nd		

Divl	Comdr	will	inspect
56	Bde	group	tomorrow
23rd	Starting	MARCHE	10.30
aaa	Added	all	concerned

FROM PLACE & TIME 66 Divn

* This line should be erased if not required.

2520—W 908—203,000—10/9/17—R.P.Co.—(E2123).

32A

2nd SAI	10.30 ✓
~~B~~ SALTMB	10.45 ✓
Bde HQ	
Sigs	11.15
Train	11.30
4th	12.00

Army Form C. 2121
(in pads of 100.)

MESSAGES AND SIGNALS.

No. of Message..............

Prefix.............. Code..............m | Words. | Charge.

Office of Origin and Service Instructions

Sent

At..................m.

To..................

By..................

This message is on a/c of:

app. 8

.... *Service.*

Copy

(Signature of "Franking Officer.")

Recd. at..........m.

Date........ 28

From ....

By ....

TO 66 Div

Sender's Number.	Day of Month.	In reply to Number.	AAA
* BS 502	22	G 687	

~~Suggested programme for tomorrows inspection by~~

G O C aaa 2nd SAI 10.30 aaa SALTMBy 10 45 aaa

~~Bde HQ~~ SA F Amb 11.00 aaa Bde HQ 11.20 aaa

542 Co ASC 11 40 aaa 4 SAI ~~[illegible]~~ 12.15

From S A Bde

Place

Time

The above may be forwarded as now corrected. (Z)

Censor. Signature of Addressor or person authorised to telegraph in his name.

Lieut

* This line should be erased if not required.

(4715) Wt. W3253/P511 1,113,336 Shts. 2/18 C. & Co. (.684)

App. 8A(o)

27

Copy No. 4

SECRET.

66TH DIVISION ORDER NO. 130.

22nd January 1919.

Reference Maps:-
LIEGE, 1/100.000.
MARCHE, 1/100.000.

1. On 30th, 31st January and 1st February, South African and 199th Brigade Groups (less Field Coys R.E.) will march to HUY and MARCHE respectively in accordance with attached table.

2. All formations will march in "three's". Distances between units as laid down in S.S.724 will be strictly maintained.
All marches will be completed by 15.00.

3. Advanced Parties will proceed by lorry on 28th January. Details to be arranged by Brigades with 66th Division 'Q'.

4. Brigades will arrange direct for inter-relief of all detached parties and Guards at present found over captured German material.

5. On completion of move, 430th Field Coy. R.E. will be affiliated to 199th Infantry Brigade and 432nd Field Coy. R.E. to South African Infantry Brigade.

Done 6. ACKNOWLEDGE.

Lieut Colonel.
General Staff,
66th Division.

Issued through
Signals at 2100

DISTRIBUTION.

No. 1	War Diary.	No. 12	Train A.S.C.
2	" "	13	A.D.M.S.
3	File.	14	9th Glouc. R. (Pioneer Bn.)
4	S.A. Brigade.	15	X Corps.
5	198th Brigade.	16	D.A.P.M.
6	199th Brigade.	17	66th M.T. Company.
7	C.R.A.	18	D.A.D.O.S.
8	C.R.E.	19	Camp Commandant.
9	Signals.	20	A.D.C.
10	A & Q.	21	
11	100th Bn. M.G.C.	22	

MARCH TABLE TO ACCOMPANY 66TH DIVISION ORDER NO. 130.

Serial No.	Date.	U N I T.	F R O M.	T O.	REMARKS.
1.	Jan. 30th.	'A' Bn. 199th Brigade. 'B' Bn. 199th Brigade.	H U Y.	BOIS-ET-BORSU ODEL. ATRIN.	
2.	-do-	'A' Bn. S.A. Brigade. S.A. Field Ambulance.	MARCHE.	MAFFE. MEAN. CHARDENEUX.	Billeting officers to report to H.Q. No 7 M.G. Squadron (Chau. 1 mile N.E. of MEAN) for information regarding available billets.
3.	Jan. 31st.	Serial No. 1.	BORSU &c.	MARCHE.	
4.	-do-	Serial No. 2.	MAFFE &c.	H U Y.	
5.	-do-	199th Brigade Group (less Serial No. 1).	H U Y.	BOIS-ET-BORSU. ODEL. ATRIN.	
6.	-do-	S.A. Brigade Group (less Serial No. 2)	MARCHE.	MAFFE. MEAN. CHARDENEUX.	As for Serial No. 2.
7.	Feb. 1st.	Serial No. 5.	BORSU &c.	MARCHE.	
8.	-do-	Serial No. 6.	MAFFE.	H U Y.	

D.H.Q. 28.1.19.

SECRET.

66th Divn.
8717/A.

S.A. Infantry Bde.
198th -do-
199th -do-
"G"
C.R.A.
C.R.E.
Signals.
100th Bn.M.G.C.
Train.
A.D.M.S.
9th Gloucester R.
X Corps Q.
D.A.P.M.
66th M.T. Co.
D.A.D.O.S.
Camp Commandant.
A.D.C.

Reference 66th Division Order No.130 dated 22nd Janry.1919.

1. SUPPLIES.

During the progress of the moves, the supply arrangements will be as under :-

Serial No. in March Table.	Unit.	Date of drawing.	For Consumption	Refilling Point.
1.	A Bn. 199 Bde.) B Bn. 199 Bde.)	30 Jan.	31 Jan.	Church - BOIS-ET-BORSU.
2.	A Bn. S.A.Bde.) S.A.Fld.Ambce.)	30 Jan.	31 Jan.	Cross Roads - MAFFE.
3.	Serial No.1	31 Jan.	1 Feb.	MARCHE.
4.	Serial No.2	31 Jan.	1 Feb.	HUY (South Station).
5.	199 Bde.Group (less Serial No.1)	31 Jan.	1 Feb.	Church - BOIS-ET-BORSU.
6.	S.A.Bde.Group (less Serial No.2)	31 Jan.	1 Feb.	Cross Roads - MA FFE.
7.	Serial No.5	1 Feb.	2 Feb.	MARCHE.
8.	Serial No.6	1 Feb.	2 Feb.	HUY.

2. TRANSP ORT.

To supplement existing transport, lorries will report as follows :-

At Headqrs., 199th Bde., HUY, at 16.00 hours, 29th. .. .. 11 lorries.

At Headqrs., S.African Bde., MARCHE, at 16.00 hours, 29th. .. .. 8 lorries.

These lorries will remain with Brigades and be under their orders until the moves are completed, but will return to park immediately after completion.

P. T. O.

25A

8.

3. AREA STORES.

Area Stores will not be removed either from HUY or MARCHE Area. They will be handed over to Area Commandants concerned and copies of all receipts forwarded to these Headquarters.

Lieut.-Colonel,
A/A.A.& Q.M.G.,
66th Division.

25.1.19.

SOUTH AFRICAN INFANTRY BRIGADE.
Order No. 269

Secret.
Copy No. 18
27/1/19.

10.

24

App. 9

Reference Maps:,

MARCHE)
LIEGE.) 1/100,000.

1. On the 30th, 31st. January and 1st. February, 1919, the South African Infantry Brigade Group, less 432 Field Co. RE. and 1st. South African Infantry will move to HUY in accordance with the attached MARCH TA[BLE]

2. All formations will march in threes. Distance between Units as laid down in SS 724 will be strictly maintained.

3. Staging area during the move will be HAFFE, MEAN, CHARDENEUX.

4.(a) Billets in HUY will be taken over as follows:

2nd. SAI.	from 5th. Connaught Rangers,
	A Coy. King's Liverpool Regt.
	and 45 Rue AUGUSTINE.
4th. SAI.	from 9th. Manchester Regt.
	B, C, & D. Coys. King's Liverpool Regt.
SALTMB.	Chateau, BEN AHIN.
SAF Amb.	from 2/3rd. W. Lancs. F.A.
542 Co. ASC.	from 544 Co. ASC.

(b) Billeting parties as detailed below will proceed direct to HUY by lorry on the 28th. January. Lorries will leave Square, MARCHE at 10.00 hours:

Brigade HQ.	1 officer and 1 NCO.	
Each Battalion	1 " " 10 other ranks.	
SAF Amb.	1 " " 1 NCO.	
SALTMB.	1 " " 1 "	
542 Co. ASC.	1 " " 1 "	

Rations for 30th. will be carried on the man.

(c) Billeting parties to arrange billets in the staging area will proceed as follows:

4th. SAI.	1 officer,	3 NCOs.	on 28th. January.
SAF Amb.	1 "		" " "
2nd. SAI.	1 "	3 NCOs.	" 30th. "
SALTMB.	1 "	or NCO.	" " "
542 Co. ASC.	1 "	" "	" " "

Parties proceeding on 28th will leave by lorry from MARCHE at 10.00 hours. Transport arrangements for party on 30th. will be notified later.

5.(a) All duties in the HUY area at present found by the 100 Brigade will be taken over by the South African Brigade on the 29th. January. The Duties are shown in Table A. Personnel will proceed by lorries leaving Square, MARCHE at 10.00 hours on 28th. January. Rations will be carried for 29th. January inclusive.

(b) All duties in the MARCHE area at present found by the South African Brigade will be taken over by the 100 Brigade on the 30th. January as shown in Table B. 2nd, SAI, and 4th. SAI. (S.A. Scottish) will arrange to accommodate relieving personnel on the night 28/29 Janua[ry]

(c) 8 lorries will be available for the move of the South African Infantry Brigade Group. These are allotted as follows:-

<u>On 30th. January.</u>	4th. SAI.	7 lorries.
	SAFAmb.	1 lorry.
<u>On 31st. January.</u>	2nd. SAI.	4 lorries.
	4th. SAI.	3 lorries.
	SAF Amb.	1 lorry.
	SALTMB.	1 lorry.
<u>On 1st. February.</u>	2nd. SAI.	6 lorries.
	Bde. HQ.	1 lorry.
	SALTMB.	1 lorry.

6. Rations during the move will be issued as follows:

Serial No. in March Table.	Unit.	Date of Drawing	For Consumption	Refilling Point.
1.	4th. SAI.	30th. Jan	31st. Jan.	Cross Rds. MARCHE
2.	SAF Amb.	"	"	"
3.	2nd. SAI.	31st. Jan	1st. Feb.	"
4.	SALTMB.	"	"	"
5.	542 Co. ASC	"	"	"
6.	4th. SAI.	"	"	HUY (South Station)
7.	SAF Amb.	"	"	"
8.	2nd. SAI.	1st. Feb.	2nd. Feb.	"
9.	SALTMB.	"	"	"
10.	542 Co. ASC	"	"	"

7. Area Commandant, Town Major, and staffs will remain in MARCHE until relieved.

9. All area stores will be handed over to relieving Units, and receipts forwarded to this Office.

10. On completion of move the 430 Field Co. RE. will be affiliated to the 199 Brigade and the 432 Field Co. RE. to the South African Infantry Brigade.

11. Brigade Headquarters will close at MARCHE at 10.00 hours on 31st. and open at HUY on arrival.

12. Acknowledge.

[signature]

Capt.,
Staff Capt.,
S. Afr. Inf. Bde.

Issued through Signals at 1130 hrs.
to:

No. 1. 1st. SAI.
2. 2nd. SAI,
3. 4th. SAI,
4. SALTMB.
5. Bde. Educ. Off.
6. Staff Capt.,
7. Bde. Sig. Off.
8. Bde. Transport Off.
9. SAF Amb.
10. 430 Field Co. RE.
11. 542 Co. ASC
12. 66th. Division.
13. Bde. Major.
14. 198 Infantry Bde.
15. 199 " "
16. Area Commandant. MARCHE
17. Town Major, MARCHE.
18/19 ✓ War Diary.

A.

Nature of party to be relieved.	By whom found.	Location.	By whom to be relieved.
Guard. 1 NCO & 3 men.	9th.Manch. Regt.	Guarding barges on MEUSE, in own and 432 Field Co.RE.area	S.A.Scottish.
"	"	Material at 333 RUE DE LA MOTTE.	"
"	"	Material near Brigade Theatre.	"
"	"	At VANDEN RIELOOMS Store, RUE ST.PIERRE.	"
" (night only)	"	MT. vehicles in Post Office Shuare.	"
2 NCOs & 6 men	"	RE.material on lest bank of MEUSE.	"
1 NCO. & [illegible] men	5th Connought Rangers.	Timber at GARE,HUY, (Sud)	2nd. S.A.I.
X Corps concentration Camp. 2 off. 18 men.	18th (LH) King's L'pool Rgt	X Corps Concentration Camp.	1st. S.A.I.
1 NCO & 3 men.	5th.Conn. Rangers.	17 barges in own area.	2nd. S.A.I.
2 Off. 18 O.R. ..	9th.Manch. Regt.	X Corps Concentration Camp.	1st. S.A.I.
1 " 11 O.R.	"	Town Major's Office,HUY.	2nd. S.A.I.
1 man.	18 (LH) Kings L'pl Regt.	"	do.
109 men	do.	R.S.O. HUY (HALTE REPAS)	S. A. Scottish.
15 O.R.Guard.	9th.Manch. Regt.	NAMUR.	2nd. S.A.I.

B.

Nature of Party to be relieved.	By whom found.	Location.	By whom to be relieved.
Railway Guard. 1 NCO, 3 men.	4th.SAI.	AYE.	
Guard on RE.stores 1 NCO. 3 men.	do.	MARLOIE.	
Dump Guard. 26 other ranks.	2nd.SAI.	CINEY.	
Dump Guard. 1 officer and 1 platoon.	do.	MELREUX.	
Area Commandant, 1 off. 3 O.R.	1st.SAI.	MARCHE.	
Area Commandant. 1 off. 3 other R.	2nd.SAI.	HAFFE.	
Town Major. 1 off. 3 O.R.	4th. SAI.		
2 "	1st. SAI.	MARCHE.	
1 "	2nd. SAI.		
1 Cpl.	RAMC.		

MARCH TABLE.

Serial No.	Date.	Unit.	Starting Point.	Time.	From.	To.	Route.	Remarks.
1.	30th.	4th. S.A.I.	Road Junct. N. of R. in MARCHE.	09.00	AYE.	MAFFE.	MARCHE - MEAN - MODAVE - HUY.	1. Midday halt will be from 11.30 hours to 13.00 hours.
2.	"	S.A.B. Amb.	No.1 Kilo stone N. of MARCHE.	10.00	MARCHE.	CHARDENEUX. MEAN		2. Units will arrange to reconnoitre routes in order to select suitable halting places.
3.	31st.	2nd.S.A.I.	do.	09.30	"	MAFFE.		
4.	"	SALTMB.	do.	09.45	"	MEAN.		
5.	"	542 Co. ASC	do.	10.00	"	CHARDENEUX		
6.	"	Serial 1	Cross Rds.MEAN.	09.30	MAFFE	HUY.		
7.	"	" 2	do.	09.45	CHARDENEUX MEAN	"		
8.	1st.Feb	" 3	do.	09.30	MAFFE	"		
9.	"	" 4	do.	09.45	MEAN	"		
10.	"	" 5	do.	10.00	CHARDENEUX	"		

Army Form C. 2123. 14
(In books of 100.)

"C" FORM.
MESSAGES AND SIGNALS.

No. of Message ....

app. 10 (e)

Prefix .... Code .... Words 66	Sent, or sent out.	Office Stamp.
Received from .... By	At .... m.	ARMY SIGNALS 19 SZA 27. 1. 19
Service Instructions	To	
Priority	By	

Handed in at YFF Office .... m. Received .... m.

TO SA Bde

*Sender's Number.	Day of Month.	In reply to Number.	AAA
G 442	27		
Ref	my	G 5217	of
22nd	aaa	Owing	further
orders	regarding	demobilization	
received	from	4th	army the
move	of	199	Bns
SA	Bde	from	is
cancelled	aaa	1st	SA
Infy	will	be	prepared
to	move	to	CINEY
and	9th	GLOSTERS	to
SEILLES	at	SHORT	notice
aaa	addsd	199	Bde
SA	Bde	1st SA Inf	9th
Glosters	reptd	Train	adms Q

FROM
PLACE & TIME 66 Divn

* This line, except **AAA**, should be erased, if not required.

(3287) Wt. W54/P738. 691,000 Pads. 3/18. A.P.Ltd. (E3013)

"A" Form
MESSAGES AND SIGNALS.

Army Form C. 2121 (In pads of 100.) 14

No. of Message..............

Prefix.............. Code...............m

Office of Origin and Service Instructions

Words. Charge.

Sent

At...................m.

To.....................

By.....................

This message is on a/c of: App. 11 *Service.*

(Signature of "Franking Officer.")

Recd. at...........m. 18

Date.................

From..................

By....................

TO
1st S A I | S A F Amb | 66 Division | Area Cdt MARCHE
2nd S A I | 430 Co RE | 198 Inf Bde | Town Major
4th S A I | 542 Co ASC | 199 Inf Bde | MARCHE
S A L T M Bty | Bde Sig Off | |

Sender's Number.	Day of Month.	In reply to Number.	AAA
* BS 536	28		

Brigade Order 269 cancelled aaa acknowledge

From SA Bde

Place

Time

The above may be forwarded as now corrected. (Z) Major

Censor. Signature of Addressor or person authorised to telegraph in his name.

* This line should be erased if not required.

(4715) Wt. W3253 P511 1,113,336 Shts. 2 18 C. & Co. (E.684)

14.

App. 12 (o)

16

SECRET.

Copy No. 4

66th DIVISION ORDER NO. 131.

Reference Maps:-
LIEGE, 1/100,000
MARCHE, 1/100,000

27th January, 1919.

Reference 66th Division Order No. 130 dated 22/1/19.

1. Owing to further orders regarding demobilization and future moves of the Division which have been received from Fourth Army, the moves of 199th Infantry Brigado and S.A. Brigade Groups to MARCHE and HUY respectively, are cancelled.

2. The 1st S.A. Infantry will move to CINEY being relieved at SEILLES by9th Bn. Glouc. Regt. who will take over the administration of the Concentration Camp for demobilization. Relief will be carried out in accordance with the attached march table.

3. All formations will march in 'throe's'.
Distances between units as laid down in S.S. 724 will be strictly maintained All marches will be completed by 15.00 hours.

4. 1st S.A. Infantry will leave a party in SEILLES Camp to hand over to 9th Bn. Glouc.R.

5. Commencing on February 1st, all British Infantry Battalions will be demobilised at the rate probably of 10 a day; in the case of Pioneer Battalion 15 a day.

6. Supplies.

The supply arrangements will be as follows:-

UNIT.	Date of drawing.	For Consumption.	Refilliong Point.
9th Bn. Glouc. Regt.	29th Jan.	30th Jan.	HAILLON.
do.	30th Jan.	31st Jan.	ANDENNE.
1st S.A.Inf.	30th Jan.	31st Jan.	HAILLON.
do.	31st Jan.	1st Feb.	EMPTINNE.

P.T.O.

(o) 12 (o)

(2)

7. **Transport.**

To assist moves 6 lorries will report at Headquarters 9th Glouc. R. CINEY and 6 lorries at Headquarters 1st S.A.I. SEILLES at 16.00 hours on 28th January. These lorries will remain with the Battalions until the move of each is complete whereupon they will immediately return to Park.

8. ACKNOWLEDGE

[signature]

Lieut Colonel.
General Staff.
66th Division.

Issued through Signals at 23.00 hours.

DISTRIBUTION.

Copy No. 1	War Diary.	No. 12	Train A.S.C.
2	"	13	A.D.M.S.
3	File.	14	9th Bn. Glouc. R.
4	S.A. Brigade.	15	Canadian Corps.
5	198th Brigade.	16	D.A.P.M.
6	199th Brigade.	17	66th M.T. Coy.
7	C.R.A.	18	D.A.D.O.S.
8	C.R.E.	19	Camp Commandant.
9	Signals.	20	1st S.A.I.
10	A & Q.	21	A.D.C.
11	100th Bn. M.G.C.	22	Fourth Army

MARCH TABLE TO ACCOMPANY DIV. ORDER NO. 131.

Date.	Unit.	From.	To.	Remarks.
Jan. 29th.	9th Glouc. R.	CINEY.	HAILLON.	
Jan. 30th.	9th Glouc. R.	HAILLON.	SEILLES.	Not to enter ANDENNE before 11.45 hours.
	1st S.A. Infantry.	SEILLES.	HAILLON.	To be clear of ANDENNE by 10.30 hours
Jan. 31st.	1st S.A. Infantry.	HAILLON.	CINEY.	

SOUTH AFRICAN INFANTRY BRIGADE. **WAR DIARY** *or* **INTELLIGENCE SUMMARY.** (*Erase heading not required.*) FEBRUARY, 1919. Copy No 1

Army Form C. 2118.

Instructions regarding War Diaries and Intelligence Summaries are contained in F. S. Regs., Part II. and the Staff Manual respectively. Title pages will be prepared in manuscript.

V.d 35

Place	Date	Hour	Summary of Events and Information	Remarks and references to Appendices
MARCHE. AREA.	Feb.		Training arrangements under Battalion arrangements continued during the month, where not interrupted by moves, special parades etc.,	
	1.		Lieut. Col. E.F.THACKERAY, CMG.,DSO., relinquishes command of the SAI. Brigade. Brig. General W.E.C.TANNER, CMG.,DSO., resumes command of the SAI. Brigade.	
	2.		Church Parades as usual.	
	[illegible].		Lecture by Lieut. Commander EVERARD, RN., - Subject: "THE NAVY'S WORK - THE SUBMARINE". 74 Officers and [illegible] other Ranks attended.	
	8.		N.Z.Rugby Football team visited MARCHE to play return match with S.A.Bde. Result N.Z.3. S.A.8.	
	9.		Church Parades as usual. 66th. Division Order No. 13[illegible] received - S.A.Brigade to be concentrated in HUY area. 1st. SAI. to move by March route from CINEY, via OHEY, HAILLON, to HUY on 10th. Feb. Orders for remainder Brigade Group to be issued later.	App. 1. (d).
	10.		General Tanner and Brigade Major at CINEY. Move of 1st. SAI. from CINEY postponed. 66th. Division GS.[illegible] received. Exchange of Guard duties among Brigade Groups.	App. 2. (e).
	11.		1st. SAI. move to HUY from CINEY by lorry.	
	1[illegible].		Lt. Col. E.F.THACKERAY, CMG. DSO., assumes command 4th. SAI. General the Rt. Hon. LOUID BOTHA, P.C., arrived in MARCHE. 2nd. SAI. provided Guard of Honour. General BOTHA inspected Brigade (less 1st. SAI. and 4th. SAI., at 1[illegible].15 hours. General Botha remained for the night in MARCHE and proceeded to HUY following morning. Maj. General H.K.BETHELL, C.M.G., DSO., Commanding 66th. Division, accompanied by Brigade Major, S.A.Brigade, visited 4th. SAI. at AYE. 66th. Division Order No. 1[illegible] received. S.A.Brigade Group less 1st. and 2nd. SAI. to move to HUY.	

13

2/1

D. D. & L., London, E.C.
(A10266) Wt W5300/P713 750,000 2/18 Sch. 52 Forms/C2118/16

SOUTH AFRICAN INFANTRY BRIGADE. **WAR DIARY** *or* **INTELLIGENCE SUMMARY.** (*Erase heading not required.*) FEBRUARY, 1919. Army Form C. 2118.

Instructions regarding War Diaries and Intelligence Summaries are contained in F. S. Regs., Part II. and the Staff Manual respectively. Title pages will be prepared in manuscript.

Place	Date	Hour	Summary of Events and Information	Remarks and references to Appendices
MARCHE AREA.	Feb. 14.		General Botha inspected 1st. SAI. at HUY. Brigade move order 870 issued. Move of Brigade Group less 1st. and 2nd.SAI. from MARCHE to HUY by lorry. 66th. Division [illegible] received. Administrative instructions re Divisional Order No. 1[illegible].	App. [illegible] App. [illegible] (c)
	15.		A & B. Coys. 4th. SAI. move to HUY by lorry.	
	16.		C & D Coys. 4th. SAI. moved to HUY by lorry. H.Qrs. S.A.Brigade closed at MARCHE at 11.00 hrs. and opened at HUY 1[illegible].00 hrs.	
HUY AREA.	17.		Divisional Commander at HUY conferring with BGC. and C.O. 1st. and 4th. SAI., SAFA. moved to TIHANGE. H.Q. in hospital building.	
	18.		Disciplinary Order from Major General, Commanding 66th. Division. received.	App. [illegible] (c).
	2[illegible].		Church Parades as usual.	
	2[illegible].		Rugby Match 1st. SAI. vs. 2nd. SAI. at MARCHE - Draw. No score.	
	26.		Rugby Match 1st. SAI. vs. 2nd. SAI. at HUY (RETURN MATCH) Draw - No Score.	
	27.		Orders received for commencement of scheme for moving to England weekly parties of 100 other Ranks SAI. and 10 Other Ranks SAFA. for demobilization on Compassionate grounds (QMG.691 (QA-AX/54,2.)	App.7. (c).
	28.		66th. Division Warning order (wire No. Q[illegible] of 28th.) received. 1000 of 2nd. SAI. to entrain at HUY for England, on 2nd. March.	App 8. (c)

[signature]
Brig. General,
Commanding,
S. Afr. Inf. Bde.

14

2/2

D. D. & L., London, E.C. (A10266) Wt W5300/P713 750,000 2/18 Sch. 52 Forms/C2118/16

2/3

appx

file

WD

11

SECRET. Copy No. 4.....

66th DIVISION ORDER No. 133.

Reference Maps :-
LIEGE, 100/000.
MARCHE, 100/000.

8th February, 1919.

1. It has been decided to concentrate :-

S.A.Bde in HUY Area.
Cadres of 199th Bde in ASSESSE Area.
R.E. Group in CINEY Area.
Cadres of 100th Bn M.G.C. } in CINEY.
Cadres of 9th Bn Glouc.R. }

2. In order to facilitate the transfer to the Demobilization Concentration Camp, SEILLES, of the large drafts detailed for demobilization from the 199th Bde, preliminary moves as per attached Table will take place commencing February 10th.

3. Orders for moves subsequent to February 13th will be issued later.

S.A. and 198th Bdes H.Q. will move to HUY and WAGNEE respectively, move will .. be completed probably by Feb. 16th.

4. Arrangements for the inter-relief of guards at present found by S.A. and 199th Bdes and 9th Bn Glouc. R. will be notified separately.

5. ACKNOWLEDGE.

J P M Mostyn

Lieut-Colonel,
General Staff, 66th Division.

Issued through
Signals at 16.00

DISTRIBUTION.

Copy No. 1.	War Diary.	12	Train A.S.C.
2	" "	13	A.D.M.S.
3	File.	14	9th Bn Glouc. R.
4	S.A. Bde.	15	Canadian Corps.
5	198th Bde.	16	D.A.P.M.
6	199th Bde.	17	66th M.T. Coy.
7	C.R.A.	18	D.A.D.O.S.
8	C.R.E.	19	Camp Commandant.
9	Signals.	20	A.D.C.
10	A & Q.	21	1st S.A.I.
11	100th Bn M.G.C.	22	

Recd 9/2/19

Table shewing Locations of Marching Units at 15.00 on Undermentioned Dates.

Date.	43[illegible] Fld.Coy. R.E.	432 Fld.Coy. R.E.	100th Bn M.G.C.	9th Bn Glouc. Regt.	1st S.A. Infantry.	18th Bn K.L.R.	2nd Conn. Rang.
Feb. 9th	WAHA	HUY	SENINCHAMPS HAVERSIN HAID.	SEILLES.	CINEY	HUY	HUY
Feb. 10th	x HAVERSIN	EVELETTE	"	GESVES.	OHEY-HAILLON	SEILLES	"
Feb. 11th	ACHENE	CINEY ≠	Concentrate in HAVERSIN & HAID	CINEY ≠ %	HUY	"	"
Feb. 12th	"	TAVIET.	"	"	"	"	"
Feb. 13th	"	"	"	"	"	ASSESSE	SEILLES.

x Accommodation to be arranged by O.C., M.G. Bn.

≠ 9th Bn Glouc.R. to be clear of MAIBE by 10.15 hours. 432 F.Co. not to pass MAIBE till 10.45 hours.

% Accommodation from Town Major.

66th Division.

No. G.S. 59

S.A. Brigade.
198th Brigade.
199th Brigade.
9th Bn. Glouc. R.

1. Guards at present found by Brigades are as shewn on attached list.

2. The relief of these guards (~~reference D.O. 133 para. 4~~) will be as under, and will be arranged direct between Units concerned.

3. Reliefs to be complete by noon February 15th.

Serial 1.	By 9th Bn. Glouc. R.
" 2.	" 198th Brigade.
" 3.) " 4.) " 5.)	As at present.
" 6.) " 7.) " 8)	By 199th Brigade.
" 10.) " 11.) " 12.) " 13.)	As at present.
" 14.	By S.A. Brigade.

J. [illegible]
Captain.
General Staff, 66th Division.

D.H.Q.
10.2.19.

Copy to:-
'Q'.

GUARDS OVER ABANDONED GERMAN MATERIAL.&c.

Brigade.	Serial No.	Place.		Strength of Guard. Off.	N.C.Os.	O.Rs.	Material guarded.
S.A. Bde.	1.	CINEY.			2	18	Guns, Rations, Ammunition.
"	2.	AYE.			1	3	8 Heavy guns.
"	3.	NAMUR.	(a)	1	2	30	For D.D.S. & T. Fourth Army.
			(b)		2	6	Barrack Police.
			(c)			4	For Area Commandant.
"	4.	SPA.		3	-	45	
"	5.	SCLAIGNEAUX.				14	Ration Dump.
"	6.	ASSESSE.			1	3	) Canadian Corps asked to relieve.
"	7	SORINNE LA LONGUE.			1	3	-ditto-
"	8	10 Kilo. stone on NAMUR - MARCHE Road.			1	3	-ditto-
198th Bde.	9	ROCHEFORT.			1	3	Guns, Ammunition.
"	10	HOUVET.			1	3	Train.
"	11	GENDRON.			1	3	Dump.
"	12	WANLIN.			1	3	Ammunition Dump.
199th Bde.	13	HUY.			6	18	Barges, Ammunition.

D.H.Q.
10.2.19.

2/6

8

Acknowledge receipt

SECRET.

Copy No. 4

66TH DIVISION ORDER NO. 134.

Reference Maps:-
LIEGE, 1/100,000.
MARCHE, 1/100,000.

13th February 1919.

1. S.A. Brigade Group will move from MARCHE to HUY as follows:-

		From.	To.
February 15th.	S.A. Brigade H.Q.) 4th S.A. Infantry.)	MARCHE.	HUY.
	542 Coy R.A.S.C.	MARCHE.	MAFFE.
February 16th.	542 Coy R.A.S.C.	MAFFE.	HUY.
February 17th.	S.A.M.C.	MARCHE.	HUY.

2. 2nd S.A. Infantry will remain in MARCHE until further orders.

3. ACKNOWLEDGE.

F.P. [signature]
Lieut Colonel,
General Staff,
66th Division.

Issued through
Signals at 12.00

DISTRIBUTION.

Copy No. 1	War Diary.	No. 10	A & Q.
2	" "	11	100th Bn. M.G.C.
3	File.	12	Train A.S.C.
4	S.A. Brigade.	13	A.D.M.S.
5	198th Brigade.	14	9th Bn. Glouc. R.
6	199th Brigade.	15	Canadian Corps.
7	C.R.A.	16	D.A.P.M.
8	C.R.E.	17	66th M.T. Company.
9	Signals.	18	D.A.D.O.S.
		19	D.A.D.V.S.
		20	Camp Commandant.
		21	A.D.C.

2/7

SOUTH AFRICAN INFANTRY BRIGADE.
Order No. 270.

7

Map reference:-

MARCHE } 1,/100,000.
LIEGE }

Secret.
Copy No. 13
14-2-1919.

---

1. On 15th. February, 1919, the 4th. South African Infantry, Brigade Headquarters, and 542 Co. ASC. will move to HUY.

2. On 17th. February, 1919, the S.A.F.Ambulance will move by lorries to HUY, except Transport.

3. 4th. S.A.Infantry and Brigade Headquarters will move by lorries, with the exception of Transport.

4. 45 lorries will report at 09.00 hours to 4th. S.A.Infantry, and 4 lorries at 08.30 hours to Brigade Headquarters. Number of lorries for S.A.F.Ambulance will be notified later.

5. 542 Co. ASC. and Transport of 4th. S.A.Infantry and Brigade Head-Quarters will move off as follows:-
Brigade Headquarters pass 2nd. S.A.Infantry Stables 09.00 hours.
542 Co. ASC. pass 2nd. S.A.Infantry stables 09.30 hours.
4th. S. A. Infantry pass 2nd. S.A.Infantry Stables 10.00 hours.

6. Staging during the move for 542 Co. ASC. and Transport will be as follows:-
542 Co. ASC. night Feb. 15/16 - MAFFE.
4th. S.A.Infantry night Feb. 15/16 - MAFFE.
Brigade Headquarters Transport night Feb. 15/16 - MEAN.

7. S. A. F. Ambulance Transport by staging area as follows:-
Night Feb. 17/18 - MAFFE.

AREA STORES. These will be handed over to Town Major, and copies of receipts forwarded to this Office.

BILLETS. Special care will be taken to see that all billets are properly cleaned on leaving.

SUPPLIES. Units will see that their Transport are issued with rations for 15th. and 16th. February before move commences.

A.G. Emery
Lieut.,
A/Staff Capt.,
S. Afr. Inf. Bde.

Issued through Signals at 14.00 hours to:

1. 1st. SAI.
2. 2nd. SAI.
3. 4th. SAI.
4. SALTMB.
5. Staff Capt.
6. Bde. Sig. Off.
7. Bde. Transport Off.
8. S.A.F.Ambulance.
9. 542 Co. ASC.
10. 66th. Division.
11. 198 Infantry Brigade.
12. 199 Infantry Brigade.
13. War Diary
14. do.
15. Brigade Major.
16. Town Major.
17. Area Commandant.

66th Divn.
8717/Q.

6

ADMINISTRATIVE INSTRUCTIONS issued in connection with 66th Division Order No.134 of 13.2.19.

1. MOVE OF TRANSPORT.

(a) Transport (less S.A.M.C.transport) will move on Feb.15th and 16th, staging night Feb.15/16th at MAFFE.
(b) Transport of S.A.M.C. will move on Feb.16th and 17th, staging night Feb.16/17th at MAFFE.

2. SUPPLIES.

(a) Supplies for consumption Feb.16th :-
(i) by units moving to HUY on Feb.15th will be carried on the lorries referred to in Serial No.1 of para 3 below.
(ii) by units moving to MAFFE on Feb.15th will be carried on supply wagons.

(b) Supplies for consumption Feb.17th :-
(i) by all units moving (except S.A.M.C.) will be drawn from dump at HUY South Station on Feb.16th, and delivered by affiliated Train Coy.
(ii) by S.A.M.C.(less Transport) will be carried on the lorries referred to in Serial No.2 of para 3 below.
(iii) by transport of S.A.M.C. will be carried on supply wagons, which will move with S.A.M.C. transport.

(c) Supplies for consumption 18th Feb. by S.A.M.C. (and transport) will be drawn as in 2(b)(i) above.

3. LORRIES FOR MOVES.

These will be detailed to report as under :-

Serial No.	Date.	Unit.	Number of Lorries.	Hour of Start.	From	To	Remarks
1.	Feb.15	S.A.Bde.HQ 4th S.A.I.	49	08.00 hours	MARCHE	HUY	
2.	Feb.17	S.A.Bde. Fld.Ambce.	5	"	"	"	

All above lorries will return to Park immediately on completion of journey to HUY.

6 TM 16
1 FAmbs.
Stores
& ??

R.Potter
Major,
D.A.Q.M.G.
66th Division.

14.2.19.

Copies to:- G.
S.A. Inf.Bde.
Div.Train.
A.D.M.S.
66th Div.M.T.Co.

Q.M.G. (Q.A.).
XXXXX AX/54/2

Q.M.G. 691 (Q.A.)
AX/54/2

3

[illegible]rth Army.

---

1. Instructions have now been received to the effect that the demobilization of South African Units will be carried out by desparsal drafts at the rate of 200 per week.

Embarkations will take place at HAVRE on Monday in each week.

The destination in ENGLAND for desparsal drafts from South African Units will be PERHAM DOWN CAMP, TIDWORTH.

The port of disemberkation will be WEYMOUTH.

2. Each weekly quota of 200 will comprise drafts from South African Units as follows:-

Unit.	No. of all Ranks.	Formation Administrating.
44th Brigade R.G.A.	20.	First Army.
50th Brigade R.G.A.	20.	First Army.
1st S.A.Inf. Bde.	100.	Fourth Army.
S.A.Field Ambulance.	10.	Fourth Army.
S.A.Signal Units. (XV)Corps)	10.	Fifth Army.
S.A. General Hospital.	10.	G.O.C. LofC Area.
92nd Railway Operating Coy.	10.	D.G.T.
93rd -do-	10.	D.G.T.
84th Miscellaneous Trades Coy.	10.	D.G.T.

3. Weekly quotas will be despatched to HAVRE by rail under arrangements to be made by Formations administrating units concerned ~~xx~~ with Local Traffic Offices so as to arrive at HAVRE on Saturday in each week. The first quota will arrive at HARVE on Saturday, 1st March 1919.

4. Shipment from HARVE to WEYMOUTH will be carried out on Monday in each week under arrangement to be made by G.O.C. L of C Area.

5. (a) Personal equipment, arms and accoutrements will be disposed of as directed in G.H.Qs 6081.

(b) When the Units themselves are broken up further instructions will ~~xxxxxx~~ be issued.

(Sgd) R.W.MAY, Brig-General.
for Quartermaster General.

G.H.Q.
22nd Feb.1919.
Copy to B.C. HARVE.

S.A. Bde

The first quota of 110 men will report to R.T.O. HUY by midnight Feb 28/March1st and travel to HAVRE by the 2nd Army leave train.

Future weekly quotas will travel by the 2nd Army leave train from HUY at midnight each Wednesday/Thursday

Capt
Demob. Officer
66th Div.

27th February.1919.

www.ingramcontent.com/pod-product-compliance
Lightning Source LLC
Chambersburg PA
CBHW082356010526
44111CB00041B/2592